Lineages of Modernity

For Laurent

Lineages of Modernity

A History of Humanity from the Stone Age
to *Homo Americanus*

Emmanuel Todd

Translated by Andrew Brown

polity

First published in French as *Où en sommes-nous? Une esquisse de l'histoire humaine*
© Éditions du Seuil, 2017

This English edition © Polity Press, 2019

This work received the French Voices Award
for excellence in publication and translation.
French Voices is a program created and funded
by the French Embassy in the United States and
FACE (French American Cultural Exchange).

Polity Press
65 Bridge Street
Cambridge CB2 1UR, UK

Polity Press
101 Station Landing
Suite 300
Medford, MA 02155, USA

ISBN-13: 978-1-5095-3447-0

A catalogue record for this book is available from the British Library.
Library of Congress Cataloging-in-Publication Data

Names: Todd, Emmanuel, 1951- author.
Title: Lineages of modernity : a history of humanity from the Stone Age to
    Homo Americanus / Emmanuel Todd.
Other titles: Ou en sommes-nous? English
Description: Cambridge : Medford, MA : Polity Press, [2019] | Includes
    bibliographical references and index.
Identifiers: LCCN 2018037566 (print) | LCCN 2018046524 (ebook) | ISBN
    9781509534494 (Epub) | ISBN 9781509534470 (hardback)
Subjects: LCSH: Civilization--History. | Ethnohistory. | Families. | Social
    structure. | Democracy--Social aspects.
Classification: LCC CB151 (ebook) | LCC CB151 .T5313 2019 (print) | DDC
    909--dc23
LC record available at https://lccn.loc.gov/2018037566

Typeset in 10.5pt on 12pt Sabon by
Servis Filmsetting Ltd, Stockport, Cheshire
Printed and bound in Great Britain by TJ International Limited

For further information on Polity, visit our website: politybooks.com

CONTENTS

CONTENTS

FOREWORD

Nobody who reads Emmanuel Todd could have been surprised by the election of Donald Trump. Before the businessman and reality television star shocked the world by becoming President of the United States, the French social scientist and public intellectual had anatomized the conditions that made such a disruptive event possible: the polarization of American society as a result of the hollowing-out of American manufacturing by globalization, and the failure of a foreign policy that masked the limits of American power with what Todd called 'theatrical micromilitarism'.

Had Todd written his pessimistic analysis in 2014, he would have been prophetic enough. But he published it in 2001, in his book *After the Empire: The Breakdown of the American Order*. At the time, conventional wisdom held that the post-Cold War emergence of the United States as the sole remaining superpower had inaugurated an age of 'unipolarity'. European and Japanese alternatives to Anglo-American neoliberal capitalism had failed. Countries that wanted to grow needed to obey the rules of the Washington Consensus – liberalization, deregulation and privatization. And history had ended, according to Francis Fukuyama. Liberal democracy was the final outcome of humanity's political evolution, and the chief threat to the human race in the future would be boredom.

This was not the first time Todd had been at odds with the elite consensus on both sides of the Atlantic. A quarter of a century earlier, following the US withdrawal from Indochina, the Soviet Union appeared to many to be more powerful than ever. In 1976, in response to claims that the Central Intelligence Agency downplayed the Soviet threat, President Gerald Ford appointed then-Director of Central Intelligence George H. W. Bush to organize a 'Team B' of outside experts who, after re-evaluating intelligence reports, claimed that the CIA had consistently underestimated Soviet strength.

In the same year, then only twenty-five years old, having examined Soviet social indicators such as increasing infant mortality rates, Todd published *The Final Fall: An Essay on the Decomposition of the Soviet Sphere*. As in 2001, when writing about underlying American weakness, in 1976, when writing about underlying Soviet weakness, Todd was prematurely and unfashionably correct. If *Untimely Meditations* were not the title of a collection of essays by Nietzsche, it would make an apt summary of Todd's work.

That work is virtuosic in its variety and impressive in its depth, ranging from a study of the elites of pre-First World War Europe, *Le Fou et le prolétaire* (1979), to social developments within Muslim societies, *A Convergence of Civilizations: The Transformation of Muslim Societies Around the World* (with Youssef Courbage, 2007). In an age of growing distance between scholastic university research and clickbait Internet punditry, Todd has managed, against the odds, to be an influential public intellectual as well as a rigorous scholar. Although Todd denies paternity of the term, his influence is said to have led French president Jacques Chirac to invoke the idea of 'the social fracture' in his 1995 campaign. And in 2015, the prime minister of France, Manuel Valls, denounced Todd's controversial book *Who Is Charlie? Xenophobia and the New Middle Class*, in which Todd argued that public demonstrations of solidarity with the victims of the terrorist attack on the staff of the satirical magazine *Charlie Hebdo* disguised currents of xenophobia and reaction in French society.

For nearly half a century, between publishing his insightful analyses of the Soviet Union, the United States and France, Todd has been constructing an impressive body of thought linking the values of historic and contemporary societies to different family systems. In *Lineages of Modernity: A History of Humanity from the Stone Age to Homo Americanus*, Todd unites his complementary roles as anthropologist and historian, scholar and public intellectual. The French thinker puts Anglo-American civilization at the centre of modern global history, writing that 'it was England and her daughter America who were, and remain, the true revolutionary nations'. Todd notes the paradox that it was the very fact that the individualistic Anglo-American family was primitive, in anthropological terms, that made possible the incubation of liberal modernity in Britain and its settler states. And he presents another paradox: at the very moment that the rest of the world is catching up with a previous wave of Anglo-American liberalism, Brexit and the Trump presidency may represent the next phase in Anglo-American liberal evolution, a check upon ultra-liberalism: 'The choice for advanced societies does not lie between elitism and populism, between openness and closure, but between negotiation and disintegration.'

For my part, I would hesitate to argue that a thinker who has been right so often about contemporary societies like the Soviet Union and the United States is wrong about the contemporary world. Whether readers agree or disagree with Emmanuel Todd, in *Lineages of Modernity*, they will find a worldview as revolutionary as the world revolution it describes.

Michael Lind

PREFACE TO THE ENGLISH EDITION

When the English language first appeared in the fourteenth century, its kingdom of 3 million inhabitants was just a tiny peripheral country on the edge of a Eurasia that had a population of 300 million. This language is now unifying the world. The Anglosphere – the United Kingdom, the United States, Canada, Australia, New Zealand – is characterized not only by its language, but by an individualistic family structure, and by a corresponding social and political temperament: in 2018–19 it had more than 450 million inhabitants. British globalization in the nineteenth century, followed by American globalization in the twentieth, generated a worldwide economic organization. Yet Britain remains an island and continues to amaze Europeans with its particularism – its habit of driving on the left, its royal family, its humour, its general refusal to conform. Solving the paradox of a culture that is not only tiny but particularistic, one that created the United States and shaped the world, is the central focus of this book.

I had to start from the emergence of *Homo sapiens* and reconstruct the history of the family systems of our species before I finally understood that, as so often, the problem was basically the solution. It was *because* it was peripheral and residual that England succeeded. Its dynamism, and even more so that of America, is the dynamism of the original *Homo sapiens*. Elsewhere, successive civilizations have had time to imprison themselves in complex constructions that are liable to paralyse human creativity.

The principle of conservatism of peripheral areas, familiar to linguists and anthropologists before the Second World War, explains why archaic anthropological, family, ideological and political systems remain as isolated pockets on the periphery of historical territories, while, conversely, the most elaborate constructions can be observed in the centre of the continental regions where they form continuous blocks. On a map of Eurasia, the nuclear family appears as a peripheral, and therefore archaic, phenomenon. The central mass of the continent is occupied by dense, communitarian, patrilineal, anti-individualistic anthropological systems.

We can agree with many previous scholars that individualistic social systems nourish human creativity and experimentation. But we must accept that individualism is not an invention of modernity. It is the original state of humankind. If it is abolished, history grinds to a stop. The confinement of the individual in compact family blocks across the mass of Eurasia very gradually produced, between 2500 BCE and 1800 BCE, an educational, technological, economic and social paralysis. If history began in Sumer – with the city, writing and the state – it did so at a time when the family was not too oppressive, the status of women was elevated and children were brought up to be free. At the very most, in the middle of the third millennium BCE, we can detect a first densification of the family due to male primogeniture – a primogeniture that would be observed one and a half millennia later in China and more than three and a half millennia later in Japan and Germany. Primogeniture and the stem family, invented to transmit the family's possessions, initially produced a cultural and economic acceleration before leading, via an initial fossilization and then even more complex mutations that entailed a confinement of men and women, to a paralysis of history. As the geographical successor of Mesopotamia, Iraq is so weak and dominated today that it has become a training ground for various armies; in that country, the family, slowly developed over five thousand years of history, has become communitarian, patrilineal and endogamous, with rates of marriages between cousins in the order of 35 per cent. Meanwhile, England, which was for a long time on the margins of the civilized world, has kept its original nuclear family type, while acquiring agriculture, writing, the city and the state, all elements of civilization from the Middle East that passed via Greece, Rome and France. Protestantism has completed the purification of its nuclear family type, now 'absolute' in my terminology, destroying the undifferentiated and flexible kinship network that initially framed it. This, then, was the anthropological basis for the English take-off: the flexibility of the family system. My model of history, at this stage, is built on the ideas of Alan Macfarlane, who was my PhD examiner at Cambridge. But in my view England is not unique; its archaism is the remnant of a form that was once common to the whole of the human species, the survival of a concrete universal. In this preface, I extend to England this notion of the concrete universal, which I had not dared apply to any country other than America (see chapter 11), and I contrast it with the abstract ideological universal of France.

In the United States, the English family type, albeit somewhat transformed by cultural waves from the heart of Eurasia, instead reverted more closely to the original type of humanity. This is why it is *Homo americanus* who appears in this book as the most legitimate successor of the original *Homo sapiens*.

This is the solution to the paradox of the Anglosphere, a peripheral archipelago surrounding Eurasia, but one whose individualistic dynamism has driven the history of the world since the English political revolutions of the seventeenth century and the industrial revolution of the late eighteenth century.

The English and the Americans

The hypothesis of a *Homo americanus* who is dynamic because he is close to the naturalness of origins does not seem too difficult to accept: continental Europeans perceive Americans not only as modernizers and experimenters, but also as a bit simple, not to say brutal and boorish. The English present us with the opposite image of sophistication, self-control and reserve, none of which suggests any naturalness. The contrast between the inhibited Englishman and the feisty American woman is a classic figure in cinema.[1] Yet, beneath the tangible surface of a certain English rigidity – self-control, social control – stemming from the earlier adoption by the higher social strata of more continental, more authoritarian family forms, and doubtless even more from Protestantism of a Calvinist hue – it is not too difficult to detect an English naturalness: a naturalness that has allowed and still allows England to speak to all human beings, and to be universal in a concrete way, like America. To begin with, let's note, for the record, the liberal economic system and the theory behind it. In England, they attained a strength and a level of abstraction that transformed the world, but in fact only modernized and formalized the spontaneous behaviour (predation, labour, acquisition and savings) of the original *Homo sapiens*, the hunter-gatherer and experimental farmer with little inclination for bureaucracy or Bolshevism. If we then proceed to more cultural matters, we find England affecting the world through its individualistic spontaneity. It invented the novel, then those so-called popular genres of crime and science fiction. The pop music of the 1960s, for its part, did more to undermine the strength of the Soviet regime than CIA-funded magazines.

As far as I am concerned, the most convincing proof of English naturalness is philosophical empiricism, because philosophy is supposed to distance us from the banality of the world. I come from a French family where the reading of A. J. Ayer's *Language, Truth and Logic* was the equivalent of deciphering a Torah passage at your bar mitzvah. I fully accepted the way my family transmitted to me the idea of the superiority of British empiricism over continental rationalism, but I must admit that I have always perceived this philosophical empiricism as mere common

Table P1   Distance from Anglosphere values

	Authority	Equality	Endogamy	Feminism	Total distance
Denmark	0	0	0	0	0
France (Paris Basin)	0	0.50	0	0	0.50
France (total)					1.25
Sweden	1	0.50	0	0	1.50
Russia	1	0.50	0	0	1.50
France (periphery)	1	0.50	0	0.50	2
Germany	1	0.50	0	1	2.50
Japan	1	0.50	0.50	1	3
China	1	0.50	0.50	2	4
Iran	1	0.50	1.50	3	6
Saudi Arabia	1	0.50	2	4	7.50

sense – the common sense of a *Homo sapiens* who doesn't want his mind to get muddled by words, who doesn't want to lose touch with the reality of the world. One could extend the list of examples of English naturalness, such as the importance in its high culture of poetry, an archaic literary form. English humour itself, more than just a particularism, is perhaps connected to the idea of staying in touch with the healthy roots of human nature. To abstain from laughing or smiling are things that have to be learned; the spirit of seriousness, unfortunately, is a cultural achievement.

In fact, is not the particularism of the English itself the manifestation of a certain human archaism? The original group always thinks of itself, as we shall see, in contrast with other groups: it is simultaneously separated, open and assimilative. The strong and early self-consciousness of the English did not prevent them from building America and absorbing into it those people who were fleeing from the over-dense, suffocating family systems of Eurasia, or the political autocracies that loured over them. Anglo-American liberal democracy will also appear in this book as a peripheral archaism that succeeded.

The Anglosphere, then, is not simply dynamic. Across the whole world, its temperament touches the buried, free and flexible heart of original humanity, however transformed it has been by the history of the local culture, however constrained by the ways in which individuals and groups have been forced into rigid patterns. But to touch something does not mean that, as if by waving some magic wand, you can set it free. Throughout Eurasia, a transformation did after all take place, and it now seems that human beings in those parts of the world, far from being natural, are very unlikely to turn English or American overnight.

Distance from others

By 2017, in keeping with its tradition, or rather with the aptitude for change that stems from its particular family structure, the Anglosphere, once again, was starting to change. The absolute nuclear family, fostering the autonomy of children and uninterested in the issue of equality, tends to create major breaks between one generation and the next. That is why, in the eighteenth, nineteenth and twentieth centuries, the United Kingdom, and then the United States, were capable of getting rid of their peasants and then their workers in a few generations; since the Second World War, they have struck us as first social, then liberal, and soon no doubt they will seem national. By 1979–80, Margaret Thatcher and Ronald Reagan were symbols of the neoliberal turnaround. Brexit and the election of Donald Trump might also appear one day as the beginning of the Anglosphere's shift into its next stage.

The whole world is surprised, incredulous, shocked. How could those Anglo-Americans who had proposed, or imposed, their neoliberalism and globalization on us do such a terrible thing as become protectionist, or nationalistic? At the present stage, only the United States presents the two symptoms – with a surge in protectionism and 'America first' – since, for the British, free trade has been a matter of identity since the mid-nineteenth century. This was hardly the case under Cromwell, a great protectionist, and we can already sense in Jeremy Corbyn's Labour Party the demand for a new focus on the industrial resources proper to the United Kingdom.

The world press is naively speculating on the emergence of new champions of free trade and the universal, as if China, Germany or (let's be really creative) the European Union, despite being in political, economic and ideological collapse, could produce ideological values that were simultaneously liberal and universal.

It is therefore at this stage important for the Anglosphere nations to position themselves, in terms of deep values, in relation to the world away from which they are temporarily moving. In the first part of this preface, I mentioned the seductiveness of Anglo-American culture to all the peoples of the world, suggesting an answer to the question, why do people love you? There remains the complementary question: why do people hate you, or, in a more moderate, targeted and pragmatic way: who are you close to, who are you different from? Who will your friends be, and who your enemies?

This book considers politics and the economy as superstructures and seeks the fundamental factors behind the movement of history in deeper layers of social life. Thus, the educational subconscious explains, first, the democratic moment as stemming from mass literacy and, subsequently, the clash of elitism and populism as arising from the new stratification that has divided advanced societies into those educated to higher, middle and primary levels. In this representation of history, the origin of the rise in educational levels can be found in Jewish and then Protestant religious transformations. It identifies, beneath the ideological preferences of the various regions and nations, the unconscious action of old family values that should have been swept away by urbanization but which nonetheless end up being re-embodied in the multiple dimensions of social life in the electronic era.

These hidden family values explain the persistence, in continental Europe, Russia, China, Japan and elsewhere, of specific ideological temperaments, essentially resistant to the non-egalitarian liberalism of England and the United States. These national cultures are studied in detail in this book, in their historical depth, and in their interactions with the religious and educational layers of social life.

I would like to add here, in an attempt to glimpse the conflicts that lie ahead of us, a brief assessment of the anthropological distance between the Anglosphere and some of the other nations of the world. Most of the latter have been chosen for their strategic importance, but some smaller ones, such as Denmark or Sweden, are merely typical of this or that anthropological form.

Classical geopolitical analysis focuses on the conscious forces of social, political and economic life, mainly military and commercial rivalries. These two fields in which power is expressed do not correspond so closely these days. If we take the American point of view, Russia will appear militarily effective, but economically harmless; Germany, a formidable economic aggressor with a trade surplus of 8 per cent of GDP, is militarily harmless; China could perhaps just about be considered a double threat, economic and military, if its economy were not so dependent on globalized capitalism, and its army on Russian technology.

What I want to do here is very different. We can sense that the American and British national impetus is on the point of breaking the old alliance systems inherited from the Cold War, but we can also see that the elites of Washington and London are struggling to achieve the right adjustment of friendships and enmities, a little as if there were definitely sporting fixtures in the offing, but the teams had not yet been drawn up. Typical of this is the incredible Russophobia of the English elites, at the very same time as it is the European Union that is threatening the independence and integrity of the United Kingdom by its insistence on not settling the Irish border issue. The same determined anti-Russian hostility is paralysing the protectionist reorganization – anti-Chinese and anti-German – of the American economy.

Anthropological analysis can contribute to a clarification by measuring the objective distance that lies between the deep values of nations. It is not a question here of explicit, theoretical, official political values, but of latent family values: the relationship to authority and equality, the relative closure of the group by endogamy, and the status of women.

I have therefore roughly estimated for each of the nations in Table P.1 *the distances between their latent family values and those of the absolute nuclear family of the Anglosphere*, which is liberal with regard to parent–child relations, indifferent to the principle of equality, exogamous and feminist. I have summed up these distances in a last column to obtain an overall distance. The data and developments that allow me to draw up this table can be found, as regards the advanced countries and China, throughout this book. For Iran and Saudi Arabia, I refer to the essay I wrote with Youssef Courbage on the demography of the Muslim world, *A Convergence of Civilizations*.[2] But in fact this table condenses forty-five years of research into, and familiarity with, family systems across the world.

We see that the Anglosphere is similar only to Denmark and the France of the Paris Basin in the dimension of authority, since no other nation in the table is characterized by the nuclear family and pure individualism. We also observe that the Anglosphere, indifferent to equality, and in this respect followed by Denmark alone, is situated in this dimension (on the family level, and not the economic or social level), equidistant from all other nations, whether these be egalitarian (France of the Paris Basin, Russia, China, Iran, Saudi Arabia) or inegalitarian (France of the periphery, Sweden, Germany, Japan). Endogamy is strong only in Iran and, even more, in Saudi Arabia. I mentioned the tolerance found in bygone days for some marriages between cousins in China and Japan. The scale of feminism is probably the most familiar, since women's emancipation is on the agenda of international organizations even if the reality of its development as studied in this book is often very different from what the fantasies of the UN or NGOs might suggest. All in all, we discover – and this comes as no surprise – an Anglosphere that is close to Scandinavia and the France of the Paris Basin, but, more unexpectedly, a little further from Germany than from Russia. Admittedly, as I explain in Chapter 18, Russia, authoritarian, egalitarian and communitarian, may appear to be the antithesis of the Anglo-American world, which is liberal, indifferent to equality, and individualistic: the anthropological contrast seemingly coincides with military rivalry. But the feminist dimension, as we will see, brings these strategic rivals closer together.

The most violent discordance between geopolitical alignment and anthropological distance is found in Saudi Arabia – communitarian, endogamous and anti-feminist to the highest degree. This ally and priority customer of the United States achieves the maximum score of 7.5 for its anthropological distance. If we accept the equation *maximum incomprehension + intimate association = hatred,*

we won't find it too difficult to understand 11 September 2001.

More usefully when it comes to the future, such a tabulation can serve as an introduction to Chapters 16 and 17, where we will see how the United Kingdom and the United States stand out in terms of fundamental values from Germany and the mainland of Europe as a whole. In fact, anthropological analysis explains the ongoing split within the Western camp between a national and liberal component and an authoritarian continental component.

I must nevertheless point out that this sketch of human history, written by a Frenchman whose central focus is the Anglo-American dynamic, gives full importance to Germany, whose role in world history is considerable. Without Lutheranism and its demand for literacy for everyone, I would have needed to write a quite different sketch of history.

The crisis and the limits of anthropology

The division into primary, secondary and tertiary educational orders guarantees a persistent tension between the democratic principle and the oligarchic principle in all advanced societies, and therefore in British and American societies as they are now focusing more on national interests. In the postscript to this book, which appeared in the French edition, I follow others in emphasizing the need for a negotiation between those with a higher education and those with a primary education, between 'somewheres' and 'anywheres', in David Goodhart's terms. A viable world cannot fail to integrate the aspirations of some people to openness with the aspirations of other people to security. The choice for advanced societies does not lie between elitism and populism, between openness and closure, but between negotiation and disintegration. The existence of a massive intermediate category, schematically referred to here as 'those with a secondary education', reveals, rather reassuringly, that the fierce ideological struggle between Remainers and Brexiteers, between Trumpists and Clintonians, tends to exaggerate (due to the very dynamics of political competition) the dualistic character of social opposition. There is a vast world of people who are neither 'open' nor 'closed', but in search of an individual flourishing that does not exclude security.

The predominance of the national principle, the necessary framework for interclass negotiation, seems to be inevitable in the long run, since belonging to a territorial and linguistic group (the nation, these days) is, from the anthropological point of view, necessary for human life. A strange parallel comes to my mind. The Third International, socialist and workerist, collapsed in 1914 because the slogan 'Workers of the world, unite!' was unable to prevail over more primordial national identifications. In a world of open, explicit rivalries between the United Kingdom and continental Europe, between the United States and China, the implicit slogan of globalization, 'Higher educated of all countries, unite!' will probably not seem very convincing in the face of the need to belong to a territorial group. To those who doubt this, I recommend a meditation on the behaviour of football crowds at World Cup matches.

Anthropology also explains how Brexit and Trump emerge from a liberal and non-egalitarian tradition, and that the deep meaning of these emergences is not that they pose a 'danger to democracy'. The innumerable essays currently being published in the United States, comparing Trump with Orbán, Putin, Lukashenko or Erdoğan, appear, in the light of historical anthropology, ridiculous. Let's be reasonable: if the crisis of 1929 produced leaders as different as Roosevelt, Chamberlain, Blum and Hitler, how could the current crisis in neoliberalism lead to a convergence in 'illiberal democracy' or a uniform autocratic system?

There is indeed a crisis in the Anglo-American world, but these essayists wrongly insist on presenting it as a decline in liberal democracy, even though it was the inegalitarian trends of the years 1980–2015 that had endangered this same liberal democracy. The current contestation of the system should rather, in spite of certain unpleasant xenophobic aspects, be analysed as a return to the sources of primordial democracy. The non-egalitarian liberalism of the Anglosphere is still in place, and in principle it prohibits any serious drift into authoritarianism. Xenophobia, as explained in Chapter 11, is part of the original foundation of democracy, a political system that derives more from a group's self-awareness than from internal egalitarian values. This indeed is why the Anglo-American populations, structured by the liberal but non-egalitarian values of the absolute nuclear family, moved over to modern democracy more easily than the French of the central regions, who are certainly more radical in their political demands but are rendered anarchic by the values of the egalitarian nuclear family.

However, we do not see family structures as a unique and absolute determinant. We have to admit that the inegalitarian upsurge of the Anglo-American world in the years 1980–2015 had gone 'too far', i.e. beyond the natural social potential of the absolute nuclear family. The latter defines brothers and sisters as different from each other, but in no way unequal in principle, as was the case in the German, Japanese, Rwandan or Basque stem family. If the empirical study of history allows us to discern the laws of association between family and ideology, it also obliges us to observe moments of dissociation when economic, social and ideological evolution becomes independent and transcends its determinations. This 'take-off' permits the temporary emergence of extremist systems, each of which, however, retains the characteristic features of its original matrix: the runaway ultra-liberalism of the years 2000–15 may have ended up leading to an increase in the mortality rates of White Americans aged 45 to 54, but it wasn't Stalinism or Nazism!

Reflections on the Anglo-American revolution

I would like to end this preface with a confession: I have a sense of inadequacy concerning my description of the dynamics of the Anglo-American world, which I thought I had finally grasped after a prolonged investigation that began in Cambridge in 1971. My variables, admittedly schematic, are nevertheless important and allow quite a rich representation of societies, with family structures, the relation to the values of freedom and non-equality, group consciousness, racial sentiment, religious traditions, educational stratification, and levels of economic inequality and political authority, all leading to the un-Marxist view of the struggle between educational classes. But I have the feeling that, by superimposing my variables methodically, I have missed something essential. The description of an Anglo-American world that goes too far in economic inequality, i.e. beyond the natural social potential of the nuclear family, may put us on the trail of a more fundamental 'going too far' or 'going even further'.

Everything went too far in the Anglosphere: market freedoms, inequality, the denial of the nation. The radicalism of the globalist project, more and more detached from the old English conceptions of property, freedom and social responsibility, was, on the eve of Brexit and Trump, just about to present a clean slate, a new world of uprooted megalopolises filled with people from anywhere and everywhere. But even individualism, in the philosophical or religious sense, as the fundamental value of the Anglo-American world, may be going too far, or at least even further – I really do not know – and actually redefining human nature. Even though the question of rising inequality is still completely unresolved, the standard of living of working people continues to stagnate or fall, young adults are being trapped in a new poverty and the Black question in the United States and the European question in the United Kingdom are still not settled, the ideological debate on the overcoming of the duality between man and woman has become a burning issue. I am not speaking here as a reactionary ideologue, since I rejoice in the emancipation of women, fully endorse the legalization of same-sex marriage and am perfectly well aware of the universal moral dimension of the demand for transgender recognition. But, whether real or invented, the duality between man and woman has always been used by human societies to structure themselves, starting with the sexual division of labour among hunter-gatherers. To manage without it will constitute a revolution that goes beyond all others.

While studying the Anglo-American societies engaged in this ultimate transformation of social life, I suddenly thought of Burke and his passionate denunciation of the 'metaphysical' principles of the French Revolution, principles that he thought were indifferent to the nature of real human beings. There is indeed something metaphysical about the Anglo-American world's quest for a society that abolishes differences between the sexes, or the genders, depending on your ideological point of view. Something more radical than the desire of the French revolutionaries at the end of the eighteenth century to cut their national territory up into equal departments and to abolish their traditional calendar. But this is exactly what Burke had refused to see: it was England and her daughter America who were, and remain, the true revolutionary nations, capable of dreaming the next step that human beings will take and the world that will follow.

INTRODUCTION:
THE DIFFERENTIATION OF FAMILY
STRUCTURES AND THE INVERSE
MODEL OF HISTORY

The West lies in thrall to a strange sense of helplessness, despite a technological revolution that had apparently made everything possible. Goods,
images and words can circulate freely and quickly. There are harbingers
of a medical revolution that will allow human life to be wonderfully
extended. One Promethean dream leads to another. Between 1999 and
2014, the proportion of Internet users worldwide increased from 5 per
cent to 50 per cent. Countries have been transformed into villages and
continents into districts.

In the most developed countries, however, the sense of decline is
spreading, together with an inability to arrest it. In the United States,
the median household income fell during the same period from $57,909
to $53,718.[1] The mortality rate of White Americans aged 45–54 has
increased.[2] The revolt of the White electorate led, in November 2016, to
the election of an unlikely and alarming candidate, Donald Trump.

In various ways, other democracies seem to be following America
down this regressive economic and social path. The rise in inequality and
the decline in the standard of living among the younger generation are
virtually universal phenomena. Populist political forms of a new kind
are rising up almost everywhere against the elitism of the upper classes.
However, we can sense a certain variety in these imitations. While Japan
seems to be turning in on itself, Europe, with Germany now at the helm,
is turning into an immense hierarchical system, even more fanatical than
the United States in its devotion to economic globalization.

There is no economic mystery

The economic explanation for these phenomena is easy to find. Critical
analysis has largely managed to account for them since the early 1990s.
Free trade and the free movement of capital, while permitting a rise in

1

the rate of profit, have also led to a depression in ordinary incomes, a rise in inequalities, a deficit in global demand worldwide, and, at the end of a mad dash, the return of economic crises. Far from being emancipated by technology, the most advanced of the world's inhabitants are once more falling under the yoke. Job insecurity, declining living standards, sometimes even life expectancy: our modernity closely resembles a march towards servitude. For those who experienced the dreams of emancipation of the 1960s, the collapse of these hopes, in barely a generation, is astonishing.

Those interested in the economic mechanics of these phenomena have an abundant literature to refer to, including work by Joseph Stiglitz, Paul Krugman and Thomas Piketty on the dynamics of inequality and its depressive effects.[3] Note that some economists have taken their discipline to its very limits: James Galbraith has revealed that ultra-liberals now rely heavily on the state to enrich themselves, while Pierre-Noël Giraud has demonstrated that the logic of the *Homo oeconomicus* could lead to the claim, in certain quarters, that some human beings are 'useless'.[4]

Still, most establishment economists are feeble or indeed conspicuously absent when it comes to the criticism of free trade. They dare not suggest that free trade might be moderated by a few mechanisms of control. Too daring a critique would jeopardize their positions in academia, or – even worse – in the profession's prize-giving system.[5] This passivity is no great theoretical loss. We can find all we need on the real effects of free trade in Friedrich List's *The National System of Political Economy*, which dates back to . . . 1841. This is a classic: we can also read John Maynard Keynes's articles as well as a more recent book by Ha-Joon Chang, a Korean based in Cambridge, England.[6] In my *L'Illusion économique*, written in 1997, I emphasized the depressive effect of unregulated trade on a globalized economy.[7] We should also remember, quite simply, that Adam Smith, in *The Wealth of Nations*, did not envisage an untrammelled free market that would deny the reality of nations and their higher interests.

In spite of the high quality of all these studies, we must admit that the regression of the advanced world is not, as a purely economic phenomenon, a very interesting subject of study. What continues to fascinate me, on the other hand, is the feeling of powerlessness that persists despite our efforts at understanding: we have the diagnosis but we do nothing; we just passively witness the unfolding of the economic sequence.

The great recession of 2008–9 gave the impression that a return to a Keynesian type of action with the restoration of tariff barriers was necessary. Insufficient demand is in fact the central concern of Keynes's famous *General Theory of Employment, Interest and Money*, and a minimum of common sense leads to the conclusion that, without protectionism, a revival in the domestic economy leads to the creation of demand for one's neighbours rather than for oneself. For a short time, American, English and French newspapers all came together to celebrate Keynes's comeback. Robert Skidelsky, the greatest of his biographers, even wrote a book with the title *Keynes: The Return of the Master*.[8]

The years 2010–15, however, forced us to realize that this lucidity had evaporated. During the 2016 US presidential election, the eruption of the debate on free trade and protectionism led by Bernie Sanders and Donald Trump took establishment journalists and politicians by surprise and made eminent economists very angry. Sixteen Nobel laureates and two hundred members of the most prestigious American universities petitioned against Trump and in favour of free trade, without succeeding in convincing the American people, whose living conditions, insensitive to the beauties of the theory, were continuing to deteriorate. How can we explain today the persistent intellectual backwardness of those specialized elites who, after denying the deadly effects of free trade in the United States and Europe, are now denying Trump's election? How can we explain this multidimensional refusal of the reality of the world, by serious people who have studied their subject at length? That's the real mystery.

Between 2010 and 2016, then, the march to inequality resumed and the global shortfall in demand became ever more threatening. The growth rate in emerging countries fell, reaching zero in Brazil. China itself, the factory of the world, is suffocating in an industrial pollution worthy of the nineteenth century, teetering on the verge of a crisis with incalculable geopolitical consequences. In this floundering economic world, whose political systems are in disarray, we are warned ever more insistently, day by day, that populism is a threat to our 'values' and that we must defend them. But what values, basically? Inequality? Poverty? Insecurity? Ah, no, sorry: it's 'liberal democracy', a now hollow concept emptied of its founding values – i.e., the sovereignty of the people, the equality of human beings and their right to happiness.

Thus, what we need to explain is not strictly speaking economic. It is rather the absence of any *real* awareness, i.e. one that would lead to action – this absence is what the historian of the present must understand. But in order to do so, we have to admit that the movement of history is not limited to the economic sphere alone, and that certain vital transformations occur in the deeper layers of social life.

The structures I am going to discuss are banal, obvious even, but we will be forced to admit that they are even more decisive for human actions than is the economy: they include education, religion, the family and, finally, the nation, which represents only the belated and current form of group belonging, without which the life of *Homo sapiens* is deprived of meaning.

3

I will be putting forward an anthropological vision of history, but let me make it clear that I will not be professing the slightest scorn for economics: however insignificant the establishment economists may be, whether they are academics or mercenaries of the banking system, this must not lead us to reject economic analysis as such. Let us keep in mind the very useful postulate of the rational individual, the selfish *Homo oeconomicus*; but let us never forget that *Homo oeconomicus* does not act in a vacuum, but has capabilities and goals defined by the group, family, religion and education. There is indeed a logic of markets. It is even true, as Bernard Mandeville had stated in 1714 in *The Fable of the Bees: or, Private Vices and Public Benefits*, that capitalism uses all the least altruistic features in human beings, all that is worst from the moral point of view, to make the most efficient productive system work. In 1776, in *The Wealth of Nations*, Adam Smith delivered a less aggressive vision of this economic optimization based on an aggregation of the selfish traits of individuals. But that is precisely the point: the moral problematic of Smith should inspire us to explore the depths of a social life that goes beyond the economic system alone – depths in which the mental transformations that define the conditions of economic activity are produced.

The crisis in advanced countries

It is so easy these days to show that the immense upheaval of the world that is happening in front of us cannot be grasped by political economy. To understand this, we will stick to the most advanced countries. The current difficulties of Brazil and China rid us of the illusion that history is now decided by these countries as they catch up with the rest. It is in the United States, in Europe and in Japan that the rules of the game of economic globalization have been defined. It is this 'triad' which, since 1980, has put to work the newly literate working populations of the Third World, crushing its own workers' wages and raising (to put it mildly) the overall rate of profit. The domination of the ageing advanced world is perhaps even better expressed by its ability to attract a labour force trained elsewhere, sucking in from its periphery workers, technicians, computer scientists, nurses, artists and doctors as it needs them, thus ensuring its own survival by a veritable act of demographic predation. This plundering of human resources is much more serious than that of natural resources, because, on a certain level, it jeopardizes the development of those countries that are now taking off, by depriving them of their executives and middle classes.

Thus, world power has not shifted decisively. In fact, it is in that old European power, Russia, that the only independent force in the globalized system has managed to maintain itself. The protagonists of the Second World War are still at the helm of world history. But they themselves are experiencing a shift of such magnitude that it is necessary to speak of an anthropological mutation comparable to the Neolithic revolution even more than to the industrial revolution. Like sedentarization and agriculture, the transformation under way is causing an upheaval in the way of life of the human species in all its dimensions. Let us look at its most important elements.

- *Massive enrichment* of all, but especially of the middle and working classes, between 1920 and 1960 in the United States, between 1950 and 1990 in Europe and Japan; sudden rise in the standard of living, with countless psychological effects.
- *Sudden drop in birth rate between 1960 and 1980.*
- *Increased longevity* and ageing populations on a scale never seen in history. The median age of Europeans fluctuated between 20 and 25 years until the middle of the twentieth century. In 2015, it was 41.7 years.[9] That of the English who carried out the 1688 Revolution was about 25 years. The industrial revolution in Britain brought it down to 20 years in 1821, and it was still 22 years in 1871. But in 2015 it reached 40 years. In 1900, the median age of Americans was 22.9 years; in 1950 it was 30.2 years. The increase in post-war birth rates temporarily brought it back to 28.1 years around 1970. It rose to 38.3 years in 2015, an increase of ten years in just forty-five years.
- *Dramatic increase in educational level.* The development of secondary and higher education systems – from the inter-war period in the United States, after 1950 in Europe and Japan – led to a new cultural stratification, tending to figures of 40 per cent higher educated, 40 per cent long-term educated and 20 per cent of a 'remainder' ranging from those 'without diplomas' to 'functional illiterates'.
- *Women overtaking men in educational terms* with, again, significant differences between advanced nations. This is the most impressive change in the eyes of a specialist in family structures.
- *Terminal erasure of religion*, probably including in the United States.
- *Collapse of the model of marriage inherited from religious times.*

We could extend the list and give many more examples of fundamental transformations.

If we take these transformations, presented in Table 0.1 in no particular order, into account, we gain a singularly enriched vision of the one-dimensional individual of the economists: we can maintain the hypothesis that human behaviour is rational while wondering what happens to the

Table 0.1 Life expectancy and ageing

	Life expectancy 2015		Median age		Ageing
	Men	Women	1950	2015	1950–2015 in years
United States	76	81	30	38.3	8.3
United Kingdom	79	83	34.9	40	5.1
Australia	80	84	30.4	37.5	7.1
Canada	79	84	27.7	40.6	12.9
Germany	78	83	35.3	46.2	10.9
Sweden	80	84	34.2	41	6.8
Japan	80	87	22.1	46.5	24.4
South Korea	79	85	19	40.6	21.6
France	79	85	34.7	41.2	6.5
Italy	80	82	28.6	45.9	17.3
Spain	80	85	27.5	43.2	15.7
Russia	65	76	23.3	38.7	15.4
China	73	78	23.7	37	13.3
Middle East	71	76	20.8	26.3	5.5

Source: UN data

existential objectives of human beings when they become, statistically, richer, older, more educated, more feminine and less numerous . . .

It is of course in observing the evolution of these real individuals that we will discover the historical conditions behind the feeling of powerlessness that has swept through the most advanced societies. To grasp it in all its complexity, we will have to investigate not just the economy but three other fields of investigation, all deeply affected by this evolution: education, religion and the family. Membership in the national group is a constant, a structural element whose action we will need to assess, abstaining from fantasies about its potential disappearance and thus going against the grain of the ultimate dream of globalizing ideology. And let us immediately provide the right answer to the question asked at the beginning of this book: if we do not understand what is happening today in the world, it is because economics, as the dominant ideology, is a magician of false consciousness that hinders any complete description of the world. When historical anthropology selects the essential aspects and defines accurately their respective importance, economics deems that what is of primary importance is in fact secondary, or rather mistakes the effect for the cause and the cause for the effect.

The conscious, subconscious and unconscious levels of societies: economics and politics, education, family and religion

A simplified pastiche of Freud's model of the mind will allow us to proceed to a stratified representation of human societies and their movement. On the surface of history, we find what is conscious, the economy of economists – what the media tell us about on a daily basis, and which neoliberal orthodoxy assures us, in a bizarre reversal of Marxism, is decisive. Politics is also conscious, of course – noisily so, one might even say.

Going deeper, we find a subconscious level of society, namely education, a layer that citizens and commentators can perceive as important when they think of their real lives, but which orthodoxy refuses to fully accept as decisive, denying its powerful action on the conscious layer. Parents know that the fate of their children – economic success, survival or disaster – will depend on their academic performance. It is easy for people to imagine that an educationally efficient society will succeed economically. The achievements of Finnish and Korean schools explain the exceptional economic careers of their pupils. To the extent that the OECD (Organization for Economic Co-operation and Development) has made the comparison between the educational performances of different nations one of its statistical preoccupations, it can be said that the subconscious is no longer very far from the conscious, even if this intellectual bureaucracy finds it difficult to admit that educational performance is more dependent on religious and family traditions than on economic investment.

This is because, if we go even deeper, we find the true unconscious of societies: family and religion, in their complex interaction.

Family structures – authoritarian or liberal, egalitarian or inegalitarian, exogamous or endogamous depending on the country – determine, unbeknown to those who form them, political values and educational performances. I put forward this twofold hypothesis in the early 1980s in two books, *La Troisième Planète* and *L'Enfance du monde*.[10]

I noted that the map of communism as it stood in the late 1970s matched the map of a specific peasant family system, found in Russia, China, Vietnam, Yugoslavia and Albania; this was a form that combined a father with his married sons, and it was authoritarian as regards the relations between parents and children, egalitarian in the relations between brothers. Authority and equality, indeed, represent the hard core of communist ideology, and the coincidence between family and ideology was not difficult to explain. It resulted from a sequence at once historical and anthropological: urbanization and literacy break down the communal peasant family; the latter, once it has disintegrated, releases into general social life its values of authority and equality; individuals

7

emancipated from paternal constraint seek a substitute for their family servitude in fidelity to a single party, in integration by the centralized economy, or in KGB control (in the Russian case).

Starting from this very simple empirical observation, and from its explanation, I generalized the result obtained for communism to the competing ideologies of the era of educational and economic upswing. Then I linked each one of them – social democracy, Christian democracy, anarchism, ethnocentric nationalism, pure Anglo-American liberalism and French egalitarian liberalism – to an underlying family structure.

Educational dynamism – the modernizing subconscious, one of the main agents of the breakdown of the traditional anthropological system – seemed, for its part, to reach a maximum in regions dominated by authoritarian family systems that were favourable, or at least not too unfavourable, to women: in Germany, Sweden, Japan, Korea and Finland. But everywhere, a mechanism of diffusion led, whatever the family type, to the mass literacy achieved in Europe between the Protestant Reformation of the sixteenth century and the middle of the twentieth century.

To my great surprise, this identification of a family unconscious of ideological life, which I had arrived at in a purely empirical way, provoked violent resistance, rejection even, from specialists in the human sciences, particularly in societies that were freer in temperament and way of life. Reactions to the original publication of these two titles in French, as well as to their translations, convinced me that the relevance of the family was denied with particular vigour in individualistic societies, in France and the Anglo-American world in particular. In Japan, a country of stem families where the traditional custom, whether samurai or peasant in nature, had designated a single heir, usually by male primogeniture, the family hypothesis was not seen as shocking. The many lectures I have given in France have revealed that the southwest of that country is highly receptive to the family hypothesis. But this is because southwest France is our great stem-family area, a little Japan of our own, with its particularly strong centres in Béarn and the Basque Country.

It is as simple to explain the acceptance as it is the rejection. In an authoritarian and inegalitarian family culture, the resulting general collective constraint is obvious and comes as no revelation. On the other hand, in the liberal world, the hypothesis that ideology is determined by family structure collides head-on with the dominant ideology of individuals who think of themselves as autonomous, deciding and acting as they wish, without constraint.

The fundamental paradox of a theory that explains ideology by the family is that it suggests that *adherence to the ideal of freedom is itself determined*. This ideal flourishes in regions dominated by the nuclear family, an anthropological form that never contains more than a married couple and their children. The nuclear family is liberal in its intergenerational relations, irrespective of the appearance of any Lockean or Rousseauist political philosophy. When the peasants of the regions concerned learn to read and write, they become politically active and adhere as if 'naturally' to the ideal of freedom, even though this is predetermined. Freedom, both political and economic, then finds expression in social life and in history, in a very real and concrete way; it produces great positive effects on intellectual and scientific life. But this freedom is nonetheless an illusion. Pushing the argument to its limits, it can be said that men and women within a nuclear-family system do not have the freedom to work together to build a totalitarian society. This is lucky for them, but it poses a significant problem for the metaphysicians of human freedom.

The concept of a family unconscious thus applies fully to the case of liberal societies. In a country like Japan, where the ideological tradition includes the action of the family, the notion of the unconscious is more questionable. It is valid only to the extent that the country remains officially under the tutelage of the liberal ideology imposed by the United States.

The case of Germany, and with it a good part of continental Europe, is different. Nazism was the clear realization of the authoritarian and inegalitarian potential of a very harsh stem family in a historical phase of religious and economic crisis. But after 1945, Germany was obliged to return to the fold, and to think of itself as democratic and liberal like the Anglo-American world. It succeeded in this much better than Japan, because the absolute abomination of Nazism led to amnesia being used as a form of therapy. In this case, false consciousness has reached a maximum level, but it is not alone in Europe: Italy, whose communitarian family, predominant in the centre of the country, successively produced fascism and then a massive communist vote, finds itself in a similar situation of false consciousness. The liberal democratic language of the Italian ruling class in no way reflects the potential inherited from the country's old family structures. And, as we will see in the penultimate chapter of this book, the return of repressed European anti-liberalism, which between the two world wars produced Mussolini, Salazar, Hitler, Franco and Pétain, explains the strange, sad but logical destiny of the Eurozone.

Religion used to be on the conscious level: it explicitly defined the framework of social life, especially in the Jewish, Christian and Muslim worlds. The ebbing of belief (i.e., secularization) has changed its status, causing it to plunge gradually into an almost absolute unconscious. It hardly exists any more for citizens who think of themselves as secular, modern atheists, and are worried about its persistence in populations of immigrant origin. Sociological analysis, however, reveals that it continues to exist among citizens of the most secularized countries, as a dim echo, like a void that we must take into account if we want to understand the anxiety of advanced societies.

Curiously, this void is not the same everywhere: it is coloured by significant and varied traces of social beliefs and ways of being that stem from the vanished religious systems. In two previous books, I discussed the specific social behaviour of the French provinces, where Catholicism has been dying out since the last couple of decades of the twentieth century. In order to grasp this phenomenon of partial survival after death, I defined the concept of *zombie Catholicism*.[11] But other religions than Catholicism survive their apparent death. To understand the continuing educational and economic effectiveness of Scandinavia, or the specific xenophobia of northern and eastern Germany, the concept of zombie Lutheranism would be of crucial value. Inverse forms of the zombie phenomenon are observable: American Protestantism and Judaism are probably dead even though they think they are alive. The God of the United States has become a good pal, and American Jews have started to believe in Paradise![12]

It is usually difficult to completely separate family systems from religious systems. Religion generally has something to say about sexuality and marriage, the status of women, the authority of parents, and the equality or inequality of brothers. In this book, I will take the opportunity to study the interaction between the undifferentiated nuclear family and Judaism, between the egalitarian nuclear family and early Christianity, and between the stem family and Protestantism. In all these cases, I will retain the idea that the family predominates and is capable of favouring the appearance of certain religious forms; but I will immediately grant that an autonomous retroactive action of the emerging religion is possible, with its undeniable ability to reinforce certain features of the family system that had given rise to it. Talking in terms of a co-evolution of family and religion is undoubtedly the right way of formulating the situation.

The time of the conscious, the subconscious and the unconscious

Imagining societies as superimposing conscious, subconscious and unconscious layers leads to a new representation of history, one that is necessarily schematic but reveals a fundamental paradox and leads to a thoroughly Copernican intellectual revolution.

The model of a society with a stable structure at any given moment is only a representation. Time passes, inevitably. Each level of the structure evolves. But the pace of change is not the same for each level. We can say, as a first approach, that the more one sinks towards the unconscious depths of social life, the more slowly time passes, and the longer the forms last.

- At the conscious level of economic globalization, free trade and the financialization of the world took little more than half a century to impose their presence, if we date the trend to open markets back to the American victory in 1945. The process started to get hysterical first around 1979–80 with Margaret Thatcher and Ronald Reagan, and then around 1989–90 with the fall of the Berlin Wall and the collapse of the Soviet Union. Globalization is also a political process with a maximum degree of consciousness, since the imperial power of the United States piloted the worldwide establishment of global markets for goods, capital and labour. These conscious phenomena, which include treaties, wars, trade and the establishment of tax havens, were spread over just a few decades – six, four or three decades depending on whether we are interested in the whole of the process, its rise, or its dramatic acceleration.
- At the subconscious level, time passes more slowly. The movement of societies towards universal literacy began in Germany in the sixteenth century with the Protestant Reformation, which demanded direct access for believers to Scripture and God. There was then a circular diffusion from this initial centre, which first affected the countries that had converted to Protestantism – Scandinavia, the heart of the Netherlands, England and Scotland, the American colonies – then France, and finally Southern and Eastern Europe. In the aftermath of the Second World War, the mass literacy of the continent could be viewed as complete. The process spread everywhere, from the American and Japanese centres and the great British and French colonial cities. By 2030, younger generations will be able to read and write everywhere, including in Africa. It will have taken five centuries to reach this result – i.e., simplifying somewhat, ten times more than for economic globalization.
- At the unconscious level, the movement of family structures is even slower. I reconstructed it for Eurasia in L'Origine des systèmes familiaux [The Origin of Family Systems].[13] The evolution of the family, however, is part of the time of history, not of some immemorial past. To understand its mechanisms of differentiation and diffusion, we must start from Sumer in Mesopotamia, around 3000 BCE, and from northern China around 1500 BCE. These were periods when writing was invented twice over: this is conventionally taken to define the beginning of history in the strict sense. If we choose Sumer as ground zero and time zero for the differentiation between the family structures of Homo sapiens, we have five thousand years of evolution up until now, a multiplication by ten of the time scale

11

of literacy, and by one hundred of the time scale of economic and political globalization.

Rounding out, let us say that the economic conscious works on a scale of fifty years, the educational subconscious on a scale of five hundred years, and the family unconscious on a scale of five thousand years.

Religious time, unsurprisingly, takes as its basic unit the millennium, as does family time, but it is still twice as short on average. If we date the writing of the Bible to the eighth century BCE, we get 2.8 millennia for Judaism, 2 millennia for Christianity and 1.4 millennia for Islam. The history of Buddhism begins in the fifth century BCE if we date it back to the awakening of Siddhartha Gautama, but three or four centuries later if we take as a starting point the first written texts, i.e. between 2.5 and 2.1 millennia of development. The difference in rhythm between family time and religious time is consistent with the hypothesis of a primacy of the family structure.

Economy, education, religion and the family: research into these factors, broadened and organized by the notions of conscious, subconscious and unconscious, can produce a realistic representation of the crisis of the Western world in the wider sense of the term, i.e. including Japan and South Korea. Thus, individualistic atomization at the economic level and the incapacity of collective action at the political level will spring from the development of higher education, the disappearance of religion, and the transformation of family structures. The divergence of the Anglo-American, German, Swedish and Japanese paths can be reduced to the diversity of the original family structures, as can the Russian resistance to globalization. We will be able to impose order on a multiple modernity, which combines the rise of economic inequality and a new equality in relations between men and women, a rise in educational level and a collapse in democratic practice.

This enriched analysis will make it possible to place the dynamic West in its correct relations with the rest of the world that is now catching up with it. The West's interactions with China, which has become the workshop of the world, and with the Middle East, an energy producer and manoeuvring ground for its armies, are particularly strong. In the West, what North American and European societies require from less developed countries is not only cheap labour and oil, but an alignment with their own way of life. The ideological caddy from the West is trundling its heap of values and projects across the whole planet – values deemed to be universal: freedom of expression, free trade, the free circulation of human beings and money, women's emancipation, the right to vote, and the redefinition of homosexuality as legitimate human behaviour. Elements belonging to the conscious level of social, political and economic life, and others drawn from the unconscious, family level, are piled up higgledy-piggledy. The ongoing transformation of the Western way of life must spread to the world, and our elites are impatient at the lack of enthusiasm to follow them evident in China, India, Iran and the Arab world, especially with regard to women's emancipation and homosexuality. Our desire for the universal, attractive in itself (I am, in this, an ordinary Westerner in full agreement with our values), is unfortunately based on a false vision of the historical development of family structures and ways of life. For millennia, different dynamics have been at work in the centre of Eurasia and on its periphery. An accentuation of the divergence can be perceived, indeed, in the most recent period.

In the West, women have overtaken men on the educational front: this leads me to the hypothesis of a shift to matriarchy, though I would not claim that it is nearing completion or even succeeding. Such a phenomenon has never been observed in history: it represents an anthropological revolution, a leap into the unknown. All the same, in the West narrowly understood (the Anglo-American, Scandinavian and French worlds), the matriarchal revolution stems uninterruptedly from a family structure that initially gave women a high status. The nuclear family made the marital couple the fundamental element. In China, India, Iran and the Arab world, on the other hand, traditional family structures include a powerful patrilineal component and a very low status for women. This East/West opposition is pretty familiar. On this point, the real problem of liberal democracies, in their confrontation with the patrilineal worlds, is that they also mainly have a false view of the historical movement of family structures. We perceive the low status of women as a form of 'backwardness', a logical complement to the economic backwardness of non-Westerners. But the reconstructed history of family systems reveals that Eastern patrilineal systems are the result of a long evolution that the West, on the whole, did not undergo. In China, as in the Arab world, Iran and India, the long-term historical dynamic has for millennia involved giving women a low status. What we need to admit at this point is that the 'Western matriarchal' revolution does not find itself confronting backward family cultures in the East, but systems whose patriarchal dynamic has been opposed to theirs for millennia.

The patrilineal transformation had begun to affect Germany and Japan, and this factor will enable us to understand the demographic difficulties of these economically very advanced countries. We will be surprised to discover, in spite of this, that Russia, the bridgehead of the communitarian family towards the West, seems to be achieving a partial but very profound and large-scale shift towards matriarchy, which could make it, in the third millennium, a highly original social model not only in its authoritarian democracy, but also in its degree of women's emancipation.

It is therefore not enough to see social life as a hierarchy of conscious, subconscious and unconscious layers. It is also not enough to grasp that the pace of change slows down when we plunge into the deeper layers, from politics and the economy to education, then to religious and finally family life. We need to make the ultimate leap and to admit that the movement of the deep layers is not what we had believed.

When it comes to the evolution of family structures, it is tempting to evoke a magnificently repressed planetary unconscious. In this introduction, I will present some of the theoretical consequences of our mistaken views of the dynamics of family systems, because identifying this error will show up the pointlessness of many of the efforts made by the human sciences over the last two centuries to understand our history.

The densification and gradual differentiation of family systems

The standard model of the historical and social sciences places the emergence of the nuclear family and the 'individual' at the heart of the upswing of the West. Millions of pages have been written on this theme by thousands of authors. The liberation of the individual, that atom of creativity, is said to have occurred in Europe from the Middle Ages onwards, at a date that changes depending on which variant of the liberal canon we refer to. I am here presenting an obviously simplistic model: I hope the reader will forgive me. But it would be ridiculous to stick to an outmoded description.

Over a long first phase, the nuclear family emerges from the stifling mass of the great family of the past. The simple but stable association of a man and a woman – the Adams and Eves of modernity – permits the rise of an initial individualism. This conjugal couple produces children, quickly raised and liberated, who become, as adults, 'individuals', admittedly imperfect, but free actors in economic, social and political life.

In a short second phase, recent and still with us since it began in the 1960s, the 'pure individual' is finally born, released from the nuclear family itself. In this second phase of individualism, the conjugal bond between man and woman is replaced by temporary conjunctions between individuals who no longer consider the durability of the relationship – ranging from a night to a lifetime – or the sex of their partners as essential factors. Divorce, new relationships, homosexuality and sex changes all become structural elements in the family system.

Forty years of research on family systems have made me realize, by accident, that the first phase of this standard model – from the complex family to the conjugal couple – was a factual absurdity. The original family was nuclear and this anthropological form was therefore never,

14

properly speaking, invented: it was that of *Homo sapiens* in the native state. However, the communitarian-family forms that bind the couple in patrilineal kinship ties and dominate the mass of Eurasia are creations of history. Their existence results from experiences and crystallizations spanning five millennia, in a process that began in Mesopotamia with the birth of the city and writing. An equivalent process, occurring later but of the same nature, is observable in Chinese history. It had its equivalent in Africa, without it being possible to discern, in this continent, any link with writing or the city.

The development of agriculture always seems to lie at the origin of the densification and the structuring of family groups by bonds between males, a phenomenon that we may designate with the neologism *patrilinealization*. Embryonic forms of this mechanism can be identified on the central Mexican plateau occupied by the Aztec Empire, or in the Andes under the Inca Empire on the eve of the Spanish conquest.

Since the emergence of *Homo sapiens*, the family has evolved from simple to complex and not from complex to simple. The lowering of the status of women is an essential element in the way it has grown more rigid. The most western part of Europe has largely escaped this transformation, even though Germany and southwest France, like Japan, saw the development of the stem family, that first stage of patrilinealization, and central Italy even witnessed the emergence of the exogamous communitarian family, the second stage of the same process. In northern France and England, only the mediaeval nobility and sometimes the upper stratum of the peasantry were affected by the beginning of a stem-family mutation.

There have been exceptions to this mechanism of densification of the family and lowering of the status of women. An inverse process of simplification can be observed here and there at various moments in history. Northwest Europe has its own particular history, which includes, in England, Holland and northern France, an increasingly nuclear type of family by means of the destruction of the network of undifferentiated kinship (or bilateral or cognatic kinship according to standard Anglo-American anthropological terminology) which framed it in its original shape.[14] We can even identify regional episodes where there is a reversion of patrilineality towards bilaterality, i.e. from complexity to simplicity, a mechanism of reversion that includes a rise in the status of women. I will study what for us are the most significant examples, including the one that occurred at the beginning of our era in Rome, Hellenistic Greece and Judea. But I will also show, in Chapter 2, that Africa, which I did not include in Volume I of *L'Origine des systèmes familiaux*, conforms to the general model and has not escaped the dominant historical process: a patrilinealization and a complexification of the family over time.

An 'inverse model' of history

The discovery of a gradual densification of family forms has incalculable consequences for the interpretation of human history. This 'inverse model', as opposed to the 'standard model', opens up the possibility of an equally inverted perception of several historical fields and a better understanding of what we are, here or elsewhere: in Europe, America, China, Japan, Russia, the Middle East or Africa. The question 'Who is more evolved?', or 'Who is ahead?' becomes very complicated, difficult to answer and self-contradictory. The economically backward Middle East has the most complex and 'evolved' forms of family, as the endogamous communitarian family, which combines the father with his married sons and then encourages marriage between the children of these brothers, is the result of five thousand years of evolution. North America, the leader of economic globalization and of the opposition to it, represents – even more than England or the France of the Paris Basin – the nuclear-family form closest to the original model of *Homo sapiens*. If we turn to East Asia, we must also admit that the Japan of the Meiji Revolution in 1868 had a family system that, although not nuclear, was less distant from the original type of *Homo sapiens* than the one predominant in China. The Japanese stem family in peasant milieus designated a single heir and combined at most two married couples; it was therefore simpler than the Chinese communitarian family, which ideally combined a father with all his married sons and could have three or more couples living together.

The technological and economic modernity of the West coincides with rather archaic family systems. As regards way of life, *Homo occidentalis* is a primitive figure, not too distant from the ancient common background of humanity, the hunter-gatherers who originally populated the planet. This archaism was regulated rather than abolished by the Christian conception of sexuality and marriage, as well as by feudal or state-based guidelines for inheritance.

The inhabitants of the so-called 'emerging' countries do, of course, lag behind technologically and economically. But as far as their family customs are concerned, Chinese, Indians, Arabs and Africans are 'advanced' populations – they have been shaped by five thousand years' worth of developing complex communitarian and patrilineal family systems, including a lowering of the status of women.

The West believes that its modernity is . . . well, modern. Women's emancipation, however real, is only the radicalization of a primitive state of humanity. *Homo sapiens* was hardly hostile to abortion. The same could be said of the struggle for the rights of homosexuals, since the residual primitive hunter-gatherer communities studied by anthropologists rarely appear homophobic.

16

What the 'West' demands of the economically emerging world at the heart of Eurasia is therefore not just a mere catching-up. Technology, education and the economy must make progress in those regions. Fortunately, we can observe a global convergence of many of the indicators that concern the conscious or subconscious levels of social life: the economy is advancing, education levels are rising in the former Third World, and the birth rate is declining. Even secularization is progressing, in spite of powerful fundamentalist spasms of resistance in the Hindu and Muslim worlds. In Iran, the mosques are already empty.

But what is required in the field of the family is, at the heart of Eurasia, a historical retreat, the deconstruction of systems that had taken thousands of years to develop. The nuclearization of family structures, in cultures where the merging of couples in the extended family and the lowering of the status of women had been regarded as progress, as a newly sophisticated way of life, can only produce resistances, reactions and rejections that are incomprehensible if we stick to the standard model of human evolution. In India, China, Vietnam, Kosovo, Georgia and Armenia, the proportion of female babies is declining because modern prenatal sex screening techniques are used to perform selective abortions of foetuses of the female sex.

Anchored in a false vision of history, our perception of the present is a mere absurdity, producing misunderstanding, intolerance, violence. As for the future . . . How can we reasonably foretell future developments in the globalized world if we project into the future trends that do not exist in the present, or are rather the direct opposite of the real trends? Over the last five thousand years, the movement of human societies has been, not everywhere but most often, directed towards the submission of the individual and the lowering of women's status. True, we are currently living through an attempt to reverse the process. But it starts from a limited area, the periphery of Eurasia, which, far from the centre of gravity of human history for the last five thousand years, mainly escaped the patrilinealization and densification of its family fabric.

Providing an accurate description of history rather than explaining it

The West is not only suffering from rising inequality and economic paralysis. It is engaged in an anthropological transformation that combines, to mention only the essentials, higher mass education, accelerated ageing, an elevation in the status of women and perhaps even matriarchy. So if we want to grasp the meaning of our malaise, we must look down on history from above – but so as to plunge into its unconscious depths. To try to understand, to know 'where we have got to', I will be attempting an overall outline of human history that, starting from the emergence of *Homo sapiens* in Africa, will set family and religious anthropology at its heart.

I will not, however, be trying to explain human history in any philosophical and absolute sense. My work on the evolution of the family, from nuclearity to patrilineality, and my later studies of the way ideology is defined by family structures, leads only to 'fragments' of explanation. Admittedly, laying bare the reasons behind the contemporary disarray in the unconscious layers of social, family and religious life is, in a sense, to explain. But there can be no question of completely systematizing the explanation, of rigorously prioritizing the levels, or even claiming that family structure, the variable in which I am a specialist, comes first. And, as I said, I do not reject the idea of a specific economic dynamic. The logic of *Homo oeconomicus* can be deployed only within anthropological frameworks, but globalization connects and contrasts very different anthropological frameworks in a specific way. The dynamics of states also has its logic: their confrontation through diplomacy and war – hot wars, cold wars, economic and ideological wars – defines a largely autonomous field of study. This is why geopolitics has its own value as a description and explanation of certain elements of history.

To pretend to integrate all the fields of analysis, all the determining factors, or all the logics into a coherent total model would be very pretentious.

What I propose here is more simply to break away, without any dogmatism, from the narrow vision of economists and politicians, and to give an enriched description of globalization. An accurate, extensive description is already a great contribution towards an understanding of what we are currently experiencing.

Thus, in the most advanced societies we shall see how family and religious changes precede a stagnation in the educational level and a fall in birth rates – phenomena that are themselves harbingers of a crisis in the economy and the state. We will see how the West ventures out on the new paths of matriarchy but is mistaken in thinking that it has explored, in the past, the paths of patriarchy. Its attempt to move beyond the nuclear family of the founding days, by granting a higher status to women than to men, would indeed be its first radical invention, comparable but opposite in meaning to the invention of patriarchy that started in Mesopotamia at the beginning of the third millennium or in China in the middle of the second millennium BCE.

The principle of divergence

This enriched empiricism will allow us to grasp the persistent diversity of the world – quite the opposite of an economicism that fosters a uniform vision of societies. It is axiomatic that *Homo oeconomicus* is the same everywhere. It would be an understatement to say that, for neoliberal theory, *Homo oeconomicus* belongs to similar societies, since the ideal type of such a human being exists only outside society. In Margaret Thatcher's words, 'there is no such thing as society'. The universalism of the rate of profit forces us to forget the anthropological diversity of the world. In the aftermath of the collapse of Soviet communism, the major political and economic decisions of the 1990s were taken on the basis of a generalized hypothesis of convergence: free trade was bound to unify the planet, the single currency was bound to homogenize Europe. What we observed next, in the reality of history, was of course the opposite, a divergence of economic performance and standards of living. Why? Because, while the human being is universal in an ultimate anthropological sense – there is one species *Homo sapiens* whose primordial characteristics I will describe below – societies are diverse in their values and modes of organization.

Economic globalization in fact accentuates differences, and is in itself a factor of divergence: societies that are forced to compete, obliged to adapt and threatened with disintegration all end up by falling back on themselves in one way or another. To survive, they draw new strength from their original values. Pushed too far, free trade fuels universal xenophobia.

It is probably here that using family models to grasp history seems most indispensable. For what the development of the human family reveals over the past five thousand years is, starting with an original anthropological type common to the species, a strong tendency towards differentiation, in other words a slow but powerful divergence between concrete human groups.

I do not want to sound too melodramatic. Today, there are elements of convergence in the world: the spread of literacy in the former Third World, combined with the plateauing out of higher education in the most advanced societies – in the United States since 1965–70, in France since 1995, for example – has led to a reduction in the educational gap between nations and to an intellectually more homogeneous world. Birth control is leading everywhere to a decline in birth rates, which has already abolished the binary opposition between the old developed nations and the least developed countries. By 2015, the birth rate in the United States (1.9 children per woman) was higher than that of China (1.7), and that of France (2.0) was higher than that of Iran (1.8). With education and birth rate, however, we are only on the subconscious level of social life, even if the birth rate has a major impact on the underlying family structures. This is already better than sticking to the economic consciousness of politicians or journalists, but it is not enough. Deeper down, at the unconscious level of family structures, a tendency to divergence leads the societies of the world to differ in new ways.

A comparison between the most advanced societies suffices to demonstrate this. Despite high and comparable educational levels, their birth rate indicators diverge in proportions that imply different destinies. By 2015 (again), the United States, with 1.9 children per woman, the United Kingdom (1.9), Australia (1.9), Sweden (1.9), France (2.0) and Russia (1.8) were not too far from the threshold of 2.1, which essentially makes the replacement of one generation by the next possible. On the other hand, Germany (1.4), Japan (1.4), and South Korea (1.2) had reached rock-bottom values that prohibit the natural renewal of the population and require either the use of mass immigration or the acceptance of demographic decline. We will see how these differences are easily explained by the subterranean persistence of distinct family values, those that concern the status of women in particular.

In *Le Mystère français*, published in 2013, Hervé Le Bras and I were obliged to note the perpetuation, across the 550,000 square kilometres of France, of different systems of customs and manners in most recent times. Despite the acceleration of internal migration, despite the disappearance of complex households in some provinces and the collapse of Catholicism in the areas where it had survived, regional heterogeneity persists. Homogenization, via television, the TGV express train and the Internet, has not prevented the persistence of diverse cultures, stimulated rather than erased by economic globalization. The way these cultures adapt to stress is differential because regional societies continue to integrate individuals more or less effectively, and are therefore more or less able to withstand the shock of economic competition. And all this has happened within a single nation, unified by its administration and by its language. How can it be imagined that the different nations that play a part in globalization – the United States, Britain, Sweden, Germany, Japan, Russia, China and Korea – will do any less well, in terms of cultural permanence, than the provinces that make up France? The question of the balance of powers is nowadays combined, in geopolitics, with the issue of the latent conflict between different systems of customs, without any clear understanding of the factors at play or the stakes involved. The hypothesis of universality and convergence poisons international relations, since the stronger party, or the one that believes itself to be such, requires the other to align with its values and way of life as well as submitting in economic and military terms.

Imperialism and feminism

The map of the American imperial system, with its dominant English-speaking constellation and with its advanced bases in Europe and Asia, is always strangely reminiscent of the map of certain family systems: all are characterized by a status of women that is either originally high (United Kingdom, France, Netherlands, Norway, Denmark, Spain, Australia, Philippines, Indonesia, Thailand), or else not too low in historical terms (Germany, Japan, South Korea). A central Eurasian bloc (Russia, Iran, China, India) continues, long after the fall of communism, to resist American domination. It seems to mark a kind of geopolitical continuation of the continental patrilineality that gave rise, between 3000 BCE and 1700 CE, to extended and dense family systems. But we must not oversimplify: the Russian communitarian and patrilineal family system is of very recent origin. It permitted women to maintain their high social status, and today, as I have said, it is showing signs of a matrilineal inversion. But that is the point: does the anthropological shift in Russia, combined with the reaffirmation of a German anthropological difference, not announce a realignment of geopolitical affinities?

In the Arab-Persian world, as well as patrilineality we find an endogamous preference for marriage between cousins. Its family systems are those that lower the status of women the most, and tie the individual into the closest bonds of kinship. By virtue of the anti-feminism and anti-individualism that dominates it, northern India, where the family is exogamous and communitarian, is close to the Arab-Persian world.

Despite the hegemony of 'economicist' thinking, it is clear that the geopolitical field is imbued with notions or concepts of an anthropological order: that is why the West bombards the Middle East with demands to elevate the 'status of women'. The strangest case is surely that of a Russophobia focused on the issue of homosexuality. In the midst of the Ukrainian crisis, the Anglo-American press and many others in the West criticized the Putin regime for its homophobia. Who would have imagined, at the time of the wars of Louis XIV or Napoleon, or during the First or Second World War, such a fixation on sexuality in international relations? Far from bringing people closer together, globalization leads to conflicts that, more than those of the past, call into question the very foundations of life in certain of the dominated societies.

Impossible futures

This book describes, very schematically, the historical movement of the last 100,000 years in an attempt to grasp current developments and 'say something' about the changes that we are experiencing at the beginning of the third millennium. It is not a question of predicting the future. How would that be possible? Our advanced societies have no equivalent in previous history. Never have human groups of such a size been so rich, so old, so educated, so devoid of collective beliefs. The frequent (but not universal) educational backwardness of male individuals is an absolute novelty, as is what is known as 'very low low fertility'. Our enriched description of history so far, however, will allow us to depict the history still to come as if in a photographic negative: it means, in fact, that we can consider some futures as improbable or downright impossible.

- For instance, the survival of democracy as we knew it in the twentieth century seems unlikely in the current conditions of educational stratification and stagnation. But the return to a genuinely oligarchic government, a system that was based on mass illiteracy, seems equally unlikely.
- The full convergence of nations whose unconscious value systems persist is another impossibility.
- The fundamentally archaic character of Western anthropological structures, whose present-day modernity, as we shall see, is often only a fundamental return to their primordial basis, allows us to exclude the hypothesis of a social disintegration that would follow changes in the way of life.
- Identifying the mechanisms of continuity of anthropological systems will help us understand why constant but reasonable flows of emigration and immigration do not pose problems of equilibrium and perpetuation for the anthropological systems concerned. On the other hand, we will have to admit that above a certain threshold of emigration in the Middle East, in the Baltic countries or in Ukraine for example, or a threshold of immigration in Germany, these flows may destabilize the societies of arrival and departure. However, we cannot predict much more than the appearance of sociological black holes, of sizes, depths and natures that are difficult to define.

We can therefore anticipate certain elements of the future concerning, for example, family structures, the end of the religious sphere, the return of economic protectionism, and the appearance of zones of anarchy, but without being able to describe how all these elements fit together and preserve a balance between themselves.

We will also be able to minimize the risk of error, both in our photographic negative and in our projection of trends, by focusing the analysis on the most advanced society. I said earlier that the developed world – the triad formed by the United States, Western Europe and Japan, to which must be added Russia – was still the master of the global game, and continues to define the future. But, inside the triad, the United States, despite its difficulties, continues, for better and for worse, to play its role as leader. Its population continues to grow and it remains the locus of fundamental innovations. And it is essential to take this into account.

The Anglosphere at the heart of modern history

Before the United States, England set the transformation of the world in motion with the invention of representative government, the industrial revolution and the organization of a first wave of globalization before the First World War. It is probably time for us to admit that 'the Anglosphere' lay at the heart of the history of the years 1700–2015. Let me point out that this term has only an anthropological sense for me: it allows me to bring together a language and a family system that is absolutely nuclear. The notion of the Anglosphere frees us from the implicit 'Germanism' of the concept of 'Anglo-Saxon world', which, as I have noticed, can annoy Americans of Italian, Jewish or Japanese origin. The absolute nuclear-family system predisposes its members, as Alan Macfarlane was the first to see, to every form of radical individualism.[15]

It is relatively easy to admit the economic primacy of the Anglosphere over the last three centuries. The absolute nuclear family, capable of radically dissociating the generations, was the anthropological precondition for the uprooting, over a few decades, of the English peasantry. The industrial revolution began in Britain between 1780 and 1830: the use of coal by the steam engine released an energy potential never before seen in history. We can follow the spread of the new mode of production by the dates of economic take-off of the various nations, as estimated by William W. Rostow: 1830–70 for France, 1840–70 for the United States and Germany, 1870–85 for Sweden, 1880–1900 for Japan, 1890–1900 for Russia, 1900–10 for Canada, 1905–15 for Australia, 1950–60 for China, and 1960–65 for Korea.[16] The predominance of the United States in the economic globalization that followed the Second World War is another obvious fact.

The model of an economic transformation driven by the Anglosphere is therefore easy to accept. More difficult for us to accept is the model proposed by Daron Acemoglu and James Robinson, of a modern political history that began not with the French Revolution of 1789, but with the Glorious Revolution of 1688. And yet it was the latter that established the liberal institutional bases for the economic take-off.[17] Like Voltaire in his *English Letters* (also known as the *Philosophical Letters*), the revolutionaries of 1789 looked to Albion: England was the model to emulate, the nation to catch up with, in the political rather than the economic field at a time when the industrial revolution was not yet a given. The central character in the *English Letters* was Newton (1643–1727), and perhaps it is simplest to admit that England was also the heart of the scientific revolution of the seventeenth century.

It is in the familial and religious unconscious of this Anglosphere – defined not so much by language as by a nuclear but non-egalitarian family structure, as well as by an adherence to a Protestantism of Calvinist variety – that we will find the origin of the decisive changes, positive and negative, that affected the planet.[18]

England and America will together form the central element of this outline of human history. An in-depth analysis of their histories will allow us to confront in the most direct way possible the paradox of a modernity – technological, political and economic – that arose from an archaic anthropological background. The case of America will appear even more significant than that of its mother nation. This is because the American family of the years 1700–2000 seems the closest to the original type of *Homo sapiens*.

Science here sheds light on a very common intuition, perhaps even a cliché: we will understand why America constantly strikes us as simultaneously modern and primitive, capable of defining our future while appearing to us so unsophisticated in its way of life, so natural in its way of being.

At the current stage of history, in a context where technological breakthroughs coexist with educational stagnation and a decline in living standards, one logical mistake must however be avoided: we should not confuse the idea that America is in the lead with the idea that it defines 'progress'. This was unambiguously true until around 1965. But at that date the United States, before the rest of the world, fell into an educational stagnation, and if it is in the lead these days, it is often because it is ahead of the rest in its journey towards deeper stagnation. This is how the demographic performances shown in Table 0.1 should be interpreted. We see from this table that life expectancy in the United States is far from being the highest. But in this respect, the best results obtained by East Asia and Europe do not indicate that these two regions have 'overtaken' the United States in an absolute historical sense. They simply benefit from the most advanced medical techniques, while they have not yet reached the stage of complete educational stagnation. Japan, Korea, Germany and France can be expected to go through stages of regression long since traversed, and sometimes overcome, by the United States. Each of these nations will do so in its own way, in accordance with the principle of divergence that is one of the structural elements of the history described in this book. Nations with ultra-low birth rates could not, for example, envisage any American-style social stabilization. I will examine, in the conclusion of this book, the delicate question of whether American society might experience a new start.

The real question raised by Germany and Japan: the role of the stem family and primogeniture in history

Before deciding, in the case of the United States, between the assumptions of regression, stagnation or a new start, I will need to qualify, in the body of this book, the model of the nuclear family as the only one capable of inventing the future. The examination of history will indeed force us to formulate not only the hypothesis of a mechanism of innovation generally derived from the nuclear family, but also the idea that there is a principle of acceleration associated with the stem family.

Before the English political, scientific and industrial revolution, there had been the Protestant Reformation and mass literacy, which came from elsewhere. Religious crisis and educational upswing originated in Germany – let us say in 1517 if we select Luther's ninety-five theses as the zero point of these upheavals. Now the Germanic world is the land of the stem family rather than of the nuclear family. But another question arises immediately: are we sure that the stem family was fully developed in Germany, in all strata of society, when the Reformation began? After all, primogeniture was really practised there by the nobility only from the thirteenth century onwards.

Above all, we must not imagine a fixed or even stable anthropological milieu in the history of Europe. It is of course essential to have a typology defining the various family systems and allowing us to map them out. But this instrument should not make us forget that these 'systems' are actually 'dynamic', in constant evolution, most often in the sense of strengthening their characteristic features. This notion of a 'dynamic system' is particularly important if we focus on Germany and Japan, whose family types, far from being stable, have been constantly emerging since the Middle Ages. The history of the Japanese and German stem families demonstrates the growing development of their constituent features between the fourteenth and eighteenth centuries and an increase in their rigidity in the nineteenth century – and sometimes even in the twentieth.

Let us leave the periphery of Eurasia, whether German or Japanese, for a while, and head to its heart; let us plunge into its past, right at the start of history.

In Sumer, Mesopotamia, very shortly after the appearance of writing around 3300 BCE, we can identify the first rules of primogeniture, as we can in Egypt just a little later or in China a millennium and a half later. A microscopic scrutiny of the first human economic upswings does not reveal homogeneous family compositions but, almost immediately, the combination of a nuclear basis with 'stem' elements. In the avant-garde societies of Sumer, Egypt and ancient China, the first accumulation of an intellectual and physical capital led to the invention of transmission rules. We can thus see the appearance of laws or practices of primogeniture, and embryonic forms of the stem family. With its principles of undivided inheritance and lineage continuity, the stem-family type facilitates the accumulation of knowledge and an acceleration of progress.

Let us return to the most recent modernity.

After the English and then the American upswings, the spectacular way in which Germany and Japan – the two great stem societies of the present day – have caught up with them shows that the question of a specific interaction between stem family and development must be posed, along with the connection between nuclear family and innovation. In 2006, for example, the United States filed 22.1 per cent of triadic patents (registered simultaneously in America, Europe and Japan), the United Kingdom 2.3 per cent, Japan 29.1 per cent, Germany 7.4 per cent and South Korea 9.8 per cent.[19] With 360 million inhabitants between them, the two great nations of the Anglosphere, where the absolute nuclear family holds sway, produced 24.4 per cent of patents; with only 257 million inhabitants between them, the three largest stem-family nations filed 46.3 per cent. It is thus necessary to reflect on the historical role of the stem family, whether in its embryonic or its mature form.

Forwards to the past

At the end of my life as a researcher, it is disturbing for me to come to such a reflection on the historical interaction between the absolute nuclear family and the stem family because, in a way, this is exactly where I started, or rather where my teachers made me start. When I arrived in Cambridge in the early 1970s, Peter Laslett had just discovered the nuclear family in seventeenth-century England and was still struggling, more and more feebly it has to be said, against the idea that the stem family could ever have existed anywhere.[20] Lutz Berkner had just shown, from eighteenth-century Austrian local censuses, that the stem family presents three generations – grandparents, parents, children – only at certain stages in its development cycle.[21] Frédéric Le Play (1806–82), inventor of the stem-family concept, had just been exhumed, to be challenged and then legitimized by the immense historical survey launched in Europe and Japan between 1965 and 2000. A systematic review of the past shows the importance of primogeniture as a stage of human history, since it is found not only in Sumer, in the upper classes of ancient Egypt and in mediaeval China, as I have said, but also among the Indian salmon fishermen of the northwest coast of America, and among the Maori and the original Hawaiians. It remains very common in the most 'archaic' part of Africa from the point of view of family structures.

The stem family quickly became an obsession for Le Play. As a reactionary in a turbulent France, he was as it were hypnotized by its values, the father's authority over the son and the inequality of the brothers, a combination that seemed to him to embody a principle of order and hierarchy. He emphasized its potential for economic dynamism and its ability not only to pass on knowledge, but also to liberate into social life adventurous younger sons, the d'Artagnans of the economy or culture.

However, liberal thought had begun to hate the stem family long before Le Play. As early as the end of the seventeenth century, John Locke (1632–1704) criticized Robert Filmer (1588–1653) for his apology for primogeniture and the power of the father in *Patriarcha, or the Natural Power of Kings*, published posthumously in 1680.[22] American and French revolutionaries in the eighteenth century focused on birthright as a major target. Progress and the stem family were later considered by progressive thinkers to be polar opposites. Historians therefore had some difficulty in defining the proper place of primogeniture in the process of development. And indeed, we will see that the stem family can produce, depending on the circumstances, dynamism or paralysis.

Anthropologists mostly ignored Le Play, who is not mentioned in Robert Lowie's (1883–1957) fine survey of the history of ethnological thought.[23] The anthropologist Elman R. Service (1915–96) was, to my knowledge, the first to have understood his importance as a significant figure. In his book *Origins of the State and Civilization*, Service makes primogeniture a central element in the stabilization of chieftaincies and the development of the state.

The stem family, as a mode of organization, either noble or peasant, no longer exists. Three-generation households are no more than statistical leftovers in Germany, Japan, Korea and southwest France. But we must, at the beginning of the third millennium, recognize two phenomena: the persistent technological dynamism of nations where the stem family was dominant, and the deep demographic crisis of these countries now that their birth rate indices are around 1.4 or less.

Moreover, the underground permanence of 'stem family' and 'nuclear' values is about to disrupt the unity of the 'Western world', born as it was around 1945 from American military conquest rather than from any cultural convergence. The re-emergence of values of authority and inequality in Germany and elsewhere is giving a new shape to Europe. Thus, without the hypothesis of a return of the anthropological repressed – the family unconscious – we will not understand the gradual transformation of the continent into a rigid hierarchical system. The liberal and democratic revival that is rousing the Anglosphere, expressed by the Brexit vote as well as by the election of Donald Trump, seems to me difficult to explain without recourse to the hypothesis of a permanence of the liberal and non-egalitarian (but never inegalitarian) values of the absolute Anglo-American nuclear family.

The crisis of the Western world is therefore twofold. It does not take the same form in the Anglosphere as it does in countries characterized by a traditional stem family. It would be absurd to detect an ultra-individualistic thrust in Germany, Japan or Korea, a feminism tending to matriarchy or a deficiency of collective action. The crisis of the stem-family nations is specific. It assumes varied forms since, as we shall see, Japan and Germany now diverge, for reasons that lie largely outside the anthropology of family structures. Opening this book with the concept of a crisis in the Western world, we will close it by issuing that world's death certificate. By way of compensation, we will have to admit that Russia is undoubtedly much more Western than the conflicts of the moment suggest.

The methodology of my work is not new. This outline of human history focuses on a few key areas – family, religion, education, ideology – which, observed as closely as possible, make it possible to assess the nature and extent of what we are experiencing. The variables I work on – the structure and development of the domestic group, the status of women, infant mortality, current birth rates, final number of offspring, literacy rates, the proportion of the population with a higher education, theological conceptions, religious practices, political voting patterns, and sexual norms – were those I was inspired to study by my years of training in Paris and Cambridge. They were those of the French school of the *Annales* and the Cambridge School of Historical Anthropology, two schools that were not very different at the time. That is where I studied, and then took my doctorate. I remained a loyal student, faithful to the lessons of my teachers – Emmanuel Le Roy-Ladurie, Peter Laslett, Alan Macfarlane, Pierre Chaunu, Tony Wrigley, Pierre Goubert, Jacques Dupâquier, Michel Vovelle, Lawrence Stone, François Furet, Jacques Ozouf and Akira Hayami. I may add here that my gratitude to Anil Seal, my tutor at Trinity, without whom I would never have survived intellectually, remains absolutely intact. My only originality probably lies in applying a methodology designed to understand the seventeenth and eighteenth centuries to an analysis of the world of today.

A simplified family typology

In this book, which strives to understand the crisis of the most developed parts of the world, and especially that of its greatest powers, we will content ourselves with a simple typology of family systems.

The *pure nuclear family* (unstable according to Le Play) essentially consists of a couple and their children. The latter must move away as teenagers and then establish, through marriage, autonomous domestic units. This type is found in all the Anglo-American countries where it also includes the absolute freedom to test, since parents can share out their property as they see fit between their children. That is why, in the case of England, the United States, Australia, New Zealand and English-speaking Canada, we talk of an *absolute nuclear family*. The France of the Paris Basin adds to this nuclearity of the household an egalitarian inheritance rule, which leads to the concept of the *egalitarian nuclear family*, also applicable to southern Italy, central and southern Spain and central Portugal. These two variants of the nuclear family consider paternal and maternal relations as equivalent, but of secondary importance.

The *nuclear family with temporary co-residence* also has the ultimate goal of independence for its married children, but it provides them with a phase of co-residence with the previous generation for a few years, according to three possible modes: either with the parents of one or the other spouse, it does not matter which (*bilocality*), which I will sometimes call an *undifferentiated nuclear family*; or with the parents of the groom (*patrilocality*); or with those of the bride (*matrilocality*). The *bilocal variant* is observed in the Philippines and in Belgium. The *patrilocal variant* is typical of the nomads of the Eurasian steppe (Turkish and Mongolian groups), the Nahua-speaking populations of the central Mexican plateau, the populations speaking Quechua and Aymara in Peru, Ecuador and Bolivia, and southern India. The *matrilocal variant* dominates Southeast Asia, including Burma, Thailand, Cambodia, Malaysia, Sumatra and Java.

The *stem family* names a single heir, usually the eldest of the boys, who takes most of the family property. The young couple cohabits, according to more or less strictly defined formulae, with the parents of the husband (patrilocality), allowing the appearance of households that, when he has children, contain three generations. This type of stem family corresponds to a *level 1 patrilineality*. A boy is privileged, but a girl can succeed in the absence of sons and, above all, sons who are non-heirs are in fact treated like girls. The principle of dominant masculinity cannot be systematized. This classification includes Japan, Germany, Korea, the southwest of France and, with a strong feminist twist and little cohabitation, Sweden. Today, the cohabitation of generations and the inequality of inheritance have largely disappeared in cities on the formal level, but we will see that the values of authority and inequality have survived very well, somewhat mysteriously, after the disappearance of the large peasant households that displayed them. However, we can observe, among a few minor groups, *bilocal stem-family types*, which in principle name the 'absolute' elder, whether boy or girl, as the heir, as in the Basque country, among the Ibans of Borneo or in certain villages in Tohoku in northeast Japan, and *matrilocal stem-family types*, where the eldest daughter is chosen (the Garos in the Assam hills, the Aegean islands, northern Portugal).

The *exogamous communitarian family* (patriarchal according to Le Play, the *joint-family* of northern India) establishes the equivalence of the brothers and a general principle of male superiority. All sons are ideally combined with the father and find their wives outside the original group. Girls are exchanged between patrilineal complex households. At the death of the father, the inheritance is more or less rapidly divided equally between the brothers. The system defines a *level 2 patrilineality*: this time, all men are superior to all women. This type is found in China and Russia, the latter (rather like Sweden in its stem-family category) with a strong feminist residue. This system is particularly recent in Russia, hardly going back to the seventeenth century. As in the case of the stem family, the latent values of the family structure survived the disappearance of the large peasant households of the nineteenth century. There are also *matrilocal communitarian variants*, for example among the Hopi Indians of the southwestern United States, as well as *bilocal communitarian* variants, notably on the northwestern edge of the Massif Central in France. In the Massif Central, however, these non-patrilineal communitarian types have, like the patrilocal communitarian family, favoured a strong communist vote.

In northern India, the exogamous communitarian family reaches an anti-feminist level equal to or perhaps higher than that of the Arab world, expressing itself by the excessive mortality of female foetuses or girls even more than by the sequestration of women.

It is hardly possible to understand the crisis of the most advanced parts of the world without referring to the opposite fantasmatic pole that now comprises the Muslim and, more specifically, the Arab-Persian world. To situate it anthropologically, we need to define the *endogamous communitarian family*. As in the case of traditional Russian or Chinese families, its ideal development cycle involves a father and his sons. But the marriage model is no longer exogamous, but endogamous, demanding, when possible, marriage between the children of two brothers. If an ideal cousin of the right age does not exist, any other first-degree or even distant cousin is desirable. In the central

Arab world, the rate of first cousin marriages hovers at around 35 per cent. It falls to 25–30 per cent in Iran, Egypt and the Maghreb, but reaches 50 per cent in Pakistan. Marriage between the children of two brothers expresses the strength and continuity of their affection. This horizontal axis is the fundamental link of the Arab family, and it was tragically revealed by the drift into terrorism of the Kouachi brothers and then the Abdeslam brothers.[24] This pathological manifestation must not hide the fact that, in 99 per cent of cases, the residual fraternalism of the second generation, as it becomes assimilated, simply leads to warmth and security. The strength of the masculine principle here goes up a notch further: we reach a *level 3 patrilineality and a maximum egalitarian value*.

Finally, the *family type of southern India* is circumscribed on the map but demographically significant since it concerns a population of around 350 million individuals (the figure for 2015). I have already mentioned it above as a nuclear-family type with patrilocal temporary co-residence. But this *nuclear family with patrilocal co-residence* is complemented, in Tamil Nadu, Karnataka, Andhra Pradesh and Maharashtra, by a specific endogamous mechanism that encourages *marriage between the children of a brother and a sister* (preferential marriage between *cross cousins*) but forbids marriage between the children of two brothers or the children of two sisters. In Tamil Nadu, the heart of Dravidian India, the *oblique marriage* between a man and the daughter of his elder sister is also well represented. Oblique marriages and cross cousin marriages express the importance of the affection between brother and sister. The brother–sister bond moderates the patrilocality in establishing the young couple, who co-reside for a while with the parents of the husband, then settle nearby. The principle of masculinity is therefore relativized. Let us add that no value of equality is observable in this anthropological type whose principal brother–sister axis excludes any principle of symmetry. Southern India, despite its rather exotic kinship from the point of view of the European exogamous and bilateral system, and thanks to the absence of the principle of equality and the relatively high status of women, encompasses several elements that are very compatible with the Anglo-American world. It would therefore not be absurd to give southern India the status of associate member or junior partner in the Anglosphere. But I will give it a level 1 patrilineality, comparable to that of the German or Japanese stem family.

The last point to keep in mind when following the description of the history set out here is this: the 'inverse model' of the history of the family reveals a fundamental historical sequence leading from the undifferentiated nuclear family (level 0 patrilineality) to the stem family (level 1 patrilineality), then from the stem family to the exogamous communitarian family (level 2 patrilineality), and finally to the endogamous communitarian family (level 3 patrilineality).

— 1 —

THE DIFFERENTIATION OF FAMILY SYSTEMS: EURASIA

About 200,000 years ago, the so-called *Homo sapiens* type emerged in Africa, with its essential physical characteristics (its two-legged posture and its brain size). Its predecessor, *Homo erectus*, which appeared on the scene 1.8 million years ago, had already mastered fire (around 400,000 years ago, plus or minus 100,000 years). A step up the ladder of evolution, *Homo habilis*, identifiable 2.4 million years ago, knew how to use cut stones as tools.

The history of *Homo sapiens* continued with the species spreading out across the whole planet. These hunter-gatherers left their home continent some 100,000 years ago and moved into the southern fringes of the Middle East. They reached southern India around 60,000 BCE, then Australia, southern China and Southern Europe around 40,000 BCE. *Home sapiens* moved into Western Europe some 25,000 years ago. At the same time, the Bering Strait was crossed. South America was entered 15,000 years ago; Scandinavia, northern Siberia and Canada 10,000 years ago. Finally, just 6,000 years ago, Austronesian-speaking peoples moved from Taiwan to colonize the Philippines, Borneo, Malaysia and Indonesia, eventually reaching Madagascar around year 0 and New Zealand around 1250–1300 CE. These Austronesians were agriculturalists. All these dates are controversial and tentative, especially those concerning the settling of China and America.[1]

The great migration of hunter-gatherers did not establish a definitive map of human settlement. The invention of agriculture triggered new movements because it is a naturally expansive activity. The masters of the new techniques quickly realized that newly cleared land was particularly productive, and the first peasants set out in turn to conquer the earth, dominating, assimilating or eliminating the hunter-gatherers they found on their way. So human beings were restless – especially as the invention of nomadic breeding, which followed that of agriculture, triggered even more movements, several times over, using donkeys, horses, camels and dromedaries.

There are few questions that inspire one to dream as much as the original migrations of hunter-gatherers. The fossil remains of humans and their productions are no longer the only data at our disposal for reconstructing their history. Modern genetics can reconstruct their ancient movements. The analysis of the human genome may one day lead to a definitive map and chronology of the mechanism of dispersal. For the time being, archaeologists and geneticists often disagree, and the geneticists themselves have not really come to any agreement. This new science is prone to indulge in an element of poetic licence. Analyses point to genetic bottlenecks occurring when human beings first moved into the Middle East, and when they crossed the Bering Strait and the Isthmus of Panama: each time, the small size of the migrant group led to what is known as a 'founder effect' caused by 'depletion' of the genome. Africa, it seems, retained a maximum genetic diversity, resulting from the long and chaotic emergence of the human species on this continent.[2]

Nowadays, again, we are increasingly aware of the hypnotic effect of a genetics that claims to have identified immutable biological characters at the deepest levels of the human being. The male Y chromosome and the female mitochondrial DNA have succeeded the blood groups A, B, AB and O as ways of essentializing group membership, delineating these groups ever more finely and allowing us to study lineages according to sex. The fascination that these stable and transmissible characters exert over us is quite legitimate. Differential sex-based genetics has, for example, led to the discovery that Judaism was transmitted to Europe by male individuals from the Mediterranean.[3] This new patrilineal element will lead us, once we have tackled the rabbinical debates on the role of fathers in the education of children and on the conversion of women, to a reasonable interpretation of why a belated Jewish 'matrilineality' appeared on the scene (I return to this question below).

The historian of social forms must, however, be cautious and often sceptical when noting advances in population genetics. In most cases, the analysis of genes invisible to the naked eye does not go much further than the examination of trivial phenotypic differences such as skin colour or facial features. Recent genetic maps show that Africa, southern India and Australia were populated in ancient times and closely related in terms of genome. But we have known for a long time that these are also the regions where the skin of individuals is darkest – the effect of a genetic proximity that has not been affected by a long stay at higher, less sunny latitudes. Anthropology at its most traditional also revealed the similarity between the Dravidian faces of southern India and those of the Australian Aborigines, which without any shadow of a doubt establishes the close relationship between the two populations.[4] Recent genetics confirms here what everyone already knew, and adds nothing to the accuracy of dating.

The analysis of secondary genetic differences between human sub-groups, however, is of real interest in several areas, first and foremost when biological variations have medical implications. Note the vulnerability of African children to measles and the tendency of Australians of British origin to suffer from skin cancer.[5] Specifically heterosexual transmission of the HIV virus in populations of African origin is an essential piece of data when it comes to prevention. But we have to admit that, for anyone interested in the social elements of human history over the last 10,000 or 12,000 years – including sedentarization, the invention of agriculture, the diversification of family structures, and the emergence of the city and the state – this genetic research is most often quite useless. The separation of the groups is too recent for genetic differences to have become big enough to cause a divergence in instincts, aptitudes and tastes.

What history shows us, on the contrary, is an astonishing ability on the part of the scattered human populations to invent similar techniques and social forms and pass them on to one another. Agriculture was born in the Middle East, China, New Guinea, Africa, and Central and South America. Each of these agricultural emergences led, in each of the populations concerned, to an invention of the patrilineal principle. The highly typical custom of transmission involving inheritance by the eldest son is found in every shape and size: we find it, at different dates, in Africa, the Middle East, China, Japan, Polynesia, Europe and among the Indians of the American Northwest. The history of human family systems can, for the most part, be written without any reference to biology.

The Neolithic revolution

The dispersal of hunter-gatherers, then, was followed by sedentarization and the invention of agriculture by several separate human groups. The Middle East made the first big leap, with sedentarization and the emergence of agriculture first occurring in the Fertile Crescent around 9000 BCE. It was followed by China, in the Yangtze and Yellow River valleys, around 8000 BCE. Neo-Guinean horticulture also developed from 7000 BCE onwards. It is now accepted that there was an autonomous sub-Saharan zone of emergence in West Africa between 3000 and 2000 BCE. In central Mexico and northern Andean America, two zones emerged between 3000 and 1000 BCE. Some researchers identify a pole of innovation in the eastern United States around 2000–1000 BCE. The invention of agriculture also came in many different shapes.

Six thousand years after the invention of agriculture, the differentiation of family types began, first with the emergence of primogeniture in Sumer, southern Mesopotamia, during the third millennium BCE. According to

35

the model I am going to present, most of the differentiation in human family systems has occurred over the past five thousand years. Here, I will merely be describing this history of anthropological types in broad outline; for the details and the demonstration, the reader is referred to Volume I of my *L'Origine des systèmes familiaux*, where I analyse and methodically map the family structures of 215 populations of Eurasia; its general introduction includes the groups from America and Africa that are indispensable to the general demonstration.[6] *L'Origine des systèmes familiaux* (henceforth OSF) is the main database on which the following description of family diversification is based.

However, in Chapter 2 of the present book I will add some results from Volume II (forthcoming) of *L'Origine des systèmes familiaux*, which will be devoted to Africa, the Americas and Oceania, but only for the human groups that, densified by agriculture, have survived European colonization: in the Central and Andean Americas, in New Guinea, and especially in Africa. These populations today comprise millions of people; they have been caught up in economic globalization and it would be unjustifiable to exclude them. Moreover, the significant populations of African origin in the United States, the United Kingdom and France, and those of Mexican origin in the United States, are, along with many others, being drawn into the most advanced modernity and a knowledge of their original family structures cannot fail to be of interest.

From the nuclear family to the Eurasian communitarian family

Our reconstitution of the history of family systems starts out from the geographical localization of types on the eve of urbanization. It uses an interpretative logic that was quite commonplace for linguistics and anthropology prior to the Second World War: *the principle of conservatism in peripheral areas* (PCPA). This powerful explanatory hypothesis makes it possible to read history in space: the most archaic forms (linguistic, architectural, culinary or family) survive on the periphery of cultural spaces. Once the great age of certain types has been established by geography, we can refine and date the sequence of transformations using the written documentation that has survived.

The PCPA was temporarily overshadowed by the structuralist moment initiated jointly by Claude Lévi-Strauss (1908–2009) in 1947 and George Peter Murdock (1897–1985) in 1949.[7] Ignoring the PCPA was the fundamental reason why anthropology was unable to produce any synthetic explanatory propositions. But there is nothing to stop us resuming analysis in terms of mapping and the PCPA, taking it up from where pre-war anthropology had left it – albeit on the basis of a body of data greatly enriched by monographic research between the 1960s and the 2010s.

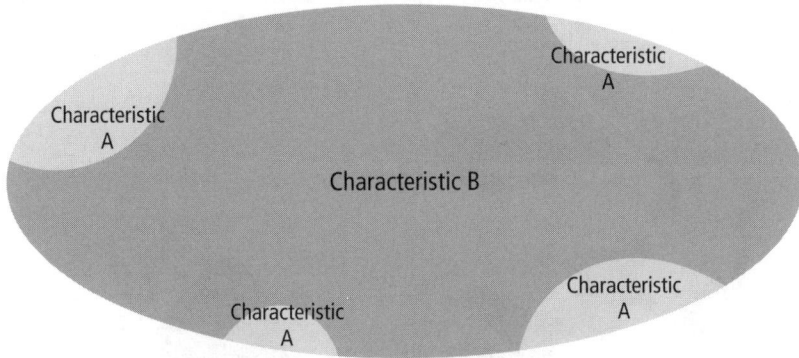

Figure 1.1   The conservatism of the peripheral zones
Source: Emmanuel Todd, *L'Origine des systèmes familiaux* (Paris: Gallimard, 2011), p. 24.

If a characteristic A distinguishes several pockets placed on the periphery of a characteristic B that covers a continuous central space, we can suppose that A represents the ancient characteristic, which in the past occupied all the space under consideration, and B a central innovation that has spread to the periphery without completely submerging it. The greater the number of residual pockets A, the more certain we can be of our interpretation. The global map of family systems is irrefutable. On the periphery of Eurasia, we find nuclear-family systems inserted into undifferentiated (or bilateral, or cognatic) kinship structures that treat maternal and paternal kinship as equivalent. An undifferentiated kinship system contrasts with a patrilineal system, which selects the male lineage for the transmission of status and property, and with a matrilineal system, which favours the female lineage.

Let us take a look at Map 1.2. If we move around Eurasia in a clockwise direction, the nuclear family, inserted into an undifferentiated kinship system, can be identified in southern Italy, in central and southern Spain, in Portugal, in northern France, in England, in the coastal parts of the Netherlands, in Iceland, Denmark, southern Norway, northern Sweden, the Lapland groups of Scandinavia and Russia, among the Chukchi, Yukaghirs and Eskimos of the Siberian northeast, among the Ainu people of northern Japan, in the Philippines, Indonesia, Cambodia, Thailand, Burma, among the Aborigines of the Andaman Islands, in Sri Lanka, and among the Christians of southwest India. This is the conservative, archaic characteristic A in the theoretical diagram drawn in Figure 1.1, embodied here in the reality of anthropological structures. The innovative characteristic B, namely patrilineality, is found in the communitarian families of central Italy, Serbia, Russia, China, Vietnam, northern India,

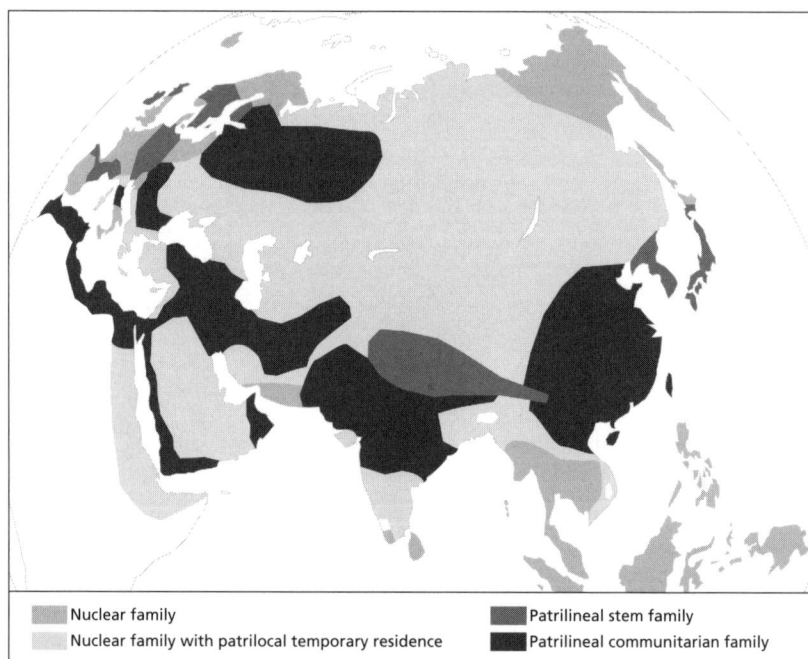

Nuclear family
Nuclear family with patrilocal temporary residence
Patrilineal stem family
Patrilineal communitarian family

Map 1.2   The main family systems in Eurasia
Source: Emmanuel Todd: *L'Origine des systèmes familiaux* (Paris, Gallimard, 2011), p. 103.

Pakistan, Iran, eastern Turkey and the Arab world. The family types of steppe nomads – Mongols, Kazakhs, Turkmen – are characterized by a flexible patrilineal organization, which brings together nuclear families related by males (nuclear family with patrilocal temporary residence), living in mobile camps. Together, patrilineal communitarian and patrilocal nuclear-family types comprise one magnificent bloc, all of a piece and occupying the heart, and indeed the greater part, of the mass of Eurasia.

Observe on Map 1.2 the intermediate position of the stem family: distinct in Germany, Sweden, Japan and Korea, and intertwined with the egalitarian nuclear family in Occitania and the north of the Iberian Peninsula, and with the absolute nuclear family in western Norway and Scotland. The Tibetan stem family, meanwhile, is set on a high-altitude frontier.

On the periphery of the patrilineal bloc, some matrilineal forms can be found in Kerala (southwest India) and in isolated pockets in southern China. In Southeast Asia, the (matrilocal) nuclear family of the young couple remains close to that of the wife's parents, a frequent phenomenon in Burma, Cambodia and Malaysia, and even more marked in Thailand,

38

Sumatra and Java. The kinship systems of Southeast Asia, however, are described by anthropologists as undifferentiated in the vast majority of cases, with the exception of the matrilineality of the Menangkabau of Sumatra. Religion is here clearly disconnected from the family fabric since these countries can be either Buddhist or Muslim.

In *OSF* I interpreted the matrilocality of Southeast Asia as the effect of a reaction to the waves of patrilineality – Indian, Chinese, then Arab – which have transformed Asia. As the sociologist Gabriel de Tarde (1843–1904) would have put it, this reaction was a *counter-imitation* and, if we prefer the terms used by the ethnopsychiatrist George Devereux (1908–85), we could speak of a *dissociative negative acculturation*. Patrilineal innovation – i.e., the primacy of men in the definition of lineage – is rejected. Conversely, the reaffirmation of the role of women turns them, in a way not required by the undifferentiated original, into the key element in the transmission system of identities and goods, leading to a matrilineal counter-innovation. The matrilineal formula abolishes, just as surely as the patrilineal principle, the undifferentiated nature of the kinship system, but it leads to paradoxical anthropological constructions in which women constantly oscillate between the authority of their brother and that of their spouse.

Matrilineal types find themselves, like the stem family, on the advancing front of the patrilineal principle, and that is why these forms are often close to one another on the map, or even mixed together. Primogeniture can even be matrilineal, as among the Garo of the mountains of Assam in northeast India. Here, it is an eldest daughter who succeeds. Among the Khasi, who are all close, it is the youngest daughter who is designated (ultimogeniture). Most often, the elder son plays a special role in the mechanics of matrilineal family systems.

Geography here provides us with the key to history. We can read the effects of time directly in space; we can see the patrilineal shift transforming the shape of the family, moving in waves towards a periphery that is never reached. Once it is complete, the patrilineal shift leads to the weightiest anthropological type, the communitarian family, an association between the father and his married sons. If it is not completed, it produces only male primogeniture and the stem family.

A careful examination of patrilineal family systems across Eurasia, however, reveals that between the fully communitarian poles of the Middle East, China, northern India, Russia, Serbia and central Italy that we noted above, there are vast spaces occupied by kinship systems that may indeed be patrilineal but which are content to bind nuclear families without the emergence of any large community households. The steppe from Mongolia to Ukraine is by far the largest geographical mass in which nuclear families are held together by patrilineal links. But Albania and northern Italy (apart from the Veneto) also belong to the category

39

'patrilocal nuclear family'. A complete model of diffusion must explain why Eurasian patrilineality is heterogeneous in this way. To do so, we must resort to historical sources.

The surviving literature reveals, in various zones of emergence and agricultural densification, several poles of patrilineal innovation. Each time, male primogeniture represents the first stage of the transformation. We see it invented in Sumer in the third millennium BCE, and in China at the turn of the second and first millennia BCE. In both cases, the innovation seems endogenous. On the other hand, we can sense the influence of Mesopotamia in the primogenitures that appeared later in northern India and in Europe: the double share of the eldest, a typically Sumerian custom, is found in the Indian laws of Manu and in the Bible, two texts that could not fail to inspire to foster the idea of primogeniture where they actually were read.[8]

Male primogeniture makes it possible to transmit real estate, whether it be tiny or immense, without dividing it. The emergence of a densely settled rural world, crowned by a political system that controls the whole of the regional space, is the basic condition for it to emerge, among the peasantry as well as the aristocracy. As long as there are new lands to be conquered, the emigration of children, whether nobles or commoners, as and when they reach adulthood, renders the privilege of the eldest useless. When land becomes scarce, this privilege may appear. The stem family then develops as a logical consequence of primogeniture: in a peasant environment, the choice of a single heir gradually leads to the co-residence of two adult generations, in accordance with a mechanism that tends to become rigid. What we can see here is a first example of the way a characteristic and a family system tend to become accentuated over time.

Historical and anthropological data reveal a stem family that prefers to designate the eldest son as the heir in 75 per cent of cases. If we do not just count the stem-family types observed in Eurasia, but weight the calculation with their respective demographic masses, we obtain a male primogeniture that organizes 95 per cent of 'stem' humanity. So this family type clearly expresses the emergence of the patrilineal principle. But the latter is still, at this stage, only imperfect. For if a man does not have a son, a girl will be the vector responsible for transmitting the family property, a phenomenon that can be observed in the ancient Middle East and ancient India, and in Japan and Europe between the fourteenth and the nineteenth centuries. In addition, male primogeniture a priori classifies younger sons with daughters in the same category of non-heirs. For these reasons, the stem family represents only stage 1 of patrilineal emergence. The kinship systems corresponding to the stem family are still usually placed by anthropologists in the 'undifferentiated' or 'bilateral' or 'cognatic' category.[9]

Around the vertical axis defined by male primogeniture, paternal and maternal relations are of equal importance. But the spread of the imperfect patrilineal principle of the stem family will lead in stages to its being systematized and accentuated.

In northern Sumer and ancient China, patrilineality was transmitted to neighbouring nomads whose kinship system was undifferentiated. These livestock farmers could not fail to admire, envy and imitate the technical and social innovations of sedentary civilizations. The nomadic pastoralists, however, had no reason to adopt primogeniture, whose primary function is to transmit an immovable property, farm or fief. However, they had found an innovative application of the principle of male superiority: they could use it to balance the sons' positions in the life of the group. Their households, which remained nuclear, would now be linked to each other by the patrilineal principle. In the Middle East, clan genealogies gave the Amorites of the Syrian Desert, then the Arameans, then the Arabs, the social and military architecture that allowed them to conquer Mesopotamia and northern Africa. In the heart of Asia, the patrilineal clan gave the Huns of the Turco-Mongolian steppe and all their successors the instrument that ensured their military superiority over their sedentary neighbours in China, northern India and Eastern Europe.

The patrilineal principle defines an order, a way of classifying all men, all warriors. A clan is an army in civilian life, or, more precisely, a civil society made for war. Conquest is its destiny. Its predatory vocation was theorized by Marshall Sahlins in 1961. But in 1954 Frank Lorimer had already pointed out, on the basis of African data, that unilinear systems (that is, patri- or matrilineal) favoured high birth rates and led groups to a demographic expansion that itself entailed competition for control of food resources.[10] It would be unfair, however, to forget Rome in the description of the universe of predation and conquest engendered by the patrilineal clan.

Rendered militarily irresistible by their now symmetrical patrilineal organization, the nomads of the desert and the steppe were able to enslave the sedentary Mesopotamians and Chinese who, respectively, had educated them. They then paid their patrilineal debt, so to speak, by transforming the stem family of the sedentary populations into a communitarian family by political domination (OSF, pp. 146–54, 555–8). The patrilineal communitarian family added to the authoritarianism of the stem family the symmetry of the brothers in the nomadic clan. The sequence was repeated in northern India (OSF, pp. 227–32), where the 'stem' innovation was not independent, and perhaps in northwest Russia, very belatedly, since from the thirteenth century onwards, the influences of the German stem family and the Mongol patrilineal clan were there superimposed (OSF, p. 368).

41

The symmetry of the sons, now associated together in farming, makes the patrilineal principle absolute. In the absence of male heirs, the family cannot survive. Women's status goes down another notch. This defines a stage 2 of patrilineality. But the evolution continues with an autonomous accentuation of the characteristic over time. A stage 3 of patrilineality is gradually achieved in the Middle East and in northern India where the situation of women falls to significant levels of oppression.

The map of patrilineality and Eurasian communitarianism has now been completed. The sociologists and anthropologists of the nineteenth and twentieth centuries traced it, people by people, region by region. The demographic weight of the Chinese, Indian, Arab and Russian peasant masses reduced the importance of the nuclear and patrilineal systems of the nomads of the Eurasian steppe and the Middle East. Still, the Soviet and subsequently American armies were able to put to the test the martial abilities of the patrilineal Pashtun clans of Afghanistan. The predatory efficiency of the clan can also explain the inability of Westerners to control Somalia and, to some extent, the sudden expansion of Daesh between Iraq and Syria.

The late emergence of the stem family in Europe, Japan and Korea

On both the edges of the Eurasian community, the European stem families of the West, on the one hand, and their Japanese and Korean counterparts, on the other, are beautifully symmetrical.[11] In the West as in the East, male primogeniture appeared in the Middle Ages.

In Europe, the Franco-Norman aristocracy in the eleventh century took the innovative step of adopting primogeniture (*OSF*, pp. 439–40). The stem form certainly affected peasant communities from the thirteenth century onwards, but it was implanted in depth only in certain regions: in the Germanic world, Occitania, Catalonia, the Basque Country, Sweden, and western Norway. In these regions, in the post-industrial age, we will continue to find still active 'stem cultures'. In the Paris Basin, the population has resisted primogeniture: it can even be said that it has defined itself against it. Here, the egalitarianism of the common people opposed noble primogeniture (*OSF*, p. 455). In Germany, strangely but logically, the reverse has occurred: peasant primogeniture finally became identified with the very notion of servitude, so, from the fourteenth century onwards, the aristocracy asserted its freedom by returning to the principle of equality and division of property, which became a marker of noble identity (*OSF*, pp. 440–1). David Le Bris has observed a similar phenomenon of elite egalitarianism in mediaeval Toulouse.[12] In Chapter

8, I will study the impact of Franco-Norman primogeniture on the English family system.

In Japan, the nobility began to practise male primogeniture in the thirteenth century, during the Kamakura period (*OSF*, p. 180). Birthright then spread through the peasantry until the nineteenth century. The shift to the stem family occurred later in Korea, and began only in the mid-fifteenth century (*OSF*, p. 192).

In the context of the outline sketched out here, attentive to the phenomena of cultural divergence, it is essential to understand that the appearance of male primogeniture occurred late in Europe and on the eastern fringes of Asia. It is even more important to understand how gradual and slow the spread of the stem family was. Thanks to Akira Hayami for Japan and to Dionigi Albera for the Alpine Arc, we have a clear vision of the process. In Japan, the systematization of primogeniture spanned centuries, culminating in the late nineteenth century with the Meiji Revolution, which finally enshrined it in the national civil code and applied it to the imperial family itself.[13] Dionigi Albera, meanwhile, has identified a very late spread of the stem family up until the nineteenth century in the French Alps.[14] The Irish stem family is also of very recent origin, since the principle of undivided property, long forbidden by the English, was applied on the island only after the Great Famine of the years 1844–7 (*OSF*, pp. 396–7, 453). One of the important lessons of the anthropology of family systems is that the history of the West and of Japan is very brief.

— 2 —

THE DIFFERENTIATION OF FAMILY SYSTEMS: INDIAN AMERICA AND AFRICA

The hypothesis of an original undifferentiation in family and kinship systems applies outside Eurasia. I will confine myself here to an examination of the populations that survived the European conquest, in America, New Guinea and Africa, and that are currently playing a part in the process of economic globalization.

Indian America

As demographic and anthropological masses, only those peoples that practised sedentary agriculture in America in the fifteenth century CE resisted the shock of European colonization. We will of course need to analyse the anthropological systems of the populations that were at the time living from gathering, hunting, fishing and even slash-and-burn agriculture – in North America, the Amazon and the southern cone of the American content – if we are to gain an overall understanding of the process of differentiation of family types, and I will do so in Volume II of *L'Origine des systèmes familiaux*. However, this would be of little use here, in a book whose purpose lies in identifying the social dynamics at work today. Hunter-gatherers and itinerant farmers were marginalized or crushed by the European conquest. On the other hand, even a cursory examination of Nahua-speaking groups in Mexico or of Aymara and Quechua speakers in Peru, Ecuador and Bolivia is of immediate interest. These languages were those of the Aztec and Inca Empires, and they are still spoken by numerous peasant populations, which continue to constitute the demographic background of their respective countries. Even where Castilian has prevailed, old family systems have survived or adapted.

The central Mexican plateau and the Andean highlands enable us to verify the association between endogenous agricultural development and patrilineal transformation. Ethnographic studies have revealed that groups in these areas are intensely patrilocal: over 80 per cent of young households who temporarily co-reside with their parents do so on the side of the husband's family.[1] The subsequent separation of generations is only very relative, since the newly autonomous household settles down nearby. The youngest son remains to take care of his elderly parents. Thus, in the emergent areas of American agriculture, we find the same combination of patrilineality and state construction as in Mesopotamia, China and India. The combination of the three variables – agriculture, patrilineality, the state – is not fortuitous, since around these poles, the Indian populations that have survived, on the outskirts of Mexico, in Colombia and Venezuela, show rules of residence that are hazier, sometimes bilocal and often predominantly matrilocal.

Two differences with Eurasia, however, must be noted: the absence, in these areas of patrilineal emergence, of male primogeniture, and of any fully developed form of communitarian family. No rule of succession by the eldest son existed in the Aztec or Inca Empires. Among the Indian populations of the American continent, male primogeniture appears to be well defined only among certain groups of salmon fishermen on the northwest coast of North America; these were not conversant with agriculture but were sedentary and highly organized. The Kwakiutl are the typical example.

With regard to agricultural populations, the fact that we do not encounter primogeniture in them can be explained in two ways: either because it has never existed in these regions, or because it has disappeared.

The absence of observations during and after the European conquest does not prove that the privilege of the eldest did not exist in the Andes or on the Mexican plateau in the more distant past. After all, in Mesopotamia, in China and in northern India, the family observed in the twentieth century by anthropologists was communitarian, but it had been superimposed on an erased history of stem families. In all these cases, however, we find in the old codes the trace of ancient primogeniture. And the invention of writing is always associated, in Eurasia, with the emergence of the stem family. On this point, a precise examination of the Mayan and Aztec texts remains necessary. But we may have another kind of trace at our disposal. As David Robichaux has shown, *ultimogeniture*, in which it is the last-born who succeeds, reaches a high level of formalization on the Mexican plateau. Robichaux even refers to a 'Mesoamerican stem family'.[2] Now I myself had come to the conclusion, in *OSF* (pp. 140–2), that the ultimogeniture of the nomads of the steppe had followed primogeniture in China, and was in fact an inverse mirror image of it. The hypothesis of extinct stem forms cannot be ruled out in the case of Central America. And it is far from impossible that the case of the Andes is pretty similar. Jean-Louis Christinat describes a

45

well-formalized mechanism of ultimogeniture in an Aymara community in Peru, albeit with one qualification: if the youngest child is a girl, she takes over the home and assumes responsibility for the parents.[3]

There were no fully developed communitarian families in the Andes or on the Mexican plateau between the sixteenth and twentieth centuries, either. There is some confusion over this point if we survey the full range of monographic studies, but it seems that patrilocality in those areas is never more than the mere aggregation by proximity of nuclear families (OSF, p. 71). It is, in one sense, quite normal: we do not find in the history of pre-Columbian America, as in Eurasia and Africa, nomadic populations that have acquired the patrilineal principle from sedentary peoples, developed a symmetrical clan organization, and then transformed by conquest the stem families of the sedentary people into a communitarian system.

Thus, the actually observable data suggest a specific Amerindian path to patrilocality and patrilineality, one that does not include the communitarian family. The invention of agriculture, on the other hand, does seem to have been a necessary condition.

We are here only at the stage of forming hypotheses. We cannot as yet say that the evolution towards patrilineality is very ancient in Central and South America. It is not impossible that it even occurred *after* the Spanish conquest. A local sixteenth-century census concerning a Nahua population reveals that brothers-in-law and sons-in-law were frequently found in complex family aggregates, proof of a persistent undifferentiation or bilaterality in the kinship system.[4]

What is certain, however, is that the patrilocal zones of the central Mexican plateau and the Andes emerged from a mass of family systems dominated by nuclear and undifferentiated peripheral types, which were thus peripheral with regard to the Amerindian agricultural poles of development. To illustrate this peripheral nuclearity and undifferentiation, my introduction to Volume I of L'Origine des systèmes familiaux mentioned the Dene groups of the Canadian Arctic Shield, the Shoshone in the interior basin of the Rocky Mountains, the Nambikwara of the Amazon, and the Yaghan of southern Patagonia (OSF, p. 19). In the immediate vicinity of patrilocal poles, as on a first radiating circle, there were many family systems with matrilocal temporary co-residence, particularly in the Amazon and in the south of what is now the United States. Many secondary problems remain to be solved, such as the autonomous matrilineal emergence of certain populations in northwest America such as the Haida, neighbours of the Kwakiutl – we here observe, yet again, a close relation between matrilineality and primogeniture – but it is clear that the systematic study of the Indian populations will confirm without any particular difficulty the hypothesis of the original character of the nuclear family, enclosed in an undifferentiated kinship network. This evident fact explains why American anthropologists such as Robert Lowie and

George Murdock could so easily view the nuclear family as paramount in human experience.[5]

New Guinea

The Papuan people of New Guinea also owe their demographic mass and their survival to agriculture – horticulture in this case. The third largest island in the world has a population of 10 million inhabitants (2015 figures), three-quarters of them Papuan. This was a centre of agricultural emergence, and also a place of patrilineal innovation, something that I can mention only in passing. In general, sons share out their inheritance, but there are very clear traces of primogeniture.[6]

Sub-Saharan Africa: a question of method and ideology

I must rather apologetically admit that the following presentation of the history of African family systems is somewhat rudimentary. It is more like a research programme than a completed study. It is, however, indispensable to this outline of human history.

First, of course, because Africa exists in itself, as a developing continent whose relative demographic weight is growing on a global scale. Then, and especially (in the context of this book, which accepts the leading role of the Anglo-American world), because a correct vision of the original African societies is particularly necessary. The United States at the beginning of the third millennium still seem unable to escape from their original racial organization, which had designated the 'Blacks' as a separate human category. It is therefore essential to verify that the family development laws identified for Eurasia and Indian America also apply to the African continent. And this verification will free us from the dead ends and illusions that present the current American situation as resulting from a Black specificity. It is America itself that manufactures 'African-Americans'.

To understand the endogenous character of American racial conceptions should certainly not lead us to convict the United States specifically. *Homo americanus* is presented, in this outline of human history, as very close in its way of life to the original type of *Homo sapiens*. Its fixation on 'Blacks' only highlights the tendency of any human group to define itself against other human groups. It is not America but humankind that must strive to solve this problem of racial, ethnic and national organization. I will come back to this point in the next chapter, when I attempt a general reconstruction of the anthropological system of the original *Homo sapiens*.

Murdock's *Ethnographic Atlas*

The geography of African family types allows us to confirm on a large scale the hypothesis that the nuclear family came first.[7] This continent also provides us with a good example of the historical disconnection between technological and economic development, on the one hand, and the evolution of family forms on the other.

Sub-Saharan Africa is the last part of the world to reach the stage of universal literacy, and it is only just beginning its demographic transition, since, between 2005 and 2010, the birth rate remained at 5.4 children per woman, compared with a global rate of 2.6.[8] But its family systems are among the most advanced if we consider their distance from the original nuclear type. On the eve of the European conquest, there were people on the African continent who did not generally use writing but were organized into extremely complex family systems.

Let us start with the simplest, and the most decisive, phenomenon: the nuclear character of the family among the African peoples considered the most 'primitive': the Pygmies of the equatorial forest and the !Kung Bushmen of southern Africa.[9] The !Kung, in particular, have been frequently studied by ethnographers, and are considered by Peter Gluckman and his co-authors of *Principles of Evolutionary Medicine* as the population closest to the ancient biological type of humanity.[10] They are characterized by the nuclear family and the reasonably high status given to women, although the latter are not considered to be similar to men. A sexual specialization in reproduction, labour and social activities in general is part of the original common background of humanity.

But we can go further. Murdock's *Ethnographic Atlas* makes it possible to map the family density and the rule of primogeniture among African peoples, and to thus outline for the whole continent a model for the differentiation of family types.[11] The importance of polygyny here adds an extra dimension to the process of complexity and divergence.

The absence of written sources, however, in principle precludes a reliable dating of most elements in the sequence. The dating of the emergence of agriculture and nomadic livestock breeding, and the settlement of the southern part of the continent by Bantu farmers, are themselves controversial issues for specialists. I will not be able to give any more precise dates for patrilineal innovations, whether stem or communitarian, matrilineal reactions, or for the rate of diffusion and reinforcement over time of the patrilineal principle or the rate of polygyny.

Murdock's *Ethnographic Atlas* distinguishes peoples according to whether their family is *communitarian* (more or less extended types F and E), *stem* (type G, which consists only of a parent couple and a child couple), or *independent* (types P, Q, R, S, if polygyny is frequent, N if it is limited, M in the case of monogamy). The continental predominance of polygyny means we cannot retain the term 'nuclear family': even in the absence of a complex association of married brothers, or of the cohabitation of a parent couple and a child couple, an independent married man moves between several wives, each of whom usually lives in a separate dwelling. In the case of the independent family, we need to keep in mind the existence of semi-nuclei consisting of the mother–children group and a man ensuring the stability of the family group as much as he can.

The *Atlas* also allows us to distinguish peoples according to the inheritance rule, with Pp in the codification indicating a male primogeniture. Murdock himself assures us that this datum is one of the least reliable of his tabulations, but the tracing of some very significant maps belies his own caution. As a synthesis of the monographs produced in a dispersed way by anthropologists involved in fieldwork, the sample is obviously bound to contain a multitude of errors of appreciation or coding. The categorization of a people will have depended, successively, on the anthropologist's glance, most often non-quantitative, and then on the coder's evaluation of the description. In the case of Africa, however, the projection of the results onto maps gives very clear results for the variables that are of interest to us. The use of points of varying sizes evoking the size of the peoples (more than 1 million individuals; between 1 million and 100,000; between 100,000 and 10,000; and fewer than 10,000) allows us to grasp both the family zones and their densities on the eve of the great demographic expansion after the 1950s.

The map of African family systems allows us to identify two poles of patrilineal innovation, located respectively in the two main zones of the emergence of agriculture. These, again, are the two areas where population density was particularly high on the eve of colonization. I leave aside a third densely populated region further to the north, Christian Ethiopia, treated in *OSF* as an extension of the Eurasian sphere. We should remember, however, that the Amhara nuclear family of the Ethiopian highlands perfectly verifies the model of an archaic nuclear form protected by its peripheral geographical position.

The West African communitarian family

West Africa was one of the places where agriculture emerged, a phenomenon identified in 1958 by George Murdock, who located the focus of agricultural innovation near the sources of the Niger, 1,600 kilometres from the Atlantic Ocean.[12] The complete autonomy of this emergence, in 3000–2000 BCE, is still controversial.[13] But later on in West Africa we find the usual association between agricultural innovation, patrilineality and communitarianism already observed in Mesopotamia, China and

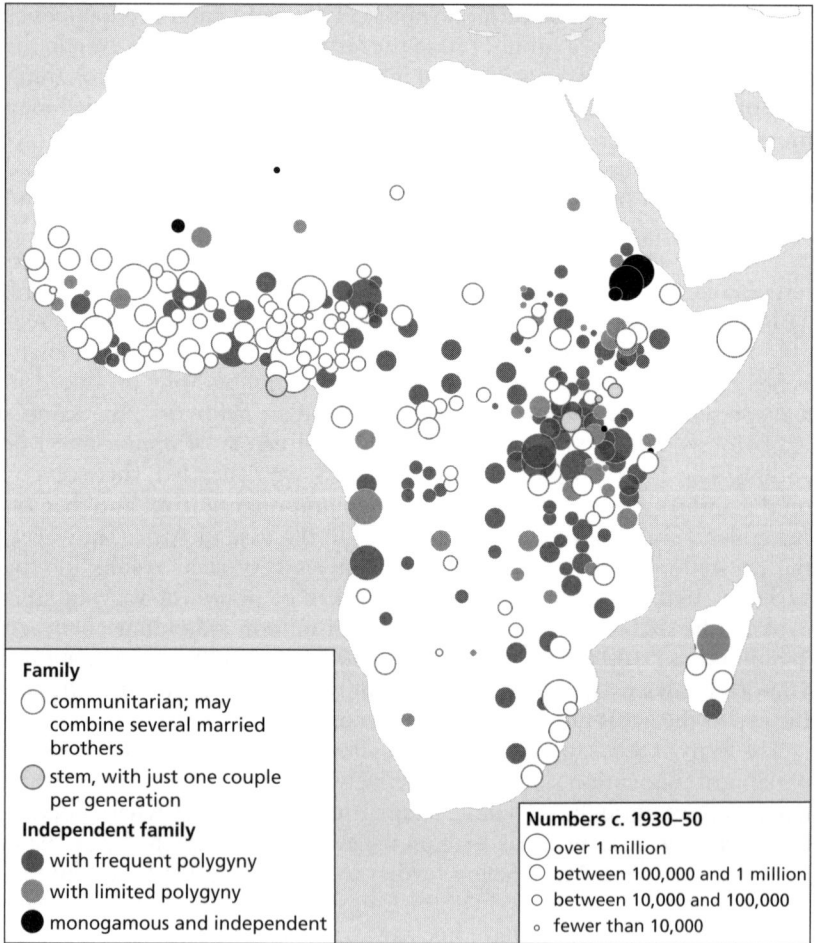

Map 2.1 Communitarian family and independent family in Africa

northern India. The data in the *Ethnographic Atlas*, projected on Map 2.1, point to a concentration of communitarian forms in West Africa, with the rest of the continent clearly dominated by various types of *independent* families. The best monographic description of the West African communitarian family probably remains that given by Meyer Fortes (1906–83) for the Tallensi of northern Ghana and Côte d'Ivoire.[14]

Around the West African communitarian and patrilineal pole, we can observe the classic scattered pockets that represent the remains of the previous stages of complexification. On the coast of the Gulf of Guinea, we find rules of primogeniture, among the Yoruba and Ibo of Nigeria for

50

example, as well as, in a plateau area, among the Bamileke of Cameroon.[15] Sometimes, primogeniture is grafted onto a communitarian-family structure and, in this case, it is only a remnant of birthright in a well-developed patrilineal system which combines all brothers – as is the case with the Yoruba and Ibo. The Bamileke, for their part, have a linear stem-family development cycle that allows the father to choose his successor and condemns the other sons to emigration. But these peripheral traces show us that in West Africa, a stem-family phase succeeded the original nuclear family of *Homo sapiens*, to be followed by a communitarian symmetrization of the family group.

To explain the transition from the stem-family stage to the communitarian stage, in the case of West Africa, as in Mesopotamia and China, a decisive role must be given to nomadic pastoralists. Let us imagine, again, that the patrilineality of sedentary stem forms was transmitted to nomads of the Sahel zone further north; then that nomadic invasions superimposed a symmetrical patrilineality on the sedentary stem family. According to Murdock, nomadic breeding did not appear in Africa until after 1000 CE, so this shift can only have been belated.[16] In future research, interaction with the history of regional state building will need to be examined. But here, there is doubt over the dates, and one can sense that a huge amount of work will be necessary to settle the chronology of agriculture, breeding, invasions, the history of states and the final sudden appearance of Islam.

The communitarian family represents stage 2 of patrilineal emergence, and that is why, in West Africa, as one moves away from the communitarian epicentre and approaches the coast, one can see a hint of undifferentiation in the kinship system: for example, a higher status for women, frequently found even within peoples traditionally regarded as constituting a single ethnographic unit. This gradient leads to uncertainty and debate about the patrilineal or non-patrilineal nature of the kinship system, as for example among the Wolofs of Senegal or the Yoruba of Nigeria.[17]

As we approach the coasts, we can also observe classic matrilineal responses to patrilineal innovation. In southern Ghana and Côte d'Ivoire, the Ashanti, also the subject of ethnographic study by Meyer Fortes, belong to this periphery of the patrilineal communitarian bloc. In the textbooks, they represent a classic case for the structural study of matrilineality, with women torn between their husbands and their brothers.[18]

Incomplete stem-family forms in the eastern highlands

The highlands of East Africa, south of Ethiopia, constitute a second region where agriculture developed. The proximity of the Egyptian focus a priori stops us from considering it to be autonomous. But in this zone we can observe a high incidence of primogeniture, which even so shares the space with rules of egalitarian division between sons. Here we are clearly in a zone of patrilineal emergence, and, yet again, primogeniture seems to be at the heart of the process. One main pole is visible, centred on the Rift and Great Lakes region. In the highlands of East Africa, according to data from Murdock's *Ethnographic Atlas*, primogeniture is combined, apart from rare exceptions, with the independent family. The husband and his wives do not cohabit with the previous generation. The data thus refer only to an emerging stem family. The notion of co-residence may be ambiguous, however, in an area where the habitat

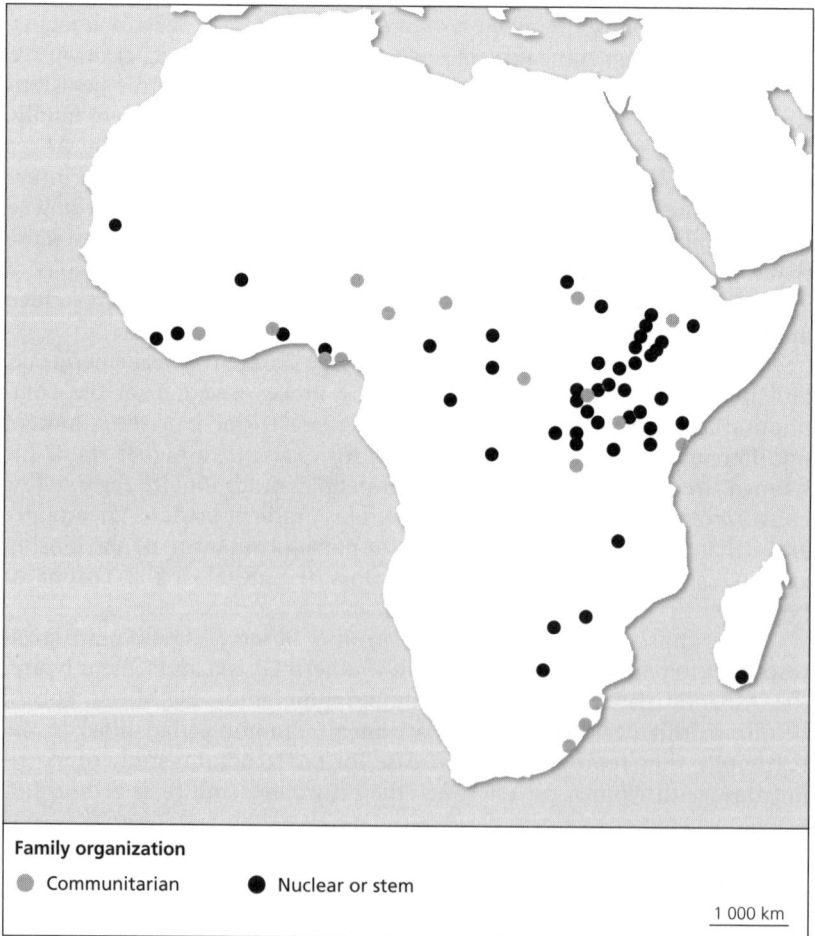

Family organization

● Communitarian   ● Nuclear or stem

1 000 km

Map 2.2   Transmission of land by male primogeniture in Africa

is light, consisting of huts with varying degrees of agglomeration. The direct examination of the fieldwork monographs alone will make it possible to decide. We can already note that the strength of authoritarian and inegalitarian concepts among the Hutus and Tutsis, in Rwanda and Burundi, suggests a well-developed stem system.

Can we conclude that primogeniture in the Africa of the Rift Valley and the Great Lakes is endogenous? We know that it does not come, like so much of the knowledge of agriculture, from the north, because it is not found in Ethiopia. On the other hand, it is not impossible that Bantu-speaking populations from Cameroon, able to conquer thanks to their possession of iron metallurgy, introduced it into the region. The Bantu groups joined up with the agricultural populations of the Great Lakes at a date (yet another one) still to be determined, and it is likely that they had already reached the stage of primogeniture when they left the eastern fringe of West Africa.

In the south, archaic forms: the 'matrilineal belt' and a high status of women

The southern part of Africa, south of the equatorial forest, long remained populated by hunter-gatherers of which the 'nuclear' !Kung Bushmen are merely a residual group. Today, the bulk of the population, south of a diagonal line from Gabon to Tanzania, is the result of the late Bantu expansion from present-day Cameroon. This is why the Bantu languages today define a huge space whose linguists strive, in agreement or in conflict with archaeologists, to trace the exact process of differentiation. Let us place this expansion between 500 BCE and 500 CE, without any illusions, just to give an idea of the order of magnitude involved. The deadlines of 100 BCE and 1000 CE would also have their supporters.

Having set out from Cameroon, as has been said, these expansive pioneers could not fail to carry level 1 patrilineal stem forms or level 0 nuclear forms, which were therefore relatively feminist in nature. Level 2 communitarian patrilineality did not yet exist in West Africa when they left it. The migrants did of course evolve, but in a way that was different from, and especially less rapid than, the populations of the zones of ancient agricultural sedentariness in the west or northeast of the continent. Cartography makes it possible to check this set of hypotheses.

South of the equatorial forest and the densely populated Great Lakes area, patrilineality ceases to dominate family structures. As the anthropologists usually put it, a 'matrilineal belt' occupies a vast space from southern Gabon to southern Tanzania.

This matrilineal belt is made up of fluid family systems in which the matrilineality of the transmission of goods and status does not, in most

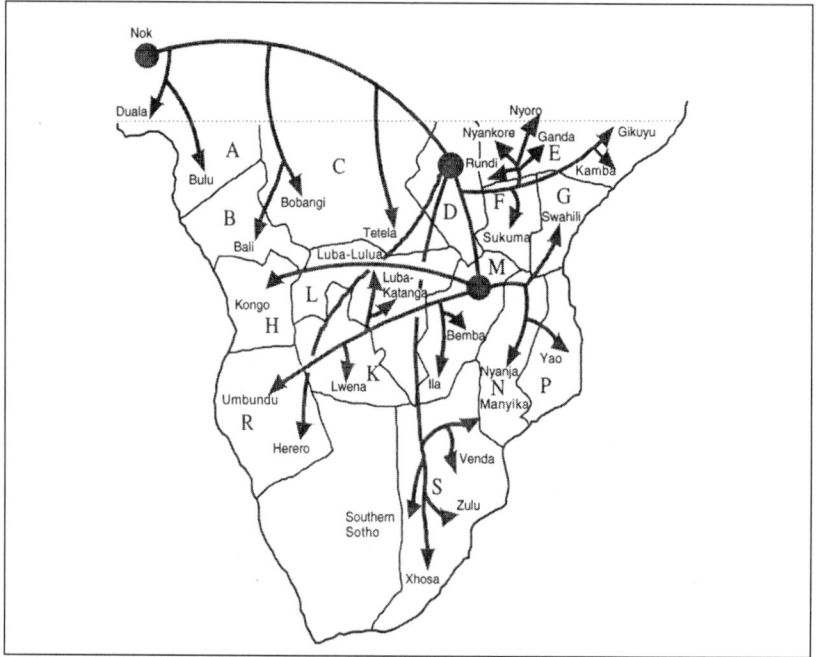

Map 2.3   A possible representation of the Bantu migration

Note: An already old attempt at a geo-genealogy of Bantu languages. It is outdated in the view of many linguists but I feel it will be more useful to specialists in family structures. *Source:* This is the general map presented by Luigi Luca Cavalli-Sforza, Paolo Menozzi and Alberto Piazza, in *The History and Geography of Human Genes* (Princeton, NJ: Princeton University Press, 1994), p. 166.

cases, lead to the constitution of large, compact, stable households. The map of the density of households (Map 2.1), taken from data in the *Ethnographic Atlas*, also clearly reveals how the independent family predominated in the matrilineal area.

Audrey Richards has described the potential variations in the family structures in this region, with instability and variability being common to all of them.[19] Among the Mayombe of western Congo, matrilineality in the transmission of status and property can be combined with patrilocality in the formation of marriage: the wife comes to live in the village of her husband, but, at adolescence, the children return to the village of their maternal uncle. East of the matrilineal belt, among the Bemba, initial marriage is matrilocal, as among the Yao of Mozambique, Malawi and Tanzania.[20] Marriage is unstable among the Yao, but more durable among the Bemba, where the status of men is higher. Marriage with the maternal uncle's daughter often increases the stability of the

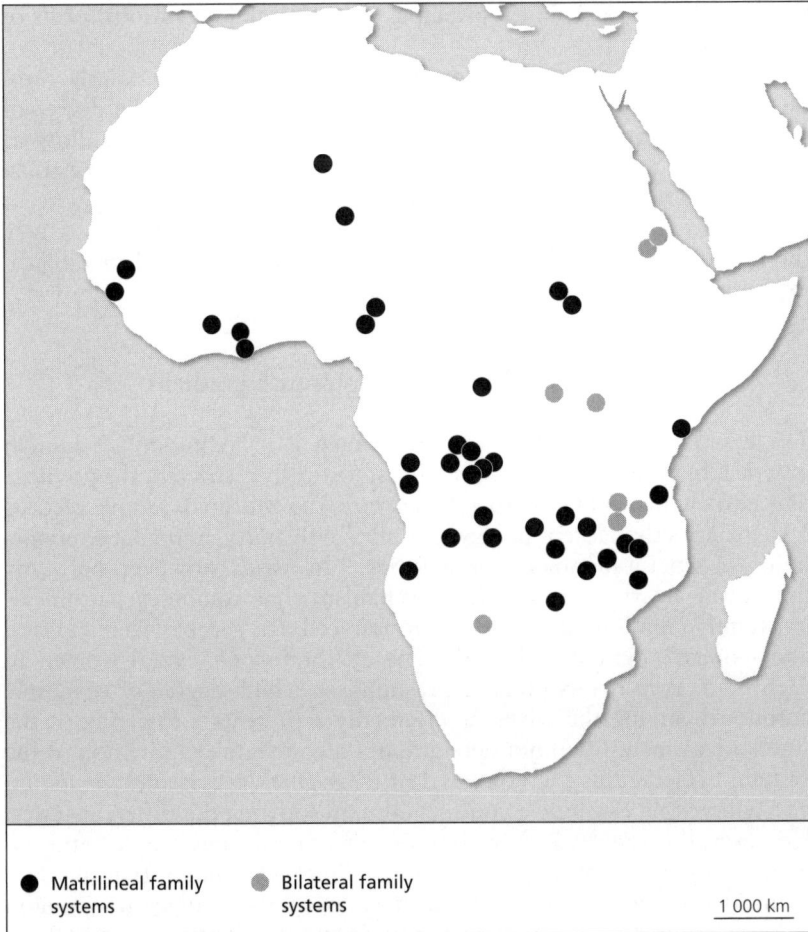

Map 2.4 Matrilocality and bilaterality in Africa

family system. It usually affects older siblings. But whatever the solution, matrilineal systems involve tensions: a woman is always torn between her allegiances to her husband and to her brother.

Matrilineal forms of family organization most often confer a particular role on the older brother.[21] In Africa, horizontal inheritance, from elder brother to younger brother, is the most common characteristic of matrilineal systems, as it is of patrilineal communitarian systems in the west, but not of primogenitures in the east. Bordering in the south a patrilineal world where primogeniture has been or remains an important characteristic, the matrilineal belt can only be the effect of a reaction to the spread of the patrilineal principle of level 1 and its various forms of primogeniture.

At this stage, however, we must resist the vertigo of scholarly complexity and highlight the simple variables that best target the degree of evolution of anthropological forms. Two statistical indicators allow us to locate the usual characteristic of family archaism in southern Africa: a higher status of women. The first indicator, the rate of polygyny, is familiar to Africanist anthropologists. The use of the second, namely the rate of infection with the HIV virus, represents the anthropological exploitation of a tragic demographic variable.

Polygyny and its northwest/south gradient

The marriage of a man to several women is a commonplace human practice, but one that usually remains statistically restricted, the privilege of a narrow male elite. In *Social Structure*, the Murdock sample records 193 societies that accept polygyny, only 2 polyandry, and a large minority of 43 strictly monogamous societies.[22] In Africa, however, polygyny lies at the heart of a complex mechanism that combines patrilineality, family communitarianism, a pronounced age gap between spouses, and women's agricultural work. The attribution of several women to each man, even if this practice presupposes a high degree of economic autonomy among the wives, undoubtedly represents a lowering of the status of women. I will not here attempt a complete examination of the system; I reserve this for Volume II of *L'Origine des systèmes familiaux*, and will simply examine a continental map showing the different states. However, this is already enough to demonstrate the innovative nature of mass polygyny and its connection to patrilineal communitarianism.

In Africa, the proportion of women living in a polygamous union varies according to the country, ranging between 10 per cent and 50 per cent. In several very small populations, it is absolutely never found. Such rates are made technically possible by large age gaps between spouses. If men marry late and women early, a balanced marriage market can be established only by associating each man who has been married for a short time with several women who have been married for longer. The mechanism involves the transfer of widows to younger brothers or cousins of the deceased husband, who will be significantly older on average than his wives. The higher the age gap between spouses, the higher the rate of polygyny.

DHS (Development and Health Survey) reports can be used to map the intensity of polygyny at the state level at the turn of the third millennium (Map 2.5). The existence of a West African pole is immediately visible. In Senegal, Guinea, Burkina Faso and Togo, the proportion of women

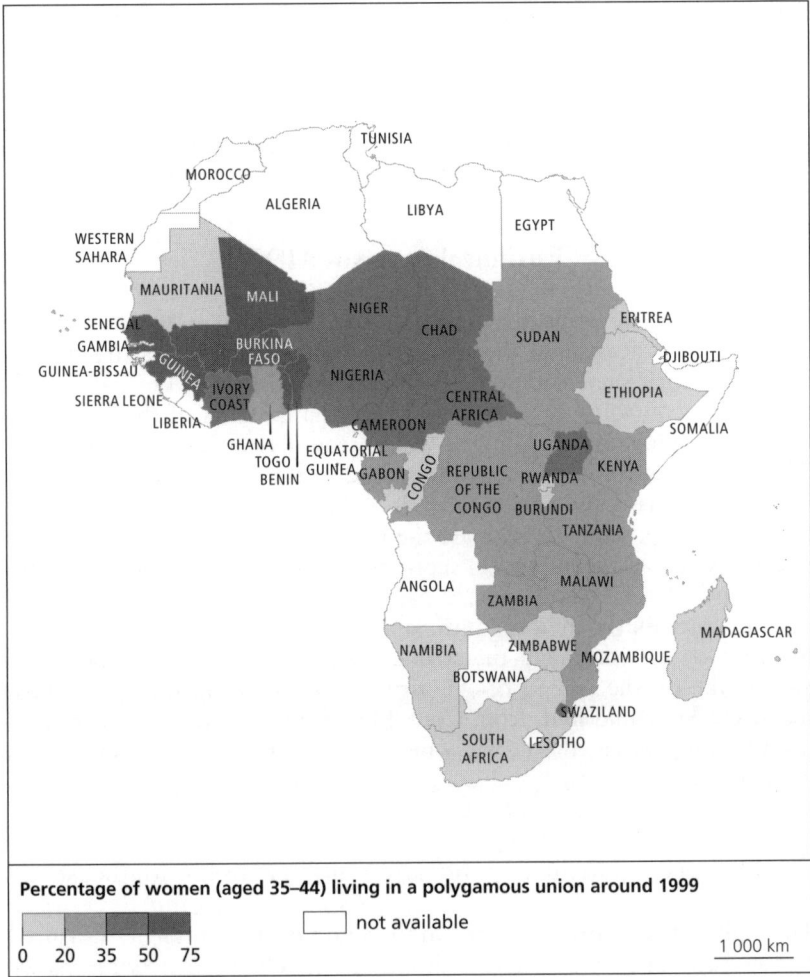

Map 2.5   Polygyny in Africa

aged 35 to 44 living in polygamous unions is higher than 50 per cent. The rest of the map reveals a structure of radiating circles, with polygyny rates declining from west to east, and, once we reach the east, from north to south. In the most southerly countries, the rates fall to 10 per cent, even lower in some areas within these states. The regularity with which the rate declines suggests a mechanism of diffusion. The older maps published by Ron Lesthaeghe in *Reproduction and Social Organization in Sub-Saharan Africa*, which go down to the level of regions, confirm this geographical spread across several parameters. We can see, in particular, that the average age gap between spouses exceeds seven years in the region of maximum polygyny.[23]

The map of polygyny in Africa is one first synthetic approach to the status of women, which decreases from the northwest to the south. In conventional anthropological terms, it may be said that the intensity of the patrilineal principle decreases from northwest to south.

Patrilineality versus AIDS

The spread of infection by the HIV virus provides us with a second, more indirect measure of the status of women. Their sexual freedom is negatively correlated with male domination and the level of patrilineality. Where control over women is weak, the freedom of the local way of life has unfortunately allowed widespread dissemination of the virus. Where this control is stronger, the spread of the disease has been better contained. This is the reason why the HIV-positive rate of the population makes it possible to evaluate the level of patrilineality of the family system. With accidents and exceptions, the highest HIV-positive rates are found in the regions where patrilineality is weakest. Again, East Africa, particularly in the south, appears only weakly patrilineal. In the west of the continent, the stronger level of patrilineality has acted as a brake on the spread of the virus. If we zoom in on the regions, however, we would find, from Côte d'Ivoire to Cameroon, higher HIV-positive rates along the coast, which is more feminist and sometimes matrilineal.

The recent patrilineal innovation in the extreme southeast

The high status accorded women in the south of the continent, measured by low rates of polygyny and high HIV-positive indices, now means we can raise in its proper form the question of the origins of the small patrilineal and communitarian pole isolated in the extreme southeast, the area where Bantu groups migrating south eventually confronted Dutch or British colonizers heading north. This pole – which includes the Venda, Thonga, Swazi, Zulu and Pondo groups – still affords women a high status, and thus corresponds, like Russian communitarianism, to a very recent patrilineal transformation. The history of colonization tells us of a frontal shock between Europeans and African groups in the middle of transformations affecting families and warfare: the Zulu people had achieved fame through its organization and military efficiency. For this region, we also have accounts of the explosion of warfare in the African environment and of the migrations of peoples fleeing the conquest – very

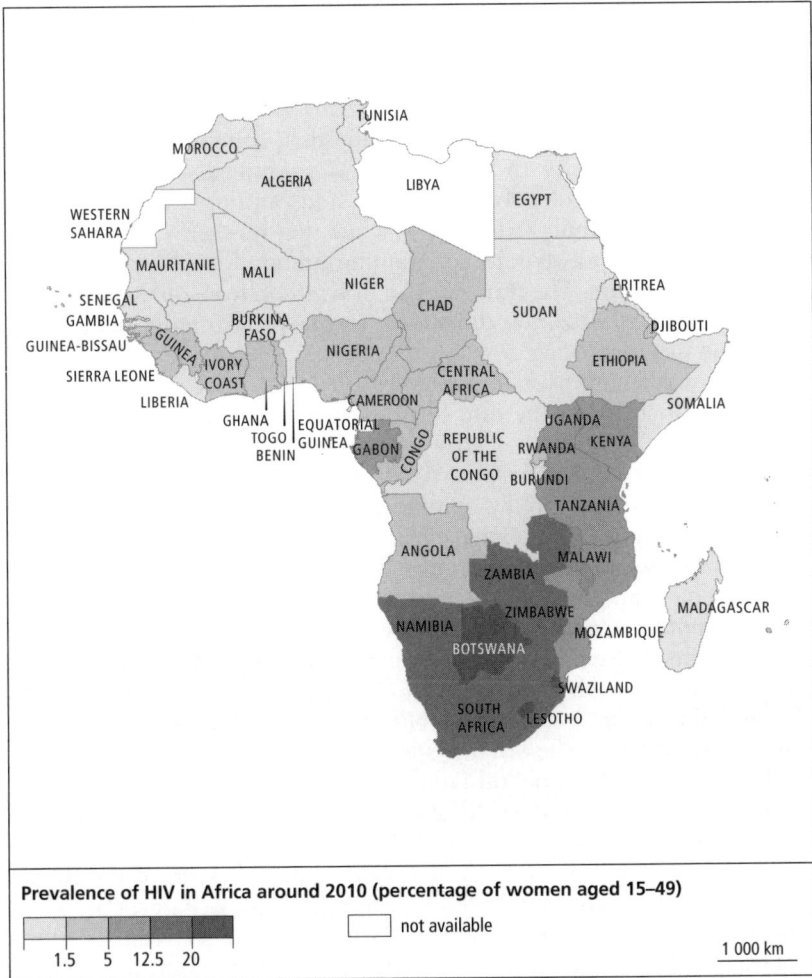

Prevalence of HIV in Africa around 2010 (percentage of women aged 15–49)

not available

1.5   5   12.5   20

1 000 km

Map 2.6   The spread of AIDS in Africa

reliable signs of an endogenous patrilineal transformation that had reached its peak in the nineteenth century.[24]

By way of conclusion: the nuclear family and the flexibility of the original *Homo sapiens*

While we are still waiting for a detailed analysis of all these changes in the west, northeast and south, some data and several maps have allowed us to highlight the original character of the simplest family and the high status given to women in sub-Saharan Africa in the most distant past. Again, the archaic, primordial character of the nuclear family and undifferentiated kinship systems is verified. The historical sequence 'nuclear family then stem family then communitarian family', leading from simplicity to complexity, is confirmed. It is radicalized in Africa by the rise of polygyny, which adds an important element of complexity to the family structure. The fact that brothers can have many wives endows the polygynous communitarian family with a particularly massive architecture. The transmission of widows, from older to younger brothers, adds a horizontal dimension to the vertical movement of the succession of generations.

The strengthening over time of the patrilineal principle is expressed here by an increase in the rate of polygyny. The fact that plural marriage reveals a geographical structure of radiating circles, reaching its maximum in the interior of West Africa and its minimum in the south of the continent, does not in my opinion express any direct diffusion of the polygynic principle, but an intensification over time of patrilineality, and therefore of the polygyny associated with it, in a population that must originally have practised plural marriage at a rate of 5–10 per cent.

This hypothesis forces us, once more, to move away from the vision of a highly standardized original nuclear family. Monogamy undoubtedly dominated, but it was not, as in the Christian societies of Europe, an absolute obligation. A statistically but not morally dominant monogamy is probably typical of the original species of *Homo sapiens*.

The inventory of peripheral family forms shows that, more generally, no rule is absolute in the world of the original nuclear family. Take the example of one of the most peripheral and archaic groups ever to be studied by ethnographers, the Indians of the Great Basin of the Rocky Mountains, of which the Shoshone were one of the main groups. Their 'backwardness' horrified the writer Mark Twain: he was usually funny and progressive, but he became a vulgar racist on his comments on them, and unhesitatingly compared them to the Bushmen of Africa.[25] These particularly primitive Indians occupied the interior of a mountain range far to the north of the pole of development of agriculture and patrilineality located in Central America. In the late 1930s, Julian Steward wrote a survey of all that was known about them.[26]

Steward notes their undifferentiated kinship system. The nuclear family is the unit of gathering and hunting in a social world without any formal organization. However, it is a nuclear family of a very undogmatic kind. The young couple joins the parents of the wife until the birth of the first child, then decides whether to return to the husband's original group or to go elsewhere. The conjugal family is central, but polygyny is quite common, although at levels far below what can be found today in West

Africa or even in the East – probably close to the lower rates in the south. Polyandry – a woman with several husbands – is also widespread, which Steward rightly interprets as a sign of gender equality in this society. Divorce is common, leaving the mother to look after the young children. Older parents can co-reside with an adult child. Everything is fluid, optional, reversible.

On the other side of the world, let us take a look at the Philippines, a set of islands roughly symmetrical to Great Britain when compared to Sumer, the historical heart of Eurasia. Some fragments of writings derived from Dravidian models from southern India have been found in the major island of Luzón, but the region only really entered history with the Spanish conquest in the sixteenth century. The ethnography of the Agta hunter-gatherers, like that of Tagalog farmers, reveals an undifferentiated kinship system. The family type is nuclear in both cases, but it allows for a temporary co-residence of the young couple with the parents of one or the other spouse. In the case of the Agta, the conjugal couple is part of a mobile local group. Among the Tagalogs, solidarity between brothers and sisters is very important. For the Agta, the average age at marriage was 18.4 for women around 1980 and 21.7 for men.[27] We can consider the average age at marriage in the Philippines as representative of the Tagalogs, the majority population of the country: in 1948, it was 22.1 years for women and 25 for men.[28] Here we have a very general law: in nuclear-family systems, age at marriage can never fall very low because a woman-child and her husband-child would be unable to enjoy an independent life. Only communitarian-family systems can envisage young women of 16 getting married, as in some Russian peasant communities of the nineteenth century, or even girls of 15, as in northern India in the 1970s.[29] An age range of between 18 and 22 for women to get married seems to characterize the nuclear-family systems of the periphery.

At the end of this simplified reconstitution of the process of differentiation of family forms, we are in a position to define an original type, of which we can find traces in the entire periphery of the planet, in populations that can be primitive or advanced. We are approaching, in a way, a characterization of *Homo sapiens* as an animal species. But in order to grasp this correctly, we need to combine two dimensions: a central norm and a high coefficient of variability around this norm.

The central norm is nuclear and monogamous: at the beginning, there is the conjugal couple. But with this element of analysis alone, we cannot distinguish the original hunter-gatherers from the English or the Americans after the Second World War, for example.

That is why it is necessary to take into account a second original element: flexibility. This includes the possible temporary co-residence of newlyweds with their parents, the recuperation of isolated elderly people by their children, or their elimination if food grows scarce. It makes infanticide possible too, for the same reasons. It allows polygyny, polyandry, divorce and, as we will see later, homosexuality. *Homo sapiens* was very free. Western man, partially shaped by Judaism and Christianity, lost much of this freedom, which was probably necessary for the survival of hunter-gatherer groups.

The pre-existence of an experimental hotchpotch in the original *Homo sapiens* species, a real toolbox of conceivable forms, explains the emergence, over time, of differentiated family norms and types, whether they are complex and rigid communitarian forms, patrilineal and matrilineal, or purified nuclear types, basically no less rigid if they absolutely forbid the co-residence of different generations or require the strictest monogamy.

The family household, however, simple or complex, does not exist in a vacuum. To obtain a complete reconstruction of the original anthropological system of *Homo sapiens*, we will need to describe, in the following chapter, the structuring of its territorial groups by matrimonial exchange.

— 3 —

HOMO SAPIENS

The principle of conservatism in peripheral areas has enabled us to discern, on the maritime fringes of Eurasia, in southern Africa, and in a large part of America, the remains of the first human family system, one that was nuclear and centred on the conjugal bond. This was enough to establish a radical break with its neighbour in evolution, the chimpanzee, so close in terms of genetic code (with a 99.6 per cent shared heritage). The conjugal bond is actually unknown among chimpanzees. In chimpanzee groups, females are covered by several males successively. There is no stable link between a male and a female or between a father and his offspring – and the latter cannot in fact be determined. One of the important lessons of social anthropology is that there is no simple connection linking the genetic distance between species with the distance between their social organizations. Monogamy predominates in humans and most birds, and a communitarian pansexuality among chimpanzees.[1]

The sharp family contrast between *Homo sapiens* and *Pan troglodytes* (the common chimpanzee) clearly explains why the adaptive strategy of the human animal, as defined by the theory of natural selection, was a success. A stable couple means that children can enjoy a long upbringing, including time for the organism to grow to its final state outside the womb: this is necessary in the case of human beings because of the size of their brain. A fully developed skull would not 'get through' during childbirth. The parental couple also provides much of the transmission of knowledge accumulated by the adult community. Lifespan is essential here.

Homo sapiens is also distinguished from the chimpanzee by superior longevity, another factor that facilitates cultural transmission. There is a 'grandparent' stage in the life cycle of humans, and the possibility of an educational process that includes three generations. Michael Gurven and Hillard Kaplan recently assessed the normal potential life expectancy of the basic form of *Homo sapiens*, combining all of the current

63

demographic data available on residual hunter-gatherers. They calculated a modal age at death of 70 years old for humans. A generally very low life expectancy did not prevent those who had survived their childhood from reaching advanced ages.[2] The hunter-gatherers survived only in marginal areas, most often unsuitable for agriculture. They cannot therefore be completely representative of the hunter-gatherers of the past, who lived in areas that enjoyed more clement weather and were richer in the natural production of plants and animals. But this is precisely why the results obtained by Gurven and Kaplan can be trusted: the living conditions of the original hunter-gatherers were much more favourable. Their conclusion is reliable: after the very high mortality rates of youth, the hunter-gatherer has a body that can remain in good working order up to the age of 70.

The modal age at death of wild chimpanzees is 15 years, that of chimpanzees living in the greater comfort of captivity 42 years, that of the !Kung 74 years; for the Swedes living in the period 1751–9 it was 72 years, and for the Americans of 2002, 85 years.[3] At all levels of technological and social development, human beings remain similar.

The original couple

The equivalence of paternal and maternal relationships in the original kinship system should not lead us into the illusion that there was a symmetrical relation between men and women in primitive society. The conjugal family, an effective tool for the education of children, includes a principle of the sexual division of labour. Women make children. Men protect the mother, the child and the group. A dimorphism of size and form, moderate in comparison with that of other species, but perfectly real, expresses the specialization of the sexes. Men are stronger and always dominant, although size dimorphism was lower among hunter-gatherers than among farmers.[4]

The study of residual hunter-gatherers allows us to refine the image of the original pair, even though surviving human predators are frequently influenced culturally by nearby peasant groups. This is particularly evident for the Pygmies of the Equatorial Forest and the Bushmen of southern Africa, two populations influenced by the surrounding patrilineality.

With these reservations, we can identify a constant: hunting, when it uses throwing weapons and involves the shedding of blood, is a function of men. Alain Testart has shown that this rule, to which there are very few exceptions, transcends all material and economic conditions.[5] Women dominate in gathering activities. If the consumption of the products of gathering usually occurs within the nuclear family, meat is shared by the entire local group. The masculine principle frames collective life.

Alain Testart refused to give this specialization by sex a naturalistic explanation. He rejected the interpretations of those anthropologists who wanted to see the exclusion of women from hunting as the effect of the immobility that results from bringing children into the world and giving them their first education. Testart considered sexual specialization as a primordial manifestation of ideology, associated with the taboo on menstrual blood. The question is of little importance to us. Universality, even if it is ideological, here defines a characteristic of the original species. The fact remains that the recent integration of women in certain societies into the army or police forces, and thus the acquisition of the right to violent bloodshed, seems rather to justify Testart's distinction between nature and ideology.

The equivalence between paternal and maternal kinship, the sexual division of labour: these explain the status of the women of original times. This status was high, but different. One hesitates to speak of equality because a principle of male domination, based on physical strength, is always observable. This force is not only a constraint. In her study of the !Kung, Lorna Marshall says that women were protected by men rather than oppressed. She suggests a certain harmony, and even a balance in couples, since her study ends with the description of a furious !Kung woman beating her husband on the head with his foraging stick. The man had forced her to accompany him, while she wanted to visit her own parents instead.[6] Marshall says she has never seen a man hitting his wife in this community. Equivalence and difference, in other words complementarity: this was probably the original configuration for the two partners of the human couple.

Encampments, bands, villages and peoples

The family of *Homo sapiens* was nuclear but never isolated, apart from certain phases of gathering or hunting, periods that were always followed by regroupings. We now need to move up above the level of the nuclear family to attempt a complete reconstruction of the *anthropological system* of *Homo sapiens*. What we observe, on the periphery of the inhabited world, in both peasant and hunter-gatherer populations, are aggregates of families.

The band, the hamlet and the village all constitute a first level of regrouping. Local monographs reveal the importance of horizontal links between brothers and sisters (brother–brother, brother–sister, sister–sister) in the composition of groups and mutual aid. This is true of hunter-gatherers such as the !Kung Bushmen, Dene, Shoshone and Agta, and also nomadic Lapland breeders and Tagalog farmers. These populations have not been transformed by the destruction of the bilateral kinship network, which I will study in the following chapters where I discuss the transformations in way of life brought about by Judaism and early Christianity, then by the Protestant Reformation.

Basic demographics partly explain this horizontality. Admittedly, a generally low life expectancy did not, as we have seen, prevent men who had survived their childhood from often reaching the age of 70 and remaining, until that age, net producers rather than consumers of resources. However, their mortality increased after the age of 40, at first slowly, then at an accelerating rate. In a world of survival, the importance of physical resistance led to emphasizing the horizontal relations between young people, whether men or women.

The specific resources of older people can only play a role where the accumulation of capital likely to produce an income is possible. It is agriculture that generally paves the way to accumulation and the power this confers on the old. However, we should be wary of any mechanical explanation that forgets the inventiveness of the human mind: among Australian Aborigines, who were not acquainted with agriculture, the gathering done by women produced an income that maintained, within a polygynous system, the dominant position of quite elderly husbands.

Flexibility of the local group

Flexibility is the word that best evokes the life of hunter-gatherer groups described in the classic work edited by Richard Lee and Irven Devore, *Man the Hunter*.[7] These groups are mobile, composed according to variable criteria that always leave room for choice, in particular a choice between paternal and maternal relations. We no longer believe in Radcliffe-Brown's original patrilocal and patrilineal horde, even though some groups show this kind of patrilocal inflection, that is, a certain preference for the association between a father and his sons. Murdock had already noticed, in the overall set of undifferentiated systems, important fluctuations between patrilocality and matrilocality. Few undifferentiated systems operate in a statistically bilocal way with 50 per cent of young couples going for the patrilocal option and 50 per cent for the matrilocal option when it comes to proximity of residence to their parents.

The particular importance given to hunting explains in some cases the patrilocal inflection, as in most Eskimo groups. This asymmetry in no way prevents their belonging to the world of bilaterality. Eskimo kinship terminology, which distinguishes brothers from cousins but does not differentiate between the paternal and the maternal sides, is typically bilateral and nuclear. This is just the same as in our own culture, and that is why the nomenclatures of European kinship fall, according to the practice of anthropologists, into the so-called 'Eskimo' type.

The fact remains that this original fluctuation between patrilocality and matrilocality opens up the possibility of subsequent developments, patrilineal or matrilineal, capable of radicalizing an originally moderate inflection and making it more rigid. A bilateral kinship system will allow up to 70 per cent of patrilocal choices; a patrilineal kinship system will produce patrilocality rates ranging from 75 to 99.9 per cent.[8]

Exogamous families, endogamous peoples

Beyond the band or the hamlet – associations ranging from a few dozen to about one hundred individuals – we can always define a larger human entity, occupying a certain territory and using a common language. It is within this population that the exchange of spouses takes place. It defines an endogamous space. For the !Kung studied by Lorna Marshall in 1952–3, this set consisted of about one thousand individuals.[9] This population, although influenced by the patrilineality of the surrounding farming and breeding peoples, was devoid of any stratification and of any formal political organization. Marriages took place inside a society without any firm structure but in which alliances between close cousins were avoided, whether they were on the side of the mother or of the father. This population without a political organization thought of itself as 'us', distinct from other similar populations, 'them'.

One could follow, throughout history, the extension of this basic population of matrimonial exchange from the district bringing together a few villages to the region, then to the nation. In a world of believers, religious belonging – Catholic, Protestant, Orthodox, Jewish, Muslim or Buddhist – also most often defined an endogamous space that complicated territorial and linguistic endogamy. Moreover, the disappearance of belief generally finds expression in a break with religious endogamy and a proliferation of interfaith marriages. Today, in Western Europe, the United States, Russia, China and Japan, and despite all the talk of globalization, the statistics of matrimonial exchange define, better than in any other previous historical phase, the nation as a reference endogamous space. Districts, regions and religions have faded out as primary integrators.

It would be wrong, however, to imagine, at any time and in any place, a completely closed endogamous space. Some porosity is intrinsic to the *Homo sapiens* system. Contacts at the margins, and the immigration of individuals, everywhere create exceptions, which can be tiny or huge. Territory and language define only a statistical endogamy. Why? Because the functioning of the original family system (exogamous, as we shall see), excludes a priori any absolute closure of the population. A family system is not fundamentally a lineage descending from the past to the future (which is how we often think of our own families), but a group of families exchanging spouses within a territory. However, the great number of exchanges leads to a high probability that there will be an occasional break in the group's usual endogamy.

Relative to his kinship, *Homo sapiens* is indeed exogamous from the beginning, finding a spouse from outside his or her immediate family group. I concluded in Volume I of *L'Origine des systèmes familiaux* that a *tempered exogamy* was the original marriage system (*OSF*, pp. 595–7). Beyond the taboo on incest in the narrow sense, which prohibits unions between brothers and sisters or between children and forebears, peripheral and archaic populations avoid as much as possible marriages between cousins, at least of the first degree, regardless of their level of development. I call this exogamy 'tempered' because it is not absolute, revealing rates of marriages between first cousins that sometimes reach up to 10 per cent.

Marriage between cross cousins, that is to say between the children of a brother and a sister, is frequently allowed, even though it is not often practised. At the beginning of the twentieth century, James George Frazer made an inventory of peoples entering into this type of marriage.[10] The imperative of exogamy therefore weighs particularly heavily on parallel cousins, the children of two brothers or the children of two sisters. The meaning of the distinction is clear: in the view of early human beings, the children of two brothers, or two sisters, reproduce particularly well the identity of nature between the brothers or between the sisters. Marriage between cross cousins reveals, for its part, the importance of the brother–sister axis in the organization of elementary groups. The union of their children perpetuates their complementarity. Most of the permitted alliances highlight a horizontal family axis in the structuring of archaic populations: men exchanging their sisters, fraternal polyandry, sororal polygyny. All these types of horizontality were found among the Great Basin Indians inventoried by Steward.

Tempered family exogamy

G. P. Murdock's *Ethnographic Atlas* confirms the overwhelming dominance of quadrilateral exogamy – a ban on the four types of first cousins – in the American, African and Oceanian populations. Really effective preferential marriage systems – with rates of unions between first cousins ranging from 25 to 50 per cent – are typical of historically evolved populations: the Arab-Persian world for quadrilateral endogamy, and southern India for marriage between cross cousins. There are, however, cases of a high degree of endogamy in some Amazonian populations such as the Makuna of northwestern Amazonia, with rates of cross cousin marriages that vary between 30 and 50 per cent depending on the type of sample.[11] The asymmetrical marriage between a man and his mother's brother's daughter (MBD), which Lévi-Strauss placed at the heart of his system (his typical 'elementary structure'), is not much found across the world, as Laurent Barry has shown.[12] And when it does exist, it seems to be a consequence of the asymmetry engendered by the patrilineal shift (*OSF*, p. 595). Far from reflecting a state of nature, the elementary exchange of structuralist thought is a creation of history.

The central position of Muslim endogamy in the ancient world, where it spread out from the Middle East, is an indication of its innovative character. If we delve into the past of Mesopotamia, where it is not found, we realize how belated it was (*OSF*, pp. 580–2).

Original exogamy survived better than the nuclear family. Among residual hunter-gatherers – the Bushmen of southern Africa, the Shoshone of the Great Basin of the Rocky Mountains, the Agta in Luzon in the Philippines and the Eskimos in the subarctic zone – quadrilateral exogamy still dominates, as in Western Europe, in all Anglo-American and Latin American areas, and in the bulk of Southeast Asia, which is nuclear and undifferentiated (Muslim Malaysia aside). Only a few peoples of the Paleo-Siberian northeast, with nuclear families and undifferentiated kinship systems, seem at first sight to accept endogamy. A critical review of the data suggests that this was actually a toleration of marriage between first cousins that did not exceed 10 per cent (*OSF*, pp. 163–4). In Japan, first cousin marriage was as high as 7–10 per cent in the aftermath of the Second World War, but this seemed to be a creation of history and this rate has since collapsed (*OSF*, pp. 187–90). But even in the patrilineal and communitarian world, quadrilateral exogamy continues to predominate: in Russia, Serbia, China and Vietnam, as well as in northern India. In sub-Saharan Africa, too, neither patrilineality, nor communitarianism, nor polygyny has stopped quadrilateral exogamy from still affecting 60 per cent of the peoples for whom information is available in the Murdock sample. Cross cousin marriages are well represented in Africa only in the matrilineal belt, but probably with moderate effective rates. The Tswanas, in the extreme south, practise quadrilateral endogamy, but this is certainly a recent innovation, in an area characterized by belated patrilineal communitarian innovation.[13]

Exogamy is definitely one of the most resistant elements in the original anthropological system of *Homo sapiens*. The strong endogamies of southern India and the Arab-Persian world, however, prevent us from seeing this resistance as anything absolute.

The taboo on incest is original: the Westermarck effect

The description of *Homo sapiens* as naturally exogamous with regard to marriages between cousins complements and expands the conclusion reached by Edward Westermarck in 1891 for brother–sister unions. In *The History of Human Marriage*, this Finnish Swede, based at the London School of Economics, put an end to the fantasies of his anthropological predecessors (English, German, French and American scholars combined) on the immorality of primitive customs. Indeed, Westermarck destroyed the assumptions common in his day of a primitive sexual promiscuity, original incest, and archaic family communism. He also made fun of 'Bachofen, McLennan, Morgan, Lubbock, Bastian, Giraud-Teulon, Lippert, Kohler, Post, Wilken and several other writers'.[14]

The Westermarck effect suggests that the incest taboo is not a fact of culture but an unconscious behaviour inherited from the process of natural selection. This taboo has 'all the characteristics of a real, powerful instinct, and bears evidently a close resemblance to the aversion to sexual intercourse with individuals belonging to another species'.[15] This prohibition was selected by evolution as a competitive advantage because endogamous involution – taken here in the narrow sense of marriage within the nuclear family – results in the elimination of the less socially effective bearer groups.

Westermarck is a universalist Darwinian. He uses the hypothesis of natural selection to define and explain what is common to the whole human species and not, as is often the case with the 'degenerate' Darwinism of current sociobiology, to imagine a competition between races and a selection within the human race.[16] He is obviously right against later thinkers such as Freud, Lévi-Strauss and so many others who wanted to see the avoidance of incest as a fact of culture. Alas, the history of the human sciences is filled with these intellectual regressions. In the context of the present study, which takes family structures seriously, the neglect suffered by Le Play between 1900 and 1970 comes immediately to mind.

We are very well placed, in the West at the beginning of the third millennium, to confirm the Westermarck effect. All sexual taboos are currently disappearing, with the exception of two: those concerning paedophilia and incest, respectively. A demand for the acceptance of paedophilia was briefly made in the 1970s by various worldly fantasists, who saw it as a final advance in the process of sexual liberation, but it quickly reverted to its status in the zone of forbidden activities. The imperative of protecting one's offspring seems to be deeply rooted in human nature. As for the taboo on incest, right in the middle of the sexual revolution it became completely unconscious and all the more effective. Even though the prohibitions of the Church on marriages between cousins have disappeared from the civil legislation, never has the number of such marriages been so infinitesimal. And indeed, nobody has ever claimed that sexual experimentation within the nuclear family was necessary to the evolution of customs.

Westermarck is remembered today only for his conception of a natural taboo on incest, but he had in fact understood the main aspects of the family life of archaic human beings. In his book he describes a monogamous primitive couple and suggests that the complex forms of family life are products of history. Original monogamy and the relative stability of the couple that comes with it are no more facts of culture than is the taboo on incest:

> Considering that the union lasts till after the birth of the offspring, and considering the care taken of this by the father, we may assume that the prolonged union of the sexes is, in some way or other, connected with parental duties. I am, indeed, strongly of [the] opinion that the tie which joins male and female is an instinct developed through the powerful influence of natural selection. It is evident that, when the father helps to protect the offspring, the species is better able to subsist in the struggle for existence than it would be if this obligation entirely devolved on the mother.[17]

He repeatedly notes the resemblance between the families of primitive peoples and the families of the moderns of his own age:

> There is thus a certain resemblance between the family institution of savage tribes and that of the most advanced races. Among both, the grown-up son, and frequently the grown-up daughter, enjoys a liberty unknown among peoples at an intermediate level of civilization.[18]

Further:

> As to the history of the forms of human marriage, two inferences regarding monogamy and polygyny may be made with absolute certainty: monogamy, always the predominant form of marriage, has been more prevalent at the lowest stages of civilization than at somewhat higher stages; whilst, at a still higher stage, polygyny has again, to a great extent, yielded to monogamy.[19]

Having myself come to the almost too surprising conclusion that the lifestyles of Westerners and primitives are very close to one another, I find it reassuring to note that a researcher had come to almost the same conclusion a little more than a century ago, using the data and methods available in his day.

But we can only accept Westermarck's conclusions if we include the dimension of flexibility in the characteristics of the human species – the

71

plasticity that makes the evolution of forms possible, as I mentioned in the previous chapter.

We can now present this combination of *norm* and *plasticity* in a formula describing the anthropological matrix of *Homo sapiens*. Let N be the nuclearity of the family, M monogamy, E exogamy, and U the undifferentiation of the kinship system. Let us add a fifth element V, the possibility of variations, likely to affect all the others (an action noted *). This gives us:

$$\text{Matrix of } Homo\ sapiens\text{: } (N + M + E + U) * V$$

Without this variability V, we would not be able to understand the ability of the species to cover the entire planet at the technological stage of gathering and hunting. The economic adaptability of *Homo sapiens* cannot be conceived without this variability of the family system, and in particular the relationship between men and women: the sexual division of labour, which assigns gathering to women and hunting to men, does not prevent some peoples from being predominantly hunters while others are primarily gatherers.

Undifferentiation as a general concept

At this point, we can give a simplified description of the original anthropological system of humanity, as an ideal type. The family is nuclear, albeit without any dogmatism – young couples or elderly parents can be temporarily added to it. Women's status is high. The kinship system is bilateral, or undifferentiated, giving the mother's kin and the father's kin equal places in the definition of the child's world. Marriage is exogamous, seeking spouses beyond cousins of the first degree, but again without dogmatism. Divorce is possible. Polygyny too, and sometimes even, though more rarely, polyandry. Interactions between the families of the brothers and sisters are frequent and structure the local groups. No relationship is completely stable. Families and individuals can separate and regroup. There are two levels of aggregation above the family:

1 Several nuclear families, most often related, constitute a mobile group.
2 These groups of families exchange spouses with each other within a territory comprising perhaps a thousand individuals. The existence of an external limit to the exchange of spouses defines an endogamous territorial group whose boundaries are, however, porous.

The concept of undifferentiation is generally used by anthropologists to describe kinship systems that are neither patrilineal nor matrilineal, but leave individuals free to use paternal and maternal filiations prag-matically. We can at this stage generalize its use to all elements of the family structure that have not been polarized in the course of history by a stable dichotomous choice.

Take the *co-residence of generations*, a positive value for the German stem family or the Russian communitarian family, a negative one for the French egalitarian nuclear family and the English absolute nuclear family. All nuclear-family systems for which a *temporary co-residence* of young adults or the elderly is possible can be said to be undifferentiated, in this dimension of co-residence: they include most hunter-gatherers, Icelanders, Walloons, Poles, Tagalogs and Javanese.

In the case of *inheritance*, it is the absence of the inequality–equality polarity that will define a family system as undifferentiated. The stem family opts for inequality, the communitarian family for equality, just like the egalitarian nuclear family. The English absolute nuclear family appears here as undifferentiated, alongside the Tagalog and Javanese family forms.

The model of *marriage* can also reveal either differentiation or undif-ferentiation. The indissolubility of marriage suggests differentiation, the possibility of divorce undifferentiation. Polygyny, below the 10 per cent level, evokes a tempered, undifferentiated monogamy. Between 15 and 50 per cent, polygyny presupposes a norm and comes under the concept of differentiation. Strict monogamy and African-type mass polygyny rep-resent the opposite poles of differentiation.

Tempered exogamy, which prefers leaving the family group of origin but accepts the possibility of marriage between cross cousins and some marriages between parallel cousins, can be said to be undifferentiated. The obsessive exogamy of the Christian world is differentiated. The endogamy with a high rate of marriages between cousins of the Arab-Persian world or of southern India also suggests, in the opposite sense, differentiation.

We can also use, for the description of sexual life, the adjectives 'dif-ferentiated' and 'tempered' (rather than 'undifferentiated', which could be confusing). The first overviews derived from the Murdock sample show that, in primitive human groups that have not been transformed by one of the great universalist religions, if male/female sexuality dominates – this is a necessity for reproduction – a certain indifference to homo-sexual preferences is dominant, an indifference that seems absolute with regard to female homosexuality. Anal sex, a central Christian phobia, seems to have held no terrors for *Homo sapiens* in original times.[20] The right concept for original *Homo sapiens* thus seems to be a tempered heterosexuality, highly compatible with that of tempered monogamy.

In actual fact, most of the basic behaviours of *Homo sapiens* seem to have been of the 'tempered' type. In 1922, Alexander Carr-Saunders noted the coexistence of norms and variability in the treatment of the weak, children and elderly parents, among hunter-gatherers.[21] Children are produced and raised with love – how could it be otherwise given that the species survived? – but abortion, infanticide and exposure are possibilities that make it possible for the group to survive if it faces a scarcity of resources. The same goes for old people, who are generally well treated, but sometimes abandoned or even killed when a borderline demographic situation is reached. In every respect, the *Homo sapiens* of original times seems to have been simultaneously moral and pragmatic. Darwin had very clearly understood, in his second major book, *The Descent of Man*, that the existence of a collective morality was for the basic human group a competitive advantage for survival.[22] His successors have highlighted the pragmatic nature of this morality of the species, which should not hinder the survival of the group.

Homo sapiens, as I have reconstructed this species, appears undifferentiated in all dimensions, with a system of kinship that is, in the most classic sense of the word, undifferentiated. But the tempered exogamous marriage, tempered monogamy, possible temporary co-residence, and absence of any rule of egalitarian or inegalitarian inheritance in the species all require a broader definition of the concept of undifferentiation. The concept of *generalized undifferentiation* allows us to portray human history as a long process of differentiation, with a polarization of anthropological forms and of the specialization of types, a process in which certain forms have shown more capacity for survival and expansion than others. I will show its liberating potential by applying its corrosive power to some great fantasies of European history.

The Celts, Germans and Slavs of original times

One of the curses that affects the historian of Western Antiquity is the abundance of names of peoples that are void of meaning. We can situate on the map of Europe Celtic, Germanic and Slavic groups, for various periods prior to the acquisition of writing. And we certainly have data on their knowledge of agriculture, animal husbandry, metalworking, pottery and other elements of material life. But the existence of ethnonyms makes us too easily prone to essentialize peoples to whom we attribute, without being able to specify them, various social and mental characteristics. The current existence of French, German and Russian temperaments – an indubitable fact – is projected retrospectively onto those Celtic, Germanic and Slavic origins. The hypothesis of the original undifferentiation of *Homo sapiens* allows us to read the surviving documents correctly: these include, for the two centuries either side of year zero, Strabo's *Geography*, Caesar's *Gallic War*, Tacitus's *Germania*; for the sixth and seventh centuries CE, *The History of the Franks* by Gregory of Tours, and the Frankish, Burgundian and Visigothic legal codes; for the beginning of the twelfth century, the Russian *Primary Chronicle*; and for the twelfth and thirteenth centuries, the Icelandic sagas.

However, the data obtained, although very incomplete, all refer to an original undifferentiation: a high status for women, flexibility in a bilateral kinship system, exogamy (probably tempered), monogamy but tolerance for polygyny. The Germanic codes even allow us to grasp the link between the nuclear family and the bilateral kinship network: *Wergeld*, compensation paid to the family group in case of assassination of one of its members, favours the nuclear family, but it takes more distant kinship into account, on a bilateral basis affecting, on the paternal and maternal sides, equivalent compensations (*OSF*, pp. 340–6 and pp. 427–38).

From then on, Celts, Germans and Slavs are no more than different varieties of *Homo sapiens* and very similar to each other. The divergence of languages (all of them Indo-European) has not led to any divergence of social types and mentalities.

Pierre Guichard has noted the persistent horizontality and fluidity of kinship in the nobility of the Carolingian era, i.e. before the emergence of the stem family from the eleventh century.[23] The terms he uses, citing German and English writers, could be applied, without much adaptation, to the original hunter-gatherer groups, whose kinship systems were undifferentiated.

The Romans and the Greeks, the other major players in European history, cannot be placed in this category of original undifferentiation. Their family systems had polarized features. Their contact with the patrilineality invented in Mesopotamia was substantial, but, as we will see in the next chapter, it did not prevail: indeed, in their cases we will need to describe a certain reversibility in the process of differentiation. The emergence of the Jewish and Christian religions, furthermore, will enable us to raise the question of a co-evolution of family structures and religious systems from a certain date.

Division into peoples: the notion of relative identity

To speak of *Homo sapiens* as a single animal species, selected by natural evolution, distinct from all others, should not make us lose sight of the natural fragmentation of this species. Concrete men and women always belong to a higher order entity, the people. The general undifferentiation of their original anthropological structures cannot lead us to the conclusion that the various Celtic, German or Slavic groups did not exist in history, with their interactions, peaceful or violent. Ethology has identified the human species as characterized by a marked potential for internal, *intraspecific* aggression.[24] But it is not really necessary to resort to Konrad Lorenz to formalize this characteristic of the species: it had already been grasped in 1767 by Adam Ferguson, in his *An Essay on the History of Civil Society*. This representative of the Scottish Enlightenment (with David Hume, Adam Smith and James Watt) was probably the first to integrate into his view of human beings concrete ethnographic records concerning, in particular, North American Indians:

> Late discoveries have brought to our knowledge almost every situation in which mankind are placed. We have found them spread over large and extensive continents, where communications are open, and where national confederacy might be easily formed. We have found them in narrower districts, circumscribed by mountains, great rivers, and arms of the sea. They have been found in small islands, where the inhabitants might be easily assembled, and derive an advantage from their union. But in all those situations, alike, they were broke into cantons, and affected a distinction of name and community. The titles of *fellow-citizen* and *countryman*, unopposed to those of *alien* and *foreigner*, to which they refer, would fall into disuse, and lose their meaning.[25]

Ferguson empirically notes the dialectic of 'us' and 'them', regardless of the level of group development. He does not make the mistake of attributing this fragmentation to differences of essence or of nature between human groups. There is no reference here to the notion of race or colour. Human groups are always in conflict because they are all equally human.[26]

Ferguson realistically associates the internal morality of the group with hostility to outside groups, a simple and powerful observation.

> These observations seem to arraign our species, and to give an unfavourable picture of mankind; and yet . . . [t]hey are sentiments of generosity and self-denial that animate the warrior in defence of his country; and they are dispositions most favourable to mankind, that become the principles of apparent hostility to men. . . .
> Without the rivalship of nations, and the practice of war, civil society itself could scarcely have found an object, or a form.[27]

We can verify the living relevance of this conception by noting how peace between European nations contributes to social disintegration. We understand better, after reading Ferguson, the need for the most advanced societies to create an internal Muslim group or demonize Russia in order to recover their balance, which is ultimately threatened by reconciliation between the nations. The perpetuation of a separate Black group in the United States is based on the same logic of the species.

War is of course observable throughout human history, but the finding is not as trivial as it seems. It leads much more surely than Freud's late generalities on the death instinct to a simple and effective formalization of one of the fundamental problems of the species. Group cohesion depends on hostility to other groups. Internal morality and external violence are functionally associated. Thus, any drop in external violence ultimately threatens the morality and internal cohesion of the group. Peace is a social problem.

In the rest of this book, I will treat as axiomatic this way in which human groups define one another reciprocally. The most important thing is not accepting the notions that external war or internal racism in a society are normal human phenomena, unfortunately non-pathological with regard to the constituent features of the species. The essential point is to understand that there is no absolute identity for any group that would be independent of its relation to other groups. France really began to exist in the fourteenth century only by its conflict with England, American Whites exist only in relation to Blacks, the Greeks were only Greek as compared to barbarians, Athenians as compared to Spartans, Christians as compared to pagans and Jews. Human societies have, of course, intrinsic characteristics: economic system, family structures, religious beliefs, political organization. But none can be conceived and described without external references not only that contribute to the fixing of its characteristics in a long process of reciprocal influences or rejections, but that also give it its internal cohesion, the mobilization of a group solidarity of the group against an 'other', outside or inside it. There is no absolute identity: the identity of a group, in the species *Homo sapiens*, is always relative.

— 4 —

JUDAISM AND EARLY CHRISTIANITY: FAMILY AND LITERACY

Neither Judaism nor Christianity emerged in societies whose family systems were complex, dense, clearly patrilineal or matrilineal. But to understand this fact, we must first get rid of the image of the family as projected by the Bible. This is a subject about which I personally have made many mistakes, having been hypnotized – like so many others – by biblical genealogies.

In the Bible, primogeniture organizes the separation of peoples and the genesis of Israel on the basis of a single humanity begun by Adam and Eve. The idea of the first-born is an obsessive theme in the story of the ten plagues of Egypt and the Exodus. The double share of the elder appears as a rule of inheritance in Deuteronomy. The Bible therefore seems to be describing a patrilineal primogeniture. I saw this literary stem family as the anthropological foundation of monotheism, where the powerful image of fathers found in the Bible supported the image of a single and demanding God. Much later, from the sixteenth century onwards, in Germany and Occitania, Protestantism, as a religion of the Father rather than of the Son, also seems to have been favoured by the emergence of primogeniture. In Japan, between the twelfth and sixteenth centuries, the monotheism of the sect of True Pure Land Buddhism (Jodo-shinshu), which became the central tendency of Buddhism in that country, was also linked to the birth of the stem family.[1] But a universal association between primogeniture and a single god is far too simple a theory. It is inapplicable to early Christianity and Islam, two monotheistic religions whose success it would be difficult to attribute to the stem family. As for Judaism, though it did dream of the stem family in its sacred texts, its people did not, at any stage of its history, seriously practise it.

Representations of the ancient Jewish family are most often a carica-ture. The reading of the Bible is in fact conditioned by two a priori models that rule out any realistic perception of the family structures of the Jews of Antiquity. First, there is the 'standard model' of family history, which searches in the past for complex structures and continually comes across the emergence of the nuclear family wherever it looks. Then there is the 'Bedouin model' that observes the nomadic Arabs of the Near East and finds a patrilineal, communitarian and endogamous family, which it tries to see as a belated form of Abraham's wandering family. If we add Jacob's marriage with his matrilateral female cross cousins Leah and Rachel, it becomes an open-and-shut case: the ancient Jewish family was patrilineal, communitarian and endogamous.

In France, a popular version of the stereotype can be found in André Chouraqui's *La Vie quotidienne des hommes de la Bible* [*Daily Life in Biblical Times*].[2] There are, however, many scholarly forms of the same illusion. In 1991 Baruch Halpern gave us the full works: a clan organization, patrilineal and endogamous, that supposedly disintegrated to allow the nuclear family to appear – and with it, of course, individualism and moral responsibility. This happened in Judea between Hezekiah (727–698 BCE) and Josias (639–609 BCE).[3] Halpern studiously ticks all the boxes of the standard model: he does not forget the parallel between the ancient Jewish family and the families found in Arab villages in the present state of Israel. The Judean religious revolution of the seventh century – one king, one holy city, one temple, one God – was, of course, in his view one manifestation of the rise of individualism.

This preconception about the nature of the family poisons all literature about ancient Israel. It even affects the work of the great archaeologists and historians who, over the last fifteen years, have freed us from the biblical narrative, demonstrating that the journey of the patriarchs from Ur, then the exodus from Egypt, and finally the powerful kingdom said to have preceded the division into a northern state, Israel, and a southern state, Judea, are just literary myths. *The Bible Unearthed* by Israel Finkelstein and Neil Asher Silberman, and *Israel's History and the History of Israel* by Mario Liverani are based on a reality independent of the holy text, namely the peoples of Palestine in the Iron Age (i.e. from the twelfth century BCE). But these impressive works are still influenced by notions of clan and lineage drawn from the old social anthropology. And these concepts are projected onto the past by historians who, even when they do not explicitly say so, have the patrilineal clan in mind, and who are probably unaware of the existence of fluid and undifferentiated forms of kinship.[4]

Primogeniture, although benefiting the older son, could have served as a warning to all concerned, as this element of family and domestic organization most often corresponds to kinship systems that anthropologists describe as bilateral or undifferentiated, in Germany, Japan and elsewhere. Biblical genealogies certainly exist, and *in the Bible* they are predominantly patrilineal. But the Bible is not a field monograph patiently assembled by a Cambridge anthropologist: it was and remains a religious, family and ethnic project, written over a long period of time. Only direct observation, by other means and thanks to other sources, of the real Israelite, Judean or Jewish populations, between the Iron Age and the beginning of our third millennium (CE), can allow us to say whether this biblical blueprint has ever been implemented, in the Promised Land or in the world of the diaspora.

The Jewish nuclear family of original times

Christophe Lemardelé has managed to see things from another and truer perspective. In a pioneering article, he accepted the inverse model of family history and observed the actual data provided by archaeology and by the texts. He hypothesized a shift in the ancient Jewish family from nuclearity to complexity.[5] All the conditions for the application of the inverse model of family history are indeed met, and in particular the clearly peripheral and conservative character of the Land of Canaan within the Near East. The patrilineal principle emerged in Mesopotamia in the third millennium BCE; it spread westward, but only with great difficulty penetrated the highlands of ancient Israel. The small houses of the early Iron Age, around 1000 BCE, excavated by Israeli archaeologists, could contain only nuclear families.[6] So why should we imagine anything other than a delay in the acquisition of primogeniture and the first patrilineal principle by these 'backward' populations living on the margins of the Fertile Crescent, in the highlands? Two and a half thousand years later, the Alawite, Druze and Christian Maronite populations, which occupy the heights immediately to the north, are still characterized, when compared to the patrilineal, communitarian and endogamous world of the surrounding lowlands, by 'archaic' characteristics: residual nuclearity, a higher status of women, weaker endogamy, and inheritance systems that retain non-egalitarian traits (OSF, pp. 484, 500–1).

James George Frazer noted in the biblical account a contradiction between the – obsessional – rule of primogeniture and the actual form of succession practised by the characters involved, who are forever transgressing this rule. The archetype of this literary figure is the stealing of Esau's birthright by Jacob, with the help of his mother. There are many examples of heirs who are not elder sons, and of women who are stronger than men. The specific role of the last born is typical of the original nuclear family (Frazer called it 'natural'), a system in which the youngest child is responsible for the parents because his elders have left one after the other to start their own families on new lands.[7] *Homo sapiens* was mobile, early agriculture was expansive. To explain the contradiction, Frazer postulated an ancient nuclear family the functioning of which was not understood by the later writers of the Bible. In his view, the scribes invented legends to explain the role of the younger sons, a role that appeared to them as the expression of a dysfunction in the normal system of primogeniture. The explanation can perhaps be applied to the genealogies of the kings. Archaeologists have very recently shown that Solomon's kingdom was in reality neither very great nor very glorious, and he himself was not actually David's eldest son. The Patriarchs, those literary characters, were simply invented. However, there is nothing to stop us imagining, even more simply than Frazer does, a contradiction that was still a live issue at the time the Bible was written: primogeniture was then a new concept, one that penetrated the scribes' culture from above, while the undifferentiated nuclear family of the Judeans resisted this innovation. This tension can be found in the form of religious myths in this or that part of the Bible.

The neo-Assyrian and neo-Babylonian epoch: primogeniture and patrilineality

Let us try out a chronology that would take the double share of the elder son in Deuteronomy as its main pointer. The rule is very specific and, as such, could lead us to a very simple origin. It was, in the Near East of the first millennium, extremely commonplace, having spread everywhere from Sumer. It affected the law codes of the neo-Assyrian Empire. We can therefore imagine either that the Israelites acquired it from their contact with the Assyrians, who destroyed the kingdom of Israel in the north in about 720 BCE, or that it was later adopted by the exiles of Babylon after their deportation by Nebuchadnezzar in 598 and 587 BCE. The return from exile was even later, extending, according to Liverani, from 539 to 445 BCE. Now, specialists agree that Deuteronomy was composed between the seventh and sixth centuries BCE, and Deuteronomy includes the double share.[8] At that time, Babylon's inheritance rules had already been egalitarian for quite some time (*OSF*, pp. 525–31). An acquisition of primogeniture resulting from the confrontation with the Assyrians, which lasted from 859 to 627 BCE, seems much more likely.

But it is also clear that the Jews who later returned from Babylonian exile, liberated by the Persian conquest, were obsessed with lineage and blood purity. They took back control of Jerusalem and Judea and rebuilt the Temple (consecrated in 516 BCE). Their obsession with genealogy guarantees that they brought back from Babylon a regenerated patrilineality, regardless of primogeniture. So, overall, we need to imagine the whole of the neo-Assyrian and neo-Babylonian phases as the time when a patrilineal ideology spread towards Palestine, then more precisely to the south, towards Judea. The persistent centrality of primogeniture proves that this patrilineality, however, never went beyond level 1, the form that in general does not lead to a questioning of the bilaterality of the system of general kinship. What we must postulate for Israel in the period from the seventh to the fourth centuries is an attempt to superimpose primogeniture onto an undifferentiated family and kinship system.

Did the peasants of Judea reach the stage of a fully developed stem family, with co-residence of generations within the household? This is doubtful: neither the Assyrian conquest of the kingdom of Israel in the north, nor the Babylonian conquest of Judea in the south was the kind of conquest that structure rural life in a good way. The deportation of those who worked the land by the Assyrians, and the deportation of the elites by the Babylonians, cannot fail to have created chaos in the towns and countryside. Primogeniture therefore probably never affected anything other than the religious or ideological sphere. This is important, but it excludes the hypothesis of a Judean rural society organized at any time by the stem family.

Hellenistic and Roman times: a bilateral reversion

With the conquest of the Persian Empire by Alexander between 334 and 328 BCE, the political and cultural wind changed direction. From the Assyrians to the Persians, it had blown patrilineality from east to west. From the Hellenistic period, it blew bilaterality from west to east. In the Hellenistic era and then in Roman times the entire Mediterranean basin was engaged in a *general reversion of the systems of kinship towards bilaterality*, which we are forced to observe even though we cannot fully explain it. Systems in the process of patrilinealization swung back to a relative equivalence of men and women.

Classical Greece and Republican Rome had patrilineal family systems. The Athens of Pericles confined women to *gynaecea*. The Romans certainly respected their wives more, but the Roman *gens* was a patrilineal clan (agnatic, according to Latin terminology) and, as we said above, as an institution it came with the usual potential for predatory expansion. Even Egypt, which was still relatively feminist, had seen an embryo of male primogeniture develop in its upper classes several times over.

But in the Hellenistic period, as Sarah Pomeroy notes, the situation of women started to improve.[9] According to William Harris, girls' education started to be a matter of interest for families.[10] The growth of gender equality was particularly spectacular in the Hellenistic Egypt of the Ptolemies (*OSF*, pp. 571–5). I have studied in detail the nuclear and bilateral reversion of the Roman family and kinship system under the Empire in *L'Origine des systèmes familiaux* (*OSF*, pp. 346–57). Finally, in 533 CE, the Code of Justinian enacted equality in inheritance for boys and girls. Though first written in Latin, this text was promulgated in

Constantinople, the heart of an empire in which Greek was now the spoken language.

Judea, brought into the sphere of domination of the Hellenistic kingdoms – the Ptolemies and the Seleucids – and then part of the Roman Empire, must have been affected by this reversion to bilaterality. We have to accept, at the very least, that its evolution towards patrilineality was arrested. This is indeed what we observe with the development of the rabbinic Judaism that followed the destruction of Jerusalem and the Second Temple by the Romans in 70 CE: patrilineal and matrilineal traits begin to coexist in Jewish texts. We must be aware, however, that, at that time, the populations of the diaspora in Egypt, Syria, Asia Minor and, secondarily, Rome were already demographically more important than Judaea.[11] The diaspora was essentially urban and seems not to have followed a rule of primogeniture, since no rural inheritance was to be transmitted *undivided*. Although it is not an exclusive determining factor, urban civilization was a good framework for the nuclear and bilateral reversion of the family system.

The *trompe-l'oeil* of Jewish matrilineality

It was towards 200 CE that there appeared, set down in the Mishna, the celebrated rule whereby membership of the Jewish people was transmitted by the mother.[12] It would therefore be easy to imagine that Judaism evolved towards to matrilineality in reaction to the conquering patrilineality of the Middle East. And why not? Shaye J. D. Cohen, who has established with certainty that this rule emerged only belatedly, can find no reasonable explanation for it and concludes that it was initially a scholarly whim – but a whim that laid the basis for the future. Nevertheless, before giving up on the mystery, he comes close to the truth: 'Intermarriage was not a severe problem in rabbinic society, and even if it was, the logical response would have been the institution of a bilateral system, requiring both a Jewish father and a Jewish mother for an offspring to be reckoned Jewish by birth.'[13] But that is precisely the point: in the diaspora, the fathers were Jewish and that was not the problem.

A group seeking to protect its identity cannot fail to demand cultural orthodoxy from its women; a group whose men are mobile and which takes its women from abroad even more so. For such was the mechanism of dispersion, for the Jews, as it had been for the Greeks who had colonized the western basin of the Mediterranean in the eighth and seventh centuries BCE. A large proportion of migrant men married women whom they encountered where they settled. As we have seen in Chapter 1, the genetic makeup of Ashkenazi Jews reveals a predominance of European mitochondrial DNA, transmitted by the mother. The rule of matrilineality, therefore, probably arose only to compel Jewish men to demand that their wives convert. Originally, it expressed no aspiration to matrilineality. It was the father's religion that must be passed on, a requirement expressed by rabbinic Judaism's emphasis on the father's responsibility for the religious education of his children.[14]

We must also assume that pagan women were attracted by the family values of Judaism, as they would be later on by those of Christianity. 'The people of Damascus planned to massacre the Jews of the city but had to keep their plans secret because all of their wives, except for a few, had gone over . . . to the Jewish religion.'[15]

The oldest conversion ritual to have come down to us is recorded in the Babylonian Talmud. Shaye Cohen describes this remarkably simple ritual. Converts, male or female, must answer a single question: they are asked if they are aware that they are seeking to join a persecuted group and need to answer with just a few words: 'I know' and 'I am not worthy'.[16] No detailed theological verification is required. The point is to ensure that the wife, who is not the central figure in religious transmission, enters the Jewish community and withdraws from the non-Jewish world.

The educational patrilineality of Judaism

Around 63–65 CE, shortly before the destruction of the Temple, the Pharisee High Priest Joshua ben Gamla ordered every Jewish father to send his 6- or 7-year-old sons to primary school to learn how to read the Torah. This was undoubtedly the founding act of the Judaism familiar to us: that which survived the disappearance of its territorial roots and developed into a very literate diaspora (this is the world studied by Maristella Botticini and Zvi Eckstein over the period that extends from 70 CE to 1492). A millennium and a half before Luther and Protestantism, we thus find a religion that required mass literacy for theological reasons. According to Botticini and Eckstein, who are undoubtedly following Catherine Hezser on this point, the Jews of Judea were rather less literate than the Greeks and Romans at the time of the destruction of the Second Temple.[17]

William Harris attempted to evaluate literacy rates of the Greco-Roman Empire at the apogee of its cultural evolution.[18] In Italy, this seems to have been well below 20 per cent for men and 10 per cent for women.[19] The figures given by Harris for the Empire are generally lower in the west and higher in the east: they suggest an overall average of 10 per cent maximum. This was better than nothing, but, as Harris notes, it is much less than England in the years 1580–1700.

Botticini and Eckstein, paradoxically, do not give literacy rates for their study period of a millennium and a half.[20] They undoubtedly over-estimate the educational achievements of rabbinic Judaism. But these were still considerable. To show this, we can cite the literacy rates of Jews and non-Jews in Russia at the time of the census of 1897; this was a country where mass literacy was just beginning. The literacy rate for males over the age of 10 was only 28 per cent for the population of the Russian Empire, but 65 per cent for Jews (including both Yiddish and Russian).[21] Rates among the over-60s, i.e. those born before 1837, bring us a little closer to the original Jewish culture, with its imperfections and its patrilineal educational tendency: 54 per cent of men were literate, but only 15 per cent of women. We are close to the world dreamed of by Joshua ben Gamla in the first century of our era. In the next chapter, focusing on Germany and the Protestant Reformation, I shall study the rise of literacy for humanity as a whole.

Bilinearity

If we combine educational patrilineality and religious matrilineality, we get an idea of the Jewish family during the emergence of rabbinic Judaism. The coexistence of patrilineal and matrilineal imperatives defines what is called, in anthropology, a bilinear system, typical of cultures that have been influenced by patrilineality but have, for the most part, resisted it, retaining a relatively high status for women despite the absorption of patrilineal traits. We must, moreover, admit that the urban transformation of the Jewish population excludes the hypothesis of a truly complex family. What we know about the Jewish way of life, in its various adaptations, from Iran to Morocco, from Spain to Russia, suggests the pragmatism of the undifferentiated nuclear family: tempo-rary co-residence with the parents, the taking in of elderly forebears, the choice between geographical mobility and stability, the intensity of relationships between siblings, and the absence of a strict principle of equality in the distribution of inheritance. A patrilineal bias is certainly evident in education, and a symbolic emphasis on primogeniture is main-tained by a reading of the Torah. But overall, the family type remains nuclear and undifferentiated.

Censuses of Jewish ghettos in Germany in the seventeenth century show nuclear households in houses structured by bilateral ties of kinship, expressed by the way that young couples sometimes opted for matrilo-cal, and sometimes for patrilocal, places of residence.[22] As a result of the Russian environment, further east, patrilocality was stronger.[23] One must also assume a patrilineal influence of the environment among the Jews of the Arab-Persian world. The marriage model, however, reveals

85

that a strong resistance was put up by the original undifferentiation of Jewish family culture.

The tempered exogamy of Judaism

The endogamy of the Jewish people has often led to an erroneously endogamous representation of the Jewish family. The absence of a ban on marriages between cousins and the possibility of union between uncle and niece (oblique marriage) has contributed to this categorization, as has the geographical proximity of origin to the Arab populations that today practise family endogamy. But we are here faced with a myth. The immigration of numerous and varied Jewish groups to the modern state of Israel has made it possible to measure precisely family endogamy for populations from Europe or the Arab-Persian world. In around 1955, Israel had a first-cousin marriage rate of only 1.4 per cent for Jews of Ashkenazi origin and 7.9 per cent for others, mainly from the Arab world.[24]

These levels are certainly higher than the rates among Christian populations in Europe (below 1 per cent), but they definitely point to a tempered exogamous model. This is evident in the case of Ashkenazi Jews of European origin. But the rate of less than 8 per cent among the Jews of the Arab-Persian world, subject to the influence of the surrounding endogamous world (with an average of 35 per cent), is actually very low. Moreover, Christians in the Middle East, explicitly exogamous before the Arab conquest, but subject to the same endogamous cultural pressure as local Jews, did not do any better. Myriam Khlat found that Christians in Beirut in 1986 had a rate of first-cousin marriages of exactly 7.9 per cent.[25]

Jewish culture seems to have practised, like that of Rome and many other populations, a de facto exogamy, which, without prohibiting marriages between cousins, generally avoided them. In *The City of God*, St Augustine set out a theory of this unconscious exogamy:

> And with regard to ... marriage between cousins, we have observed that in our own time the customary morality has prevented this from being frequent, though the law allows it. It was not prohibited by divine law, nor as yet had human law prohibited it; nevertheless, though legitimate, people shrank from it, because it lay so close to what was illegitimate, and in marrying a cousin seemed almost to marry a sister.[26]

At this stage, we can define the Jewish family system as undifferentiated and nuclear, differing from the original type of *Homo sapiens* only in its patrilineal inflection and in its (rarely realized) dream of primogeniture.

The true Jewish family innovation: the protection of children

The Jewish religion, however, modified the functioning of the undif-ferentiated nuclear model by introducing what were in ancient times completely new prohibitions on abortion and infanticide. The Bible strongly supports a high birth rate: it thus breaks with the pragmatic attitude of *Homo sapiens* who, spontaneously Malthusian, thought in terms of a balance between population and subsistence and did not feel bound by any 'Thou shalt not kill' if there was a food shortage. It is reasonable to assume that this innovation provided the ancient Jewish population with a high birth rate, which partly explains the level of emigration and the numerical growth of the diaspora even before the Roman conquest.

Jewish morality at the end of the first century, seen by Flavius Josephus and Tacitus

Both Josephus the apologist and Tacitus the critic mention the rejec-tion of infanticide. Flavius Josephus captures the mixture of respect for women and the patrilineal inflection that underlay it; Tacitus is worried about conversions and reveals, by denouncing them as abomi-nations, which innovations might attract people to Judaism: internal group solidarity, morality and respect for children.

FLAVIUS JOSEPHUS *Against Apion* (c. 93 CE)
'But, then, what are our laws about marriage? That law owns no other mixture of sexes but that which nature hath appointed, of a man with his wife, and that this be used only for the procreation of children. But it abhors the mixture of a male with a male; and if any one do that, death is its punishment. It commands us also, when we marry, not to have regard to portion, nor to take a woman by violence, nor to persuade her deceitfully and knavishly; but to demand her in marriage of him who hath power to dispose of her, and is fit to give her away by the nearness of his kindred; for, says the Scripture, 'A woman is inferior to her husband in all things.' Let her, therefore, be obedient to him; not so that he should abuse her, but that she may acknowledge her duty to her husband; for God hath given the authority to the husband. A husband, therefore, is to lie only with his wife whom he hath married; but to have to do with another man's wife is a wicked thing, which, if any one ventures upon, death is inevitably his punish-ment: no more can he avoid the same who forces a virgin betrothed

87

to another man, or entices another man's wife. *The law, moreover, enjoins us to bring up all our offspring, and forbids women to cause abortion of what is begotten, or to destroy it afterward; and if any woman appears to have so done, she will be a murderer of her child, by destroying a living creature, and diminishing human kind*; if any one, therefore, proceeds to such fornication or murder, he cannot be clean. Moreover, the law enjoins, that after the man and wife have lain together in a regular way, they shall bathe themselves; for there is a defilement contracted thereby, both in soul and body, as if they had gone into another country; for indeed the soul, by being united to the body, is subject to miseries, and is not freed therefrom again but by death; on which account the law requires this purification to be entirely performed.'

On the education of children:

'Nay, indeed, the law does not permit us to make festivals at the births of our children, and thereby afford occasion of drinking to excess; but it ordains that the very beginning of our education should be immediately directed to sobriety. It also commands us to bring those children up in learning, and to exercise them in the laws, and make them acquainted with the acts of their predecessors, in order to their imitation of them, and that they might be nourished up in the laws from their infancy, and might neither transgress them, nor have any pretence for their ignorance of them.'[27]

TACITUS *Histories* (106–107 CE)

'For all the most worthless rascals, renouncing their national cults, were always sending money to swell the sum of offerings and tribute. This is one cause of Jewish prosperity. Another is that they are obstinately loyal to each other, and always ready to show compassion, whereas they feel nothing but hatred and enmity for the rest of the world. They eat and sleep separately. Though immoderate in sexual indulgence, they refrain from all intercourse with foreign women: among themselves anything is allowed. They have introduced circumcision to distinguish themselves from other people. Those who are converted to their customs adopt the same practice, and the first lessons they learn are to despise the gods, to renounce their country, and to think nothing of their parents, children, and brethren. However, they take steps to increase their numbers. *They count it a crime to kill any of their later-born children*, and they believe that the souls of those who die in battle or under persecution are immortal. Thus they think much of having children and nothing of facing death.'[28]

The Christianity of original times

When we think of Christianity in relation to Judaism, we try in general to grasp the metaphysical innovations of the religion founded by Christ and St Paul. Two latent but never dominant concepts in pre-Christian Judaism, the immortality of the soul and openness to non-Jews, immediately spring to mind. The quotation from Tacitus presented in the box contains these two elements, since it targets converts to Judaism and mentions the immortality of the souls of warriors and the tortured. We can also sometimes wonder whether, in these words, Tacitus is aiming his criticism at Jews or at Christians, between whom, at the time, there was barely any difference.

According to Flavius Josephus, Jewish sects differed in their ideas about immortality: Essenes and Pharisees granted it to the souls of the righteous, but the Sadducees denied it.[29] For him, all are Jews. From many sources, we also know that conversions to Judaism were common at various times in Antiquity. The immortality of the soul and the conversion of non-Jews could therefore have fundamentally constituted only options within Judaism; in this regard, Christianity was just one sect among others.

On the other hand, while the Christian rejection of circumcision and food prohibitions distances us from metaphysics, it brings us closer to a sociological perception of religion. Regardless of any conception of the hereafter, the abandonment of circumcision and food prohibitions abolishes the idea that the Jewish group was separated from the rest.

What can we learn from a comparison between the two religions, the mother and her daughter, when we look at the way they viewed the family?

Christianity comes from a Jewish background in the context of the Greco-Roman world, and its initial association with the nuclear family has never posed any problem of interpretation. It has often been noted, indeed, that the Gospels radicalize the nuclear characteristic of the ideal family. Jesus's message is explicitly anti-familialist: 'And the brother shall deliver up the brother to death, and the father the child: and the children shall rise up against their parents, and cause them to be put to death. And ye shall be hated of all men for my name's sake: but he that endureth to the end shall be saved.'[30] At this stage, however, as we have just shown, Christian nuclearity was still a Jewish nuclearity.

Studies in historical sociology, which attempt to model rigorously the quantitative growth of Christianity in the Roman Empire, show that there was a huge number of converts from Judaism – until much later than is generally admitted. Rodney Stark has used his knowledge of the sociology of American sects to understand Late Antiquity. In his view, in

89

the middle of the second century CE, the Church was still dominated by believers with Jewish roots and he estimates the conversion rate of Jews in the diaspora at 20 per cent.[31] He was followed by Maristella Botticini and Zvi Eckstein, whom I have cited above for their contribution to the history of Jewish education: they see these conversions to Christianity as one of the major causes of the numerical collapse of the Jewish people between 65 CE and 650 CE.[32] Stark's view is that it was mainly Hellenized Jews from the diaspora who converted, while Botticini and Eckstein think that it was the peasants of Judea, who were frightened by the cost of the education demanded by Joshua ben Gamla. The Botticini–Eckstein model provides an efficient explanation for the near disappearance of the Jewish population in Palestine. But the geographical coincidence between the map of early Christianity and that of the Jewish first-century diaspora essentially proves that Stark was right. The closeness, up until the foundation of the modern state of Israel, of Jewish and Christian communities at the extremities of the sphere of ancient Christianity, as in Ethiopia or Kerala in southern India, suggests a Christianity that emerged out of diaspora Judaism – i.e., is evidence that Christianity sprang from an essentially Jewish anthropological matrix.

Christian innovation 1: radical exogamy

We must note, however, that the earliest Christian representation of the family – the couple and their children, the high status given to the wife – combines and crystallizes all the current developments in the Roman Empire of the first centuries of our era. Even before the emergence of Christianity, as we have seen above, Jews, Greeks, Egyptians and Latins all seem to have embarked on a common reversion of the family to its nuclear stage, and of kinship to its undifferentiated stage. Equality between boys and girls in inheritance as set out in the Code of Justinian in 533 would, moreover, suggest an explicitly bilateral, rather than undifferentiated, kinship system, affirming as it does the equivalence of the paternal and maternal sides.

The initial anthropological dynamic, nuclear and bilateral, is therefore one of family rather than religion. The importance of the family was accentuated by the nuclear Christian vision. Here we are confronted with a typical case of the co-evolution of family and religion. The Christian religion strengthens or protects the nuclear-family type. That is why twentieth-century anthropologists would find, in the most remote and isolated Christian groups, among the Christians of Kerala and among the Amharas of Ethiopia, a family that is still nuclear in an environment that is no longer so (OSF, pp. 220, 486). The strengthening of the anthropological type by religion also affects the model of marriage:

early Christianity was marked by a new and radical exogamy. Here, it distinguished itself clearly from Judaism, where exogamy was tempered. But once again, a non-religious – and Roman – point of departure can be detected at work in the anthropological dynamic.

The Christian taboo on consanguineous marriage is a dynamic principle that progresses with time. The Church also restricts the possibility of unions with in-laws. Let us confine ourselves for the time being to blood relatives. Initially limited to first cousins, the prohibition was extended to the descendants of first cousins at the Councils of Epaone (in 517) and Clermont (in 535). In 721, the Council of Rome targeted all kinship, in practice to the seventh degree of Roman computation. The fever of these prohibitions then cooled down, lulled by the inapplicable nature of the phobia. In 1215, the Fourth Lateran Council reduced the ban to just those born from first cousins.

The Christian obsession with consanguinity, however, predated this conciliar legislation. St Augustine had been, as we have seen, a particularly creative anthropologist on the matter. In *The City of God* (written between 413 and 426), we find a long discussion of the historical enlargement of the taboo of incest, which prefigures Claude Lévi-Strauss at one point: the father of the Western Church defines exogamy as an indispensable agent for the extension of social bonds between men. A generation earlier, Ambrose of Milan, his model, had already written about the ban on marriage between cousins. But he presented himself as the continuation of a dynamic initiated by imperial power rather than by the Church. For, as early as 295, Diocletian had forbidden marriage between uncle and niece (sister's daughter). In a letter of 393 to his friend Paternus, Ambrose also alludes to an edict of the emperor Theodosius, which can be dated to between 379 and 395 but is now lost: 'Indeed, the emperor Theodosius also forbids first cousins by the father and by the mother to unite in marriage.'[33] Did this stem from a dynamic of the state, or from the deepest strata of society? The Church, in any case, did not lie behind the movement towards radical exogamy, even if it took charge of it and gave it its full importance between the sixth and eighth centuries. Here again, as in the case of bilaterality, we can speak of co-evolution, of an initial family dynamic strengthened by religion.

Western monogamy is another point of application, even if monogamy was already an absolute rule (not tempered) among the Greeks and Romans. The Church nevertheless made it a central element of its doctrine, consistently and vigorously forcing German invaders to abandon the tempered version of monogamy that characterized them. Ashkenazi Jewish culture, born in the Moselle and Rhine valleys in the tenth and eleventh centuries, also gave up the occasional polygyny permitted by the Bible.

Christian innovation 2: feminism

I mentioned above the rise in the status of women in the Hellenistic and then Roman worlds, from the second century BCE onwards. Here again, the Christian feminist transformation first appears as an effect of the change in family structure before becoming a cause of its intensification. In actual fact, the high status of women, absolute monogamy, bilaterality and radical exogamy constitute a systemic whole in motion.

The role of women in the conversion to Christianity of the middle and upper classes of the Roman Empire is a historical commonplace. Its central symbol is the irresistible emergence of Mary in Catholic worship. Alexander of Alexandria was the first to define her as 'Theotokos' (mother of God), in 325; this title was confirmed by the Council of Ephesus in 431.

Peter Brown, followed in this respect by Rodney Stark, gave a particularly detailed vision of the role of the Christian woman. In his view, she represented a gateway into Christianity for the pagan family, and conversion narratives tell of many husbands who were their wives' 'followers' into the new religion. According to Brown, the predominance of women in the new religious movement becomes clear from 200 CE onwards.[34] The Church encouraged widows, who in those days were often still young women, to remain chaste and not to remarry. When they were rich, they became benefactors of the Christian clergy.

The specific influence of women would be reasserted, with little difference in each case, when barbarian, Germanic and Slavic Europe converted. The role played by Clotilde in Clovis's decision to convert in 498 would be echoed by Olga of Kiev in 957, though not until the time of her grandson Vladimir (980–1015) did the ruling classes of Kievan Russia accept Christianity.[35]

Note that the conversion of Kievan Russia to Christianity predated the acquisition of patrilineality by Muscovite Russia, and also predated the Mongol conquest. The patrilineal communitarianism of Russia would not be fully realized in peasant circles until between the mid-seventeenth and the nineteenth centuries (OSF, pp. 364–6), seven or eight centuries after Christianization. Perhaps the feminist characteristic of Christianity, encapsulated in an Orthodox Marian cult just as intense as its Catholic counterpart, slowed down the spread of the patrilineal Russian characteristic. Orthodox feminism thus helps explain the paradox of Russian culture: the combination of a fully developed patrilineal family organization with a relatively high status attributed to women.

As Brown notes, Christianity broke with the religious and educational patrilineality of Judaism. The rabbis, for their part, remain faithful to a conception of the study of the Torah that excluded women. But the separation of Christianity and Judaism became truly spectacular in connection with every aspect of sexuality. Christianity invented the notion of a sexuality that was in itself bad, and needed to be limited or abolished.

Christian innovation 3: anti-sexuality

Judaism had opposed the Greco-Roman sexual and family practices that were relatively lax, or more likely similar to those of the original *Homo sapiens*. Jewish religious morality condemns adultery, homosexuality and infanticide. But Judaism at the beginning of the first millennium was essentially familialist and did not reject sexuality as such. After all, as we have to agree, the sexual act is necessary for procreation, and, as we have noted, the Bible supports big families: 'Go forth and multiply.'

Christianity took over this heritage. It converted the Greco-Roman world to a family morality of the Jewish type, protective of children. It also benefited very early on, like Judaism (as noted by Rodney Stark), from a competitive advantage of birth rate compared to the pagan world, which was always ready to get rid of unwanted children, and thus lived under the constant threat of depopulation. But the Church went further than the rabbis, or rather, took a new direction: sexuality itself was defined as bad. Abstinence and asceticism constituted for the Church of Antiquity a vast field of experimentation, which included the invention of mass monasticism. The sexual instinct ceased to be a promise of life, and instead became a symptom of our inability to rise above our animal condition. To renounce sexuality meant asserting freedom from our impulses (here we are very far from a conception of sexuality as 'liberating', as it was in the 1968 student movement). In addition, for women, chastity – irrespective of all metaphysics – would be the means to escape the risks of pregnancy and childbirth, i.e., in the context of the time, a way of greatly improving their life expectancy. The marriage age of women in upper-class Roman society rose in a Christian environment, and their mortality rate declined correspondingly.[36]

What we have here is a radically innovative religion: defining the chaste man and woman as *essentially* superior to the married couples who ensure the reproduction of the species was a transformation of considerable violence. We will see in the following chapter how, from the sixteenth century onwards, it ended up affecting the family structures of Christian Europe, whether nuclear, stem or communitarian.

The Christian anthropological transformation was, as we have said, all of a piece: chastity, feminism, absolute monogamy and radical exogamy walked hand in hand. I will not venture to explore the deep psychological link between chastity and exogamy – the two elements that seem a priori

93

the farthest removed in this list; I will simply note that St Augustine himself instinctively connected them:

> And on this account, even when the world was full of people, though they did not choose wives from among their sisters or half sisters, yet they preferred them to be of the same stock as themselves. But who doubts that the modern prohibition of the marriage even of cousins is the more seemly regulation – not merely on account of the reason we have been urging, the multiplying of relationships, so that one person might not absorb two, which might be distributed to two persons, and so increase the number of people bound together as a family, but also because there is in human nature I know not what natural and praiseworthy shamefacedness which restrains us from desiring that connection which, though for propagation, is yet lustful and which even conjugal modesty blushes over, with anyone to whom consanguinity bids us render respect?[37]

Christian innovation 4: poverty as a limit experience

There is another innovative star in the Christian mental constellation – an unexpected one, since it seems far removed from the anthropology of the couple. This new element is the love of the poor. Judaism before Christianity, and Islam after it, were concerned by the fate of people suffering economic difficulties. But Christianity really made social degradation an obsession. Indeed, it seems even to have needed it. Peter Brown, who has studied in succession the conception of the sexuality prevalent among Christians of the Later Empire and their relation to poverty, is struck by the interaction of the two elements in the emerging mental system:

> Because of this, the most vocal advocates of Christianity in the late fourth and fifth centuries tended to focus attention on extreme states of the human condition. It is no accident that the torrent of Christian preaching on outreach to the poor coincided with a sharp elevation of forms of total sexual renunciation – of virginity, of monastic withdrawal, and even, in certain circles, of clerical celibacy. . . . Outreach to the poor and the adoption of virginity and celibacy were both held to be actions that went against the normal grain of human nature. Both were tinged with a sense of heroic *démesure* that demonstrated the supernatural superiority of the Christian religion, which could inspire its adherents to do such extraordinary things as abandon sex and love the poor.[38]

The strategic growth of the Christian group took place within what might be called the urban middle class of the Empire. The upper class did not 'invade' the Church until the latter had become a state monopoly. But neither group wanted to become poor, not even those wealthy Christians who donated most of their property to the Church. These reasonably comfortable or very wealthy people turned the poor, perceived as physically degraded, into a symbol of humanity and an object of charity. This represented an absolute break with the Greco-Roman ideal, which had focused on the glorification of well-nourished and healthy bodies.

It is crucial to identify, as does Brown, the same extremism at work in the sexual and social conceptions of Christians. This great historian enables us to sense why this doubly radical view was necessary for belief in the resurrection of Christ and his divine nature. But we must also understand why this in many ways frightening extremism did not hinder the expansion of the Christian group. How could the horror of sexuality and the love of the poor, considered hitherto as physically repugnant, attract so many people whom historians of the mid-twentieth century would have defined as provincial bourgeois? Only 10 per cent of the inhabitants of the Roman Empire, of course, were Christians on the eve of the establishment of the Catholic Church as a state religion by Constantine between 312 and 337, followed by his successors. But in the context of the urban population alone, this proportion was more important.

Is Paradise the real reward?

Christianity promises the righteous eternal life, of which the resurrection of Christ is the symbol. We have seen that Judaism, without being formally hostile to the concept, was somewhat sceptical, or rather saw it as a secondary element of the doctrine. Its sects varied on this point, without their theoretical disagreement excluding any of them from what was then 'Judaism'. How then did belief in eternal life become the true driving force behind conversion to Jesus's message?

In this piece of historical anthropology that we are conducting here, it is more reasonable to grasp the dynamics of faith on Earth, and to start from the elementary observation that a religion is not only a personal belief, but above all the sharing of a belief by a group of human beings on Earth. So let us agree that before it rewards us in heaven, a religion rewards us here below. We must understand why sexual asceticism and the love of the poor, extremist and deviant views for Antiquity, gave the individuals constituting the Christian group a positive reward during their lifetime.

To ask the question today, in a Western world that ideologically values sex and wealth, is crucial. For us, sexual asceticism and the love of the poor are now, again, incomprehensible extremist deviations, to be classified perhaps under the rubric of mere masochism. Today, sexual freedom and banking reign. This is where Rodney Stark's work proves to be essential.

Influenced by the rational choice school, Stark has grasped the fact that the aberrant beliefs and behaviours of religious groups, whether masochistic or not, and the opprobrium that they bring upon their members, can for the individuals concerned be more than compensated by the group cohesion produced by stigmatization. The psychological cost of belonging to a religion, demanding for oneself but ridiculous in the eyes of the outside world, is so high that adherents can be sure that they belong to a group of exceptionally reliable people. The internal loyalty of the group is the true reward of the believing individual. This gratification is immediate, more secure and tangible than the promise of the hereafter. The argument developed by Stark applies to early Christians or Mormons in the United States, but we can see how it can also contribute to a better understanding of the survival of the Jewish people, who no longer appear to have persisted through history *despite* persecution but *because of* persecution.

We can reformulate this from a Durkheimian perspective. What the individual finds in the bizarre monotheistic religious groups of Late Antiquity – whether they were circumcised and refused to eat pork, or were disgusted by sexuality and fascinated by the degradation of the body of the poor – is a sense of belonging to a moral human group. In the chaos of the great ancient cities – Alexandria, Antioch and Rome – Judaism and then Christianity were, as Stark says, refuges.[39] Christianity certainly offered, for later on, eternal life, in which its adherents could believe as a group. But what it immediately gave was an end to loneliness, a sense of belonging to a world of solidarity, and – in very concrete terms – psychological and even economic security. The Gospels, if read without prejudice, give the game away: there is a long series of miracles to do with food and health, and these point to a better earthly life rather than to eternal life.

Judaism does not generally promise eternal life, but among its faithful, in Antiquity and the Middle Ages, it fostered a courage and a contempt for death that yield nothing to those of the Christian martyrs. Its enduring power suggests that *Homo sapiens* is, in the end, more afraid of loneliness than of death.

The two monotheisms and their families

In the case of Judaism, as in the case of early Christianity, we find an association with the nuclear family, an anthropological form less capable than the patrilineal clan of ensuring, in the context of the unbridled

96

urbanization of Late Antiquity, the mental and physical security of its members. Nothing prevents us from linking this nuclear family to the religious individualism and the moral responsibility dear to Baruch Halpern, cited above. The Jewish family of Antiquity was certainly not really any more nuclear than that of the original *Homo sapiens*, but we must recognize too, with Darwin, that he already possessed an individual morality. The first theory of natural selection had pointed out, with good sense, that an internal morality of the basic human group was necessary for its survival and that it constituted, in the animal kingdom, a competitive advantage. The altruism of the individual, within the group, did not wait for civilization to come along; it had already made itself manifest in human beings, as the left-wing Darwinists of the early twentieth century pointed out.[40] Long before Darwin, however, Ferguson had pointed to the connection in *Homo sapiens* between the morality of individuals who constitute a local group and the internal conflicts of the human race in general, as mentioned above.

With the monotheistic religions from the end of the ancient world, we therefore need to conclude that group morality was transformed and intensified in urban milieus, rather than appearing for the first time. Judaism and Christianity shared various common and central elements from the point of view of family behaviour: the rejection of adultery, homosexuality and infanticide. On the other hand, it is difficult to see how the Christian addition of a negative view of sexuality and the promotion of celibacy that resulted from it could constitute additions to the group's morality. The refusal to procreate contains an antisocial element.

More generally, the definition of the group and, at its heart, of the relation of family to kinship is not the same for Jews and for Christians.

Judaism includes the principle of a closed ethno-religious group. Judaism has also kept alive, around the nuclear family, the undifferentiated kinship network and its solidarities. One can hardly speak of absolute individualism in this world of brothers, sisters and cousins. If this rich and warm network of kinship were to survive in an urban environment, however, it needed the cement provided by a religious belief that kept it separate from other groups. Once again, family and religion appear to be solidary and in co-evolution with one another.

Early Christianity militated for an open and expansive group. Its ideal type of nuclear family was, from the outset, more feminist, well-regulated by the equality of children and by a rule of absolute exogamy that attacked the undifferentiated kinship network. The absolute impossibility of marriage between cousins was aimed explicitly at the dilution of the kinship group. We can therefore, in the case of Christianity, suggest that a step forward was taken in nuclearity. We could point to a stronger individualism if an obvious counterpart to the shrinking of active kinship had not been the rise to power of a formidable clerical bureaucracy, aspiring to chastity for itself but responsible for administering the sexual lives and the marriages of the mass of believers.

In the case of Judaism, nuclearity implies a rather high level of individual responsibility, but the tempered character of exogamy authorizes a closed conception of the group; the dream of primogeniture found in the Bible, meanwhile, fosters the idea of a differentiation of human groups. In the Jewish family, which dreams of birthright even if it does not practise it, brothers are solidary, but they are not 'equal'. Like brothers, peoples are therefore perceived as different. The fondness of the Bible (read here as an ideological text) for younger brothers, however, indicates the extent to which the difference – between brothers, then between peoples – cannot lead to domination, a situation that is admittedly not very likely for a people that is always in the minority, and most often oppressed.

But it would, I think, be a mistake to find only differentialism in the Bible and not to feel that Jewish individualism, combined with the dream of primogeniture, leads in its own way to a universal conception of humankind.

The two stages of the universal

There exists, floating in Western consciousness, a common representation of Judaism that is admittedly monotheistic but also differentialist (the Chosen People) and of a Christianity that has acceded to the universal. The model can be based on a standard historical interpretation: when Jewish monotheism, differentialist in nature, confronted the universal Greco-Roman Empire, it ended up giving birth to the universalist monotheism of Christianity. This too simple representation derives in large part from European narcissism, which considerably reduces the temporal depth and geographical space of Jewish history. Judaism's confrontation with the universal did not, in fact, begin with Rome. It came much earlier, since the first Israelite or Judean visions of the Empire were neo-Assyrian and, later, neo-Babylonian. If we accept the idea that the Jewish religion was born from the confrontation between Assur and Babylon, then we must admit that the universality of humankind was, just as much as the differentiation of nations, foundational for Judaism. This is the reason why the biblical narrative immediately gives all peoples one set of parents, Adam and Eve, and traces the genealogical history of their differentiation. The cousin peoples enumerated by the Bible, differentiated by primogeniture – a concept that came from Mesopotamia – are in fact all those who were incorporated into the neo-Assyrian or neo-Babylonian empires. For anyone interested in the family's imprint in history, it is important to understand that while primogeniture separates brothers, it also favours the memory of their common origin, and therefore the notion of a unity of the human race. It defines a universal rooted in time, vertical rather than horizontal. And then, remaining anthropologists and, to the end, realists of terrestrial life: how could the very idea of existence in the diaspora, that is to say among peoples who needed to be trusted, have been possible for the Jews without their latent, but profound, belief in the universality of humankind?

Certainly, Christianity has gone further into the universal and, if we cannot here deprive Judaism of a certain priority, we need to accept that its religious progeny made a qualitative leap. The fundamental anthropological structures of the Late Roman Empire were specifically different from Assyria and Babylon. It seems that its cities were indeed dominated by a prototype of the egalitarian nuclear family, the same that could later be observed in parts of Europe from the Late Middle Ages in the Paris Basin, in southern Italy and in Andalusia. The predominance of apartments in Rome points to nuclear families. The equality of inheritance among all children, defined, as we have seen, by the Code of Justinian, seems to be something of a prefiguration of the French *Code Civil*, which itself drew on collections of customs from the sixteenth century (*OSF*, pp. 346–55). When Christianity imposed itself beyond the Jewish communities of the diaspora, it entered a family environment dominated by the idea of equality between brothers, and probably capable of taking further the idea of an equivalence between human beings in general. But here again, an evolution of the family preceded that of religion, since the emergence of a nuclear and egalitarian Roman family preceded the Christian transformation of the Empire.

— 5 —

GERMANY, PROTESTANTISM AND UNIVERSAL LITERACY

Homo sapiens is defined primarily by brain size and intellectual abilities – as an animal species able to observe, understand and accumulate knowledge. Certain decisive steps, as we have seen, preceded the *Homo sapiens* type, such as the use of tools and the invention of fire. But technical progress grew exponentially after the emergence of *Homo sapiens* around 200,000 BCE. The expansion of the species across all continents, its sedentarization in various places, the invention of the agriculture, towards 9000 BCE in the Middle East, permitted a considerable increase in the human population. The emergence of cities followed, with the appearance of writing around 3300 BCE in Mesopotamia and 3000 BCE in Egypt. In China, agriculture was invented around 8000 BCE, writing around 1400 BCE. In Central America, agriculture emerged around 4500 BCE and Mayan glyphs were conceived in the early fourth century BCE.

Writing, initially ideographic, spread from its Mesopotamian home. Towards the west, it became simplified and reached the consonantal stage in Phoenicia around 1200 BCE, then the alphabetic stage in Greece around 800 BCE. In the history of the diffusion of writing, the Latin alphabet, like the later Cyrillic alphabet, was just a variant of the Greek system. To the east also, writing advanced, with the creation, towards the third century BCE, of Brahmin semi-syllabaries, probably based on a Semitic script such as Aramaic; these written representations combine vowels, consonants and syllabic signs. The syllabaries of southern India followed; derivative forms of these made the transcription of Southeast Asian languages possible.

The original Chinese linguistic area extended only to Korea, Japan and Vietnam. To the Chinese ideograms, Japan added syllabaries that came to maturity in the ninth century CE; Korea invented a true alphabet, with consonants and vowels, in the fifteenth century; Vietnam ended up adopting, between the seventeenth and the twentieth centuries, a transcription into Latin characters. In Indonesia, syllabaries of Indian origin were replaced by Arabic writing from the fourteenth century and then by a Latin transcription in the twentieth century. In the Philippines, from the seventeenth century onwards, the Latin alphabet provided a basis for the written form of Tagalog, the most widely spoken language on the main island of Luzon. Mayan writing had reached the syllabic stage in the seventh century AD and was followed by other similar systems in Central America, including the Aztec script.

The great civilizations of Antiquity were based on writing, but literacy seems not to have reached much more than 10 per cent of the population. William Harris, whom we have already cited in the last chapter, was the first scholar bold enough to advance estimates: according to him, literacy rates along the male populations in the most advanced cities in the Hellenistic world, such as Rhodes or Teos, would have not exceeded 20–30 per cent.[1] Not only was ancient literacy very partial; it was prone to fall. This is what happened in the West in the Late Roman Empire; the decline accelerated after its collapse. In Europe, the upward movement in the literacy rate finally resumed in the High Middle Ages (eleventh–thirteenth centuries), though the current state of research has not yet discovered when it reached the level of literacy that had been achieved by the Roman Empire.

Let us be sensible again: let us decide that literacy is the central axis in human history. This idea was commonplace in the eighteenth and nineteenth centuries, shared by Condorcet and Hegel, and indeed by almost all the thinkers of civilization who preceded the current economistic necrosis in the human sciences. We see a dramatic acceleration in the advance of literacy in the sixteenth and seventeenth centuries. This positive break in the trend quickly led to the breaking of the ceiling of 10 or 20 per cent of literates, which had until then represented the upper limit of development for human civilization. The practices of reading and writing finally emerged from the cities and spread to the peasants. Thresholds of 30, 40 and 50 per cent were reached, and exceeded, by men and then by women, until universal literacy was finally achieved for the younger generations in around 1900 in Europe and around 2030 for the entire planet.

The decisive break took place in Germany. It was the consequence not only of well-known factors such as the invention of printing and the Protestant Reformation, but also of a change in the family system.

From Protestantism to literacy

Printing in movable type was perfected at Mainz on the Rhine by Gutenberg in about 1454; the Protestant Reformation was launched by Luther in 1517, when he posted his Ninety-five Theses on the church

101

door in Wittenberg, Saxony. The link between these two events and mass literacy is historically self-evident. Printing led to a drastic reduction in the cost of reproducing texts. Right from the start, the Reformation sought to establish, for each human being, a personal dialogue with God, without the mediation of the priest; like Judaism a millennium and a half earlier, it demanded that the faithful be given direct access to the sacred texts.

As Egil Johansson, the Swedish pioneer of the historical study of literacy, puts it:

> The Bible was printed in its entirety in German in 1466, in Italian in 1471, in French in 1487, in Dutch in 1528, in English in 1535, in Swedish in 1541, and in Danish in 1550. . . . Luther's version of 1543 of the complete Bible from the original languages, Hebrew and Greek, appeared in no less than 253 editions during the lifetime of the translator. To start with, the translations of the Bible were important principally for the church services and sermons. It was not until the 17th century that the ability to read, which had been aimed at by the reformers, gained more ground among the masses. Thus, a clear difference rapidly appeared between Protestant and non-Protestant Europe. Whereas in Catholic and Orthodox Southern and Eastern Europe there were still very few people who could read – less than 20 per cent – there was a drastic increase in Protestant Central and Northern Europe. An intermediate position was held by Northern Italy and parts of France with a certain literate tradition since the Middle Ages, at least in the commercial towns. . . . In Protestant Europe it can be estimated that about 35–45 per cent of the population could read at the turn of the century in 1700.[2]

Luther wanted literacy to be supervised. Parochial schools, run by sacristans, had the job not only of ensuring that pupils could read, but also of imposing the orthodox version of the doctrine. His *Little Catechism* was published in 1529, in the aftermath of the Peasants' War of 1524–6, in which the rural areas in southern Germany had interpreted the message of the Reformation a little too freely for his taste. In Protestant Germany, literacy thresholds of 50 per cent were not exceeded until the seventeenth century, but substantial results had been obtained as early as the sixteenth century. In Württemberg, the number of parish schools had increased from 150 in 1559 to 400 in 1600.[3] In the Germanic space, religious competition led to only a slightly slower spread of literacy in regions that had not adopted the Reformation and remained Catholic.

From the seventeenth to the twentieth centuries, literacy spread in radiating circles from the Protestant world in all directions: into France via the northeast of the Paris Basin, into Russia via the Baltic.

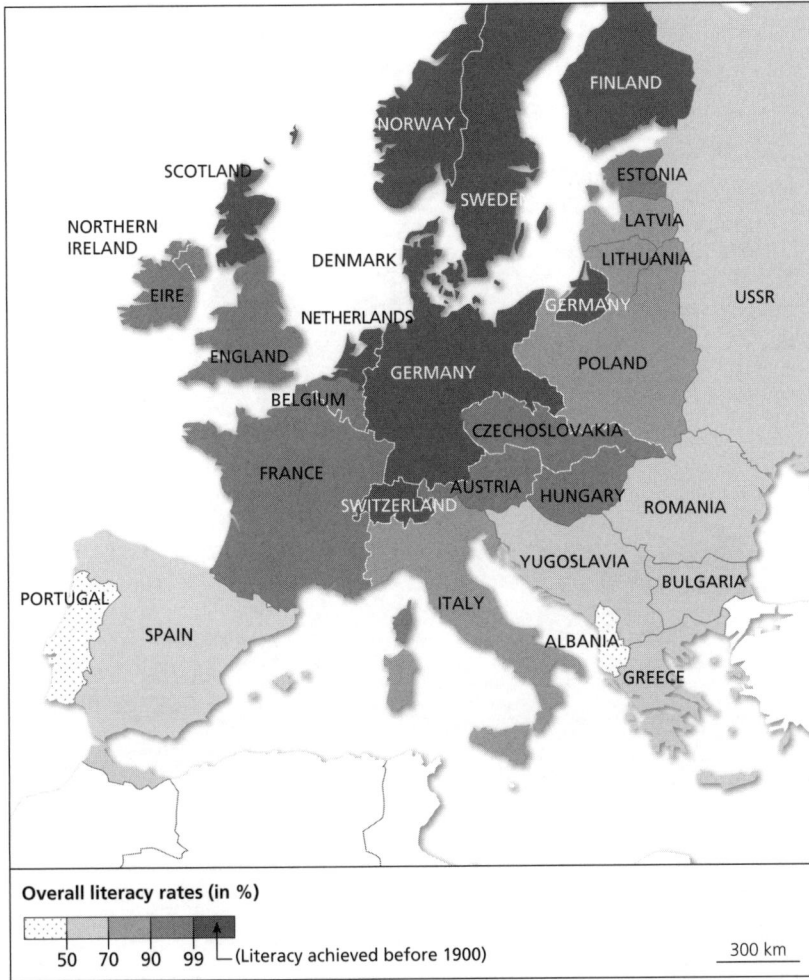

Map 5.1 Literacy in Europe around 1930
Source: Emmanuel Todd, *La Diversité du monde. Structures familiales et diversité* (Paris: Seuil, Points Essais, 2017), p. 354.

By 1930, the map of European literacy rates remained centred on its initial German pole and, more generally, on the Lutheran world, with the addition of Calvinist Scotland. But the mechanism of dissemination did not stop in Europe. The United States, Australia, New Zealand and English-speaking Canada, largely made up of emigrants from Britain between the seventeenth and nineteenth centuries, benefited from high levels of literacy from the time they came into being. Latin America

103

Map 5.2 The stem family in Europe

Source: Emmanuel Todd, *La Diversité du monde. Structures familiales et diversité* (Paris: Seuil, Points Essais, 2017), p. 356.

inherited, in this respect, the time lag and slower rhythms of Spain and Portugal. But colonization was always accompanied by a spread of literacy that advanced outwards from European points of entry or pressure.

Japan had its own endogenous dynamic prior to the age of the·worldwide spread of literacy, which progressed slowly but surely there during the Tokugawa era (1600–1868), only to accelerate sharply with the Meiji revolution, based on the fear of European or American colonization.

Table 5.1   Literacy rates for 15–24-year-olds in 1970 and 2000–2004[4]

Literacy among 15–24-year-olds	1970	2000–2004
World	74.7	87.5
Developed countries	99.0	99.3
Sub-Saharan Africa	41.3	72.0
Arab states	42.7	78.3
East Asia and the Pacific	83.2	97.9
South and West Asia	43.3	73.1
Latin America and the Caribbean	84.2	95.9

In the twentieth century, the whole of Asia and the rest of the world were affected by the global mechanism of the diffusion of literacy. In the first phase, regional rhythms were fixed by channels of communication and penetration of Western influence; in the second phase, and more and more clearly, by the intrinsic potentialities of local anthropological systems: family systems combining a reasonably elevated status for women and strong parental authority finally emerged as secondary poles of educational development in Kerala (southern India), southern China and Korea.[5]

Within this long history, the years 1945–2015 marked the final acceleration, bringing the entire species of *Homo sapiens* to the stage of universal literacy. Between 1950 and 2000–4, the literacy rate of the planet rose from 55.7 to 81.9 per cent for individuals over the age of 15.[6] For young people, the levels reached are even higher, and the rate of progress, between 1970 and 2000, allows us to foresee a situation where the whole world will be literate by around 2030. This end of the childhood of humanity is the real foundation of economic globalization. Never could the unification of the world's labour markets have been attempted without this prior educational unification.

The stem family and writing

The map of European literacy, centred on Germany, and the existence of an autonomous Japanese pole in Asia, point to a link between the take-off of literacy and the presence of the stem family as an underlying anthropological type. In actual fact, the ancient history of civilization already suggested a relationship between the emergence of the stem family and the invention of writing. In Sumer, where we find the first traces of writing around 3300 BCE, we also observe rules of primogeniture from the middle of the third millennium onwards. In China, writing appears in the fourteenth century BCE, and the first rules of primogeniture around 1100. In these two original centres of civilization, the periods that followed the introduction of primogeniture were, in both technological and artistic fields, periods of brilliance. Can we discern a logic in the writing/primogeniture sequence?

For the progress of human societies, one of the first problems needing to be solved is the preservation of acquired knowledge. What is invented must be transmitted before it can be expanded by subsequent generations. Now writing is, in essence, a knowledge-fixing technique that allows human society to escape the uncertainty of the oral transmission of memory. Primogeniture, with the stem family that ultimately springs from it, is also a technique of transmission: it transmits the monarchical state, the fief, peasant farming, the artisan's stall and, at a deeper level, all the techniques that accompany these elements of social structures – bureaucratic, agricultural and metallurgical. So it is not illogical to observe a historical proximity between those two instruments of social continuity, writing and the stem family.

In the case of the first ideographic systems, the link is undoubtedly very close. Mastery of this type of writing requires a laborious apprenticeship, and there may be a necessary relationship between the continuity of the stem family and the acquisition of writing. I do not mean simply a transmission from father to son within families of scribes. Just imagine the thousands of characters in the Chinese script, also used in Japan. How can they possibly be memorized in the absence of strong authority structures that act on the child, in a family system designed as a vehicle of transmission? Now let us turn to the present. Could the survival of the Chinese and Japanese systems of writing have even been possible without the existence of a high level of family and school discipline in these countries?

So there is nothing to prevent us from thinking of a historical association, in Mesopotamia, in China or in Japan, between the emergence of writing and the ordering of families by primogeniture. The case of Egypt, where primogeniture quite quickly affected the higher social categories, does not contradict the hypothesis. I will come back to the case of the Maya in Volume II of my *Origine des systèmes familiaux*.

With Germany, however, the country from which worldwide literacy ultimately started out, we leave the world of complex ideographic systems. Its alphabetical writing, originating in Rome, can be learned in one year at infant school, and there can be no question of considering primogeniture and stem family as indispensable for the transmission of the Latin alphabet. On the other hand, the stem family *can* contribute to an explanation of the speed and power of the development of mass literacy in the Germanic world. It has been said many times: the stem family is essentially a mode of transmission. Where it holds sway, acquired knowledge is rarely lost, but is, on the contrary, effectively transmitted to the next generation.

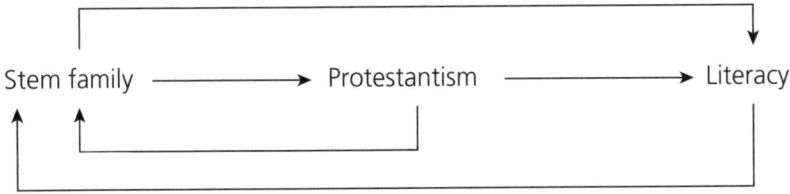

Figure 5.1   Stem family → Protestantism → Literacy

At this stage of the analysis, which concerns a very recent past, we can no longer be satisfied with observing a rough and ready coincidence in time and the simple determination of one variable by another. We will try to disentangle the complex interactions between three major elements, – family, religion and education – admitting from the outset that the mechanisms of causality between variables can function, simultaneously or successively, in both directions. This is suggested by the diagram given in Figure 5.1, which I will explain in more detail in the following paragraphs.

From the stem family to Protestantism, and vice versa

A cartographic approach makes it possible to observe empirically the coincidence, in Europe, of three elements of social structure between 1900 and 1930: the stem family, the Lutheran religion and a high educational level. However, we cannot stop here, at this level of achievement, and conclude, for example, that the stem family fostered the emergence of Protestantism, which itself required that people learn how to read. We must imagine and describe more complex historical interactions.

The primary and original character of the stem family is beyond doubt. Primogeniture appeared at the end of the Carolingian Empire in France, where in one sense it founded the Capetian monarchy. We can observe its spread in the European aristocracy from the eleventh century, then in some peasant communities in Germany and Occitania from the thirteenth century. One of the peculiarities of Germany, already mentioned in Chapter 1, was an egalitarian reaction among the aristocracy due to the fact that family property was not divided and so became identified with peasant servitude. Because they are free, noble brothers must be equal. So the history of European primogeniture was complex, but it began long before the Protestant Reformation. The transformation of the family came first: we can therefore say that it was indeed the stem family that, even before it reached its full development, favoured the adoption of the Protestant religion.

107

The mechanism that leads from family organization to religious system is simple: primogeniture comes with a high level of authority in the father; it defines a son who is chosen and other children who are rejected. In such a domestic context, a theological system that affirms that the Everlasting predestines a minority to salvation and the rest of humankind to damnation can appear quite simply as normal. Various rather belated and absolutely specious theological debates claimed that Calvin alone held to the notion of predestination, attributing a less severe attitude to Luther. Between 1536 and 1560, Calvin certainly did come up with a particularly manic interpretation of predestination, since he insisted on its double character, affecting eternal death as well as eternal life. But predestination had been discussed before him, with clear and brutal frankness, by Luther in his treatise *On the Bondage of the Will*, published in December 1525 in response to *On the Freedom of the Will* that Erasmus published in September 1524.[7] In January 1526, Luther's Latin text was translated into German by Justus Jonas, under the title *Dass der freie Wille nichts sei* [*That Free Will is Nothing*]. A short excerpt will allow us to gauge the strength of the authoritarian and inegalitarian aspiration of this first phase of Protestantism:

> But [if God is] granted foreknowledge and omnipotence, it follows naturally by an irrefutable knowledge that we have not been made by ourselves, nor do we live or perform any action by ourselves, but by his omnipotence. And seeing he knew in advance that we should be the sort of people we are, and now makes, moves, and governs us as such, what imaginable thing is there, I ask you, in us which is free to become in any way different from what he has foreknown or is now bringing about? . . .
>
> What help was free choice to Jacob, and what hindrance was it to Esau, when before either of them was born or had done anything it had already been settled by the foreknowledge and determination of God what should be the lot of each, namely, that the one should serve and the other rule?[8]

The stem family preceded the Lutheran Reformation: its values – the father's authority and the inequality between brothers – provided support for the idea of the omnipotence of God and the inequality of men when it came to their salvation.

It should be noted that when Protestantism spread from stem-family areas, especially towards regions where the absolute nuclear family dominated, its dogma of predestination eventually collapsed. Thus, in the coastal areas of the Netherlands and in England, from the seventeenth century onwards, free will was imposed on a doctrine derived from Calvinism; meanwhile, Lutheran Denmark would have to wait for the nineteenth century to shed its skin and become a more liberal theology.[9]

108

Admittedly, biblical primogeniture, expressed (as we have seen) by the myth of Jacob and Esau as cited by Luther via St Augustine, had indeed preceded Capetian primogeniture. One could argue therefore, for the sake of logical purity, that the elites of the late tenth century had discovered the concept of primogeniture in the religious texts of their time, which would suggest that religion came before the family. But then it would be necessary to explain why the Merovingian kings and the Carolingian emperors had ignored the biblical precepts for centuries, briskly dividing kingdoms and empires between their sons. But enough of these secondary historical speculations.

The way that Lutheran dogma retroacted on the family is a fundamental phenomenon.

When the Reformation began, at the beginning of the sixteenth century, the stem family was far from having reached its full and definitive form in the Germanic area. It can therefore be reasonably concluded that the triumph of a metaphysics obsessed with primogeniture of divine origin, in the northern half of the Germanic area, helped to stabilize and perfect stem-family structures in later centuries.

Luther's *Little Catechism*, the first vehicle for the Protestant educational offensive, displays, right from the start, an unambiguous patriarchal familialism:

> The Ten Commandments or the Decalogue, Such as a father of a family must teach them with simplicity to his children and his servants.

It is easy to see how the father's authority would be reinforced by his new religious role in the family, finding in Biblical mythology new reasons to treat his children in an unequal way.

Here again we find the concept of *co-evolution* as an important element in historical argument. According to this concept, family and religion not only correspond to each other, but reinforce each other with the passage of time.

The study of family structures through history still has some catching up to do in Germany, and if we are to describe the stem family in that part of the world, we will have to make do with a composite image juxtaposing a small number of local monographs. A very recent study, however, verifies that within a Germanic space generally dominated by the stem family, this latter was particularly strong in Protestant zones.

The 1885 census is the first to allow a comprehensive study of the variations in household complexity in a Germany unified by Bismarck. It omits German-speaking Switzerland and Austria. But Mikolaj Szoltysek and his collaborators have established a significant statistical relationship between the complexity of families and Protestantism, a conclusion all the more reliable since, due to the prevalent clichés about Protestant individualism, these authors expected to find the converse relationship, with complexity of families equating to Catholicism.[10] But co-residence between generations was encouraged by Protestantism.

From the stem family to literacy

At the beginning of this chapter, I noted the probable relationship between the emergence of writing and the birth of primogeniture in Mesopotamia and China. In Europe, this link stretches out over history thanks to the direct action of the stem family on literacy, independent of Protestantism. Maps of Europe reveal that Protestantism was less effective in fostering literacy in areas where the family was nuclear, especially in England, than where the stem family predominated, as in Germany and Scotland. Conversely, the Catholic and stem-family areas of the Germanic world, although lagging behind their Protestant counterparts, still achieved high levels of literacy quite rapidly.

We know enough now to return to the comparison of Judaism and Protestantism, religions similar in their demand that believers be given direct access to the sacred texts, but distinct in their family substrata. The Jews, as we saw in the previous chapter, followed an undifferentiated nuclear structure, the German Protestants a stem structure. With the Bible, Judaism fantasizes about primogeniture, but it actually rests, like English Protestantism, on an individualistic family type.

Of course, the existence of the printing press in Luther's day largely explains why the Reformation spread reading more widely: indeed, it won whole countries over thanks to written materials. The Judaism of Joshua ben Gamla could generate only a literate urban diaspora, a people specialized in jobs more intellectually demanding than agriculture, dispersed among Christian or Muslim populations that remained largely rural and illiterate. Maristella Botticini and Zvi Eckstein have explained the disappearance of Judaism from the territory of ancient Israel by the lack of interest shown by ancient Jewish peasants in learning to read and write – literacy was a costly investment of no benefit to agricultural labour. Botticini and Eckstein suggest that there was a significant move of rural Jews to early Christianity because it was less educationally demanding.

Between the sixteenth and eighteenth centuries, half of the peasants in the Germanic world became Protestants; responding to Luther's injunction, they learned to read. The stem family, with its internal authoritarianism and principle of continuity, can help explain the 'total' character of Protestant literacy. But, as I have said, this differential explanation for the exclusively urban success of Judaism and the urban and rural success of German Protestantism can only be complementary. The existence of printing in the sixteenth century was obviously the main factor in the success of the Reformation in fostering literacy.

Literacy and the intensification of the German patrilineal characteristic

In terms of our analysis, do we still have one 'passive' variable, literacy, determined solely by the other two, the stem family and Protestantism? Not even that. In Germany, there was a retroactive effect of the spread of literacy on the family structure itself. By privileging the male sex, literacy for several centuries strengthened the patrilineal characteristic of the anthropological system in Germany.

This was admittedly not a general phenomenon. Because it was the first case of mass literacy, the form it took in Lutheran Germany was very special. Its study is paradoxically less advanced than the educational transformations of England, Sweden or France. However, the few monographs already devoted to German communities reveal a specific feature: a huge lag between women's literacy and men's.

Take the example of the communities of Hesse-Kassel, between the late eighteenth and early nineteenth centuries. Around 1808, the signing of the marriage certificate by either spouse, or its absence, shows an assumed literacy rate of 91.5 per cent for men but only 43.9 per cent for women (i.e., a 47.6 per cent gender gap).[11] In this region, rates were very similar for Lutherans and Calvinists. If we go further back in time, measuring the literacy of the parents of the newlyweds (parents who would have been young adults around 1780), we already find 90.1 per cent of signatures for fathers but only 24.3 per cent for mothers (a 65.8 per cent gender gap). The upward movement of women's literacy allows us to calculate a trend and to gauge, by projection towards the future, the moment when the threshold of 50 per cent literacy among young women would be crossed, in this case around 1815. But we could also, in theory, estimate, by retro-projection to the past, a rate lower than 24.3 per cent in the first years of the eighteenth century. The application of a linear function would of course lead us to much too low a figure, but it would not be absurd to imagine a literacy rate for women of between 10 and 20 per cent. For men, on the other hand, no such possibility is open: 91.5 per cent literacy in 1808 and 90.1 per cent a generation earlier form an almost horizontal line, which merely suggests that the 50 per cent line for literacy among young men was crossed prior to the eighteenth century. In Table 7.1 (see p. 132), which compares dates of literacy, decline in birth rates, and economic take-off, I dated this threshold to around 1670, simultaneously taking into account the increase in the number of schools in the sixteenth century and the case of Sweden, which I mention a little further on.

Somewhat to the east, in Halberstadt, for marriages in the period 1785–95, the lag in women's literacy was nearly as striking: 83.4 per cent

111

signatures for husbands, 36.0 per cent for wives (a gender gap of 47.4 per cent). Likewise for Magdeburg at the same time: 83.6 per cent as against 23.1 per cent (a gap of 60.5 per cent).[12]

I have not found anywhere else, at any point in history, such a large gap between men and women in the changing rates of literacy. In England, in 1775, there was 60 per cent literacy among men and 38 per cent among women (a gap of 22 per cent).[13] In Champagne, in the middle of the eighteenth century, we find 65 per cent literacy among men and 29 per cent among women (a gap of 36 per cent); in the countryside of what is now Seine-et-Marne in the middle of the eighteenth century, literacy was 39 per cent for men and 15 per cent for women (a gap of 24 per cent); for the whole of France around 1786–90, it was 47 per cent for men and 27 per cent for women (a gap of 20 per cent).[14] If we turn to a purely patrilineal and later literate society, such as China, we observe that in the 2000 census, among the over-65s, literacy was 71 per cent for men and 35 per cent for women (a gap of 36 per cent). For Russian Jews born before 1837, we noted in the previous chapter that 54 per cent of men were literate as opposed to 15 per cent of women, a difference of 39 per cent. Only in New England in the seventeenth and eighteenth centuries did the figures approach the gap found in Germany: around 1650–60, the male literacy rate was 62 per cent, the female rate 32 per cent; in 1758–62, the rates were 85 and 45 per cent respectively. The literacy gap between men and women in that highly Protestant society, puritanical at the beginning and rationalist at the end, rose from 30 to 40 per cent in little more than a century.[15] But we are a long way from the 60 per cent gaps sometimes measured in Germany.

The discrepancies mentioned for non-German societies range between 20 and 40 per cent, while German monographs reveal that women's literacy lagged behind men's by between 47 and 65 per cent, spread over centuries.

The examples mentioned do not represent the whole history of the differences in literacy rates between men and women, a history that remains to be written; rather, they provide us with soundings. With the exception of Caribbean, but not African, societies, the take-off of literacy observably begins earlier for men than for women. So at first there is a gap between men and women; then a catch-up occurs, at widely differing rhythms. The extent of the gap depends on the degree of initial patrilineality of the family system. But a wide and lasting gap, like the one typical of German history, can only have strengthened the patrilineal character of domestic organization. For a century and a half, the majority of men in Germany could read, while only a very small proportion of women could do so. Such an imbalance accentuated the decline in the status of women. When we come to discuss the development of higher education between 1960 and 2015, we will see that the specific educational and patrilineal features of the German system have been perpetuated in other ways.

Thus what we find in Germany is a retroactive effect of literacy on family structures.

A comparison with the history of literacy in Sweden, the most intensely studied country of all, also shows that a certain level of initial patrilineality was necessary in Germany for the development of the patriarchal bias due to literacy. This contrast reveals that Lutheranism, left to its dogmatic resources, would not have been able to 'patrilinealize' a family system. The confrontation with the case of Russia, whose patrilineal community family structure was perfect but still a recent innovation in the middle of the nineteenth century, will also enable us to evaluate correctly, by contrast, the power of German anti-feminism.

Swedish and Russian trajectories

Literacy spread in Sweden earlier and more rapidly than almost anywhere; and this case is also the best known. As early as the seventeenth century, the Lutheran Church in Sweden required registers to be kept in which the ability of the faithful to read and understand simple religious texts was evaluated. Reading here must be distinguished from writing, a technique that was acquired by Swedish peasants only later.

The register for the community of the Swedish district of Tuna over the period 1688–91 indicates that, between these dates, among the parishioners over the age of 50, 50 per cent of men and 33 per cent of women could read, and among the under-20s, 44 per cent of men and 41 per cent of women. There is a slight temporary regression among men, but mainly what we see is that the sexes reached a nearly equal level very early on. Egil Johansson notes that in the eighteenth and nineteenth centuries, women's ability to read exceeded that of men. In Sweden, the gap that opened up between men and women in terms of literacy was thus small – less than 20 per cent – and above all it did not last very long: little more than a decade or two. Feminism in Sweden definitely goes back a long way. In this nation, the Church was no less Lutheran than in central Germany, but the Reformation had no patrilineal impact. The stem-family form, stage 1 of patrilineality, has probably never been fully developed in this nation on the edges of Europe.

In Russia, literacy spread far later than in Germany or Sweden, with the decisive years stretching between 1880 and 1930. The 1897 census, carried out during the Tsarist era, and the (less reliable) Soviet 1926 census allow us, by comparing the age groups, to track the opening and closing of the literacy gap between men and women. Literacy reached just 13.5 per cent for subjects born between 1828 and 1837 (24.4 per cent for men, 10.9 per cent for women). It reached 29 per cent for those born between 1878 and 1887 (51.8 per cent for men, 22.7 per cent for women) according to the 1897 census,[16] but 47 per cent according to the 1926 census, which seems to overestimate the male rate (72.1 per cent for men, 25.0 per cent for women).[17] According to the same census of 1926, however, the gap between men and women had already fallen to 19.8 per cent for individuals born between 1907 and 1912 (73.3 per cent for men, 53.5 per cent for women).

In Russia, the literacy gap between men and women was similar to that in France and England, but it was reduced more quickly. This confirms the paradox of a patrilineal but relatively feminist Russia. The development of higher education under Gorbachev and Putin would show a long-term continuity – a mirror-image of the previously mentioned case of the Germany of Gerhard Schröder and Angela Merkel.

— 6 —

THE GREAT EUROPEAN
MENTAL TRANSFORMATION

We would be wrong to see learning to read as merely the acquisition of a technique. We are now beginning to measure the enlargement of brain function induced by an intensive and early use of reading.[1] Intelligent children, of course, find it easier to learn to read. But it is more important for an understanding of human history to grasp that it is mainly reading that makes children more intelligent. Like the assimilation of a foreign language, reading is a skill that is easy to learn before puberty, difficult after it. The brain seems to be modified by literacy at a crucial phase in the development of the human body.

Reading creates a new person. It changes one's relationship to the world. It allows a more complex inner life and achieves a transformation of the personality, for better and for worse. From the nineteenth century, it became apparent to the founders of 'moral statistics' that the suicide rate rose with great regularity in accordance with literacy rates.

In 1950, in *The Lonely Crowd*, David Riesman wrote an eloquent description of the psychological transformation that accompanies the regular practice of reading. According to him, reading contributes to the transformation from a traditional basic personality, formerly regulated by custom, into a new personality guided by an interior gyroscope. 'The inner-directed man, open to "reason" via print, often develops a character structure which drives him to work longer hours and to live on lower budgets of leisure and laxity than would have been deemed possible before.'[2]

David Riesman takes the Protestant reading of the Bible as a central phenomenon. The classic example in Western history is, of course, the translation of the Vulgate into spoken languages, a translation that allowed ordinary people to read what was previously available only to the priest. He then discusses the imbalances brought about by this reading: 'The over-effects I have most in mind, however, are those in individuals whose characterological guilts and tensions were increased by the power of print.'[3]

As commonly happens, it is an observation of history, rather than the 'science' of psychology, that here provides us with the best grasp of what it means to be a human being. The educational take-off of Western Europe was accompanied by an overall measurable mental transformation in many different domains: the repression of sexuality, a fall in private violence, the development of table manners and the emergence of an obsession with witchcraft all mean we can date to the years 1550–1650 the appearance in Western and Central Europe of a new kind of human being.

The 'Western marriage model' and the belated victory of the Christian rejection of sexuality

To understand the interaction between learning to read and mental transformation, let us start from the most rigorous and the easiest to quantify data, namely the long-term evolution of a demographic parameter. Towards 1930, maps of literacy and of a high age at marriage could still be superimposed on each other – see Map 5.1 (p. 103) and Map 6.1). For women, the average age at marriage was over 26 in a group of countries centred on the Lutheran world and/or the stem family, between Scandinavia and Switzerland. But even in the Protestant countries where the nuclear family predominated – England, the Netherlands and Denmark – the age of marriage for women was above 25 years. In the Catholic countries of Europe, it ranged between 25 years for Italy and 23 for France. This was, except for France perhaps, far above the original marriage age of *Homo sapiens*, as can be measured, for example, amid groups of residual hunter-gatherers or among the peasants on the furthest periphery of Eurasia. In the Philippines, the average age of marriage was 22.1 years for women among Tagalog farmers around 1948, and 18.4 years for Agta hunter-gatherers around 1980, as discussed in Chapter 2.[4]

In 1965, John Hajnal identified a European marriage pattern that was unique in its high age at marriage and the importance it accorded to a permanent non-married status. Hajnal's Western Europe is clearly distinguished in these respects from the rest of the world, Eastern Europe included, since around 1930, in Poland, Hungary or Russia, to name but three of these countries, marriage took place much earlier and being unmarried was very rare.[5] According to Hajnal, the European model was characterized by an age at marriage for women of over 23, and more often over 24, as against under 21 elsewhere. The figures he drew from the studies in historical demography available in the early 1960s

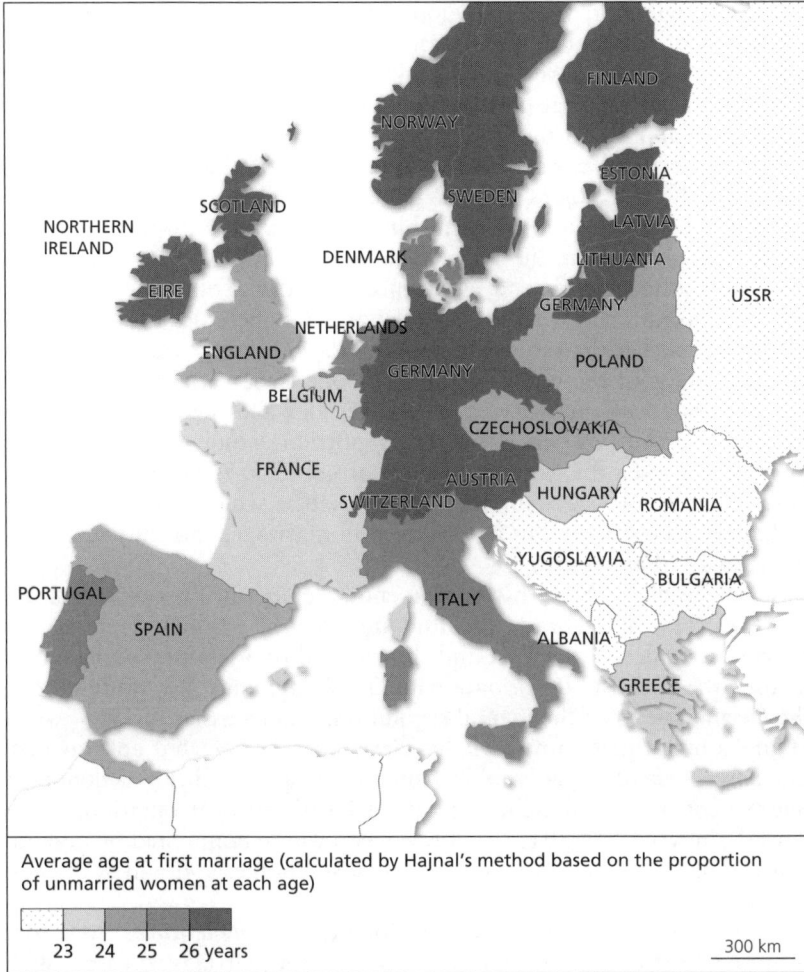

Map 6.1   Age at marriage of women in Europe around 1930
Source: Emmanuel Todd, *La Diversité du monde. Structures familiales et diversité* (Paris: Seuil, Points Essais, 2017), p. 355.

show how far back this model went. In Crulai, a Norman village where the founding study in modern historical demography was conducted by Louis Henry, the average age at marriage between 1674 and 1742 was 25.1 years for women, and 26.6 years for men. In another village in Île-de-France cited by Hajnal, in the same period age at marriage was 26.2 years for women and 27.4 for men. We are, in these two cases, in regions where the egalitarian nuclear family predominated.

117

As for England, that other region of the nuclear family, the monumental history of the English population written by Tony Wrigley and Roger Schofield now means we can go back a little further in time. From 1640 to 1649, the average age of marriage in British rural communities was 26 for women and 28 for men.[6]

Hajnal ascribed a date to the appearance of the European model using family genealogies from Württemberg, Geneva and the English nobility. His conclusion was firm but cautious: the European marriage model did not exist in the High Middle Ages, but must have appeared between the fourteenth and eighteenth centuries. Today we can refine this conclusion. The work of Wrigley and Schofield does not allow us to go back earlier than the years 1640–9 for age at marriage, but it does give us details of the older evolution of one close variable, namely the rate of permanently unmarried people. Wrigley and Schofield observe an increase from 8 to 24 per cent in the proportion of individuals who never married, between the generation born around 1555 and the generation born around 1605.[7] As for the other variables we shall be examining, a change in behaviour can be observed in marriage, and thus sexuality, between 1550 and 1650.

When he highlighted this fundamental element in European history, however, Hajnal made a threefold mistake: he resolutely placed his European model in the West and thus missed two essential explanatory factors, the Lutheran Reformation and the stem family, i.e., quite simply, the German heart of the mental revolution. It is true that in 1965, when Hajnal's hypothesis came to light, Germany was defeated and divided. The perception of its geographical and historical centrality was no longer self-evident. People thought in terms of East/West confrontation. These days (I am writing in 2017), in a European Union dominated by a reunified Germany, a revised version of Hajnal's hypothesis should not be too difficult to accept.

Let us place ourselves in the very long term (*longue durée*), one that is more Christian than Braudelian: late ages for marriage, together with large numbers of unmarried people, seem between 1550 and 1650 to have finally fulfilled, in Europe, the old project of sexual abstinence developed more than a thousand years ago on the shores of the Mediterranean by the Fathers of the Church. Our maps show us that the Lutheran Reformation was the initiator of the movement, and that the Catholic regions tagged along: the Counter-Reformation adopted a similar but slightly less austere model of the repression of sexuality. It should be noted, however, that in the stem-family regions that had remained Catholic – Austria, Bavaria, various Swiss cantons, northeastern Italy and Ireland – the model of the repression of sexuality seems to have reached an intensity worthy of the Protestant model.

The paths of discipline

The higher age at marriage, a central mental variable, did not escape the attention of Robert Muchembled, since he noted how in Artois, between the sixteenth century and 1650, it rose from 20 to 25 years for women and from 24 or 25 to 27 years for men.[8] Muchembled's focal point, however, is the way private violence was brought under control: in the thirteenth century, the rate of homicide could rise to 100 per 100,000 inhabitants, as against fewer than 1 per 100,000 today in most Western European countries.[9]

Here again, we have to note that it was between 1600 and 1650 that a first fall in numbers cut homicide rates by half.[10] Unlike Hajnal, Muchembled did not completely miss his geographical target, since in his view the original area of the transformation was Protestant Northern Europe, a zone in which he included France and the Catholic Netherlands:

> The retreat of lethal violence in Europe started in the Protestant north – Scandinavia, England and the United Provinces – but also in France and the Catholic Low Countries, before spreading to the whole western part of the continent between the seventeenth and the nineteenth centuries. As the trend is initially visible in very different types of state, including countries with little centralization, it cannot be explained in the purely political terms of the rise of absolute monarchy. Nor was it specifically Protestant. The underlying ethic, based on the responsibility and guilt of the individual, to the detriment of the law of shame and of collective honour, was also found in Catholic France and in the Spanish Low Countries, the latter characterized by an even more demanding form of Baroque Catholicism.[11]

But Germany is still absent; as we have seen, this is the effect of a lag in the historical research on this country.

Be this as it may, historical demography and the quantitative history of violence confirm, by broadening it, the initial intuition of Norbert Elias (1897–1990). In 1939, Elias showed in *The Civilizing Process* that there had been an overall change in Western behaviour, ranging from sexuality to table manners.[12]

The evolution of individual forms of behaviour mentioned so far may these days appear to represent progress: this is obvious in the case of learning to read and the reduction in levels of violence, probably somewhat less in the increase in the age of marriage and the rise in the numbers of unmarried people: sexual abstinence is no longer recognized as a positive value. But remember that late marriage and staying unmarried were the first steps in birth control that favoured a certain ability to save money, a necessary condition for the commercial and industrial take-off.

119

I would like to end this evocation of the great European mental transformation by highlighting an element that underlines its dark side and points to the irrational dimension of the Protestant Reformation and its younger sister the Catholic Counter-Reformation. Pierre Chaunu has astutely mocked teleological interpretations of the Western psychological transformation, which is too easily considered as a necessary step in the march towards progress. Chaunu had in mind the 'Max Weber' interpretations, as he put it, of a Protestant rationality 'seeking' the path of economic development, especially through the authorization of interest-bearing loans. Here is what he says:

> If the churches of the Reformation suppressed priests and monks, this was not to build a secular city, but out of the somewhat crazy desire for an overall rise in religious status. In the name of the universal priesthood, everyone was to be raised higher in Geneva, a city that looked, minus celibacy, like a large Benedictine convent where prayer and work alternated.[13]

History reveals the psychological cost of this transformation in *Homo sapiens*. Let us ignore the religious hatreds, the rise of absolutist states large and small; let us ignore the recrudescence of war, which accompanied the acquisition by the state of its monopoly of 'legitimate' violence, since the price to be paid for the internal pacification of behaviour was without a shadow of a doubt a collective reorientation of violence. Let us simply measure its consequences at the level of individuals and their anxieties, of their families and their villages. The years 1550–1650 were also those of the great witch hunt, which saw hundreds of rural communities, led by paranoid magistrates, burn at the stake thousands of old women suspected of making a pact with the Devil and (everywhere except in England) sleeping with his incubuses and succubuses. The best and most concise introduction to this central phenomenon in European mental 'modernization' is probably the one by Hugh Trevor-Roper, even though regional studies by Robert Mandrou (for France), Alan Macfarlane (for Essex) and Robert Muchembled (for Flanders) mean we can refine the picture.[14]

Trevor-Roper lists the outbreaks of this epidemic of witch-hunting on a European scale. All countries were affected, but once again the geographical distribution of the main attacks of the outbreak appears to have centred on Germany and its margins, Flanders, Lorraine, Franche-Comté, Silesia and Sweden. The Scottish and Basque poles lay outside the zone we are considering, but in both these two regions, the dominant anthropological type was the emerging stem family. Trevor-Roper does not note any significant difference between Catholic and Protestant regions. However, we cannot escape from this twofold, complementary and self-evident observation: the affected Catholic areas were usually close to the zones where the Reformation emerged, and were often characterized by the stem family.

The invention of primogeniture was also, as we have seen, the invention of patrilineality, a particularly evident phenomenon in Germany. We can therefore, without much risk of error, associate the anti-feminine frenzy of the witch hunt with the concurrent modification of relations between men and women at that time. Across the whole continent, couples got together later, in an atmosphere that denied pleasure and the flesh. In Germany, the status of women began to fall. At the origins of the great witch hunt we can identify the first emergence of the patrilineal principle.

We have to admit, however, that three countries – Sweden, where the evolution towards the stem family was incomplete, the Basque Country, where the type would be very strong but bilateral (the designated heir was the eldest child, whether boy or girl), and England, whose family type remained nuclear – deviated strongly from this interpretation of the witch hunt as one effect of the rise of the patrilineal principle. History is history, and is never simple or unambiguous. How can we deny the effect of an autonomous spread, a continental fashion for sending old women to the stake?

Destruction of the undifferentiated kinship network

We now have all the elements to be able to understand, better than at the time of Norbert Elias, the transformation of the West. I am aware that historical research on literacy, age at marriage, violence and witchcraft carried out in the period 1960–90 has given us information mainly on France and Great Britain, and not enough on Germany.

This lack of information has not, however, stopped us giving Germany its rightful place – before England, before France – in the take-off of the West. It was certainly not the starting point of the seventeenth-century scientific and political revolution that was centred on England, but it did establish the educational basis for this: namely mass literacy. Family and religious dynamics combined in Germany to raise the educational level of the entire population, including peasants. The mediaeval dynamic should have made Italy the place where things took off, but the Catholic Counter-Reformation, by tracking down the readers of religious texts, seen a priori as heretics, managed the feat of consigning the country of the Renaissance, of Leonardo da Vinci and Galileo, to a state of educational stagnation. Religious evolution, however, was probably not the only factor responsible: the flourishing of a particularly powerful communitarian and patrilineal family system in central Italy probably contributed to the success of the Counter-Reformation and the cultural paralysis of Italy (*OSF*, pp. 324–7).

121

Such a representation of history recognizes the specificity of Germany while rejecting the image of an ancient Germanic culture. The emerging patrilineal stem family separated Germany from northern France and England, stage by stage – particularly from the fourteenth century onwards. But if we go back to before the eleventh century, the 'German specificity' disappears. As was said above, we then find a nuclear-family structure and an undifferentiated kinship system – in short, a *Homo sapiens* barely modified by Christianization. In those remote times, the Church was still struggling to transform a tempered exogamy into an absolute exogamy.

A study of the great mental transformation of the years 1550–1650 will allow us to understand how lengthy – and, until the final acceleration of the Reformation, partial – the effect of the Christian religion was. The sexual abstinence dreamed of by St Augustine and the Eastern Fathers of the Church had to wait until the sixteenth century before starting to become a common social practice. Protestantism was therefore, as it claimed to be, a return to the original Christian message. It certainly achieved a mass literacy which would eventually lead, through many vicissitudes, to its own destruction. But on this point, it also followed and surpassed its mother religion, one even older than original Christianity: Judaism – and it did so by 'producing' peasants who knew how to read and write. The Reformation was, in this narrow educational sense, particularly faithful to the message of the Jews. On the whole, however, the great mental transformation pushed Christians further away from Jews, by fully realizing the Church's sexual agenda and destroying the kinship network that framed the undifferentiated nuclear family.

In spite of the biblical dream of primogeniture, the Jews, whether European or Oriental, remained close, as we have seen, to the undifferentiated nuclear-family type. Judaism had certainly introduced several innovations, in its respect for the lives of children and the elderly and in its rejection of all sexuality unnecessary to the reproduction of the species, especially homosexuality. But it never decreed sexuality to be bad in itself and never made celibacy an ideal. It remained exogamous but in a tempered manner; it was unafraid of the occasional marriage between cousins when this appeared necessary. In a Christian environment that had become hostile to kinship, it protected the solidarity of the group of brothers and sisters inherited from the hunter-gatherers, and, of course, the proximity of their children and grandchildren, first cousins or the offspring of first cousins.

An inner vertigo: the real question about Protestantism

The earliest Christianity, that of the Roman Empire, launched a first attack against sexuality and against kinship. But was the reorganization of the sexual and family life planned and set out by St Augustine in *The City of God* really applied after the great Germanic invasions? In part, yes. The struggle against marriage between cousins cannot but have failed to temper the kinship network that framed the nuclear family. The fact that the ban had to be reasserted until the early thirteenth century, however, casts doubt on its effectiveness. On another front, priestly celibacy was bound to weaken the natural dynamics of the kinship system. In this connection, the metaphysical project seems to have made real inroads into social life. In the Middle Ages, Europe had a large number of monasteries and convents, inhabited by unmarried persons, religious virtuosos as Max Weber eloquently called them – virtuosos, in this case, of sexual abstinence. The monasteries, however, were only experimental islands, refuges in a world in the grip of sin. The vast majority of society in the Middle Ages remained close to the original type of *Homo sapiens*: structured by bilateral ties that were flexible but ubiquitous. It remained bawdy and violent.

If we just stick to these visible elements, we might think that the Protestant Reformation had retreated on all fronts. It allowed priests to marry again and emptied the monasteries. Because it relied on the Bible, it permitted consanguineous unions anew. But in reality, as Pierre Chaunu so clearly recognized, Protestantism mainly wanted to clericalize the laity. The rise in age at marriage and the increase in the rate of celibacy were particularly striking across the lands of the Protestant religious crisis. Marriage rates between cousins are still lower in those areas today than in Catholic countries. In the aftermath of the Reformation, demographic change proves that abstinence was no longer reserved for virtuosos, but was allowed to all. To use the most up-to-the-minute terminology, we should probably talk in terms of 'Abstinence for All'.

By its central concept of predestination, which strictly separates the saved from the damned, by its description of the terrestrial world as corrupt, Protestantism was a renewed Augustinism. It brought to fruition the project of mental transformation presented in *The City of God*.

The Protestant transformation profoundly destroyed the undifferentiated kinship network, as demonstrated by contemporary life in countries as different as Germany, England, Sweden and the United States. It was an essential step in the emergence in Europe of pure nuclear-family types, and linear stem types, decluttered from the lateral association of relatives. However, I must admit that I have failed to analyse in a really satisfactory way the psychological mechanism that led to this destruction of the kinship network.

The first thing that comes to mind is the Protestant notion of interiority, this Reformation dream of finding in the depths of oneself a contact with God, a being who presumably does not exist and who, if he does exist, is remarkable by his silence. In the depths of their souls, Protestants of the sixteenth and seventeenth centuries found nothing but themselves, and an uncertainty as to the meaning of things. So what happens in the mind of someone who thinks that human beings are entirely distinct from animals, who is not acquainted with the notion of the unconscious, who does not understand the mechanism of the dream? We have absolutely no idea.

History tells us, however, that an utterly astonishing personality emerged from this dive into the inner depths: a personality combining anxiety, guilt, exigency and arrogance; a personality capable of inducing, in concrete social life, a paradoxical *active fatalism* capable of transforming the world by drawing on the idea of the insignificance of human beings. To sense the paradox to its fullest extent, the reader should first read the extract from Luther's *Bondage of the Will* quoted in Chapter 5: if God knows in advance what we are to do, how can we imagine that we are free?[15]

The reader should then turn to consider the vigorous economic take-offs in Germany or Sweden, though these admittedly came a little later than in England where Protestantism had rediscovered the notion of free will and softened its stance.

As far as its effect on the human psyche is concerned, Protestantism remains a mystery. But the fact that we do not fully understand a phenomenon or mechanism should not lead us to deny its existence. David Riesman, describing the transformation of the human personality through reading, only mentioned Protestantism and the reading of the Bible somewhat fleetingly. What we need to recognize, and accept as a fact, is the existence of a Protestant basic personality: turned in on itself, predisposed by its morality (sexual or otherwise) to feelings of guilt, to leading an honest and upright life, an essentially active life turned towards study and work.

Is this dive into the inner depths enough to explain how the group of brothers, sisters and cousins tended to evaporate in the Protestant mental world? Probably. But it would be imprudent to stick to a simplistic 'individualizing' interpretation. The concrete life of Protestant communities, from the seventeenth to the nineteenth century at least, also displays an incredible strengthening of the local group and its ability to control the lives of individuals. The Reformation resulted in a reinforced surveillance of manners, a phenomenon evident in the puritanical communities of New England and studied in detail in several seventeenth-century English villages, but one which certainly had its counterparts in the Lutheran parishes of Germany that have not been studied so much.[16] The registers previously used to date Swedish literacy also suggest an early, intensive supervision of individuals. I have been fortunate enough to work on some impressive early nineteenth-century Swedish records in which the pastor noted the people who left his parish or came to settle in it. This was at the beginning of the 1970s, at the time of the omnipotence of the Social Democratic Party, and I said to myself: French socialists are going to have a really hard time imitating a model of collective integration that comes from so far away.

The Protestant military state and the first nationalisms

The inner vertigo of Protestantism led, as we have seen, to new forms of community integration which replaced a destroyed kinship network. The early Protestant world did not consist of a simple juxtaposition of internal lives: from the seventeenth century, Protestant Europe suddenly revealed a formidable capacity for collective action, with the rise of the Prussian, Swedish and Hessian military states, and Dutch and English nationalisms.

On the continent of Europe, in the Protestant countries where the stem family was prevalent, younger sons were the instruments of a veritable militarization of society. Let us compare the levels of military recruitment in Sweden, Prussia and Hesse to that in the France of Louis XIV, a very warlike country but one that was again homogeneously Catholic after the Revocation of the Edict of Nantes in 1685. The personnel of the armies of the Sun King in around 1710 represented the high point of the militarization of the Ancien Régime: 1.5 per cent of the population. In Prussia, a country whose 'militarism' has become a historical commonplace, the rate reached 3.7 per cent in 1740 and 7.1 per cent in 1760, two to five times more than in France. Less well known is the fact that Sweden did better, and managed things earlier, with 4 per cent by the end of the seventeenth century and 7.7 per cent by 1709.[17] Sweden, 'the hammer of Europe', was – despite its tiny population – a great military power in the seventeenth century, not only on the shores of the Baltic but also, during the Thirty Years War, throughout the Holy Roman Empire of the German Nation. In the eighteenth century, Prussia became a major European state, a status definitively established by the Seven Years War. In the case of these two Protestant countries of the North, we are dealing with a militarization whose goal was national greatness.

In some small Protestant states, however, there was also a mercenary militarization with the more modest aim of filling the coffers. One of the best studied cases to date is that of Hesse, whose soldiers made up the bulk of the British force during the American revolutionary war. The rate of militarization of this tiny little state had reached 7.7 per cent by 1782.[18] Peter Taylor has wonderfully analysed the interaction between its family system (the stem family), and the automatic enlistment of sons who did not inherit.[19]

In England, a country where the nuclear family was universal and a liberal temperament prevailed, the military did not absorb the need for a collective born from the new Protestant interiority. The rate of militarization in Britain remained small. From 0.2 per cent in 1698, ten years after the Glorious Revolution of 1688, it reached 1 per cent in 1710, falling to 0.3 per cent in 1783. The parliamentary monarchy, which had not forgotten the seizure of power by Cromwell's New Model Army during the first revolution, carefully avoided its own militarization, at least on land. The power of the navy did not present an internal political risk. Protestantism, however, also produced a collective integration of a new kind across the Channel: the modern sense of nationhood, whose archaic religious expression is (in this case) only apparent. Every Calvinist people, formed of Bible readers, sooner or later sees itself as a new Israel, a people chosen by God. This feeling had spread through Cromwell's England during the first revolution (1642–51); our current liberals have a hard time accepting the historical significance of this upheaval, clinging as they do to the idea that modernity began, for England and the world, in 1688. They are not wrong if it is a question of setting the completed model of the liberal political and economic matrix as point zero. But even so, during the first revolution, Parliament decapitated a king, abolished what was left of communal village rights and engaged the nation in an aggressive economic protectionism, reserving its trade for its own ships.

The religious formulation of the Puritan revolution should not conceal the novelty of English national sentiment. The French are grossly mistaken when they think they invented, in 1789, the modern concept of the Nation. As Liah Greenfeld clearly saw, a flawless nationalism accompanied the economic take-off of Protestant England; indeed, she regards this liberal nationalism as the true spirit of capitalism.[20] Anyone who knows anything about English history in the seventeenth and eighteenth centuries will find it difficult to contradict her.

One could undoubtedly analyse Dutch national sentiment in the years 1570–1700 in the same terms.

The effect of the Catholic Counter-Reformation on the undifferentiated kinship network, and consequently on possible collective feelings of substitution, remains, at the present stage of research, mysterious. Of the transformation of morals by a late and darker Catholicism, domineering in its attitude towards individuals, there can be no doubt, especially, as we have seen, in the stem-family areas adjoining the Protestant world: the age of marriage rose almost as much as in Luther's world. But Catholicism also redefined itself against Protestant interiority: it demanded ever more confession and absolution. It may therefore be doubted whether the Church of Rome and its priests were as successful as the Reformation in weakening kinship ties. The very Catholic country of Ireland, until the mid-nineteenth century, and its Polish counterpart until the mid-twentieth century, remained characterized by an archaic anthropological

126

system combining nuclear family and supervision by an undifferentiated kinship system.

The fact remains that the egalitarian nuclear family of the Paris Basin, in a country that remained Catholic, was, from the eighteenth century, a pure type, freed from kinship. The Protestant path to the completely nuclear family was therefore not the only such one. In the case of northern France, Catholicism never really ceased to exist, from the seventeenth century onwards, in contact with and in the shadow of the Protestantism of Northern Europe – the most Protestant of Catholicisms, in short. It was even able to produce, in the form of Jansenism, its own Augustinian crisis, before disintegrating around 1730–50, as will be seen in Chapter 8.

Towards the economic take-off

The stem family, Protestantism, literacy, the disintegration of kinship: combined together, these four dimensions of modernity are rather unusual. Europe's take-off here assumes the shape of an anthropological transformation rather than an industrial one. Of course, we are no longer dealing only with *Homo oeconomicus*. Such an approach, as I have said, does not mean that the economy does not exist, or even that it is of less weight. Human beings have to sustain themselves and history of the *longue durée* also reveals a rising trend in their technical mastery of the world. But the empirical examination of the facts reveals that an anthropological transformation preceded the economic take-off, since the industrial revolution did not begin in England until 1770 or 1780, depending on the chosen indicator. In the following chapter, I will broaden the perspective and present economic development worldwide as a consequence of the rise in educational levels. The demographic transition – essentially control of the birth rate – will appear not in the least to be determined by the economy but to be a consequence of literacy and another religious crisis: the loss of faith.

Locating the distant origins of the economic take-off in the family and religion, two factors that evolve together, does not mean, however, that we are envisaging human beings as the playthings of their irrational passions, as opposed to the postulated rationality of *Homo oeconomicus*: family structures and religious systems have their internal logic.

We cannot even say that our interpretation takes us away from the notion of the individual. True, literacy does not create the individual as a figure which, contemporary historical sociology insists, came into being at a certain date. But literacy transforms the figure of the individual, engages it in a process of internalization and makes it more intelligent. Talking about family and religion requires us to think simultaneously about the individual needs *and* the collective needs of *Homo sapiens*.

This complementary perspective enables us to identify balancing mechanisms whose rigour is equal to that of the markets of economic theory, and whose empirical realism is vastly superior. Thus, the implosion of the undifferentiated kinship network leads to an intensification of religious or national integration. As for the Protestant surplus of interiority, it is compensated for by the fact that the local community and the state now have a greater hold over the individual.

A historical problem to be solved: the 'stem-family rate' (or family structure as a continuous variable)

If we want to describe history correctly, we can no longer be content with a static conception of family types. Observing the stem family in Europe, we saw it appear in the French and Norman dynasties of the eleventh century and start to affect the aristocracy of the Carolingian areas; it then spread vertically downwards through society, and horizontally by geographical distribution from various centres such as Toulouse in the case of Occitania, and centres as yet undefined in Germany. Studies carried out by Akira Hayami and his school show that a similar history of the stem family could be written for Japan;[21] there, vertical diffusion did not start from the theoretical summit of society, since primogeniture was not adopted by the imperial family until the end of the process of diffusion, during the Meiji Revolution. This was the apotheosis of the advance of the stem concept that had begun at the end of the thirteenth and beginning of the fourteenth century among the nobles of Kanto, the Tokyo area.

At first glance, the notion of *family type* suggests a discontinuous variable; it leads to a simple qualitative segmentation, defining territories and making cartography possible. It becomes possible to represent, on a map of Europe or Asia, the areas occupied by the stem family, the communitarian family and various types of nuclear family. Such a representation is adequate if we place ourselves, in chronological terms, at the end of the process of differentiation and diffusion: this was the nineteenth century in the cases of southern France, Germany and Japan. Occitania was undoubtedly a stem-family area, just like Germany and Japan. In these parts of the world, the concept reached the stage of a collective norm that was defined in the minds of all concerned: primogeniture and the co-residence of the eldest son were applied whenever possible in the middle strata of the peasantry, whether this peasantry owned land or was provided with stable feudal tenures. Once this cartography has been carried out anthropologically, we can move to the ideological level, and note that the political democratization of the twentieth century revealed the way that 'stem' peasants and their societies adhered to the values of authority and inequality. Ethnocentrism and attachment to the state flourished there as if they were quite natural.

However, would it be reasonable to produce a typology and a cartography of this kind for the fifteenth, sixteenth, seventeenth or eighteenth centuries? We know that these were periods when the concept of the stem family was advancing in social and geographical extent, and also in the intensity of the norm where it was applied. But we must admit that the *family type*, a qualitative concept, discontinuous in the mathematical sense, is not enough to describe this more distant historical reality. If the data allowed, we should treat the stem family like any continuous quantitative variable – i.e., just like literacy, birth rate, the proportion of Protestants, religious practice, voting for Christian democracy, social democracy or the National Socialist Party. In other words, we should allocate to each country or each region of which it is composed, for each date, a *'stem-family rate'*. Let us picture, without being able to justify it rigorously, Occitania or Germany having a 40 per cent stem-family rate around 1500, 60 per cent around 1800, and 80 per cent around 1870, a time of stabilization and the establishment of universal (male) suffrage. This rate would take into account the social and geographical extension of the family model, as well as the intensity of the norms of primogeniture and co-residence. Showing its correlation with other variables – educational, religious or ideological – would become much more precise. We would escape the dilemma of a stem family that we need to characterize – a topic discussed in Chapter 7 – as mainly a producer of dynamism *or* of social rigidity. We could say that it tends towards dynamism when it is 40 per cent or 50 per cent, and towards rigidity when it reaches or exceeds 75 per cent. The dynamism of sixteenth-century Germany and the rigidity of early nineteenth-century Germany would then become largely explicable.

If we look at the global level, and especially the heart of Eurasia, the evolution of family types often goes beyond the stem type. Where the communitarian family ends up replacing the stem family in China, Vietnam or northern India, we could similarly conceive of a rate of residual stem values, even if we are unable to calculate it in practice. We can, however, surmise that the trace of birthright, and thus the residual stem family-rate, would be higher in Vietnam or southern China than in northern China or northern India.

Our inability in practice to rigorously define a stem-family rate – or of communitarian family, or of pure nuclearity – must not lead us to commit a logical error: that of locking ourselves into a rigid typology, and concluding that arguments that do not rely on dichotomies do not make sense. Conversely, we must be aware, when we read historical reflections, that many statistical (e.g., economic) series are used because they exist, and not because they are essential to the understanding of history. Intrinsically more important variables are neglected because they are difficult or impossible to calculate.

— 7 —

EDUCATIONAL TAKE-OFF AND ECONOMIC DEVELOPMENT

With the triumph of the concept of globalization, we experienced, between 1980 and 2010, the rise to power of an economist vision of history. The statistics of the World Bank and the OECD are, of course, increasingly focused on the literacy rate and the proportion of individuals who reach the stage of primary, secondary or higher education (with the latter being labelled 'tertiary' in the most recent nomenclature). But in the models that dominate the thinking of the actors of globalization, it is the economy that determines. The quest for better remuneration on the part of families and individuals must explain the development of an education taken to ever higher levels. A good educational level in the population is becoming a decisive weapon in the economic competition between countries.

Yet what a study of the European take-off shows is that the rise in educational attainment came much earlier than the industrial revolution and the blossoming of capitalism. Above all, the primary motivation for learning to read was not economic: in Northern and Northwestern Europe, people learned to read in order to communicate with God.

The simplest way to demonstrate the fact that the educational take-off came first is to compare it with the dates of the economic take-off as defined by William W. Rostow in 1960, in *The Stages of Economic Growth*,[1] and then refined in the 1990 edition of the same book. Table 7.1 shows, for each of the countries in its sample – which includes 80 per cent of the world's population – the date of the economic take-off proposed by Rostow, highly dependent on the industrial investment rate, and the date of the educational take-off, defined here by the crossing of a literacy threshold of 50 per cent for men and women aged 20–24. In my own mind, I should say, education and industrialization are staggered in time; they are not in opposition to one another and have both contributed to our entry into modernity. To compose a more complete picture of the take-off of human societies, I have added a column showing *the date*

131

Table 7.1   Literacy, fall in birth rate and economic take-off

	A Literacy of men	B Literacy of women	C Fall in birth rate	D Take-off	D–A	B–A	C–B
Protestant Germany	1670	1820	1895			150	75
Sweden	1670	1690	1880	1870	200	20	190
Great Britain	1700	1835	1890	1780	80	135	55
United States	(1700)	(1835)	1870	1840	140	135	35
English-speaking Canada	(1700)	(1835)	1870	1895	195	135	25
Australia			1870	1900			
Germany (overall)	1725	1830	1895	1840	115	105	70
France	1830	1860	1780	1830	0	30	−80
Italy	1862	1882	1905	1900	38	20	23
Quebec	1863	1863	1905				
Japan	1870	1900	1920	1885	15	30	20
Argentina	1890	1905	1910	1930	40	15	5
South Korea	1895	1940	1960	1960	65	45	20
Russia	1900	1920	1928	1890	−10	20	8
Mexico	1910	1930	1975	1950	40	20	45
Thailand	1914	1943	1965	1960	46	29	22
Brazil	1915	1945	1965	1930	15	30	20
Turkey	1932	1969	1950	1930	−2	37	−19
Taiwan	1940	1950	1958	1955	15	10	8
China	1942	1963	1970	1955	13	21	7
Iran	1964	1981	1985	1960	−4	17	4
India	1975	2005	1970	1955	−20	30	−35

when women's fertility rates began to decline, a fundamental moment in the demographic transition.[2] Birth control too is an essential part of our modernity.

The notion of a threshold of economic, educational or demographic development, which leads to the definition of critical dates in each of these three domains, helps us to escape from the temporal flattening induced by a calculation of correlation between variables for a single date, which does not allow us to immediately grasp the causality being highlighted. For Germany I give overall dates that correspond to Rostow's initial sequence, but I have added a specific line for Protestant Germany. I have also devoted a line in the table to the dates of Quebec's cultural take-off, which was very late when compared with English-speaking Canada, because they illustrate in a particularly spectacular way the strength of religious determinism, and, in the case of Counter-Reformation Catholicism, its power to hold back progress.

132

For the countries that achieved literacy earliest, I use historical studies. Being uncertain of the figures, I have assigned to the United States and English-speaking Canada the literacy rates of England, the common matrix of English-speaking societies. This decision, however, takes into account Kenneth Lockridge's work on colonial America. The most uncertain figures relate to Germany, since the measures for the three groups of communities contained in Hans Bödeker's study only show that the literacy rate often already reached nearly 90 per cent for men in Protestant communes around 1780, and no more. The figures I propose factor in the lag in Catholic areas, and are based on a Germany that includes two-thirds Protestants and one-third Catholics. Taking into account the German-speaking Roman Catholics of the Austrian Empire would have obviously delayed the achievement of a 50 per cent literacy rate. Taking only Protestants into account would have placed Germany near Sweden or England, perhaps displaying a greater precocity than those countries: after all, Germany was the starting point of the Reformation. But the figures contained in Hans Bödeker's study reveal the existence of a few backward Protestant groups in Westphalia. Germany was at that time much larger and more varied than Sweden or England.

In the case of Japan, I start with the literacy of conscripts in 1899, given by Richard Rubinger for all regions, then I retrogress assuming a rapid catch-up in literacy over the previous years, similar to that of southern France in the nineteenth century. In the case of Sweden, France and England, pioneer countries in the historical study of literacy, I am content to follow the authors cited. I have assigned to the United States the same dates as to England: the literacy level in New England around 1700 must have been higher than the English average, and the same was perhaps true of New York and Pennsylvania; but rates in the future states located further south, slave-owning and Episcopalian (i.e., Anglican), must have been lower – enough to bring the whole figure down to the English average.

Sources:
Hans Bödeker et al., *Alphabetisierung und Literalisierung in Deutschland in der Frühen Neuzeit* (Tübingen: Max Niemeyer Verlag, 1999).
David Cressy, *Literacy and the Social Order. Reading and Writing in Tudor and Stuart England* (Cambridge: Cambridge University Press, 1980).
François Furet and Jacques Ozouf (eds), *Lire et Écrire. L'alphabétisation des Français de Calvin à Jules Ferry*, 2 vols (Paris: Éditions de Minuit, 1977).
Harvey Graff et al., *Understanding Literacy in its Historical Contexts. Socio-cultural History and the Legacy of Egil Johansson* (Lund: Nordic Academic Press, 2003).
Egil Johansson, 'The History of Literacy in Sweden in Comparison with Some Other Countries', *Educational Reports*, no. 12, 1977.

Kenneth Lockridge, 'Literacy in Early America 1600–1800', in Harvey J. Graff et al., *Literacy and Social Development in the West* (Cambridge: Cambridge University Press, 1981), pp. 183–200, and *Literacy in Colonial New England* (New York: Norton, 1974).

Richard Rubinger, *Popular Literacy in Early Modern Japan* (Honolulu: University of Hawai'i Press, 2007).

For countries where literacy has recently been achieved, I am using the data presented in Youssef Courbage and Emmanuel Todd, *A Convergence of Civilizations*, trans. George Holoch (New York: Columbia University Press, 2011), table 1.1, pp. 5–6. For the fall in birth rate in countries where literacy was achieved earlier, see Jean-Claude Chesnais, *La Transition démographique* (Paris: INED/PUF, 1986). For the fall in the birth rate in America, where the date is controversial, I follow J. David Hacker, whose most recent study summarizes the controversies: 'Rethinking the "Early" Decline of Marital Fertility in the United States', *Demography*, vol. 40, no. 4, November 2003, pp. 605–20.

For the dates of economic take-off, I use the data in the new preface to William W. Rostow, *The Stages of Economic Growth* (Cambridge: Cambridge University Press, 1960; new edn 1990).

A correlation is maximum if its absolute value reaches 1, minimum when it is zero. Table 7.1 indicates that the correlation coefficient between the date of crossing the literacy threshold of 50 per cent for men and the date of crossing the same threshold for women is +0.94. We can also see that men's literacy precedes that of women by an average of forty-three years. An analysis of correlation does not here flatten out the time scheme and allows us to define a historical sequence.

The correlation between the *date of crossing the literacy threshold of 50 per cent for women* and *the beginning of the decline in birth rate* is +0.67. The relationship is substantial but less strong. Because women's literacy precedes the decline in birth rate by thirty years on average, and that of men by seventy-three years, we can say that literacy is one of the major causes of a decline in birth rates.

Let us now turn to the interaction between education and the economy.

The correlation between *the date of crossing the threshold of 50 per cent of literate men* and *the date of the industrial take-off* defined by Rostow is +0.86. Our data allow us to add that literacy clearly precedes industrialization: the average time between crossing the literacy threshold and industrial take-off is forty-four years. Literacy is indeed a major factor in economic take-off; in fact, it is clearly the *most* important given the high level of correlation.

It would be absurd, however, to replace Marxo-liberal economic reductionism with a new educational reductionism. A study of the sixteenth and seventeenth centuries in England not only reveals, on the eve of the industrial revolution, a population learning to read and write; we also observe an agricultural, commercial, urban, financial, literary, scientific, maritime and, finally, political development, with two revolutions and the emergence of a tempered monarchy. A representative political system (tax-based) and an absolute property right became, even before the industrial take-off, the fundamental elements of the British social system, as writers such as Daron Acemoglu and James A. Robinson have emphasized.[3]

But we need to be clear about the fact that being able to read and write defines, to varying degrees, the effectiveness of all the elements of development I have just mentioned. Literacy runs through the entire intellectual, social, political and economic movement. The scientific revolution of the seventeenth century, of which England, with Newton, was the heart, cannot be conceived outside a broadly literate social and cultural ambiance, including craftsmen capable of manufacturing the instruments of observation and measurement needed by scientists. That is why literacy is such a good 'predictor' of economic dynamism: without it we cannot understand the past or the present, and without it we cannot predict the future.

The measurement of the educational progress of a society is a formidable instrument for looking ahead, in 1980 and today just as much as in 1700. The globalized world marvelled, between 1990 and 2000, at the economic growth of the 'emerging' countries. But anyone who, in 1980, took a look at literacy rates in the period 1950–80 could have predicted the emergence of China, Thailand, Indonesia, Brazil, India and, indeed, of the countries that until very recently were known as the Third World.[4] Educational globalization has, in a way, preceded economic globalization and made it possible. It was and remains much more fundamental than the spread of free trade or the free movement of capital established by political decisions taken between 1945 and 1980. Thus, the Asian, South American and now African masses could only be put to work by Western capital once they were literate. Previously, they were not exploitable in the same way. We will see later how, at present, although the educational movement of the most advanced societies does not determine the future, it does enable us to 'fit' it into a limited set of plausible futures. We will also see that no institutional dynamic can manage without educational progress and a morality of religious origin, something which the purely institutional interpretations of economic history put forward by writers such as Daron Acemoglu and James A. Robinson fail to grasp.

Why England rather than Germany?

Great Britain reached the 50 per cent male literacy threshold around 1700, and it took off economically, according to Rostow's criteria, around 1780. The rest of the Protestant world – American, German and Scandinavian – radicalized this model of a mass literacy that largely preceded the industrial revolution: the time that elapsed between crossing the educational and the industrial thresholds was 80 years in Great Britain, 115 in Germany, 140 in the United States and 200 in Sweden.

Not all the countries made literate by the Reformation took off spontaneously and automatically in the same way as England. In the case of central and northern Germany, which became literate earlier and more thoroughly, it could even be argued that the upheaval of the industrial revolution was resisted for a while. In 1846, Marx waxed ironic about the country's backwardness in *The German Ideology*. Then, like Sweden, Germany witnessed an accelerated take-off which led to it overtaking Britain in the early twentieth century. Thus, neither Protestantism nor universal literacy led directly to modern economic development.

To explain the first industrial revolution, whose decisive phase occurred in England between 1780 and 1840, other explanatory factors need to be brought in. There was, of course, the abundance of coal and iron, coupled with an excellent transport network across the island of Great Britain. But Germany is not devoid of natural resources, as was subsequently realized. Above all, England, in 1780 as today, enjoyed an extremely flexible social structure, derived from an absolute nuclear anthropological background. The English family demands separation of the generations, departure of the young; it encourages geographic and social mobility. English peasants were not tied to the land. Inheritance rules did not define equality between brothers. A culture that does not a priori attach importance to the equality of conditions in families, between classes or even within the lower classes, favours all forms of social mobility, ascending or descending. It is the ideal anthropological ground for a rapid transformation of the economic and social structure. In any case, it allowed England to witness, between 1780 and 1840, one of the most extraordinary uprootings of population ever seen in history. By 1851, its urban population was catching up with its rural population. France would not reach this stage until 1931, and only if we generously count as a city any agglomeration of more than two thousand inhabitants.

By 1891, England was 72 per cent urbanized. Covered by recent, sometimes brilliant, often filthy cities, it represented for continental Europe a real sci-fi world; indeed, the genre of science fiction was born in this futuristic society: H. G. Wells published his *Time Machine* in 1895. He described the transformation of social classes into different animal

136

species: the Eloi, heirs of the rentiers, were still human in physical terms, but they were apathetic, fed and consumed like cattle by the Morlocks, descendants of the proletarians, now living underground, a degenerate but still productive race. Ironically, this novel was written at a time when workers' incomes had begun to increase substantially after the grim stagnation of the years 1800–40. So science fiction was, at its birth, already out of date.

The stem family and industrialization

We still need to explain, however, why Germany for a time resisted the industrial revolution. The answer will lead us to a more accurate assessment of the general relationship between the stem family and development.

The stem family is a mechanism of transmission: it ensures the integrity of a land and the temporal continuity of a technique, whether this be writing or a metallurgical or agricultural process. In the world of the stem family, what has been acquired is rarely lost. The accumulation of knowledge can accelerate. But this capacity for conservation also includes an implicit potential for conservatism. A society based on the principle of the accumulation of what has been acquired is certainly endowed with the capacity for making any progress that does not entail a systemic break; it will, however, find it difficult to accept a radical change in its methods and objectives. For example, it will be more difficult to transform rural people into urban people, artisans into factory workers, or nobles into entrepreneurs. The uprooting and transformation of all these actors can only be brought about under external pressure, and at the cost of great pain. From 1870, Germany's accelerated industrial catch-up, under cultural and economic pressure from England, would be one of the key elements in the social destabilization that led to the tragedy of the years 1933–45.

Historical anthropology can find here a middle ground with the thought of Joseph Schumpeter. At the heart of the capitalist dynamic, Schumpeter identified a mechanism of 'creative destruction'. New techniques and new businesses constantly replace economic forms whose fate is always to become, at one time or another, archaic. But the stem family has no talent for creative destruction. Its goal is improvement ad infinitum. This, at least, is the function of the 'completed' stem family, a reproductive mechanism which itself has reached a certain level of perfection.

In the preceding two chapters, I mentioned the evolutionary nature of the stem family and its place in society, going as far as to suggest the theoretical necessity of conceiving, and, perhaps one day, of calculating, the stem-family rate. Notions such as the 'stem-family rate', and the 'imperfection of the stem model' allow us to conclude our reflections on the place of this anthropological type in the general problematic of dynamism and stagnation. In the case of Germany, we first saw the decisive role that the stem family played in the emergence of Protestantism and in the rise of universal literacy. But we must also admit the stem family's resistance to the industrial revolution, and finally the delayed but powerful economic take-off that it made possible.

Japan presents the same apparent contradictions. This country did not by itself achieve universal literacy, but it was capable, during the Edo period, of an amazing intellectual, artisanal, commercial and urban development, while being almost completely closed off from the rest of the world. And even if we had no knowledge of history, the current positions of Japan and Germany in the globalized economy would cast doubt on the hypothesis that the stem family is in principle opposed to development. Still, the tendency to stagnation in German and Japanese societies, in certain phases of history, also prevents us from asserting a simple association between stem family and development.

What prevents us from perceiving the nature of the real link between stem family and development is our focus on the most recent anthropological data, which describe a stem family close to the ideal type defined by Le Play: a socially dominant institution that has become crystallized and, so to speak, fossilized. Now, what we see in the long history of societies is a more subtle association between social dynamism and the emergence of certain forms of the stem family. In a very fine and minutely detailed comparative study of twentieth-century Alpine communities published in 1997, Emmanuel Matteudi clearly brought out the particular economic dynamism of rural communities whose dominant type was neither the nuclear family nor the pure stem family, but an imperfect form of the stem family.[5]

It is ultimately the too great perfection of the stem family itself that causes stagnation, a diffuse social paralysis: above a certain level of perfection, this anthropological type becomes a factor of rigidity as much as of acceleration.

— 8 —

SECULARIZATION AND THE CRISIS OF TRANSITION

In Europe, a religious revolution was the source of universal literacy, which itself led to the economic take-off. Faith nourished progress. On this continent, Protestantism brought about what Judaism had only been able to attempt on the highlands of the Middle East: it brought the whole of a population into the world of writing.

In the short term, there is no contradiction between education and religion. Lucien Febvre has shown, in *The Problem of Unbelief in the Sixteenth Century*, how the humanists of that time found it impossible to dispense with the image of a supreme being.[1] Between 1550 and 1650, Europe witnessed a revival of religious faith, the first spread of reading among the masses, the fear of the devil and the great witch hunt.

But while literacy in the first place tended to strengthen the hold of dreams and religious nightmares on people's minds, it led, a little later, to the scientific revolution. Despite the importance of Galileo, who was from Pisa, modern physics mainly developed in northwest Europe, where half of all individuals of the male sex could read. And the development of physics made it possible to call into question the idea of a God who creates and regulates all things.

Some of those who played a part in putting nature into mathematical formulae tried to overcome their religious doubts by resorting to superb paralogisms. In 1644, Descartes came up with his *cogito ergo sum*, which was supposed to lead, through many winding paths, to the acceptance of the existence of the Supreme Being; in 1670, Pascal, more simply and strangely, drew on his famous and very utilitarian 'wager'. But Newton, the true founder of physics, did not mix genres. His *Philosophiae Naturalis Principia Mathematica*, published in 1687, laid the foundations of modern science, but as a man Newton was content to remain a Christian, admittedly an unorthodox one, but conservative in his interest in, and respect for, the sacred texts.

139

Paradoxically, we can sense the presence of a French centre of gravity to the crisis of faith, rather than an English, Dutch or German one, and Catholic rather than Protestant. From the seventeenth century onwards, French elites displayed an excellent ability to doubt, expressed by *libertins* who were in those days essentially atheist philosophers. The people would follow. In the eighteenth century, the first religious collapse of a 'sociological' magnitude, the ebbing of religious observance among the masses, affected a significant proportion of Catholic areas, and in particular the Paris Basin. On the other hand, the regions controlled by the diverse variants of the Reformation – Lutheran, Zwinglian or Calvinist – were not at that stage affected by progress turning against faith in this way.

In the Germanic area, in Scandinavia and in Great Britain, Protestantism controlled regions whose family structures, stem family or absolute nuclear family, were indifferent to the idea of equality of the brothers. The areas that had remained Catholic were more diverse in their family structures. Some types did not include equal treatment for children, such as the *undifferentiated nuclear family* of Ireland, Poland and Belgium, the *absolute nuclear family* of inland western France, the *stem family* of Occitania, the northern edges of the Iberian Peninsula, Bavaria, Austria and Slovenia, and the *imperfect stem family* of the Rhineland. Other family types, on the contrary, included a strong principle of equality, such as the *egalitarian nuclear family* of the Paris Basin, southern Italy, central and southern Spain, the *communitarian family* of central Italy and the *system associating nuclear families by a patrilineal link* of northern Italy. And let us not forget the fabulous mixture of evolving types who were already sharing Brittany out between themselves.

Between 1650 and 1730, the Catholic family universe thus presented a basically varied appearance. The only feature common to the various anthropological types was exogamy, observed everywhere but probably to varying degrees of tolerance, with some marriages between cousins.

The literacy that came from the Protestant world spread by diffusion across this Catholic world controlled by priests. The Paris Basin, where family structures were nuclear egalitarian, but which itself was close to Reformation Europe, achieved literacy early on, from the beginning of the eighteenth century, even in the countryside. The number of men able to sign their marriage certificate then crossed the threshold of 50 per cent.[2] Between 1730 and 1740, the recruitment of priests collapsed in northern France. Even before the French Revolution, the birth rate began to decline in this simultaneously literate and secularized area.

In Southern Europe, with its egalitarian nuclear families, literacy at that time affected only the urban world, which around the middle of the eighteenth century lay outside the grip of the Church. Because the cities were feeding the countryside with a flow of religious personnel, which then dried up, the Paris Basin, Andalusia and southern Italy overall entered this new phase in the history of dechristianization, or rather secularization, a term that we can use as applicable to all systems, be they Christian, Jewish, Buddhist, Muslim or Hindu.

To explain the precocity of this first religious uncoupling, which affected various areas of Southern Europe that were undeveloped at the time, we need to include the family values of the regions concerned into our thinking. At the beginning of the eighteenth century, the egalitarian nuclear family of the Paris Basin, Andalusia and southern Italy defined children as free, and brothers and sisters as equals. Here, there was no strong image of the father to prop up the image of God; and there was no inequality between children to justify inequality between the priest and the ordinary person. In such an environment, the shock of rationalism was not cushioned by a psychologically deeply rooted belief. In fact, the principle of equality, in the context of an erosion of the religious interpretation of the world of the senses, seemed destined to call into question the belief in a superior being of any kind – father, king or God.

The logical sequence that can lead from the equality of brothers to the equality of all human beings and then to the non-existence of God, is not, however, a 'universal' law, that is to say, found in every place and in all historical contexts. Early Christianity, as we have seen, even seemed to present a real affinity with the egalitarian nuclear family of the Late Roman Empire. The educational context, however, was quite different.

In ancient times, Christianity followed the polytheistic mental universe in the absence of any scientific revolution and in the context of a regression of literacy. As Maristella Botticini and Zvi Eckstein have suggested, ancient Christianity had, among its first converts, Jewish peasants who had no need of the ability to read and write for their economic survival.[3] More generally, the egalitarian nuclear family of the cities of the Late Roman Empire had no positive relationship with the culture of writing.

Such, perhaps, was early Christianity, open to all, born from the ebb of reading in Antiquity, and dying long afterwards from the spread of literacy in the eighteenth century. We here discover that the Catholicism that collapsed around 1730–40, and thus triggered the process of European secularization, was implanted in a region of egalitarian nuclear families. It was anthropologically and, we will see, theologically, the true heir to the Christianity of Antiquity.

Catholicism without equality: 1800–1965

Geographically, more than half of Catholicism survived the eighteenth-century crisis, remaining in the various regions a sociologically living religion, controlling populations until the mid-1960s, particularly in regions

141

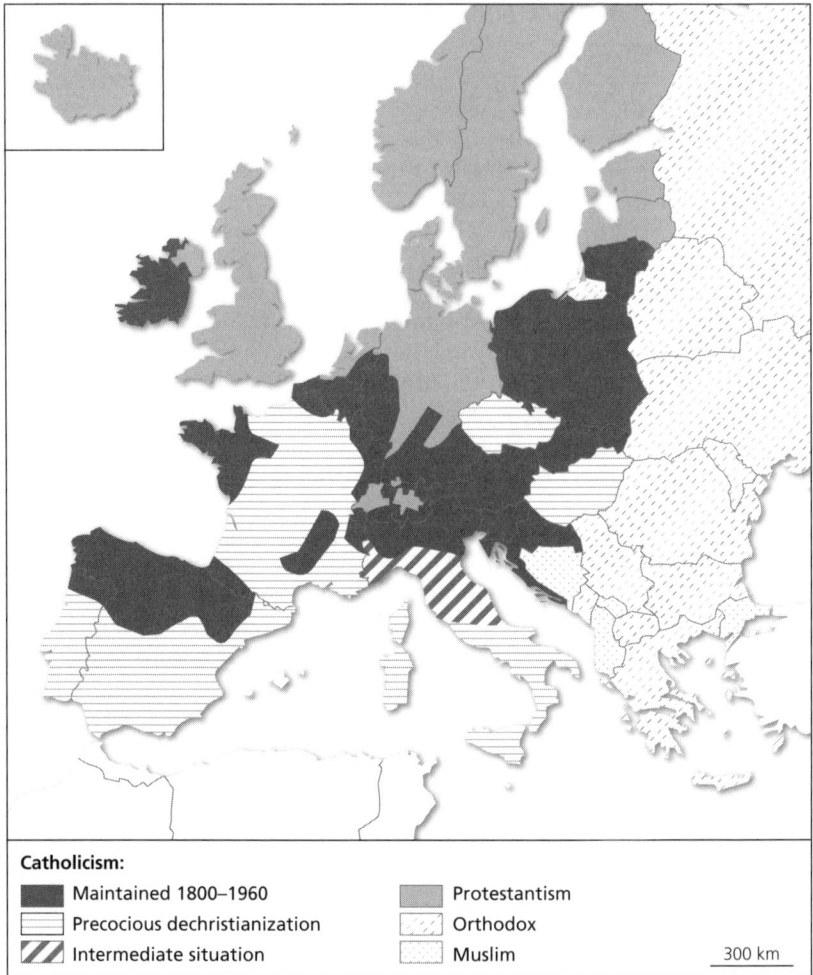

Map 8.1 Religions in Europe

Sources: For Western Europe, see Emmanuel Todd, *L'Invention de l'Europe* (Paris: Seuil, Points Essais, 1996), pp. 199–207. For religious practice in Poland, see Jerzy Kloczowski et al., *Histoire religieuse de la Pologne* (Paris: Le Centurion, 1987), p. 632, map no. 47.

where the stem family or the absolute nuclear family was the rule. As Map 8.1 shows, no perfect coincidence with any family type can be identified in this new anthropological situation.

I have extended these results to Slovakia, Croatia and Lithuania, where religious identifications are powerful. On the other hand, the Czech Republic, marked by the Hussite revolt, was integrated into the

Catholic regions that were secularized early on, just like Hungary, where Catholicism, Calvinism and Judaism coexisted. In the latter country, the fall in birth rate, in some areas almost as early as France, was an indubitable marker of secularization.

In León and Old Castile, in northern and central Italy, where Catholicism also survived until about 1960, protected by specific agrarian systems, family systems were egalitarian. However, overall, inegalitarianism and non-egalitarianism of the anthropological base became, from the end of the eighteenth century, the fundamental components of a maintained Catholicism. After 1800, the Church would adopt an attitude towards equality and authority that went completely counter to what it had originally professed. As Edgar Quinet saw so clearly in his 1845 work *Le Christianisme et la Révolution française* [*Christianity and the French Revolution*], it was the Revolution which, from 1789, bore the universal message of freedom and equality promoted by early Christianity. This shift seems absolutely logical to anyone interested in the way belief is rooted in family structures, since the French Republic was centred in the heart of the Paris Basin, with its egalitarian nuclear-family structure, just as the early Church had been centred in the proto-egalitarian nuclear family of the cities of the Late Roman Empire. In northern France, when the peasants learned to read, they started to find the principles of liberty and equality quite natural. Such is the irony of the bloody clash between the Republic and the Church: after 1791 the latter would defend an ideal of submission to the King, while waiting to declare, in 1870, the principle of papal infallibility.

The fall of Protestantism, 1870–1930

Much more literate, but lacking the anthropological principle of equality, the Protestant world largely escaped the religious crisis of the eighteenth century. It even sometimes experienced, in the sufferings of the industrial revolution, a religious comeback. In late eighteenth- and early nineteenth-century England, the petty bourgeoisie and upper strata of the working class found considerable moral support in religious faith. We find an echo of this in 'Jerusalem', William Blake's poem, printed in 1808:

> And was Jerusalem builded here
> Among these dark Satanic mills?

The Protestantism of the sects and that of Low Church Anglicanism remained the main vectors of cultural, economic and social progress in Britain. The traditional French view that progress is naturally opposed to religious faith does not apply to the country that was in the process of inventing industrial society – while waiting for science fiction.

In Calvinist and Lutheran Europe, secularization did not begin until the second pinnacle of the scientific revolution, the publication by Darwin, in 1859, of *The Origin of Species*. The subsequent collapse was a brutal affair in a world heavily dependent on a literal interpretation of the Bible and its story of creation. Between 1870 and 1930, throughout Northwest and Northern Europe, the recruitment of Protestant pastors collapsed. Secularization was finally hitting the most educated part of the continent. It opened up a phase of maximum ideological instability in Europe, including two world wars and the depths of horror represented by Nazism.

The fall of religion and the age of ideologies

By 1900, technological development seemed to be ushering in a wonderful future. But economism, yet again, has hindered the full understanding of the twentieth century. It means that the economic crisis of 1929 is continually exaggerated, and even protectionism is held guilty for its role in the genesis of Nazism. The mental crisis had begun well before that, and the First World War – it pains me to have to point this out – preceded the Second. To escape this narrowness of vision, we must remember that between 1950 and 1980 the French Historical School developed, for its study of the seventeenth and eighteenth centuries, the intellectual instruments that will enable us to understand the crises and violence of the twentieth.

The history of mentalities produced by Emmanuel Le Roy-Ladurie, Pierre Chaunu and Michel Vovelle, based on the historical demography of Louis Henry and Jacques Dupâquier, highlighted a cluster of significant interactions between literacy, secularization and a declining birth rate, on the one hand, and ideological and political crisis, on the other. And let us not forget the essential contribution of Britain's Lawrence Stone, who first suggested the existence of a causal link between literacy and revolution, in England and France as well as in Russia.

All these elements combined led to the French Revolution. Literacy and the fall of religion, in the Paris Basin and in the cities between 1740 and 1780, led to an early decline in the birth rate and, very quickly, to the ideological activation of the masses and the great Revolution; the latter had a dramatic impact on the then most populous country in Western Europe,[4] and triggered a crisis that lasted twenty-five years.

I have generalized this sequence, 'literacy, secularization, declining birth rate, ideological crisis', to the whole continent, in *L'Invention de l'Europe*.[5] The intellectual construction here is purely empirical, deduced from the observation of a fine temporal mechanism during the second phase of secularization. The collapse of religious practice in the

Protestant world, beginning in 1870, everywhere led to a decline in birth rate in the 1870s and 1890s. In the long literate regions of Northern and Northwestern Europe, where Protestantism had escaped the first phase of secularization, until 1870 the only demographic regulators had been late marriage and high numbers of unmarried people.

The religious emptiness and the psychological disturbances resulting from the modification of sexual behaviour combined, in the post-Reformation world, to favour the rise of the ideologies that led to the First World War.

Socialism, in its many variations, was not the most important element here; in Protestant Europe, it took an essentially reformist and reasonable form. It was the rise of nationalism that eventually dragged the continent into the major conflagration of the First World War. It is obvious that the epicentre of the ideological and mental crisis lay in Germany, but we must not forget that even before 1914 Britain was sufficiently febrile as to suffer, between 1914 and 1918, 740,000 deaths within four years, in complete contradiction with its military tradition, which had always been anxious to avoid engagements and human losses on the continent.

The proof of the link between the ebbing of religion and the cultural crisis – demographic and ideological – lies in the precision of the temporal sequence. From the mid-1960s, in the regions that had remained Catholic, we see the same coincidence in the sequence that led from secularization to the decline in birth rate and to an ideological transformation. This last stage of the ebbing of religion occurred, it is true, in the context of a much more general anthropological shift, the transformation of the Western world in the 1960s, which affected all the anthropological and religious areas of the West.

But what do we teach our high school students at the beginning of the third millennium, and what do our elites think they know about the rise of Nazism? That it was partly caused by the disillusions of the First World War (which is true) and partly by the economic crisis of 1929 (which is also true). But we are forgetting the main thing: the collapse of Protestant religious belief between 1870 and 1930, which was the real historical and mental backdrop of the sequence leading from the diplomatic agitation of William II to the capture of Berlin by the Red Army in 1945.

Should it not be a priority, and particularly useful at the present moment, to compare the – very similar – maps of Lutheranism and the Nazi vote in 1932?[6] Since the mid-1960s, the zones of Catholicism have been living through the final stage of European secularization. And again, the metaphysical emptiness this entails is leading, against a background of economic instability, to great anxiety and to the identifying of scapegoats.

Crisis of transition and ideologies

Between the seventeenth and the twentieth centuries, human history presents us with the spectacle of societies that are engaged, throughout the world, but at different dates and at unequal speeds, on the same trajectory of modernization: literacy, secularization, decline in birth rate, ideological crisis. Japan was the first to detach this movement from its original European and Christian sphere. At the beginning of the Meiji period (1868–1912), secularization affected the Buddhist religious system, which was quite diverse in its sects, but whose central tendency, Jodo Shinshu, had arrived at a representation of grace and salvation rather like that of Luther.[7] In it, the Pure Land of the West was the equivalent of Paradise. The pediment of mediaeval European churches also looks to the West, beyond the setting sun. The crisis of Japanese Buddhism led, in an almost classical way, to the rise of a nationalism that would lead the country to the conquest of Taiwan and Korea, to the invasion of a China too vast to be entirely conquered, and to the attack, finally, at Pearl Harbor, on an opponent too powerful to defeat. The state Shintoism developed by the elites during the Meiji period had little to do with the peaceful animism of peasant communities and the cult of rice, but it should be noted that, although Japanese nationalism defined itself against Buddhism, it did not reject religion in general.[8]

From 1950 onwards, the global spread of literacy has, as we saw in the last chapter, been accelerating, as has the questioning of traditional beliefs. At the beginning of the third millennium, we see that the Muslim and Hindu spheres are in turn being massively affected by the phenomena of literacy, secularization and a declining birth rate. We are frightened by the violence that accompanies their crises of transition to modernity; less, perhaps, by Hindu aggression against Christians in India, because they have their anti-Muslim parallels in Mumbai and elsewhere, and because we are not too sure how to handle them ideologically.

The first thing, however, would be to remember that the history of Europe in the years 1640–1945, between the first English revolution and Nazism, was also punctuated by a succession of crises combining modernization and dramatic religious change. We too easily forget, to begin with, the first English revolution, led by Cromwell, who, between 1642 and 1651, began to modernize society in the name of God, with his Bible in his hand. The Civil War was not too bloody, it is said, probably because literacy had not reached the rural masses. We then refuse to see the succession of continental ideological emergences as forming a logical sequence: the French Revolution, the nationalism of the years 1890–1914, Russian Communism, German Nazism. And yet

146

the same combination of literacy and secularization had always preceded the emergence of the new ideology. The sequence is sometimes very long, since, in the case of Protestant Germany, nearly 250 years separated the crossing of the 50 per cent literacy threshold by men aged 20–24, in around 1670, and the Nazi crisis in 1933: this is because the religious collapse did not take place until between 1870 and 1930. In France, the movement was faster: the literacy threshold was crossed in the Paris Basin in the early eighteenth century, the rapid religious decline followed between 1730 and 1780, and the Revolution in 1789. Since I cannot at the present stage date the Russian religious collapse, I must content myself with a sequence that places the crossing of the literacy threshold in 1900, followed by the Revolution of 1917.

Let us look beyond Europe again. In China, the literacy threshold was crossed in about 1940, and communism prevailed in 1949; in Iran, the crossing of the literacy threshold occurred in 1964, and the revolution in 1979. With the Iranian Shiite world, well ahead of the Sunni part of the Muslim world, we again find the Anglo-Saxon association between modernization and religion, and a revolutionary process that is not defined as against faith, but relies on its last upsurge. For let us make no mistake: *Protestant puritanism and Muslim fundamentalism* merely represent, in the *longue durée* of history, two variants of a single phenomenon, the ultimate stiffening of the faith, a step on the path to secularization.

Like a seismograph, the birth rate indicator allows us to follow the pace of mental evolution. When it dips below two children per woman, we can be certain that, in its mass, the population has left behind the old religious system, especially if, being either Jewish, Christian or Muslim, it is derived from the Bible. The injunction to encourage high birth rates and occupy territory – go forth and multiply – found in the religions of the Book is then extinguished. The birth rate in Iran in 2016 was 1.7 children per woman.

The spread of literacy always produces a moment in history during which the sons, then the daughters, can read but their parents cannot. A stage in which the authority of the family and then of society is loosened is thus, as it were, written into the programme. The decline in birth rate implies, in turn, a change in sexual behaviour, a reorganization of the relations between men and women. It contributes in its own way to the mental destabilization of populations in transition. The crisis which successively affects societies as they start to take off and make economic progress, so that we might expect them to be simply happier and more stable, is not, at this stage of the historical analysis, a great mystery.

147

Family structures and ideologies

The universality of the transitional crisis affecting societies as they 'take off' was clearly recognized in 1960 by William W. Rostow in his *The Stages of Economic Growth*.[9] The subtitle of his book was *A Non-Communist Manifesto* – rather an original one for a historical essay. Rostow was writing in the wake of the Russian, Chinese and Yugoslav revolutions, and he perceived Marxism-Leninism as a 'puddle' threatening to spread inexorably. According to him, each country, destabilized by progress, was confronted, on its ascending trajectory, by the communist threat. But in his view, all that was needed was to block the Leninist seizure of power during the transitional crisis; in this way, once the fever had passed, the peril would recede and the victory of the American conception of democracy would be assured.

Rostow was therefore quite logically a hawk during the Vietnam War, demanding, as did others, a massive military intervention. Yet 50,000 American deaths were not enough to stop the spread of communism, which triumphed locally. This was the first, dramatic failure of Rostow's theory. It failed in other respects, too, albeit in converse ways, since these other failures testified to the powerlessness of communism to take root in certain societies. They are just as important from a theoretical point of view.

Thus Rostow's model prophesied a dangerous transition crisis in Thailand, though a few insignificant communist guerrillas never managed to threaten the regime, its army or its king. The modernization of the country – educational, demographic and economic – continued, punctuated by military coups carried out under the mysterious gaze of a monarch who did nothing but was venerated by his people. The dominant ideology in Thailand today remains difficult to define.

In Cambodia, dragged into the war by American intervention, the communist insurrection mutated into a genocidal nihilism that had little to do with Marxism-Leninism. The Vietnamese army, reunited by the communists, finally had to intervene to stabilize the country – a solution accepted by the Western world with a cowardly sigh of relief.

The transition crisis is indeed, as Rostow had suggested, universal, but it takes a specific form in each different place. Why a particular form in a particular place? This is a central question for anyone seeking to understand history. In 1983, I proposed a solution to this problem, in the book that was translated as *The Explanation of Ideology: Family Structures and Social Systems*.[10] In this work, I simply applied, and took to their ultimate conclusions, the discoveries made by the historians who were my masters in the 1970s. The Cambridge School of Historical Anthropology had just established, for England, the sequence leading from the absolute nuclear family to modern liberalism, both economic and political. In

148

1965, in *The World We Have Lost*, Peter Laslett revealed the nuclear character of the English family of the early seventeenth century.[11] In 1978, in *The Origins of English Individualism*, Alan Macfarlane showed that this nuclear family was the anthropological basis for the subsequent historical development of England.[12]

My work, and especially that of the researchers who met and discussed these issues in Cambridge between 1971 and 1975, had allowed me to become acquainted in depth with the traditional peasant family forms of England, Germany and Austria, China, the Paris Basin, southwest France, central and southern Italy, Japan, Yugoslavia, Russia and Scandinavia. And I realized that the map of endogenous communism – which then included Russia, China, Yugoslavia, Albania, Cuba, Vietnam and electoral pockets in Italy, Finland and the French Massif Central, and in West Bengal and Kerala – coincided with that of the communitarian-family type. This latter was most often patrilineal and exogamous, but there were matrilineal exceptions, in Kerala and Cuba, or bilateral exceptions, in the Massif Central. The *taravad* of the Nayars of Kerala involved brothers and sisters living together without any limits, with 'husbands' visiting their wives who were members of another *taravad*. The Black Cuban family was organized around female lineages and suggested a matrilocal communitarianism. In the northwest of the Massif Central, a brother and a sister, both married, could live together.

A more exhaustive inventory of the family forms that cover the various countries of the world then revealed to me that where communitarian-family forms of one kind or another did not exist, communism's chances of success were nil. In Thailand, for example, a flexible nuclear-family system, encouraging temporary co-residence of married daughters with their parents, was the rule. Its fluidity was opposed step by step to the patrilineal rigour of the Vietnamese family system. This explains Rostow's intellectual and political failure: communism, an authoritarian and egalitarian doctrine, could flourish only in regions dominated by the authoritarian and egalitarian values of the communitarian family – in Vietnam, for example. It was, on the other hand, completely unsuited to the Thai anthropological terrain, which cannot be described as either authoritarian or egalitarian. It can be said that in Thailand, the elusive character of ideological values and the regime reflects the undifferentiated nature of family organization.

Again, in *The Explanation of Ideology*, I proposed correlating a simple family typology with ideological forms likely to appear during the crisis of transition, a little on the model of Mendeleyev's table of chemical elements:

- The Anglo-American absolute nuclear family would correspond to liberal but non-egalitarian ideologies.

149

- The egalitarian nuclear family of the Paris Basin would correspond to a belief in freedom and equality, culminating in the notion of the universal human being.
- The exogamous communitarian family would correspond to communism, authoritarian and egalitarian in nature, and universalist too.
- The stem family would correspond to authoritarian but non-egalitarian ideologies: social democracy, Christian democracy, Nazism.
- Non-exogamous family systems – the Arab endogamous communitarian family and the family found in southern India, nuclear but with a strong tendency towards patrilineal aggregation and practising a model of marriage between cross cousins – would produce specific and not necessarily antireligious transitions.

With great regularity, then, we see ideologies succeeding religions, driven by a mass literacy that is making inexorable progress. The contemporary viewer, however, cannot detect any reassuring harmony in this process: the transition crisis is often bloody. In addition, the particular form taken here and there by the transitional ideology – egalitarian, inegalitarian, authoritarian, liberal – appears oddly random. In the historical, chronologically separate paths of England (*absolute nuclear family*), France (*nuclear egalitarian in its centre*), Germany (*stem family*), Russia (*exogamous communitarian*), Japan (*stem family*), China (*exogamous communitarian*), Vietnam (*exogamous communitarian*), Thailand (*nuclear with matrilocal temporary residence*), Cambodia (*undifferentiated nuclear*), Iran (*weak endogamous communitarian*), the Arab world (*strong endogamous communitarian*), southern India (*crossed endogamous nuclear patrilocal*), and Rwanda (*polygynous stem family*), how can we perceive any orderly sequence?

To detect some logic in the maddening succession of information coming at us from all over the world, we must assess, for each country, its position in relation to the literacy threshold and the latent values contained in its family system. By so doing, we could, if not foresee the ideological future of this or that country, at least limit the range of possibilities. Such an approach would be particularly fruitful in Africa, the last continent to confront the transition crisis. The acceptance of the hypothesis proposed in 1983 would have helped us foresee the possibility of the emergence in Rwanda in 1994 of an exterminating racism as ferocious as Nazism. The Rwandan stem-family system, common to both Hutu and Tutsi, is admittedly the root cause of the country's agricultural efficiency and dense population. But it fosters the values of authority and inequality, and so is likely to produce, in a period of crisis, a racial interpretation of social problems.

150

Religion and ideology

Sometimes religion and modern ideology meld together during the transition phase. At the immediate end of the great European mental transformation, in the middle of the seventeenth century, the Protestantism of the English sects turned out to be the bearer of a liberal revolution; today we see Islamic fundamentalism and political Hinduism developing with the crossing of the threshold of 50 per cent male literacy. We should not see these overlaps of ideology and religion as the expression of overly specific anthropological or historical situations. It would be wrong, indeed, to contrast 'religion' and 'ideology' too brutally, imagining that collective religious belief is essentially fixed on a metaphysical beyond and ideology on the more horizontal objective of an ideal earthly society.

The existence, in religious systems, of concepts such as god(s), demon(s), resurrection or reincarnation, paradise, hell, and purgatory, must not make us lose sight of the fact that, for a sociologist, the rewards and punishments offered by religion are primarily earthly. Durkheim defined religion, quite brutally but with some justice, as society's worship of itself; in this way he resolutely made religion part of earthly realities.

The sociologist Rodney Stark, whom I discussed at length in chapter 4, has listed the things that a convert really finds in his or her commitment: in the case of the Christians of Antiquity, well before eternal life, these included immediate integration into a stable, moral and reliable group, which enabled him or her to escape the economic chaos and anomie of the cities of the Greco-Roman Empire. I have also mentioned the earthly reward of Judaism, a religion for which belief in eternal life is an option left to everyone's discretion. It is not impossible that some of the Protestant sects, so close to Judaism in many respects, ended up considering eternal life as a secondary element in Christian dogma. Calvin certainly declared that human beings were predestined by the Everlasting to life or death, but we often have the impression that, for many sects that have sprung from his theology, the earthly success of individuals and their families is the reality of divine election.

Just as earthly but more explicit than group integration are the economic and social programmes of emerging religions. Judaism, Christianity and Islam care about the poor and set out the obligations of the rich. The religions of the Book include a redistributive element from the outset. This is also the case of Buddhism. Religion did not wait for the ideology of modern times to come along; it was already talking about economic relations between human beings on this earth. This obvious point seems very useful when we observe in Western societies, between 1980 and 2010 – immediately after the extinction of religious faith and the ideologies of transition – the rise of a total economic irresponsibility among

151

the privileged, the 'revolt of the elites' denounced by Christopher Lasch shortly before he died.

Conversely, we should not underestimate the metaphysical irrationality of modern ideologies, the French Revolution, communism or Nazism. In their expansive phase, they fulfilled the same psychological function: the integration of individuals. Well before the realization of their programmes, they were refuges from isolation, remedies against a very earthly anomie. They never ceased to evoke a Beyond located in an indefinite future: the ideal Republic, the Communist City, the thousand-year Reich. Their first adherents, tranquilized by belonging to a group of believers, were just as capable of heroism and sacrifice as the first Christians, with slogans of the style 'Freedom or Death', even where they proposed to establish on Earth a form of servitude.

9

THE ENGLISH MATRIX OF GLOBALIZATION

By 2015, the Anglo-American world included 450 million individuals, already more than a European Union that would have only 438 million if the United Kingdom and Ireland were to leave. Projected figures for 2050 point to an Anglosphere of 560 million inhabitants as against a Europe of 444 million. I place Ireland and French Canada in this Anglo-American world because we cannot conceive the history of England without the history of Ireland, or that of Canada without Quebec, just as we cannot imagine the United States without Indians and Blacks, Australia without the Aborigines, or New Zealand without the Maori. Throughout the Anglo-American world, associated with an expanding 'we', there is an internal 'them', an enfolded 'other'.

Thus, demographic dynamics indicate that the culturally English heart of the West will soon be in the majority. But in 1086, when William the Conqueror ordered the compilation of the Domesday Book, with its census of the manors and families in the kingdom conquered in 1066, England had at most 1.5 million inhabitants, as against 6 million in France of that era (in its present territory). England did not yet have its language, since the French of the conquering class was superimposed on the Saxon of the previous invaders, which had itself supplanted the earlier Brittonic tongues, surviving in Wales, Cornwall, northwest England and a good half of Scotland. In the Church, a little Latin had survived the withdrawal of the Romans of the island around 409, after three and a half centuries under imperial control.[1]

The English language, a fusion of the Anglo-Saxon dialects spoken by the common people and the French of the aristocracy, was well formed by the second half of the fourteenth century, as can be seen in Chaucer's *Canterbury Tales*. In 1400, half a century after the Black Death, England's population reached only 3 million: at that time, France had 12 million, i.e. still four times as many. Similarly, when Voltaire celebrated English liberal modernity in his *Philosophical*

153

Letters, France had 24 million inhabitants and England 6 million; the United Kingdom of Great Britain and Ireland, plus the colonies in America, represented only 12 million. Canada then had 300,000, and the future United States of America 2 million, already more than England around the year 1100.

So even in its maturity, the English model still represented, in terms of demographic mass, only a fraction of the Kingdom of France.

It is a relatively homogeneous world. There are anthropological differences between England, Scotland, Wales and Ireland. There are subtle differences between the north and the south of England. But England alone does not present any more internal variations than a large French province. Its small size and insularity confer a unity and cohesion specific to the Kingdom. The Domesday Book was certainly an expression of Norman administrative genius, but it was possible to compile it only because England, a small country, had an identifiable natural form. In the work of seventeenth-century English statisticians such as William Petty and Gregory King, we find an early ability to think about the whole of English society, a spontaneously national approach that came with an initial conception of overall economic product.

From the nineteenth century onwards, the Anglo-American world raced ahead, expanding rapidly after the British industrial revolution and the colonization of the American territory. It was driven by population growth and assimilation into the colonies not only of immigrants from the British Isles but, from the last quarter of the nineteenth century, from all over Europe, and finally the whole world. Today, the Anglosphere has hundreds of millions of individuals of German, Swedish, Italian, Jewish, Japanese, Chinese and Korean, South Asian, Arab, South American and African origin, all of whom have adopted, over two or three generations, not only the English language but the absolute nuclear-family model.[2]

The half-billion individuals who today make up the Anglo-American world are therefore part of an anthropological system that was three hundred times smaller at the end of the eleventh century.[3] For an anthropologist, the rise of the Anglo-American world can be read as the success of a matrix that appeared in a very small kingdom between 1100 and 1650. The absolute nuclear family, although close to the undifferentiated nuclear family of origins, is not, however, exactly the same. The term 'absolute' here refers to the functional disappearance of kinship ties beyond the conjugal group and its children. Parents and adult children no longer co-reside, even temporarily; the mutual aid between brothers and sisters becomes socially insignificant; and the taboo on marriage between cousins is total.

The essentialist impasse

Alan Macfarlane's pioneering book, *The Origins of English Individualism*, tore away the veil of ideology to discern, beneath the liberal political temperament and economic plasticity of England, the family system that I call the absolute nuclear family. I sang the praises of his book in *Le Monde des livres* when it was published in 1978 but I will now be a little more critical of it. In the following lines, however, I'll be referring to the book itself as Macfarlane has nuanced his initial formulation a great deal since 1978. His insistence on the uniqueness of the English has in fact almost disappeared, as is clear from his Wang Gouwei lectures of 2012:

> England was not exceptional. There was a similar pattern over much of northwestern Europe. For example, the Normans, second-generation Vikings, were hardly distinguishable from the people they conquered in England. Much of southern Scotland was also similar, as was much of northern France, Germany and Scandinavia. If we had travelled over Europe at the end of the eleventh century we might have been surprised at its uniformity. From the twelfth century, however, a great divergence began to occur between England and much of continental Europe.[4]

However, as perhaps too loyal a student, I still feel that the holy scriptures of historical anthropology must be criticized in their original text, not taking later nuances into account. I am still convinced that an element of national prejudice was instrumental in Macfarlane's decisive intellectual breakthrough. The ways of science are indeed mysterious.

At the heart of *The Origins of English Individualism*, we find a mythi-fication not only of the English past, but also of the absolute nuclear family. The essay is built on a binary opposition between English peasants – never real peasants, according to Macfarlane, but modern individualists ever since the Middle Ages – and real, communitarian peasants of Eastern Europe, Russia, India and China. In his 'Anglotrip', Macfarlane goes so far as to suggest that many errors in the interpreta-tion of English history stem from the fact that some of the great recent British historians of the Middle Ages had Eastern European origins, such as Kosminsky, Vinogradoff and Postan, and were too fixated, in his view, on an identification of mediaeval England with Russia.

An English mediaevalist, regardless of his or her personal origins, is never obsessed with Russian history, but first looks to the west of the European continent to evaluate what, in the English social formation, draws on the Celtic past, the Roman imprint, the Anglo-Saxon back-ground or the Norman conquest. Let us forgive Macfarlane for leaving out the three and a half centuries of Roman occupation, even though they established Londinium, the first road network, a sprinkling of camps that became cities (*chester* = *castrum*) and large rural domains in the classical mode of the villa. The counter-model that we do not have the professional right to ignore, however, is France. An English mediaevalist must look to France, just as a French mediaevalist must look to England, since from the Norman Conquest in 1066 to the end of the Hundred Years War, English and French monarchies were closely interlinked, as evidenced by the common symbolism of the thaumaturgic kings.[5] On both sides of the Channel, the king healed scrofula by a simple laying on of hands.

England and France, the two oldest nation-states on the continent, were born together. They evolved as mirror images of each other; most of the time, the English monarchy kept a step ahead. In his comparative work *La Monarchie féodale en France et en Angleterre* [*The Feudal Monarchy in France and England*], Charles Petit-Dutaillis clearly shows that the Capetians played 'against' the English, resisting the expansion of the Plantagenet Empire whose administrative practice was more modern.[6] According to him, at the end of the twelfth century, France was a century behind.[7] And the Hundred Years War was only the last (mediaeval) stage of a competition that had begun in the eleventh century. The competition would resume in the eighteenth century.

Because the Île-de-France and Normandy together constitute the Seine Valley, and because England was conquered by Franco-Normans, we might even question whether, in the Middle Ages, we are actually dealing with two distinct countries. To return to Macfarlane: by refraining from comparing the English peasantry to the French peasantry, in a book that claimed to demonstrate the uniqueness and separate character of English history, he was attempting a sleight of hand. The last chapter of the essay, called 'England in Perspective', bears witness to a sublime return of the repressed, i.e. France. His need to shake English history free of its French mother (or sister, depending on the parameter chosen) was, however, irrepressible, and Macfarlane falls below the level of the tourist guide, endeavouring to explain that at every period England was different from France.

At the end, we finally catch a sight of the keystone of the whole 'system': the explicit affirmation of the insignificance of the Norman Conquest and the purely Anglo-Saxon character of England. After all these anti-historical contortions, we end up with the commonplace of 'Germanic freedom', which in any case Macfarlane draws from a Frenchman, Montesquieu (Macfarlane is no doubt unaware that the French nobility itself had a strong predisposition to fantasize about its Germanic origins).[8]

From the point of view of the analysis of family structures, it is easy to point out the absurdity of Macfarlane's claims. True, his book devotes a great deal of space to primogeniture, a very English phenomenon in his view, but he does not seem to understand that it is the source of the stem family, a non-nuclear complex model. He is convinced that primogeniture is becoming rare throughout the world, while it is in fact found on all continents. He seems to be unaware that it had first made its first European appearance in France, as Evelyn Cecil had seen in *Primogeniture*, a work published in London – in 1895. But above all, Macfarlane says nothing about the fact that the familiar expression used in English law to designate the custom of male primogeniture, the transmission of property to the eldest son, was 'borough French', as opposed to ultimogeniture, transmission to the last-born, known as 'borough English'. For the historian of the family, primogeniture is quite simply the central Franco-Norman element of English culture. Ultimogeniture is only a trace of the undifferentiated nuclear family, which allowed the recuperation of the elderly parents by the youngest of the children.[9]

We must therefore resign ourselves: neither the best of social sciences nor the best historian can escape ideology, in their conclusions or their determining factors. The breakthrough achieved by Macfarlane was the result of a national passion. *The Origins of English Individualism* was published in 1978, at the end of a period of British economic decline, a year before the seizure of power by Margaret Thatcher, whose revolution was both neo-national and neoliberal. The obsessive nationalist component of the book did not shock me at the time, perhaps because the France of the time was in good shape and I was paying little attention to national anxieties. The main reason was probably that the personal image of Alan Macfarlane, my Cambridge thesis examiner, a towering scholar and a friendly and open man, made me overlook the national narcissism of his book.

As Macfarlane later admitted, essentializing the English too much is not the ultimate solution to the riddle of the past. The rare data on the family going back to the time of the Anglo-Saxon kingdoms testify, on the contrary, to a mode of behaviour in princely families that was not Germanic but universal. Uncertain rules of inheritance, fathers and sons and brothers sharing power, horizontal successions between brothers, kings chosen from a wider, bilateral kinship, and exogamy between the princely families of the kingdoms:[10] all this can be found in other Germanic, Celtic and Slavic peoples. The above quotation from Macfarlane suggests we probably would agree on this today.

Family and collectivity in England

I will be attempting (below) a schematic reconstruction of the history of the English family since the Middle Ages, but before we plunge into these depths, we need to be sure we have an exact and complete vision of the nuclear family identified by Peter Laslett for a date well after the Middle Ages. The main sample used by Laslett, which includes one hundred lists of inhabitants, is spread over the years 1576–1821. The two oldest parishes, and the ones most important for his conclusions, were Ealing in Middlesex, near London, in 1599, and Clayworth, further north (in Nottinghamshire) in 1676. For these two parishes, we have a detailed analysis of the household structure and we find indeed that, in Ealing, only one out of eighty-five households included two couples – parents and married children – and only four of the households included adult individuals in addition to the married couple; in half the cases, these were their children, and in half a brother or sister of one of the couple. In Clayworth, not even one out of seventy-eight households simultaneously contained two married couples; eight included a collection of additional individuals, four vertically, three horizontally.[11]

With certain qualifications, the other lists of seventeenth-century residents confirm the nuclear nature of the English family. Twelve individuals lived alone in Ealing, eight in Clayworth. So we can talk of an *absolute nuclear family* at the end of the reign of Elizabeth I (1558–1603). There is still some doubt about the date, however: ninety-five of the one hundred lists of inhabitants that make up Laslett's main sample are from after 1660. However, the cultural transformation was so significant between 1550 and 1660, in England as in the whole of Western and Central Europe, that this statistical overrepresentation of the end of the seventeenth century represents a real problem for the reliable dating of the absolute nuclear family. In particular, we have no description of the absolute nuclear family until the transformation of English culture by the Protestant Reformation.

But how, in the context of the pure nuclear family, could individuals live when they were isolated by age or by the deaths of their relatives, spouses or parents: the old, the widows, the orphans? How did society treat what Laslett called the problem of 'nuclear hardship'?[12] Richard Smith, David Thomson and a few others have studied this question and provided an answer.

The local English community mastered the problem by early social taxation. The Poor Laws of 1598 and 1601 required parishes to levy a tax, administered locally by an Overseer of the Poor who, in practice, was taken from the upper or middle strata of the local peasantry. We should not imagine a marginal action affecting only a few dramatic and exceptional cases. A sample of twenty communities, a picture of which can be formed from the parish register and the poor register combined, means we can study 110,000 pension payments between 1660 and 1740. In addition, statistical analysis reveals that 5 per cent of the population received a weekly pension, a figure that rose to 8 or 9 per cent in the city and 40–45 per cent for the over-60s.[13] For the latter, the average level of the pension corresponded to the wages of a farm worker.

In the aftermath of the first neoliberal turn of English ideology, the reforms of the 1830s emphasized the duty of parental responsibility. But by the early 1840s, David Thomson found that two-thirds of women over the age of 70 were receiving a pension, half of men over 70, half of women aged 65–69, and a significant minority of women aged 55–60. Mary Barker-Read notes a mean retirement age of 70 for men, and three or four years younger for women, in the rural communities of Kent at the end of the seventeenth century and into the eighteenth.[14] Here again, we find the threshold of 70 years brought out by the study of hunter-gatherers.

In an astonishing article, Thomson has emphasized the continuity of the history of this English social security, or, better still, its cyclical nature, with the highs and lows not only of benefits, but of debates about what their level should be and the degree of responsibility of families and individuals. He estimates at 70–90 per cent of the average salary of young adult workers the purchasing power of pensions granted to elderly rural people: 'A Tudor or Stuart parishioner somehow transported to the Britain of the 1990s would recognize little about the place, but would be likely to feel at home with contemporary agonizing over welfare options.'[15]

Richard Smith, that great mediaevalist, suggests that Poor Laws in the Elizabethan era were presumably preceded by a purely local management of the pensions of the old peasants, many of them being supervised by the manorial court, the payments associating tenants and their successors who were not necessarily related to them.[16]

But we should not deduce from this collective framework that this was a closed local community. Quite the opposite. The parish most often cared for elderly people whose adult sons and daughters had left. The nuclear family encouraged this mobility. Children moved as servants between large farms while still very young. Even the sons of better-off peasants were sent elsewhere as servants under the practice of 'sending out'. The resulting geographic mobility was extreme, as Peter Laslett's pioneering study showed in his article on Clayworth and Cogenhoe.[17]

Keith Wrightson has calculated that in Terling, a particularly modern and prosperous village, admittedly located in Essex just sixty kilometres from London, the megalopolis of the time, between 50 and 60 per cent of the heads of household had no relatives.[18] Of those who married in Terling between 1580 and 1699, and subsequently had at least one child, only 25 per cent of men and 33 per cent of women had been baptized in the parish – i.e., there was a 75 per cent mobility rate for men and 66 per cent for women.[19] Neolocality of marriage was the rule: people got married and lived away from the village where they were born.

One can detect a slight matrilocal bias in Terling, since women were a little less mobile here. This matrilocality was concentrated on ordinary villagers; in the oligarchy of yeomen, dominant male primogeniture could not fail to lead to an opposite patrilocal bias. What we have here, probably, is a situation that was very general in Europe and in the bilateral kinship system: social differentiation came with an anthropological polarization which meant that patrilocality made progress in the dominant, stable group that controlled houses and land, and matrilocality increased in the dominated group that was not rooted in the soil. I have noted this mechanism in eighteenth-century communities in Artois and Lower Brittany, and at the beginning of the nineteenth century in Skåne (in the south of Sweden, opposite Denmark).[20]

The mobility of the inhabitants of seventeenth-century rural England was admittedly extreme, but we should not imagine that it contrasted with an immobility that characterized the past. The very strict rules of exogamy applied by the European populations forced people to leave their villages. The average size of English communities in the seventeenth century must have been two hundred inhabitants, a scale that implies a high level of mobility to avoid consanguinity in marital unions.[21] So here we find preindustrial rural communities that continued to operate according to the norm of *Homo sapiens*. The original hunter-gatherers, as we have noted, were exogamous and mobile. The earliest agriculture was also mobile: born in the Middle East, and for a time associated with a sedentary lifestyle, it then went on to conquer Europe, North Africa and South Asia.

State and family

The state of the Tudors and Stuarts was thus a 'strong state', whose social security system ensured the functioning of the absolute nuclear family. But this state was devoid of bureaucracy. It was effective in Europe from a very early age, but was essentially confined to the passing by a central parliament of national laws that it did not have the means to impose locally by force. Implementation of the Poor Law by parishes was more or less voluntary, run by local peasant elites.

To understand how the English state became centralized very early, the right concept we need is, in the words of Steve Hindle's appropriate distinction, 'authority' rather than 'power'.[22] This weakly predatory state was obeyed despite the absence of a repressive apparatus. This 'authority' requires two types of explanation. It can be explained first by the fact that England was a separate island, small and with a relative cultural homogeneity; but also by the respect among the lower classes for social hierarchies, the culture of deference already so clearly brought to light by

Keith Wrightson for the seventeenth century. Neither the authority of the state, nor that of the great landowners, nor that of the peasant elites, was disputed by the masses. This culture of deference is, in my opinion, the result of the absence of any value of equality in the family system.

The mechanism of the Poor Law, managed by wealthy peasants in the interest of the community, reveals the basic dualism of the typical English rural community. Inheritance practices, different for large and for small farmers, are an expression of the depth of this duality. The theoretical rule, inherited from mediaeval times, was male primogeniture. But the years 1540–1645 saw the establishment of the freedom to test, brought to completion under Cromwell during the first revolution – a revolution that was fundamentally individualistic despite its military and dictatorial outcome.[23] Monographs that have come down to the level of the rural communities highlight a twofold practice from the seventeenth century onwards. Large farmers, in general, practised primogeniture, mitigating it if they could by ensuring that some land was transferred to their younger sons. Below them, a free division of property was the practice, especially among the less wealthy. What we sometimes observe, rather surprisingly, is an unexpectedly high number of wills being made by the poorest people.[24]

The nuclear household was, however, common to all rural social categories, as the introduction of primogeniture does not seem to have had enough time to lead, in rural areas, to a co-residence of adult generations, as in Germany, Japan, southwest France or north of the Iberian Peninsula. Still, Franco-Norman primogeniture, introduced into the island by the conquering aristocracy, spread far enough down the social structure to reach the upper layer of the peasantry, the yeomen of old England, the ruling group of the elementary peasant communities. The value of inequality inherent in primogeniture was thus part of the original English matrix, but it was counteracted by the more flexible tendencies of the deepest layers of the peasant population. But the freedom to test gave everyone involved the opportunity to follow no rules at all. This freedom should not be seen as an innovation per se. It was the legal and modern form of primitive undifferentiation: the freedom of the English peasant remained the freedom of the hunter-gatherer of original times.

When we have a precise grasp of the absolute nuclear family, in the second half of the seventeenth century, the economic dualism of the village community appears to be echoed by a cultural dimension. The literacy rate among yeomen was around 70 per cent for men, except in the backward north of England where it could fall to 30 per cent. As far as the ability to read was concerned, the big farmers were aligned with the artisanal and merchant classes of urban areas. The mass of poorer peasants generally reached a literacy rate of only 30 per cent.[25]

161

Keith Wrightson has noted an opposition between the 'closed' parishes of the plains, with houses grouped together, well controlled by the peasant oligarchy and the local nobleman, and the 'open' parishes of more rugged areas, often with houses scattered in hamlets, less dominated by the principle of social deference.[26]

Cycles in English history

The most recent English historians have thus found and confirmed what Karl Polanyi had highlighted in *The Great Transformation*: the way that individualism was monitored by the Tudor and Stuart monarchies. The revolutions of the seventeenth century set up a new legal framework, theoretically capable of liberating people from the community, which was essentially rural at that time. The enclosures, implemented by Acts of Parliament in the eighteenth century, would eventually destroy the remnants of collective constraints inherited from agrarian life. Not every tradition of social responsibility, however, was broken by the English agrarian and industrial revolutions: economic individualism long remained under the supervision of the local authorities. Liberal impulses definitely continued to trigger collective reactions in England. Polanyi dedicates an entire chapter to Speenhamland case law, which between 1795 and 1834 prevented the establishment of a free labour market.

Once again, the role of local authorities appears to have been decisive, even more so than under the Tudors since it was a local decision that ended up being generalized. 'The justices of Berkshire, meeting at the Pelican Inn, in Speenhamland, near Newbury, on May 6, 1795, in a time of great distress, decided that subsidies in aid of wages should be granted in accordance with a scale dependent upon the price of bread, so that a minimum income should be assured to the poor *irrespective of their earnings*.'[27] It was not really a law, since no general set of rules was ever adopted, but the example was followed in the majority of the countryside and in some of the cities, enough in any case for the labour market to be affected.

In the early 1830s, a hard liberal phase in English history began. The Reform Bill of 1832 opened the way for the middle classes to enter Parliament. In 1834, Speenhamland case law was abolished. The moment for a strict application of Malthusian and Ricardian economic precepts seemed to have arrived. No more of the paternalism inherited from the Tudors. A first revolt of the elites designated the poor as morally culpable and destined to moral improvement by the law of the market.

The important thing here is not to assess the quality of the debate on the economic or moral consequences of this or that type of regulation, or the refusal to regulate the labour market. The important thing is to realize that the image of an English culture ultra-liberal by nature is a fiction. England was, of course, the birthplace of individualist capitalism. There is indeed a link between the absolute nuclear family and the plasticity of English society, between the lack of the value of equality and the weakness of popular reactions to the violence of the industrial revolution. But even after 1834, what we always find, as David Thomson has shown, is that this nuclear family could not have existed without the aid of a collective responsibility for the individuals removed from the elementary family nucleus, mainly the elderly but also the orphans and, in the transition phase from the countryside to the city, the workers who were in dire straits.

Thus, the Tudor state was also part of the English anthropological matrix. The absolute nuclear family and the Poor Law, i.e. the parish in action, constituted a functional whole. This is so true that the disintegration of Tudor paternalism made the structure of English households between 1750 and 1880 more complex, as Steven Ruggles has shown.[28] The effects of the industrial revolution spread beyond rural communities, and new proletarians were forced to rely more on their family ties than did the peasants. Michael Anderson has analysed this phenomenon in detail for mid-nineteenth-century Lancashire. In the Preston industrial community, he found 23 per cent of families extended beyond the conjugal family and 65 per cent of men aged 20–24 were living with their parents, compared to only 53 per cent in the surrounding countryside.[29]

England, as we have said, outstripped France in the race for political modernity, inventing political representation and the nation well before 1789. We must now question another commonplace of our textbooks, which assure us that Bismarck and Germany invented social security. No, once again, it is in England that we can observe the first European welfare state, associated with an individualistic family culture rather than a communitarian or stem-family culture.

Further in the past: Rome's imprint in the countryside

In the second half of the seventeenth century, we can discern the absolute nuclear family in all its essential characteristics, albeit firmly supervised by a village community that claims to be the local incarnation of the state. In the absence of an older sample of lists of inhabitants with details of household structures, we cannot go back further into the history of the English family with any rigour. On the other hand, we can grasp the origin of this extremely powerful and hierarchical village community. In the middle of the Middle Ages, in fact, we find the manor, which itself was most probably an heir to the Roman villa.

163

In the thirteenth century, England was dominated by an agrarian system familiar to mediaevalists, especially to specialists in the central Carolingian area located between the Loire and the Rhine. The village was grouped in the centre of its terroir, which was divided into three zones, each of which was finely divided into strips. Farmers cultivated tenures that included elements in each of the three zones. Part of the terroir was managed directly by the local lord, or by his steward, and the reserve was worked by tenants.[30] Three-year rotation meant that, each year, one of the zones was devoted to winter wheat, another to spring wheat and the third was left fallow to allow the soil to rest. All the peasants submitted to the collective discipline of the triennial rotation, even if their plots together constituted a working of the land held in their own right. Mutual support between neighbours was obviously essential. Rights of pasture and gleaning, belonging to all the members of the community without distinction, completed the strong collective dimension of the system. The local lord exercised specialized economic rights, such as a possible monopoly of the mill, the press or the village oven (the so-called banal rights). The peasants were serfs, attached to the soil, but their status was not that of slaves. They belonged to their lord, but had customary rights, including that of passing on their tenure to one or more of their children.

Max Weber noted a fundamental difference between the mediaeval serf and the ancient slave: the serf had regained the right to marriage and to the family.[31] Weber drew on Roman agronomists in his description of the Roman villa as a real barracks. It was populated by slaves, subhumans deprived of regular family and sexual life. The villa, whose archaeological remains can be found throughout the entire Roman West, was therefore, according to Weber, incapable of ensuring the reproduction of its population. In the absence of a regular supply of slaves provided by war, it was doomed to disappear or mutate into something else. The *Pax Romana*, which dried up the supply of servile labour, itself brought about a crisis and a transformation of the agrarian mode of production. This is Weber's thesis, and it is very convincing.

But Rome left the traces of this basic rural unit throughout Western Europe, and the imprint of the villa was all the more marked when the region concerned was less advanced on the agricultural level at the time of the conquest. Thus, Rome left its mark on the countryside of northern Gaul, western Germany and England.

If serfdom did not restore freedom to farm workers, it did give them back their right to marriage and the family. The serf was not a thing, a piece of movable property, transferable at will. The lord who succeeded the master of the villa, however, exercised a right of petty justice over individuals and families, with the exercise of the death penalty being reserved to the king. There were also seigneurial rights over the family:

164

these concerned the transmission of property and marriage outside the community. Ideally, the seigniory was held in fief from the king, but there were seigniories external to the feudal system, as well as free, allodial tenures.

The English manor

The English manor came a little later and was much more perfect than the French seigniory. Marc Bloch (1886–1944), who attempted to compare the two in 1936, in an unfinished lecture course, defined them as *sovereignty groups*, which combined economic functions and political organization, and were the local building blocks of the feudal system.[32]

The English manor was the most complete way in which the peasantry was divided into political cells. Michael Postan (1899–1981) echoed Frederic William Maitland (1850–1906), one of the great ancestors of the discipline, on this point, suggesting that, in the case of the English manor, 'the estate is the state'.[33] This is one of the reasons for which some of these manors have left a prodigious documentation behind in the shape of manorial court rolls, although it is true that the survival and abundance of these archives is partly due to the absence in English history of an agrarian revolution 'from below'. The manorial court, as the legal regulator of the life of peasants in the Middle Ages, was undoubtedly the original source of the juridical system in England and, beyond that, in the Anglo-American world.

The English thirteenth-century village community already displayed the social stratification of the seventeenth. Postan presents figures that were typical of southern England: 22 per cent big tenants, 33 per cent medium tenants and 43 per cent small tenants.

Such a stratification, albeit shifted downwards, at a time when slaves still existed and the majority of peasants were serfs, is evident in the Domesday Book of 1086, written in Latin by clerics and commissioners from Normandy or Le Mans to describe those Anglo-Saxon-speaking communities that had been subject to French-speaking lords for twenty years at most. Let us start with the oldest traces, the residual ancient categories: 9 per cent slaves (*servi*), 4 per cent freemen (*liberi homines*), 8 per cent sokemen (*sochmanni*, personally free but working a land oppressed by servitude). That left, for the mass of the peasants, descending the social scale: 38 per cent of villeins (*villani*), 32 per cent of bordars and cotters (*bordarii* and *cotarii*). The group of big peasants had not emerged yet from the mass of villeins.

How are we to explain the power, in England, from the twelfth or thirteenth century onwards, of the local collective organization, the existence of a peasant cell with so obvious a dominant upper stratum? The

Norman reorganization of the Anglo-Saxon kingdoms was obviously an essential factor. It was an already conceptualized feudal system that was superimposed on. and transformed, the English rural community. The Anglo-Saxon ruling class was eradicated and primogeniture imposed. The administrative and juridical spirit of the Normans and their idea of the state became part of the way of life. But the Normans in England did not create either the manor or serfdom. I have already suggested as much by referring to Rome: a 'regressive' history cannot stop at the Normans. The big estate, whether Carolingian or Anglo-Saxon, is ultimately similar to the Roman villa, so important in shaping the terroirs of Northwestern Europe. This is obvious in the case of the areas between the Rhine and the Loire, over which there is little argument. In the case of England, the eradication by the conquering Angles, Saxons and Jutes not only of the natives' language, but also of their Britonnic and Latin toponyms, has greatly obscured things. In addition, after 1890, a Germanist school exerted considerable influence in Britain, and endeavoured to blur the obvious facts. The late Victorian fantasy of an England pure of all Latinity, whether Roman or Franco-Norman, then spread.[34]

For my part, I consider that the question had been, so to speak, settled even before it had been raised, by the first great English historian of the mediaeval village, Frederic Seebohm. In his work *The English Village Community*,[35] Seebohm described the ideal type of English rural community in history. He started with Hitchin's terroir, which he could see with his own eyes, and went back to the Roman origins of the system. Seebohm, and not Maitland, is in my opinion the true genius of mediaeval British historiography. Developed fifty years before Marc Bloch's, his 'regressive' and comparative approach is impressive. The contrast he proposes between the English system and the tribal systems – Irish, Welsh or Germanic – transcends banal ethnic categories. Seebohm detects a kinship of terminology and conception only between England and the Germanic peoples of the continent who, within the Empire, had been marked by the imprint of Rome. It should be noted that one of the puerile errors of 'Germanizing' historians is almost always to forget the Roman contribution to the formation of German civilization, in the structuring of villages and cities as much as in the written form given to the language.

Be that as it may, what we discover in the depths of history, in the English manor, under the Norman imprint, is the trace of Rome. The manor is the state because it comes from Rome, which brought to Northwestern Europe all the accumulated knowledge of the Mediterranean and, beyond, Middle Eastern civilizations: writing, the city, the state and, here, more specifically, a collective organization of agriculture. True, the manor was no longer the Roman villa. The central area of land in its control no longer occupied all the terroir and it was no longer cultivated by slaves. But far from stemming from an indefinite tribal past, the simultaneously

166

individual and collective mode of production of the English mediaeval village, organized and political, drew on Rome and its principle of order. The tribal form existed only outside the political, administrative and cultural influence of Rome.

From the undifferentiated nuclear family to the absolute nuclear family

We lack several elements to describe the regional varieties of English rural life with precision, but we are nevertheless able to define an ideal type of the manor, and therefore of the local community in the thirteenth century. But this does not stop the mediaeval family from remaining, for the most part, inaccessible to us.

George Homans, however, has attempted a reconstitution based on the geographical distribution of the rules of inheritance, primogeniture, ultimogeniture or divisibility of inheritance. But no list of inhabitants confirms, as he seems to believe, that primogeniture in the thirteenth century implied an extended family.[36] Given the gradual densification of the household, which generally follows the establishment of a rule of primogeniture, the ultimate nuclearity of the English family suggests, on the contrary, that the systematic co-residence of two adult generations did not exist in the thirteenth century. We are dealing with a nuclear-family type. But can this mediaeval nuclear type be reasonably described, or imagined, as 'absolute', or did it remain 'undifferentiated'? Table 9.1 shows, on the left, the characteristic features of the ideal type of the undifferentiated nuclear family and, on the right, those of the absolute nuclear family observed in England in the second half of the seventeenth century, while in the middle is what we know and do not know about the English family system of the thirteenth century.

Table 9.1 What was the English nuclear family like in the thirteenth century?

Characteristic features	Ideal type of undifferentiated nuclear family	Family in 13th-century England	Absolute nuclear family in 17th-century England
Bilateral kinship	Active	?	Deactivated
Localization of marriage	Flexible	(Flexible)	Flexible
Nuclearity	Tempered	?	Strict
Monogamy	Tempered	Strict	Strict
Inheritance	Flexible	?	Flexible
Exogamy	Tempered	Strict	Strict

- For the Central Middle Ages, we have only two certainties, resulting from the Catholic prohibitions on polygamy and marriage with close kin: the nuclear family of the thirteenth century was already detached from the 'tempered' monogamy and exogamy of the original type.
- We cannot claim that the localization of marriage in relation to parents was flexible, but this is likely since this was still the case in the seventeenth century.
- The uncertainty is even greater for inheritance, flexible in the archaic ideal type as in the modern type. Homans's work certainly exaggerates the influence of the rules of primogeniture, which – as we have seen – in the seventeenth century, again, affected only the well-to-do peasants in an overall flexible system; but his conclusions still force us to leave the box blank.
- We do not know at all whether nuclearity still admitted temporary co-residence in the thirteenth century.
- We do not know whether bilateral kinship was still, as in the undifferentiated ideal type, active, or if it was already deactivated as it would be in the seventeenth century and replaced by the local community, now a functional element of the life cycle, with its pensions for the least wealthy of the elderly. In the thirteenth century, the Protestant transformation had not yet produced its disintegrating effect on kinship.

We have a study by Richard Smith, wonderful but unique in its kind, of sibling functioning in a Suffolk mansion between 1260 and 1320.[37] The interaction of the brothers is here evident, more significant than that between fathers and sons, and Smith emphasizes the predominance of laterality in kinship. It is a central element of the undifferentiated nuclear system, and, on the basis of this single study, we could conclude that, in the thirteenth century, the process of absolute nuclearization did not take place in the Redgrave mansion, which nevertheless provided a strong collective framework, as evidenced by the quality of the documentation it left. But at Redgrave, inheritance was shared – an archaic feature, as in most manor houses in Suffolk. Only Norfolk, immediately to the north, and Kent, south of the Thames, divided with even more enthusiasm legacies on the eastern fringe of England. In the West, Wales fully practised the divisibility of the Gavelkind. At Redgrave, we are on the eastern periphery of the central area covered by the ideal type of the thirteenth-century rural community. Nothing indicates, then, that this manor was representative. In fact, it is the converse that seems true. Indeed, the Domesday Book reveals that in 1086, two centuries earlier, Suffolk was highly atypical: 35 per cent *freemen* (English average 4 per cent), 5 per cent *sokemen* (average 8 per cent), 4 per cent *slaves* (average 9 per cent), 14 per cent *villeins* (average 38 per cent), 30 per cent bordars and cottars (average 32 per cent).[38] We are here in East Anglia, the point of arrival, as its name suggests, of the Angles.

What the highly active lateral kinship of the Redgrave mansion might prove is that at this point of arrival the 'Germanist' model applies, albeit with unforeseen consequences for its supporters. Having settled in great numbers, the theory goes, the Germanic invaders actually replaced the populations rather than taking control of existing mansions and serfs, hence the very large number of free men. But what was then left of Germanity was, ironically, the banality of a living kinship, of close brothers, something which the Anglo-Saxon royal genealogies had already brought into being and which would bring the Germanic peoples in question closer to the Celts and Slavs of Antiquity, and the Irish and Poles in the early nineteenth century.

Of the central zone, covered in the thirteenth century by open fields and grouped villages, and occupied by serfs theoretically transmitting their tenure by primogeniture, we can say nothing. I doubt whether we will ever be able to fully reconstruct the thirteenth-century family structure here at the heart of England. At this stage we are still faced with our dilemma: the strength of the local collective, the manor, suggests that an absolute nuclearization of families in this very ancient period was possible. However, so many major social changes took place between 1350 and 1650, in areas so close to family life – legal, economic, religious, demographic, educational, judicial changes – that the principle of probability would lead us to date the appearance of the absolute nuclear family to later than the thirteenth century. The years 1550–1650 would seem to have been crucial in such a process.

The transformation of the years 1550–1650

Let us set up a simplified sequence of the elements that may have conditioned the evolution of the family in English history: the weakening of serfdom began in the twelfth century, but a temporary rebirth occurred in the thirteenth, and its liquidation came about only after the great plague of 1348, which killed between 40 and 45 per cent of the population but raised wages and led to the first complete privatization of some farms. At this early stage of enclosures, cropland was converted to pasture.[39] The disappearance of serfdom, and of the rights that came with it, suggests the possibility of an increase in the mobility of the individuals with respect to their villages, and perhaps also of a distancing with respect to their kinship.

But the years 1550–1650 were, in England as in all Europe, the period when the great mental change occurred. This was when everything shifted. Led by Henry VIII, England separated from Rome between 1532 and 1536. The Protestant Reformation did not really have any effect, transforming people's minds, until the reign of Elizabeth I, which began in 1559. The history of the arts, literature and the sciences marks out the Elizabethan era as the moment of England's cultural take-off.

In the reign of Henry VIII, however, the freedom to make a will had been formalized. In 1540, it became possible to freely dispose of two-thirds of land under a 'military' obligation (the fief), and of the totality of other land. In the English Revolution, the idea of military tenure became frankly anachronistic and the Long Parliament established the complete freedom to dispose of one's property in 1645. The aristocracy, however, protected its children from this English freedom by the procedure of entails, according to which a primogeniture not subject to the freedom of individuals could be maintained over more than two generations.

From the confused and simultaneous mass of changes, one draws the feeling that an absolute nuclear family emerged between 1550 and 1650. Here we can take advantage of the considerable progress that has been made in quantitative history. Tony Wrigley and Roger Schofield have, as we said earlier, shown that there was an increase in the age at marriage, and a rise from 8 per cent to 24 per cent in the number of individuals who did not marry between the generation born around 1555 and that born around 1605.[40] This was, seen from England, the emergence of the Western European marriage model as understood by John Hajnal, described in Chapter 5.

The family can only have been transformed by this. Late marriage was, inter alia, a result of teenagers leaving their families to work on other farms than their parents'. Meanwhile, great numbers of people never married and were thus outside the reproductive cycle.

Other profound social indicators point to a change of mentality in England in the years 1550–1650, which it would be hard to believe had no relation to family life.

David Cressy observes that literacy was taking off among nobles, big farmers, tradesmen and artisans between 1530–50 and 1600, though it did not at this point reach the lower rural categories in any great numbers.[41] This was, of course, the effect of the Protestant Reformation, which required direct access to the Scriptures for everyone. The rural elites immediately hastened, in this period, to endeavour to improve the manners of the uneducated section of the population. Moralism and sternness imbued the social and political life of the time, which would give the West the word 'puritan'.

In an article on interpersonal violence between 1300 and 1800, Lawrence Stone spoke of a feverish outbreak at the end of the sixteenth century, within a general movement of decreasing homicide identified by T. R. Gurr. Stone focused on a general surge of what Durkheim would have called individualism, including the breaking of social bonds, and the isolation and anger of individuals.[42] Starting with the example of the village of Terling in Essex, where the increase of interpersonal conflicts in the courts led Wrightson and Levine to conclude that 'something' was happening, Stone generalizes:

> That 'something' was affecting not merely this single village but the society as a whole, as is shown by evidence for all the counties in the Home Circuit. Other indicators of social disintegration and anomy in late sixteenth- and early seventeenth-century England are a high bastardy rate, a high level of witchcraft accusations between villagers, a staggeringly high rate of denunciations of neighbours for sexual deviance, and a high rate of suits for slander of all kinds by neighbours (mostly women). What all this suggests is that between 1560 and 1620 there was an abrupt rise in a wide variety of indicators of social anomy and of a breakdown of consensual community methods of dealing with conflict.[43]

Internalization in individualism

If we looked only at the history of the West, at the sea fringe of Eurasia, we might characterize this phase of the years 1550–1650 in England as that of a 'rise of individualism'. In a local, restricted sense, the expression is perfectly acceptable. The broad kinship network was flexible but had nonetheless broken down and been replaced by the state, embodied locally by a community capable of caring for orphans and old people. And thus the transition from undifferentiation to absolute nuclearity might, in a way, be interpreted as a 'rise in individualism'.

But this expression poses problems as soon as we try to apply it to places where the historical tendency at that time was simultaneously in the other direction – towards an increase in the density of the family system, in other words where the constraint of an individual's closest relatives was most condensed around him or her. It becomes, for example, inoperative beyond the Rhine, the Massif Central and the Alps – everywhere, in fact, where there was during this period a rise in the power of dense and essentially anti-individualistic family structures, both in the German and Occitan stem family and in the communitarian model of central Italy.

I will keep the word 'individualism' for the study of family systems and instead use that of 'individuation' to describe the transformation of the modal personality over the years 1550–1650. The distinction is particularly important when we examine regions where concrete history simultaneously reveals a process of individuation and a fall in family individualism, as in Germany from the Reformation. The classic German opposition between the free inner man and the servile outer man, and more generally the freedom/servitude duality of Lutheran rhetoric, is a good illustration of this complex movement of individuation taking place in the ebb of individualism.

Conceptual prudence in the use of the word individualism is also essential in the case of England. The nuclear family became purer there, and a rise in family individualism can certainly be noted. The Protestant Reformation also produced, as in Germany, its effects of individuation. But in England, as much as in Germany and Sweden, Protestant interiority was accompanied by an intensification of communitarian control over morality and conduct. As I noted in the conclusion of my chapter on the great mental transformation, the Protestant surplus of individuation had its counterpart in a greater hold of the local community and the state over the individual.

Family freedom and political domination in England

We can now situate England in the development of Eurasia, geographically and historically.

England received agriculture from the Middle East around 4000 BCE. The Roman conquest and then the Norman invasion formed its rural cells and their relationship to the state.

The undifferentiated nuclear family of the 'barbarians', Celts or Germans, was transformed quite late into the absolute nuclear family. The bilateral kinship system was deactivated, and the solidarity between brothers and sisters ceased to be an essential component in the functioning of local groups. The nuclearity of the household was thus radicalized. Finally, the purified type of the English absolute nuclear family appeared, and it was hostile to the co-residence of generations.

But certain of the fundamental values of the undifferentiated nuclear family remained visible in the absolute nuclear type. The use of the will was a formalized version of the original undifferentiation. The absolute nuclear family is neither egalitarian nor frankly inegalitarian. We must, however, note the importance, in England, of the concept of noble primogeniture brought over by the Franco-Norman aristocracy. True, the ideal of primogeniture did not lead to the emergence of the stem family. But we can interpret many of the characteristics of the absolute nuclear family as resulting either from an accepted influence or from a rejection.

On the side of positive action: the vertical principle of the stem family, which insists on the link between father and son, and separates brothers, inevitably played a role in the disappearance of lateral solidarity between domestic groups, a move away from the undifferentiated nuclear family.

On the side of rejection: the stem family tends to gradually establish the constraint of a cohabitation of the father and his adult son. We can see the avoidance of cohabitation – the central feature of the English family – as an application of Georges Devereux's principle of negative dissociative acculturation, an inversion of the proposed or imposed norm.

The historical emergence of the absolute nuclear family mainly reveals how the latter cannot function in a vacuum. It forms, with a strong rural community that is able to make the maintenance of orphans and the elderly a matter of taxation, a functional whole. England seems to have invented the welfare state at the same time as the absolute nuclear family. The power of local cells is part of the English anthropological matrix, with the additional paradox of a local collective that allows for extreme mobility of men and women between communities.

This individualistic family type would never have worked in England without the existence of a superior authority, which can be understood as 'Norman power', 'aristocracy', 'gentry' or 'peasant oligarchy'. English individualism manifests itself in the context of domination. It is caught up in a social verticality. We will now see what happened on the other side of the Atlantic, where the American Revolution consciously rejected this vertical dimension and attempted to eradicate the principle of domination.

— 10 —

HOMO AMERICANUS

The American family of the seventeenth or eighteenth century can be described as nuclear, but the adjective 'absolute', applied in the previous chapter to the English family of the same period, is less suitable. Those who founded the North American colonies were, of course, British: they landed in the New World with their value systems and their forms of social organization. David Hackett Fischer has even shown that traces of the original regional cultures of the first immigrants can be found in the differences between the various colonies – East Anglia in Massachusetts, southern England in Virginia, the northern Midlands in Pennsylvania, the north of Britain in the Back Country – though he is forcing things a bit when he attempts to outline the various nuances of family organization.[1] But still, in the colonies, social organization did indeed mutate, and the family with it.

In the South, slavery polarized society. In the North, the abundance of land meant that the bulk of the population became independent peasants, and the family farm predominated. Outside the world of the planters in the South, differences in wealth between farmers, though not completely insignificant, were marginal compared to the situation in the English countryside of the same time. But right from the start, colonial America never identified with an ideal of individual freedom: everywhere indentured servants, men and women, paid for their passage across the Atlantic through years of contractual servitude.

The history of seventeenth-century Puritan settlers shows that the English sense of the local collective was transported from one side of the Atlantic to the other. However, in America, the sense of religious affiliation, voluntary in the case of radical Protestantism, replaced the vertical cell structure inherited from the mediaeval English manor. The model of a stratified local community, run by an oligarchy of better-off peasants who administered to the village the authority of the gentry (which itself controlled the country) did not apply to New England. As Kenneth

174

Lockridge suggested, an initial oligarchy did exist, but it was a moral oligarchy, defined by membership of an elite of saints, in accordance with the Calvinist doctrine of predestination and grace.[2] Even though they did not in the least believe in the equality of men – some are elected, others damned – the inhabitants of the first rural communities founded in New England participated en masse in the decision-making process. The sense of the collective found among the first Americans was just as strong as among the rural English, but it was of a different nature, more horizontal, less vertical.

A substantially enlarged family regained its importance. American economic and social life excluded the possibility of pure nuclearity. The big rural farm estates which had ensured a mass circulation of servants and the early exit of young people from their original families no longer existed. The rule of primogeniture among big farmers imploded and was replaced by a 'preferential partibility'. The very free use of the will or testament, on the other hand, was a perfectly English feature. Parents strove to distribute their assets while ensuring the viability of the farms. The system was certainly not egalitarian, but it meant that a large number of the offspring could be maintained on site.

Paradoxically, in fact, the population of the New World was initially less mobile than that of the Old World.[3] Some children did of course head off to clear the land. But for the most part, in the seventeenth century, local communities were islands of survival in a hostile world. Their goal was self-preservation rather than conquest. From the middle of the eighteenth century, local pockets of overpopulation appeared; this resulted in an increase in rural density and a socioeconomic polarization.

In colonial America, nuclear families, as Philip Greven has shown, were more often extended than in England, except perhaps in the slave-owning South where the big farm estate produced its usual nuclearizing effects.[4] To reach this conclusion, Greven, in his very fine study of the community of Andover, Massachusetts, compared the number of families registered – nuclear families – with the number of houses. He did not find enough houses. So some must have contained several families. Greven sketched out the typical 'patriarchal' family of the seventeenth century, which allowed fathers to exercise long-lasting control over their sons. Sons, meanwhile, had to house their mothers when they were widowed. Around the family, the kinship network tended to reconstitute itself because the households of fathers, sons and brothers remained close. The age at marriage was high, as in Europe: 26.7 years for the second generation of men, compared with 26–28 years in England at the same time, a phenomenon that Greven rightly interprets as a sign of the control of fathers over their sons' marriages.[5]

Inheritance, though not egalitarian, was still burdened with obligations towards brothers and sisters who were less well provided for, as

175

shown by Toby Ditz. Girls were essentially excluded from inheriting the land. Ditz called the inheritance practices in Connecticut communities 'extended cognate inheritance practices'.[6] These again allowed for cases of joint property shared between several brothers, most often on a temporary basis. This lateralization shows that, in the field of kinship as in that of communitarian functioning, a certain horizontality had again made an appearance.

The model presented by Mary Ryan for a slightly later period, a little further west, where New York State approaches Lakes Ontario and Erie, verifies in detail this model in which a pioneering family maintained both intergenerational links and links between brothers and sisters, and practised a functional separation of the sexes.[7]

The American family, then, was not at first an intensified version of the English absolute nuclear family, but quite the opposite: a very attenuated version of it, presenting in every area a reversion towards the undifferentiated nuclear family, visible in the extensions of the domestic group, the greater divisibility of inheritance, and the return to interactions between brothers and sisters. The situation in those colonial times was very far removed from the current American model of maximum deactivation of kinship ties.

It was also far removed from the current position of women in American society. All observers, including Tocqueville, noted the high status of women in the period when America was founded. Right from the start, the wives of the Puritan peasants were respected and active in religious and social life. But they were excluded from the inheritance of land and houses, whatever sect they belonged to, Congregationalist or Quaker.[8]

The sexual division of economic and social life was just as rigid among the original Protestant Americans as it was among hunter-gatherers. And it seems that the distribution of goods, initially unfavourable to American women, must be interpreted in terms of the original sexual division of labour found with *Homo sapiens* rather than as the effect of an early introduction of patrilineality. As T. Ditz has shown, the male advantage was not intended to define a lineage and so cannot be interpreted as the first step towards a patrilineal system.[9]

The fact remains that, in terms of inheritance, the initial status of American women was much lower than that of the peasants of the Paris Basin at the same time, since the latter inherited just as their brothers did. But the French system was not natural or original, since it derived, after a long history, from the sexual egalitarianism of the Lower Roman Empire as formalized in the Code of Justinian.

The settlers who founded New England had brought with them their holy book, the Bible, and they could identify with the Hebrew people even more than did the European Calvinists. They settled in their promised land, which they had to wrest from the local pagans, the Indians. In all their actions, they tried to reproduce the ancient history of Israel. Colonial onomastics is a succession of Benjamins, Jacobs, Solomons, Ezras, Sarahs, Rachels, Esthers and Rebeccas. The Episcopalians, who lived in the southern areas of New England and Pennsylvania, were also Protestants of the Anglican tradition, readers of a certain version of the Bible.

The Bible is a fantasized family story, as we have seen, but we must still wonder whether the distortions suffered by the English nuclear family during the crossing of the Atlantic owed something to it. As discussed in Chapter 4, the Bible was the unfulfilled dream of an undifferentiated nuclear-family culture. In it we find the obsessive notion of patrilineal primogeniture, but this continues to be opposed by younger sons and mothers. Applied in colonial America, the Bible was able to support a dream of patrilineal primogeniture in a society operating on the norm of a family that was no longer all that nuclear. Paradoxically, the coexistence of the Bible and an imperfect nuclear family in America backs up my vision of an ancient Israel combining 'undifferentiated nuclear family' and 'biblical stem family'.

Indeed, one cannot rule out a temporary biblical influence in America's slight reversion of the English absolute nuclear family to undifferentiation. The temporary reactivation of the kinship network, described by P. Greven and T. Ditz, is quite compatible with the vision of family relationships found in the Bible. But the erosion of the Puritan utopia, with its ideal communities founded in a savage world, inevitably led to the elimination of this factor of undifferentiation and restored the English absolute nuclear model. We can date this process.

The return to pure nuclearity

P. J. Greven's study of Andover allows us to date the emergence of the pure American nuclear model (just about visible in the third generation but clearly so in the fourth) to between 1720 and 1770. Men's age at marriage then fell to 25.3 compared with 27.1 for their fathers.[10] Geographic mobility increased, but did not reach the levels of the English parishes of Clayworth and Cogenhoe in the seventeenth century.[11] Greven observes a subsequent dispersion of nuclear families throughout New England.[12]

Further west, in Oneida County, the transition came later, as Mary Ryan's studies have shown. In fact, the whole sequence – reinforcement of the family then return to a pure nuclearity – was out of step in this region, which was still, around 1790, a frontier. Between 1800 and 1865, equality between girls and boys when it came to inheritance was finally

177

achieved.[13] Between 1850 and 1865, the frequency of family economic partnerships fell.[14]

The westward shift of the 'frontier', which accelerated in the nineteenth century, thus produced a continuous wave of the same anthropological cycle: each complexification of the family was followed, after the stabilization of the community, by a gradual reaffirmation of the nuclear model. The economic and social context of this ebb and flow remained that of small individual businesses, since the industrial revolution occurred much later in the United States than in Great Britain. Rostow dates the American take-off to 1840.[15] In the early nineteenth century, four-fifths of Americans were still self-employed; by 1870, the figure was one-third.[16] Industrial society and mass wage-earning would ensure a return to the English nuclear model.

The absolute nuclear family as an ideal type: 1950–1970

Only indeed in the twentieth century did the American family reach a state of nuclearity whose perfection came close to that of England. According to Steven Ruggle, the percentage of households with relatives living with the married couple fell in the United States from 16 per cent in 1900 to 12 per cent in 1963 and 5 per cent in 1973.[17] In these figures, we hear the echo of a march to nuclear perfection. The triumph of wage labour loosened secondary family ties – with adult siblings or with cousins – and seemed to recreate the environment, ideal for the flourishing of the absolute nuclear family, which had existed in the English village community of the seventeenth century. Capitalist enterprise replaced the big farm as a provider of wages. The local community provided schooling rather than poor aid. But social security, set up by Roosevelt's New Deal, provided pensions to the elderly. In the United States of the 1950s and 1970s, the state contributed, as it had done in Tudor and Stuart England, to the perfection of the nuclear family.

The modal relationship between men and women at this time appeared to be returning to the original *Homo sapiens* type, with specialization in equality. The husband worked outside the home; his wife managed the house, helped by her brand-new electrical equipment. This specialization led to the post-war baby boom and a rise in the total birth rate to 3.1 children per woman in 1950, and 3.65 in 1960. It had fallen to 2.30 in 1940. The rate of illegitimate births reached a historic low of 4 per cent in 1950 for the whole of American society, falling to only 1.8 per cent in its White heartlands.

The years 1950–70 saw the apogee of the absolute nuclear family in the United States: the conjugal couple, isolated from its kinship network, predominated there more than ever before.

178

We will see below that the neoliberal re-examination of the Rooseveltian welfare state is today contributing to a revival of mutual aid and a new denuclearization of the model, a phenomenon whose equivalent can be observed in England.

But on the whole, through the ups and downs of the centuries and the decades, America turned out in the long term to be less dogmatic than England in its adherence to the nuclear individualism of the family.

In the early 2000s, a study measured the proportion of individuals in the United States and the United Kingdom who had spent part of their lives in a three-generation household.[18] In the United States, this proportion was 31 per cent for Hispanics, 30 per cent for Asians, and only 18 per cent for individuals classified as White. This rate of 18 per cent, however, is not insignificant: the 'Whites' of the United Kingdom had found themselves in this situation in only 6 per cent of cases. Finally, there is one important difference I will come back to: the gap in family behaviour between Blacks and Whites in the United States. For Blacks, the proportion of individuals who had spent part of their lives in a three-generation household was 34 per cent, nearly twice the frequency observed for Whites. However, we should not draw on this gap to assume there was a specific 'Black culture': the rate for Blacks in the United Kingdom was only 7 per cent, almost identical to that for Whites – i.e., 6 per cent. The 'Black' family of the United States is truly American.

Nuclear ideal and religious revivals

A moderate religious revival accompanied the development of the American nuclear family. There was a rise in religious practice between 1940 and 1960. The rate of attendance at Sunday services rose from 39 to 48 per cent over this period. These figures, derived from opinion polls, must still be viewed with caution as they exaggerate actual practice: attendance was actually less than half those figures when checked by observations at places of worship.[19] So the data simultaneously record the rates of religious practice and of hypocrisy. But the upward trend of the 1940s–60s is indisputable.[20]

Membership in a church or sect in the United States, a country of weak vertical state integration, is an important element in horizontal social integration. Belonging to a localized religious group can be an indispensable element of security for the individual and his or her nuclear family. And the residual religiosity of the United States, stronger than that of Northwestern Europe, undoubtedly results more from the weakness of the state than from any particular predisposition on the part of the inhabitants of the New World to metaphysical speculation. The modern God of the American is not very demanding and very moderately repressive; he is no longer the God of the Bible and does not emerge from a terrible transcendence, nor does he appear as a particularly menacing authority figure. Be that as it may, the rise in religious practice in the 1940s–60s marked an intensification of local community integration at a time when the middle classes were flourishing in suburban spaces. Thus the somewhat unthreatening character of the God of America should not prevent us from taking him seriously on a sociological level: again, we need to draw a comparison, this time between the American suburbs after the Second World War and the strong English village community of the seventeenth century, structured by the Protestant religion; this community, too, was necessary for the proper functioning of the absolute nuclear family.

Let us note, finally, that in twentieth-century America, as in the seventeenth-century English villages of Cogenhoe and Clayworth, the power of the local community did not rule out an exceptional geographic mobility.[21] In the United States, the period of nuclearization of the family was also marked by an increase in geographical mobility: the proportion of the population moving from one American state to another over the previous five years had increased from 6 per cent in 1900 to 13 per cent in 1950.[22] But neighbourhood conformism and control of life by the local community were much more characteristic of American life in this period than was geographical mobility.

The moderate effect of immigration

The mass immigration of the nineteenth and beginning of the twentieth century brought to the United States men and families whose values were not those of the nuclear family: Germans, Swedes and Norwegians of the West carried the values of the stem family, while the Irish and Jews brought the values of their undifferentiated nuclear models.[23] Southern Italian families were egalitarian nuclear. In all these groups, the shock of immigration led in the first place to a reaffirmation of family solidarities, then, over three or four generations, to their eradication and to an alignment of customs with the standard American type, itself in the process of conforming again to the standard English model of the absolute nuclear family.[24]

But mass immigration distorted the English family model by giving children not just autonomy, but real centrality. The British anthropologist Geoffrey Gorer grasped this phenomenon in 1948, in a humorous essay on the American national character.[25] He shows that the process of assimilation produced, in each of the family histories, a phase during which the child could speak English as fluently as any American ('the all American child'), while the father was still hampered by his imperfect

180

control of the language. The son then became the family's cultural reference point.[26] The anthropologist sees this as a collapse of paternal power.

But he goes further. The fall of the father's authority, in his view, explains the rise of the maternal role, and of women in general, whether they be the mother, the elder sister, or the schoolteacher. Gorer thus sees America as a 'motherland'.[27] He was not the only one in those days to attribute an exaggerated power to the American woman, guilty, according to this British scholar, of having imposed that bewildering phenomenon, the prohibition of alcohol. Others have attributed acts of even greater wickedness to the American woman. In the aftermath of the Second World War, local psychiatry suggested that too great maternal power was likely to cause schizophrenia in the child;[28] some authors admittedly pointed out, to qualify the correlations which had been calculated, that working-class milieus were overrepresented among schizophrenics. This finding, however, does little to alter the terms of the debate if one takes into account the classic matriarchal deviation of the working-class world.

This theme of the schizophrenia-generating mother spread during the same period in which the conjugal family so dear to Talcott Parsons attained, in the real world of social practices, its apogee. The sexual specialization of functions was then at a maximum level, with mothers who completely ruled the roost.

It was then that the theme of the overbearing Jewish mother appeared in America, a theme which had no precedent in the traditions of Central Europe.[29] It bore witness to the distortion suffered by the Jewish family system in the United States. This family system was indeed, like other immigrant family types, liquidated, since within three generations the American Jewish family had abandoned the importance attached to close and distant kinship, i.e. its undifferentiated dimension.

Since 1965, the resumption of immigration has reactivated the well-known mechanism of a temporary complexification of family structures, since Asian and Hispanic immigrants bring with them a variety of family systems all denser than the absolute nuclear family. We can predict, in their cases, a repetition of the assimilative sequence, including nuclearization, the centrality of the child and the rise in women's status, with the proviso that the context is less favourable: in the central White world, the decline of the welfare state, and economic difficulties, have led to a certain strengthening of family interactions.

Exogamy in the United States

In America, a slight reversion to undifferentiation has also affected the marriage pattern. In the seventeenth century, the whole of Western

Europe moved away from the original type of *Homo sapiens* with the existence of a large proportion of individuals destined to remain single. America, spacious enough to be liberated from this Malthusian model, quickly returned to the natural model of marriage as an institution that could be taken for granted. In 1860, for example, the proportion of unmarried women at age 50, which reached 12 per cent in England and 13 per cent in France, had dropped to 6 per cent in the United States.

The power of Christian exogamy, however, has never lost its grip in America. Puritans, like all Protestants in Europe, theoretically loosened the Catholic ban on kinship marriage and reverted to the biblical authorization of marriage between cousins. But they did so without enthusiasm. It was in the Episcopalian South (the Anglican Church of America), among slave-owning planters on the eve of the Civil War, that marriage between cousins was most frequent: 10 per cent for first and second cousins in North Carolina.[30] I doubt whether rates elsewhere rose in any way compared to Europe.

On the contrary, between 1840 and 1920, the United States witnessed a revival of the revulsion against marriage between cousins, something which had no equivalent in the Old World. Repressive legislation contrary to the Bible was then put in place, an innovation whose origin can be traced back to the new western states, with Kansas in the lead. Martin Ottenheimer attributes this new insistence on pure exogamy to the fear of a return of natural barbarism. This is rather amusing, if I might say so, when we remember that exogamy is natural and in no way an achievement of civilization. However, we here observe only fluctuations at the margin. The overall marriage rate between first cousins probably never exceeded 1 per cent in the United States – and it fell to 0.01 per cent in the 1950s.[31] Such a rate includes the eradication of marriage between cousins in the Jewish population.

Homo americanus, Homo sapiens

We can now situate *Homo americanus* in the general history of the species *Homo sapiens*. The English absolute nuclear matrix of the seventeenth century was itself still close to the original type, in its bilaterality, its nuclearization and its exogamy, and its absence of the rule of egalitarian or frankly inegalitarian inheritance. This same English matrix departed from the original type in its prohibition of temporary co-residence of different generations and, like the whole of the Christian world, in its absolute taboo on marriage between cousins. *Homo americanus*, at first, was rather closer to the primordial form in that it relaxed the ban on co-residence; it later moved away from it, but we have the sense that it always kept open the possibility of drawing near to it again.

In fact, if we do not just define the initial matrix by the family, but include the structuring of the local group, American culture differs fundamentally from its English matrix in its absence of a strong principle of verticality – in the disappearance of a social or state keystone, a transcendent element that dictates social organization and mentalities. The American Revolution suppressed allegiance to the king and what remained of primogeniture; it abolished the regulation of local communities by the state and its Church. In America, the Protestant religion, common to all the English who had founded the new country, was fragmented into sects. To bilaterality, nuclearity and exogamy, America thus added a return to the horizontality of the primordial human group.

The groups of hunter-gatherers who originally comprised the type of *Homo sapiens* were also governed by a principle of horizontality. They rubbed shoulders, cooperated, clashed and exchanged spouses in the absence of any vertical principle of organization, whether verticality is seen in terms of stable social differentiation, of state, or of a religious transcendence common to a set of local groups.

We can, at this stage, begin to approach the American paradox.

If we look at education, technology and economics, America led the world between 1900 and 2000. But beyond this modernity, familiar to everyone, we now know that the anthropological background of America, even more than that of England, must be regarded as primitive, or, to use a less emotionally charged word, primordial. Armed with this new interpretative key, we will finally be able to understand, and perhaps even accept, many of the disturbing elements of the American social mechanism, which in reality express only the persistence across the Atlantic of a world closer than ours to the origins of humanity. The genius of America is that of the original *Homo sapiens*, which, as we have to admit, did great things.

Let us have a look at some of these features.

Geographical mobility, so characteristic of the American population, which moves from state to state at a rate that would be inconceivable in Europe, was typical of hunter-gatherers. It is a common mistake to think of the stability of peasant populations as the ancient foundation of humanity. In actual fact, agriculture itself, admittedly invented thanks to the sedentarization of various human groups in the Middle East, China, Central and South America, Africa and New Guinea, was carried across the planet by peoples who had returned to the original mobility of *Homo sapiens*. Many human groups, indeed, have long continued to practise shifting cultivation on a slash-and-burn basis.

The high level of dependence on natural resources that has characterized the American economy since the beginning, the tendency to squander soil, oil, water and forests, is reminiscent of the model of predation that characterized the original human beings. The patient improvement of a farmland, as well as the care taken over the renewal of resources, were innovations associated in history with the emergence of family types that made the continuity of lineages possible.

The physical violence that characterizes America is itself an archaism that simply prolongs the primitive human model. In the case of European populations, we now know exactly when physical confrontation was, for the most part, eliminated from interpersonal relationships. Homicide rates plummeted between 1600 and 1650. This was the period in which both age at marriage and numbers of unmarried people rose, together with the absolutist state. Robert Muchembled has shown how the monarchical state, long tolerant of private violence and inclined to hand out pardons to the guilty, finally claimed for itself a monopoly of violence.[32] The 'age of torture', as he put it, was the period of transition during which the state staged its own capacity for violence so as to forbid its subjects from resorting to violence. In England too, despite some peculiarities, the rate of homicide collapsed between 1500 and 1700.[33]

Starting out from mediaeval homicide rates of between twenty and one hundred per 100,000 inhabitants, the rate across Western Europe now fell below one per 100,000. By 1930, the homicide rate per 100,000 population was only 0.5 in England, 0.9 in Sweden, 0.9 in France, 1.9 in Germany, 2.6 in Italy, 0.9 in Spain, and 0.7 in Japan, which had a European relation to the state. It was 1.9 in Canada, which had come into being by rejecting American freedom, but it was still 8.8 in the United States.[34] America has remained more violent throughout its history, as is shown by the statistics (not easy to obtain, it is true). Between 1900 and the Second World War, the American homicide rate increased from six per 100,000 to almost ten and dropped to just over four in the 1950s to rise again to ten in the years 1970–80, falling back to five today.[35] American violence is simply an archaism, preserved by the imperfections in the state monopoly of legitimate violence and by the absence of a principle of social verticality – in short by the maintenance of a certain anthropological horizontality. The private possession of firearms perpetuates the usual carrying of knives in mediaeval Europe.

The mystery of the modal relationship between men and women in the United States can also be solved. A curious mixture of machismo and feminism, male sabre-rattling and feminine independence characterizes American culture. In more neutral language, we should describe it instead as a simultaneous affirmation of masculine and feminine roles in American life and as a structural tension in the relations between the two sexes that goes back well before the current evolution towards feminism. Before seeking the emancipation of women in history, as we shall be doing in the next chapter, we can already identify in the depths of America the perpetuation of the sexual division of labour which characterized the hunter-gatherers, combining as it did men's specialization in hunting with women's specialization in gathering and children's upbringing. However, we should here follow Gorer in accepting an initial feminist deviation caused by immigration, which has produced sons who are better adapted than their fathers to their environment – as in the aforementioned mechanism.

The most central and burning paradox of American culture remains, however, that of a modernity that constantly fails to overcome a dualist organization based on a contrast between the categories 'White and Black'. Once again, identifying *Homo americanus* as close to *Homo sapiens* allows us to escape any misunderstanding, whether scientific or moral. Indeed, what America is going through here is probably only the effect of the original mental state of *Homo sapiens*, as it had been perceived and defined by Adam Ferguson in the eighteenth century.[36] Following his lead, I noted (see the end of Chapter 3 above) that a human group is always defined in relation to other human groups. There is no absolute 'identity'. In the Old World (at least before the construction of Europe), the state principle of domination and organization into nations had tamed (or masked, or transferred) the application of this basic principle. Within each nation, the state has defined an equivalence between individuals, while it has designated and placed outside of itself some Other necessary for the self-definition of the group: the English, the German, the French, the Russian . . . In America, the state has not been able to do this; horizontality still exists, the nation is not defined by threatening nations on its borders. The Other, however, must exist if We are to exist. So the Other will be inside us. The Indians have been eliminated. So the Other will be Black.

Homo americanus: the Black version

Because this Other is inside, and has coexisted with the White We since the beginning, its culture is only American.

With Black Americans, we come up against a rare case of discontinuity in the history of family structures. As Franklin Frazier has shown in *The Black Family in America*, where he describes the difficulties in the emergence of a stable Black family organization between 1650 and 1930, the traditions of the slaves deported from Africa were methodically crushed in the United States.[37]

It was a political decision to mix ethnic groups and break up the embryos of family nuclei. In the New World, slaves were deprived of the right to a family, similar to the situation for slaves in the Roman Empire analysed by Weber. Black Americans have lost the memories of their family histories. Only a few families seem to have held on to a few myths about princely genealogies, though these seem to have been invented very late. On the other hand, any such transmission would, contrary to what we observe, have given a patrilineal bias to Black American family culture, since the majority of slaves were purchased in patrilineal West Africa. Admittedly, patrilineality is weaker on the African coast, as we have seen, but many of the individuals deported were captured inland, in highly patrilineal territory, before being transferred as livestock across the Atlantic. In certain West Indian islands, such as Haiti, these patrilineal traits have managed to survive.

The destruction of the Black family was first and foremost that of the masculine and paternal role, of which the genetic composition of Black Americans still preserves a trace. On the plantations, the White masters did not hesitate, by rape or the seduction of domination, to have sex with Black women. This is why modern genetics has measured a quarter of European descent among Black Americans, but it has also found that the male European component was 19 per cent and the female component only 5 per cent.[38] Sexual relations between Black men and White women with the quasi-servile status of 'indentured servant' were certainly not negligible, but they were overwhelmed in the statistics by Black women being used sexually by their White owners.

Frazier was caricatured later in the 1965 Moynihan Report. But he gave an objective and nuanced picture of race and family relations in American history. In his work, we find not only the theme of the predominance of women and the importance of grandmothers, i.e. an implicit matrilineal lineage in the Black family, but also the theme of the gradual fraught emergence of the status of husband and father, constantly threatened by social and economic upsets, by the abolition of slavery and then by the great migration to the North.

The attachment to religion and the Bible, so strong among Black Americans, can be partly seen as the effect of this effort to stabilize the family and the masculine role. The Bible is a patrilineal dream, a counterbalance to bilaterality, even among Jews and White Americans, and can serve as an ideological backdrop to a reconstruction of the masculine role.

If there is a prejudice in Frazier, it is the evolutionary schema leading from the matriarchal stage to the patriarchal stage, a cliché of the anthropologists and ideologues of his time derived from Bachofen, Morgan and Engels. On the other hand, Frazier achieves maximum originality when he defines class differences in the Black community. Two of his last chapters are entitled 'Brown middle-class' and 'Black proletariat'.

In Europe, industrial life led rather, among the working class, to more feminine power, to a matriarchal trend that is described in all the monographs, including the classic *Family and Kinship in East London* by Michael Young and Peter Willmott.[39] But in the United States, industry, which very early on produced a prosperous 'middle class', has instead been a chance for Blacks to stabilize the masculine role. A source of stable income gave the husband and father the authority needed to balance a nuclear family.

Thus, towards 1950, at the height of American industrial prosperity, there was not only a White world adhering to the model of an absolute nuclear family separating masculine and feminine roles, but also a Black family which, although bearing the trace of its initial matriarchal distortion caused by White domination, seemed to be converging with the White family model. Masculine instability certainly existed, since 18 per cent of Black women were divorced or separated from their husbands, compared to only 4 per cent of White women; but conversely this figure also gives us 82 per cent of Black women who had a stable husband.[40] We will see later how the destruction of the American working-class world by globalization has hit the Black American family hard. Remaining faithful to Frazier, we will then distinguish the distinct social classes that today constitute the Black American 'community'. At a deeper level, we will see how the matriarchal evolution of the American White family itself has destabilized the Black family in working-class circles.

Still, at all stages of its history, it must be emphasized, the Black family of the United States is only one of the components of American history. Blacks are only a dominated variety of *Homo americanus*.

We are now better equipped intellectually to understand why America tirelessly creates among us Europeans a dual and contradictory perception of modernity and primitiveness at one and the same time. We keep telling ourselves: they're ahead of us but so unsophisticated; we are thus unwittingly on the verge of stumbling on a simple truth.

They're ahead *because* they are unsophisticated. It was the original *Homo sapiens* who succeeded as an animal species, wandering around, experimenting, with men and women living in a state of tension and complementarity. It is Middle Eastern, Chinese and Indian patrilineal societies that have ground to a halt, paralysed by the invention of sophisticated cultures that lower women's status and destroy the creative freedom of individuals.

I will return later to the problem, which runs through this book, of the intermediate and particular case of the stem family, the first level of patrilineality, able to boost growth so long as it does not become too perfectly standardized an anthropological type. England had its stem-family component, of Franco-Norman origin, but so did America, thanks to the arrival en masse, in the decisive period of its industrial take-off, of individuals brought up in Germany and Scandinavia. Between 1870 and 1890, the Germans constituted the largest number of immigrants. And then, like Jewish culture, American culture found in a literal reading of the Bible the indispensable counterweight to its horizontality: a stern, transcendent God, the dream of a vertical stem family that never existed.

Now that we have set out the English and subsequent American anthropological matrices, and established their respective similarities to the original *Homo sapiens* type, we are in a position to understand the modernization of the world since the seventeenth century. It was then that the Anglo-American world became the leading player in the transformation of Eurasia, proposing its models and then imposing its rhythms. In the revolutions of 1642–51 and 1688, England was the first to define, on its modest scale, the institutional conditions of the industrial take-off. It 'invented' representative government, at the very same time that the European continent (and in particular France) was sinking into absolutism. In 1776, and even more in the 1820s, America 'invented' democracy. Again, we find that political transformation preceded (this time in the United States) a rise in economic power.

But what does it mean to 'invent' democracy, if there is a link between family structures and political ideologies, and if the family forms that characterized England and the United States at the time were archaic compared to those that occupied the mass of Eurasia? In the next chapter, I will show that modern democracy, based on archaic family forms, is itself largely archaic. It has been traditional since Morgan to contrast the primitive democracy of the savages with the modern democracy of the West. We will see that, in one sense, democracy is always primitive.

— 11 —

DEMOCRACY IS ALWAYS PRIMITIVE

Our analysis of the evolution of family forms, and of their effect on ideology, has helped us to define two great historical sequences.

The first sequence identified the undifferentiated nuclear origin of the family and described the differentiation of anthropological types between 3000 BCE and 2000 CE. Stem family, exogamous communitarian family, endogamous communitarian or polygynous family: these represent the successive stages of a complexification of family organization in which the last two of these types have comparable levels of complexity. We should not forget how, on the western periphery of Eurasia, pure nuclear types emerged, freed from their position in the undifferentiated kinship network. And nor should we forget the persistence, here and there on this periphery, of the original undifferentiated nuclear type.

This first sequence establishes simple relationships between family complexity, on the one hand, and space and time, on the other. The closer one gets to the centre from which agriculture emerged, the longer the time of experimentation on family and social forms (history) has been, and the more complex the family. The further away from this centre, the shorter the period of historical time that has elapsed, and the more nuclear the family.

The second sequence establishes a necessary relationship between the ideological forms that emerged as a result of literacy, then of secularization, and the various family structures produced by the previous process of differentiation.

If we combine the link between ideology and family structure with the position of family types in the space defined by the first sequence, we immediately see that individualistic, democratic and liberal ideologies are peripheral, placed in regions with short histories. In contrast, anti-individualist and authoritarian ideologies – Nazism, communism and Muslim fundamentalism – occupy more central geographic positions, in regions with a longer history.

189

Decentring democracy

We are going to break away from Western narcissism and separate the concept of liberal democracy from that of modernity, while admitting that this intellectual operation has already been performed by scholars on two occasions.

I have already commented extensively on Alan Macfarlane's work and his discovery of the link between the nuclear family and English individualism. I shall now move to the other side of Eurasia, and draw on the work of a Filipino sociologist who has identified the anthropologically archaic nature of democracy. In 1987, nine years after the publication of *The Origins of English Individualism*, Raul S. Manglapus's *Will of the People*[1] described the democracies that preceded those of the West. He sure-footedly began his inquiry with Sumer's original democracy, at the beginning and the heart of history. Where civilization began, democracy did indeed precede authoritarian political constructions.

Manglapus relies on the article that Thorkild Jacobsen wrote in 1943 on the political forms that preceded the imperial stage in Mesopotamia.[2] Sumer first appeared, like Greece 2,500 years later, as a world of cities. Jacobsen noted the persistence in the imperial era of traces of democratic life in the assemblies of inhabitants – more clearly, in the linguistic confusion between city and assembly, two concepts designated by the same word. But it was above all the behaviour of the Mesopotamian gods, survivors of a bygone era, which gave him the key to political history. Even as the earthly world became imperial, authoritarian and vertical, the gods who supervised it were free; they met, deliberated, appointed their leaders, challenged them. They were an assembly of free individuals, a primitive democracy. Jacobsen pointed out the similarity between his depiction and that of the many historians who had described early Germanic times. Macfarlane was not wrong to speak, after Montesquieu, of the freedom of the Germanic peoples, but he made the mistake of believing it to be a specific and ethnic feature, whereas it was universal in the past of *Homo sapiens*.[3]

Primitive times were thus a period of assemblies capable of appointing leaders in case of emergency. Manglapus took up and developed Jacobsen's insight and, in *Will of the People*, he set out an inventory of the democratic forms that everywhere preceded the age of domination and empires: in the ancient India of Buddhist republics, in the villages of the recent Indian subcontinent and China, in the local communities of the Inca and Aztec Empires, and among the Iroquois Indians, in connection with whom the anthropologist Lewis Henry Morgan had already referred to a 'primitive democracy'. Manglapus does not forget his own country, the Philippines, where, until the arrival of the Spaniards in the sixteenth century, no form of government had come to disturb the democratic functioning of the local communities.

Morgan, Jacobsen and Manglapus provide us with the key to an inverse history of political forms, parallel to the inverse history of the history of family forms that I am proposing. This double inversion produces a satisfactory logical order: the rise of complex family forms corresponds to the rise of authoritarian political forms, with the construction of the state at the centre of the evolution.

What is primitive democracy, in its most general form? It is the possibility for the male adult members of a people to come together in assembly to make collective decisions. This assembly is a de facto institution, but we can observe how it became institutionally formalized in the case of primitive societies that borrowed writing from the most advanced cultures of their time, such as the Greek cities and early Rome. The assemblies of the Germanic peoples, which were illiterate, did not have a formal character. However, they took decisions and elected leaders, whom we may call by the traditional name of 'kings', or 'presidents for life', if we wish to disturb the routine of an academic history endeavouring to understand modern democracy.

If we set aside the case of the matrilineal Iroquois, kinship groups were undifferentiated among the aforementioned peoples, and the automatic transmission of power through a lineage was therefore impossible.[4]

But these primitive democracies were not viscerally egalitarian, since, most often, the chiefs (the kings, presidents for life) were chosen from prestigious kinship groups. This should not surprise us, since inheritance rules at the time did not include any principle of equality or inequality. This was a world where a relative equality of conditions could exist without any structured contrast between inequality and equality having been truly thought out. One sometimes feels that it would be more accurate to speak of a primitive oligarchy.

In the absence of any principle of equality, the birth of cities, in Mesopotamia as well as in Greece, fostered the emergence of what were spontaneously oligarchic mechanisms of political representation. The sequence in which the city precedes the authoritarian state seems to have been quite universal in what is now a communitarian and patrilineal space. Before the Assyrian Empire, there was the merchant Republic of Assur; before the Russian Empire, or even the Principality of Moscow, there was, in the Middle Ages, the trading republic of Novgorod, a member of the Hanseatic League.

In just a few cases, as in Athens, there was a formalized democratic evolution – a process that I will study below. The distinction between representative democracy and oligarchy is often difficult to establish, anywhere and at any time, since the representatives are de facto an oligarchy. Be that as it may, primitive democracy, or primitive oligarchy

191

appears after the undifferentiated nuclear family, and it is flexible, fuzzy, and unstable.

The survival and development of representative institutions in Western Europe

Starting from this depiction of the original democracy, we can read the political history of Europe in an inverse form – after reading the history of its family systems in a similarly inverted way.

Let us summarize the family background first. The family was, in the Middle Ages (fifth to tenth centuries), an undifferentiated nuclear family; traces of the Roman egalitarian nuclear family had survived pretty much throughout the continent in the former imperial area.[5] In the eleventh century, primogeniture emerged in Île-de-France and Normandy and spread rapidly among the nobles and some populations, who adopted a stem-family form, in Occitania, in the Germanic area, in the north of the Iberian Peninsula, and in Sweden (very belatedly and incompletely). In central Italy, a patrilineal communitarian model of the Russian or Chinese type became the rule. In northern France, the egalitarian nuclear family ended up dominating the cities and the countryside, but in England it was the absolute nuclear family, closer to the original undifferentiated matrix, which prevailed. No 'differentiated' family form seems to have been fully defined and socially dominant anywhere before the middle of the seventeenth century, as I have shown in my study of the co-evolution of the stem family and Protestantism in Germany (Chapters 5 and 6), followed by the emergence of the absolute nuclear family in England (Chapter 9). The same work will need to be done for the egalitarian nuclear family of the Paris Basin, though we know that it had taken clear shape in the years 1560–1685 thanks to Jérôme-Luther Viret's fine study of the communes of Écouen and Villiers-le-Bel.[6]

As far as democracy in Europe is concerned, a theoretical breakthrough was made in 1992 by Brian Downing in his study of the differentiation of political forms in modern Europe.[7]

Downing's thesis consists of two stages and a few sentences:

> First, late medieval Europe had numerous political characteristics that distinguished it from other major world civilizations. These charac-teristics, the most important of which were representative assemblies, constituted a basis for liberal democracy, a . . . predisposition that can never be repeated in the modern developing world. Second, military modernization, the 'military revolution' of the sixteenth and seventeenth centuries, led to the strengthening of monarchical power in countries relying on *domestic* resources to finance modern armies.[8]

Downing's Western narcissism shouldn't alarm us any more than Macfarlane's English narcissism. In the Middle Ages, Europe was indeed very different from the rest of the world, because it lagged far behind the rest of Eurasia in its family and political development. The Middle East, India and China had long since reached the stage of the patrilineal communitarian family and political constructions with a maximum degree of authoritarianism. Mediaeval Europe abounded not only in undifferentiated nuclear-family types, but also in village or noble assemblies. Cities flourished there, particularly in Italy and Flanders, and formed the poles of crystallization of representative, highly oligarchic institutions, as Downing notes.

This urban stage, mediaeval in Europe, was characteristic of the sixth and fifth centuries BCE in Greece and the turn of the third millennium in Mesopotamia. Political representation in Europe was still alive in the Late Middle Ages, simply because this peripheral region of Eurasia was terribly backward in its historical development.

From the sixteenth century, the growth of state bureaucracies accelerated. A 'military revolution' led to a huge increase in the size of armies, which asphyxiated the feudal nobility; it was an essential component in the flourishing of absolutism. What is important for our purposes is that Downing correctly reads the meaning and geography of history in Western Europe: he identifies the spread of autocratic (anti-democratic) forms in the central part of the continent, which comes to an end at its borders. The successive military rise of the various nations allows him to set out the successive rise of authoritarian statism in a veritable sequence: Spain and Austria, then France, Sweden and, finally, Prussia. On the periphery of this central axis of development of the army and the state, representative forms are still to be found in Switzerland, the Netherlands and England. Downing methodically studies the taming of the 'estates' in kingdoms, which traditionally represented the 'orders' via-à-vis the king, i.e. the nobility, the clergy and, lastly, the commoners, the Third Estate which finally came to power in France in 1789. This model fleshes out, on the political level, the one put forward by Macfarlane.

If England was able to give birth, in the seventeenth century, to a liberal revolution, this is because enough of the primitive (or original) democratic or oligarchic representation still survived. Parliament, far from disappearing like the assemblies of the continent, ended up seizing all the power. It is true that the insular position of England protected it from a military revolution since it was up to the fleet, external to the territory, to ensure the protection of the Kingdom. Such an analysis obviously does not exclude the role of new modern factors in the development of English representative institutions, such as mass literacy or the development of commerce, craftsmanship and industry.

193

Being the methodical historian he is, Downing then notes the final failure of French and Swedish absolutism. The maintenance of a political representation for the four orders in Sweden – nobility, clergy, city dwellers, peasants – was typically peripheral, and monarchical power in this country does seem to have declined dramatically in the late eighteenth century. However, I am not sure that one can describe the nineteenth-century development of this tremendously literate and disciplined society as a return to a liberal path.

The case of France, however, is unambiguous. France seemed bent on separating from England in the seventeenth century, only to move back towards it in the eighteenth. The absolutism of Louis XIV corresponded at that time to the flourishing of the controlled monarchy in England, firmly established in 1688. Exactly one century later, the Revolution of 1789 set France back on a liberal trajectory: a bumpy ride. This mid-course correction can be interpreted as the irruption into the history of France of a people structured, in the Paris Basin, by the values of the egalitarian nuclear family and by a literacy rate that exceeded 50 per cent for men in the course of the eighteenth century.

The fact remains that, in Europe, absolutism was an innovation and constitutionalism a conservation. In the nineteenth and twentieth centuries, the failure of liberalism in a Germanic world that was highly literate but based on the stem family mainly confirms the Downing model. The real ideological innovation of that great country of the authoritarian and inegalitarian family, Germany, was – after secularization – Nazism. A decade or so earlier, the great communitarian family, at least in its central part, Italy, had invented fascism. Radical forms of the hypertrophy of the state, Nazism and fascism went much further than the absolutism of Louis XIV in France and Philip II in Spain. When we analyse the rise in sixteenth- and seventeenth-century Spanish and French authoritarianism and militarism, however, we are likely to find that the stem family – located in the south in the case of France, and in the north in that of Spain – made a particular contribution. The Basque country and Gascony provided the army, or more generally the civil service, with a regular supply of younger brothers over the centuries.

Liberal democracy, with parties alternating, was easily established in Europe only in countries where the nuclear family predominated: England, France, Belgium, the Netherlands and Denmark. The Swedish regime has produced too long a phase of social democratic domination to be considered liberal in the strict sense. The only real and important exception to the rule that the nuclear family goes with liberalism in Europe is Spain, where educational and economic underdevelopment may explain the weakness of liberal democracy. But apart from this case, the nuclear family has defined the outlines, on the northwest fringe of Europe, of a reduced but real West.

From English oligarchy to American democracy, thanks to racial sentiment

The English Revolution of 1688 did not lead the country beyond oligarchic representation. The Parliament that took power represented only a fraction of the population, even though this proportion had increased since the reign of Elizabeth, especially thanks to the actions of the Puritans who led the first revolution. It was only 4.7 per cent towards the end of the reign of Queen Anne, who died in 1714. But we should not forget that Louis XIV died the following year, leaving France at its historic peak of endogenous authoritarianism.

In proportion to the adult male population, it was still 15 per cent, enough for the functioning of the various institutions to be punctuated by elections which, as John H. Plumb showed, mobilized even the upper social stratum of the villages. To be elected, a member of the gentry needed to woo the big peasants. However, according to Plumb, there was, throughout the eighteenth century, a relative diminution in the electorate, which became less significant in proportion to the population, including in the aftermath of the electoral reform of 1832.[9] This was the effect of the agrarian and industrial revolutions, and the growth of a working population that really polarized the social structure. But this electoral narrowing, against the backdrop of economic upheaval, did not cause any political instability in England. This is no cause for surprise here: in England, inequality was not shocking – in Chapter 8, we defined the British anthropological matrix as individualistic but non-egalitarian, and this is a necessary family infrastructure for a liberal but oligarchic political system.

Eighteenth-century America pursued the converse path of an enlargement of democracy.

The English who founded America had brought their family structure with them, a structure that was nuclear but devoid of the value of equality that characterized its nuclear counterpart in the Paris Basin. We can now see how this American culture, lacking a strong principle of equality, managed to produce a democracy more quickly and rapidly than France, where the emergence and stabilization of the Republic took nearly a century, between 1789 and 1880. However, it was France that followed a sequence where family egalitarianism was transposed into an egalitarian ideology, thanks to literacy and the collapse of religious belief. But it was democracy 'in America' that Tocqueville described in his book (published in 1835 and 1840), while he himself living the beginning of a dramatic series of revolutions in a France where democracy was finding it difficult to achieve stability.

American democracy has two original objective foundations: an egalitarian agrarian morphology in the North, since the country was

195

dominated until at least the mid-nineteenth century by moderately well-off farmers, and a high educational level of the population, derived from Protestantism. But Calvinism, the theological basis of the Protestantism of American sects, does not believe that human beings are equal. In 1560, in his *Institution of the Christian Religion*, Calvin wrote: 'By predestination we mean the eternal decree of God, by which he determined with himself whatever he wished to happen with regard to every man. All are not created on equal terms, but some are preordained to eternal life, others to eternal damnation.'[10]

However, in 1776, less than a century and a half after the arrival of the first settlers, we read in the American Declaration of Independence words stating the complete opposite: 'We hold these truths to be self-evident, that all men are created equal, that they are endowed by their Creator with certain unalienable Rights, that among these are Life, Liberty and the pursuit of Happiness.'

What a path the Americans had followed, given that their original views included the firm belief that human beings were unequal! How could such an evolution – and one that occurred so quickly – have been possible?

The Declaration of Independence provides the answer to this riddle: it tells us explicitly how the transition from Calvinist inequality to democratic egalitarianism took place. It describes the Indians as 'merciless savages'. After equal human beings came non-human beings: inequality was expelled from the White social body and attached to an external element; this was the Indian in the text of the Declaration of Independence in the North, and the Black in the social reality of the South. Tocqueville had noted the strange White egalitarianism which characterized the slave-owning states of the South:

> By a singular change the democratic impulse was found to be most irresistible in the very States where the aristocracy had the firmest hold. The State of Maryland, which had been founded by men of rank, was the first to proclaim universal suffrage, and to introduce the most democratic forms into the conduct of its government.[11]

The presence of many Black slaves had sharpened the awareness in that part of the country of being equal with Whites.

The history of the United States makes it possible to link each increase in democracy to a rise in racial sentiment. Andrew Jackson, president from 1826 to 1836 at a time when America was expanding the right to vote, was a fervent defender of slavery and a strong supporter of the deportation of Indians to the west of the Mississippi. We will come across him again in Chapter 14, as President Trump's idol. In the West, between 1860 and 1900, the flourishing of a society totally devoid of traditional elites was accompanied by the extermination of 250,000 Great

Plains Indians, a carnage that occurred in the context of an apotheosis of racial sentiment.[12]

Racism cannot therefore be regarded as a flaw in American democracy; quite the opposite: it is one of its foundations. At the time the country was founded, it fostered the development of an egalitarian feeling in the White group. It subsequently facilitated, at every stage of immigration, the integration of those who were not Indians or Blacks: first, all the Northern Europeans, and then, after a period of hesitation, those who were a little dark-skinned, like the Italians, or non-Christians like the Jews. In the most recent phase, the segregation of Blacks has allowed Americans of Japanese, Korean, Vietnamese and Chinese origin to be reclassified as Whites.

And we are now able to write the magic formula of democracy in America: absence of equality among brothers + exclusion of Blacks and Indians → racial democracy.

This sequence also explains the ease with which democratic development in America was achieved, and its seemingly natural and harmonious character – all so disturbing for us French, who have to learn about the history of the revolutions of 1789, 1830, 1848 and the Paris Commune of 1871 if we are to understand this process. Democratic America is as stable as oligarchic England. No principle of equality, rooted in the family's unconscious, leads to repeated outbursts, as happens in France, of violent mass political egalitarianism.

The concept of ethnic democracy

In Antiquity, Athens had already set the example of a democracy emerging on the forceful basis of a self-assertion involving the rejection of an Other, or rather, in its case, the rejection of all others. In the midst of the rise of democracy, a law of 451 BCE required that you needed an Athenian mother and father if you were to obtain citizenship. In the fourth century, marriage between Athenians and foreigners was banned.

The United States was, from its founding to the Second World War, the archetype of a 'Herrenvolk Democracy', in the phrase used by Pierre Van den Berghe, initially to describe South Africa.[13] I will henceforth use the concept of 'ethnic democracy', which is more ideologically neutral, while specifying that the ethnic group in question must simultaneously exclude and include, i.e., in the case of the original United States, reject Indians and Blacks while assimilating Whites of all origins. The case of Asians, excluded until the Second World War, and readily included thereafter, suggests a certain flexibility in the system, which at this stage we must call anthropological rather than social. Its roots plunge into the unconscious of the life of the group, under the conscious strata of economic activity and class interaction. To describe this system, we must therefore use the key words of anthropology: the body of the citizens is defined by a rigorous White endogamy, but it practises a family exogamy that is just as severe, since White families systematically exchange spouses in a context where marriages between cousins are shunned.[14]

We end up with a slightly unexpected picture of American democracy.

England of the eighteenth century, with its non-egalitarian nuclear families and its liberal and oligarchic politics, was admittedly modern in terms of its high literacy rate and its burgeoning industrial revolution, but was still archaic in the survival and subsequent flourishing of its representative political forms.

Nineteenth-century America did not just shift this model westward. It also moved away from it, as we saw in the last chapter, and approached, at the family level, the original undifferentiated background of human-kind, from which England itself was not so distant. This background included the primitive democracy of *Homo sapiens*.

In the United States, the verticality of the English social system for the most part disappeared: aristocratic primogeniture, the monarchical state and its Church, an ancient ruling class and stable village oligarchies. It was the very idea of there being a keystone to the social and mental system that was abolished in America. Should we call this the disappearance of transcendence, of heteronomy, of a social superego? The term chosen does not really matter. We need simply note that the system that defines itself and spreads across America, with its local communities and its federated states, is much more horizontal than the English system, and much closer to the primitive groups that made up original humankind. The Founding Fathers, of course, gave this new people a written constitution, and this text was formally respected even though it was often modified by amendments. In this way, an American state and representative institutions came into being and have worked extremely well, thanks to a high level of education, the initial relative equality of economic conditions and the absence of a destabilizing egalitarian unconscious. But we have seen above that the US state has never been able truly to monopolize legitimate violence. The American population remains, in the most ordinary and archaic manner, armed, and its rates of homicide hover at between five and fifteen times what they are in Europe.

How can we fail to see the resurgence of the primordial democratic or oligarchic background in certain quirks of American political life, such as the tendency to elect to the presidency either warlords such as Washington, Jackson, Grant and Eisenhower, or representatives of prestigious lineages such as the Roosevelts, Kennedys and Bushes? As I suggested above, the terminological habit that makes us give the name 'king' to the leaders elected in the past by the assembly of warriors, often temporarily, masks the truth; if we used the term 'president' to designate the original Germanic, Greek or Roman leaders, we would have a better feel for the vitality of the primitive American base.

We are here trying to situate America in relation to the past of human-kind as reconstituted by history and anthropology. But we do not know everything about this past, and in particular about the relationship between the groups of *Homo sapiens* who, as they conquered the planet, separated and fragmented. James G. Ferguson noted that human groups exist only in opposition to each other, in the mode of *us* versus *them*. The basic ethnic group practises exogamy between families, but is generally endogamous vis-à-vis the outside world. Generally, but not totally: what we sense in the behaviour of the oldest historically identifiable human groups – Germanic, Roman and many other peoples – is the mixture of a strong ethnic identity and a no less strong ability to integrate, digest and assimilate individuals or parts of subjected peoples. If we agree to perceive America as a modernized mass form of the original *Homo sapiens* group, it can perhaps tell us what the past of humankind was like in terms of relations between tribes and peoples. This mixture of openness and racism, with the assimilation of Europeans and the rejec-tion of Indians or Blacks, is perhaps only the modern and continental consummation of an old model, fragmented but equally universal, that of an original *Homo sapiens* who was simultaneously an assimilator and a racist.

The concrete universal of America, the abstract universal of France

At this stage of the analysis, we can understand the success of America as a planetary ideal. True, it is France that produced the concept of the universal human being. But it is the Anglo-American world, not so good at theorizing the equality of humankind, that has 'globalized' the planet and given it its language.

It is not a question here of minimizing the importance of the French model. After all, France turned Europe upside down between 1789 and 1848. Thanks to its relative demographic mass, it was able, between 1793 and 1814, to raise the armies that from the west of the continent swept away the feudal regime and imposed the emancipation of the Jews. It has, in a sense, brought the whole of Western Europe to a post-religious universal stage. In 1848, having already lost its military power, France's revolution was followed and repeated as far away as Berlin and Budapest. The rationality of the French metric system has conquered the whole planet, if we ignore the few undecimalized traces that have survived in the Anglo-American world. France therefore deserves its seat as a permanent member of the United Nations Security Council. The notion of a universal human being would alone be enough to justify it.

The French, moreover, with their particularly clear vision of the principle of equality, have never ceased to help America itself to become aware of what it could be. I am obviously thinking here of Tocqueville and *Democracy in America*. But, much more recently, the works of Thomas Piketty and Emmanuel Saez on the distribution of income have brought the concept of the richest 1 per cent to the centre stage of American debates and contributed to the return of a problem of the democratic confrontation in the United States. On the persistent segregation of Blacks, Loïc Wacquant, a French scholar who teaches at Berkeley, has recently made a decisive contribution. He recognized, in the mass incarceration of young Blacks, the third incarnation of a racial system that America cannot escape. His article 'America's New Peculiar Institution: On the Prison as a Surrogate Ghetto', published in 2000, paved the way for Michelle Alexander's fine bestseller, *The New Jim Crow*, and many other texts on the current situation of Blacks in the United States.[15]

But the universal human being of the French is an abstract character – an ideological projection, in my view, of the values found in a specific family structure, the egalitarian nuclear family of the Paris Basin. The liberty of children in that part of France became, in 1789, the liberty of the citizens; the equality of brothers and sisters mutated into the equality of men and women, peoples and nations. French universalism operates according to a simple subconscious model: children are equal, adults are equal, people are equal, and there is therefore a universal human being. The need for central France to assert its values against the country's periphery, where the stem family was the rule, with its contrary values of authority and inequality, explains the clarity of the French message. But we must admit that our universal human being nevertheless emerges from a very particular anthropological base.

A similar dimension of the equality of brothers – sisters being in this case excluded – has regulated the visions of the Chinese, Arab and Russian worlds, all of which are universalist. In Russia, in the Arab world and in China, however, the family's anti-individualism has led, contrary to what has been observed in France, to a preference for the universal human being who is integrated into a closed structure – political party, centralized economy, religion, nation; a human being who is admittedly equal to others, but always ethnic. Perhaps one should speak in their case of an ideal of the universal nation.

The simple subconscious mechanism that leads from the family to the vision of the other in general can also produce, if the children are unequal, as is the case in the stem family, an equivalent determination but one that works in the other direction: children are unequal, adults are unequal, peoples are unequal, and there is no universal human being,

200

a sequence characteristic of Germany, Japan, the Basque Country and Catalonia. A large stem-family people will find itself at the top of the hierarchy; a small stem-family people will be content to assert a strong particularism. The size of the people and the interaction of geopolitical forces can define the big and small brothers.

The Anglo-American absolute nuclear family has its own sequence: children are different, adults are different, peoples are different. Inequality is not affirmed, but the notion of the universal human being cannot be taken for granted either. That is why the immigrant can be integrated on an individualist basis, but only if there is, somewhere, close at hand, an Other that serves as a foil and permits all assimilations but one.

One of the peculiarities of the Anglo-American world is thus that there is a line separating the universal human being from the non-universal human being. I am still haunted by an evening during my student years in Cambridge, at the time of the Yom Kippur War, during which a Welsh guy, a friendly, droll person, very left-wing, excluded the Arabs from his area of responsibility by uttering the fateful sentence: 'There's some place where you must draw the line.'

One of the most remarkable peculiarities of this Anglo-American line, which separates the human universal from the not quite human, is its ability to shift and include wider swathes of humankind. The Irish, the Italians, the Jews, the Japanese, the Chinese, the Koreans, very recently the Indians and – as we shall soon see – the Hispanics (a code name for other Indians from the south), end up being reclassified as Whites thanks to intermarriage, which occurs often and without difficulty. But the Blacks?

France does not have this kind of 'racial' limitation, even if it is capable of spectacular cultural xenophobia when the immigrant group brings with it a way of life that is a little too obvious and too far-removed from what prevails in France, thus casting doubt on the ideological presupposition of the universal human being. Arab family culture, being anti-feminist and endogamous, practically drives French universalism mad, because it seems to deny it. Human beings – *all* of them – should be alike.

This is the problem of French ideological greatness, which is particularist without its knowing it. French universalism does not emerge from a concrete anthropological universal, but from the dreams of the egalitarian nuclear family, rooted in a specific terroir. The French dream of the universal human being will therefore, in real social life as well as in geopolitics, constantly come up against different anthropological systems and attitudes which, according to its concept, should not exist. During the French Revolution, the Paris Basin had already needed to bring its periphery, which supported different values, up to date. But to French eyes, the entire concrete world is chock-a-block with incomprehensible and intolerable values and types of behaviour: the non-egalitarian liberalism of the Anglo-American family, the authoritarian inegalitarianism of

201

the German and Japanese families, the authoritarian egalitarianism of the Russian or Chinese communitarian family, and the more horizontal egalitarianism of the Arab endogamous communitarian family.

America does not excel, as France does, in defining human beings as similar, everywhere and in every culture. In order to feel that it exists, America will always need, existing on the other side of some mysterious line, some Other. But the American anthropological system, and the spontaneous ideology that springs from it, including racism, are closer than those of France to the original type of humankind, and thus, in a concrete sense, they are more universal. America embodies better, in its way of being, the archaic and universal *Homo sapiens*.

It is, I think, in this true naturalness that lies the deep seductiveness of America. Of course, America has offered the world its virgin lands, and its wealth, the opportunity for millions of hungry farmers to make a decent economic life for themselves, and to dream of an even better destiny for their children. America has been able to talk about the future. But America also represents, by its way of life, a sort of general human past. It appeals, far beneath the surface, to our buried instincts, to this archaic background that exists in all the human beings in all the peoples of the earth, including those whose family and anthropological structure has evolved towards greater complexification and sophistication – towards a certain norm, whether this be patrilineal or matrilineal, egalitarian or inegalitarian. The true mystery of America is that, if it presents itself to us as prefiguring the future, it also carries within itself our past. It offers us at the same time the hope of progress and the happiness of regression.

Democracy is always primitive

It is for this same reason – its primordial naturalness – that America, before France, invented modern democracy, because there it resulted from a simple application of mass literacy to the archaic human background, which includes primitive, natural democracy.

The virulent egalitarianism of France in the Paris Basin will in the final analysis have been less effective in defining a body of equal citizens than the indifference to equality found in England.

The principle of equality, built by history – the long history of a communitarian and patrilineal Roman family under the Republic, a family that became egalitarian and nuclear under the Empire – inevitably defines an abstract equality between individuals. Egalitarianism is a disintegrator of the group. Left to itself, it engenders a world of individuals, none of whom accepts subordination to the whole: anarchy, in the literal sense of the concept. Democracy, a collective phenomenon, cannot spontaneously emerge from this situation. If we go into the details of the history of France, we are even obliged to conclude that the country's stem-family periphery made an indispensable contribution to the birth of democracy, because it is this periphery that provided the country as a whole with the ideal of an individual integrated into the group together with the possibility of collective action. If we take a look at Andalusia and its anarchist tradition, and then at southern Italy and its mafia practices – two lands where the egalitarian nuclear family is the norm – we will recognize the limited democratic potential of the egalitarian nuclear family on its own. If we add that this family type came down to us by legitimate descent from Roman imperial domination, the fact that it has not spontaneously produced a democratic organization ceases to be surprising.

Anglo-American undifferentiation is more effective than French egalitarianism in fostering group self-awareness: the non-equality of children and adults implies diverse peoples, with defined identities that, under certain conditions, make it possible for democracy to put down roots. We can put this another way, in simpler if somewhat resigned terms: democracy always has an ethnic base.

Let us summarize: America invented modern democracy because most of its White inhabitants could read and write and its concrete educational egalitarianism made the equality of citizens conceivable. But it did not believe a priori in equality or inequality: it was – and remains – undifferentiated on this level. It has, on the other hand, returned to the vital feeling of group belonging, defined against an Other which is truly other in appearance, the merciless savage or the Black slave. These were the essential conditions for the emergence of the first modern democracy: a reactivation of the conditions that had produced primitive democracy, plus literacy. I admit, however, that the radical exogamy of the English and American anthropological systems, inherited from the Christian religious transformation – an exogamy that can in no way be described as undifferentiated – must have played a part in the development of the individualism of the White group, internally, just as it allowed maximum openness to the immigration and the assimilation of non-Black individuals.

We will now show, in the following chapters, that globalization can be analysed as a collapse of the notion of equality created by mass literacy, in all advanced societies, but especially in the Anglosphere. We will also note that the Western democratic revival, which began around 2000 but was affirmed in 2016 with Brexit and the election of Donald Trump, took place – as usual, we might say – in the Anglosphere, in the absence of any a priori belief in the equality of human beings. Once again, we will have to invoke the proximity of the natural background of *Homo sapiens* if we are to understand the way the Anglo-American world so easily fosters democratic practices. In both cases, however, we will find an element of xenophobia in the revival. Democracy never stops being primitive.

— 12 —

DEMOCRACY UNDERMINED BY HIGHER EDUCATION

At the beginning of the twentieth century, the United States was just one advanced Protestant country among others. Its Gross Domestic Product had certainly surpassed those of the two next largest countries on the list, Germany and the United Kingdom: by 1913, US GDP was 12 per cent higher than *the combined sum* of the GDP of these two countries: $517,383 million (1990) for the United States, as against 237,332 for Germany and 224,618 for the United Kingdom, according to Angus Maddison's calculations.[1] In comparison, France's GDP was only $144,489 million. (I am leaving the numbers in their original absurd precision to emphasize that economists should never be taken completely seriously.) The United States' technological contribution to the second industrial revolution – which combined electricity, car manufacturing and aviation – was turning out to be significant both in terms of product design and standardization of production, as evidenced by that of the Ford Model T, which was rolling off the assembly line by 1908. But the universities that counted, and scientific research in general, were still located in Europe and, more and more, in Germany.

In addition, in 1900, America was only 40 per cent urbanized, like France, while the cities of the United Kingdom accounted for 77 per cent of its population. The overall wealth of the United States was very largely due to the country's size: already 76 million inhabitants in 1900 as against 56 million in Germany, and 38 million in both the United Kingdom and France. This American population, 95 per cent literate, had natural resources that were out of all proportion to those of the peoples in Europe. But in 1900, the United States was as yet simply larger, more populous, more rural and richer than other Protestant countries. It was in the group that was racing ahead, but could not have been regarded as the leading country in the Protestant world or even the whole of the West, let alone the entire planet.

Table 12.1   Literacy in the United States and Europe around 1900

	Literacy rates (Population of over 10-year-olds, in %)
England	95
United States: Whites born in America	95
United States: Whites born abroad	87
United States: Blacks	55
Sweden	Over 95
Germany	Over 95
Austria	94
Bohemia	97
Belgium	81
France	83
Italy	52
Spain	44
Hungary	44
Poland (in Russia)	26
European Russia	19

Source: Carlo M. Cipolla, Literacy and Development in the West (London: Penguin, 1969), pp. 99, 127–8.

The second educational revolution: 1900–1940

However, it was in the United States between 1900 and 1940 that the first mass development in secondary education took place, in the form of an education that went beyond teaching pupils how to read or count. And that's when America took the lead in global development.

Enrolment rates in US high schools were still only 10 per cent around 1900; by 1940 they had reached 70 per cent. Between those years, rates of graduation from high school had risen from 6 per cent to 50 per cent. The take-off of high school education was a national cultural project – but it was conducted in a decentralized way, in terms both of setting up and of managing schools. Admittedly, programmes and curricula were, and remain, fairly uniform across the whole of the United States. Yet it was local communities rather than the central government that controlled the process. Public schooling was simultaneously homogeneous and decentralized – a typical manifestation of national action in its Anglo-American guise. The process recalls, in this regard, the establishment of the English Poor Law: the Tudor state had legislated as to the aims and objectives of this, but left the responsibility for setting things up and running them to local elites. In the United States, the national educational project was not launched, as it was in England, by a strong

205

central state (strong in people's minds, that is, since England did not have a strong bureaucracy). In America, everything happened outside the control of the federal state, and even the compulsory education laws enacted by the federated states seem to have had only a limited effect.[2] The second educational revolution, which affected high schools, was directly driven by an ideology, in this case of a democratic and egalitarian hue. But the real point was to implement a public education project, to activate the achievements of the welfare state in a broader sense.

When America entered the war in 1941, half of the younger generation had already had a full high school education. Europe, including the Protestant countries, was now lagging behind, relegated to the relative underdevelopment of primary education, even in areas where everyone could read. It was elitist state control on the old continent that blocked the development of secondary education. Claudia Goldin and Lawrence Katz have shown that the gap between the Old and the New Worlds cannot be explained either by greater American prosperity, or by the country's greater capacity to finance a lengthier education.[3] In 1955–6 again, the percentage of 15–19 year olds in education, which was nearly 80 per cent in the United States, was 25 per cent in Sweden and between 15 and 20 per cent in Great Britain, France, Germany, Denmark, Finland and Norway.

It is true that high school education provides the knowledge needed for employment in a technologically advanced society, where service activities are spreading both inside and outside industrial enterprises. Communication between individuals becomes just as important as the transformation of things. But American education was from the outset liberal, open and concerned with the development of the individual as much as the acquisition of knowledge. And, above all, this educational system showed absolutely no interest in elitist performance. As a national project, it also enabled the assimilation of immigrants by creating the all-American teen. The public high school, whose action was from 1924 onwards combined with restrictions on immigration, thus contributed to the emergence, around 1950, of an America that was not just prosperous but also culturally homogeneous.

Democracy peaks

At the beginning of the twentieth century, America was very inegalitarian in material terms. The accelerated development of industry, between the end of the American Civil War in 1865 and the beginning of the First World War in 1914, had raised the concentration of capital and income to unprecedented levels. The educational infrastructure of the country, however, remained egalitarian: 95 per cent of the adult White population could read and write by 1900, even though the proportion of Americans of both sexes who had completed higher education was only 2.5 per cent. In the period of unbridled capitalism in America, its Gilded Age, the social subconscious defined by education remained democratic, and the country's high level of political participation and its shift towards the Progressive Era at the very end of the nineteenth century are easy to understand.

The development of high school education, beginning in 1900, went against the tide of growing economic inequality and brings out the powerful underground autonomy of cultural trends in history. It was against this background of educational expansion that the economic crisis of 1929 unfolded. At that time, half of Americans had already attended, and a quarter had graduated from, high school. Thus, the dysfunction of the economic system logically led to the egalitarian political reaction of Roosevelt's New Deal. State regulation of the economy and taxation of incomes have led to a gradual but irresistible decline in the level of economic inequality. As Emmanuel Saez and Thomas Piketty have shown, the share of national income appropriated by the richest 10 per cent fell from 46 per cent in 1928 to 32 per cent in 1952, where it stagnated until around 1972. The share of the richest 1 per cent, which was 20 per cent in 1928, fell to 9 per cent in 1953, to remain stable at 8 per cent between 1963 and 1978.[4]

The third educational revolution and how it was brought to a halt

High school education was merely one stage. In the aftermath of the Second World War, upward movement continued with a third educational revolution, that of higher education. In 1900, only 3 per cent of men and 2 per cent of women aged 25 had reached this stage and obtained a BA; by 1940, this was already the case for 7.5 per cent of men and 5 per cent of women and in 1975 for 27 per cent of men and 22.5 per cent of women.[5]

Once these levels had been attained, the model of ever-increasing education for all – applicable almost perfectly to primary and more or less to secondary education – lost its validity. The expansion came to a halt. Between 1980 and 1985 the rate of obtaining a BA actually fell to 22.5 per cent for men and stabilized at the same level for women. It then rose again to reach, around 2000, 30 per cent for men and 35 per cent for women; so women were now ahead, a phenomenon that could be observed later in most countries where this revolution in higher education would be achieved. I will return to the meaning of the eventual quantitative recovery that took place at the beginning of the third millennium, albeit in a context where the meaning, motivation and perhaps even quality of the most advanced education had changed.

An assessment of the population with qualifications in higher education poses much more important methodological problems than those that one has to face for the assessment of the education provided by primary and secondary schools. The variety of subjects studied and the differentiation of levels are almost boundless. Higher education is, by its nature, multiple and stratified. This is particularly true in the United States, where, right from the start, the new student body was divided between large universities and state colleges that provided a lower-quality education.[6] The interpretation of statistics is made more complicated by their heterogeneity, and I have for my part given up trying to remove the innumerable inconsistencies, merely emphasizing the general compatibility in terms of trends and distribution of the population.

The imperfection of data must not get in our way. The question of higher education is too important for anyone who wants to understand the new stratification of advanced societies and the disintegration of the body of citizens.

In constructing my graphs, I have used, except in the case of Russia, the Barro-Lee dataset, after having checked the compatibility of the figures it proposes with those of the OECD or of various national statistical yearbooks. Despite its approximations, and even certain glaring errors for some countries, it has the merit of proposing an assessment

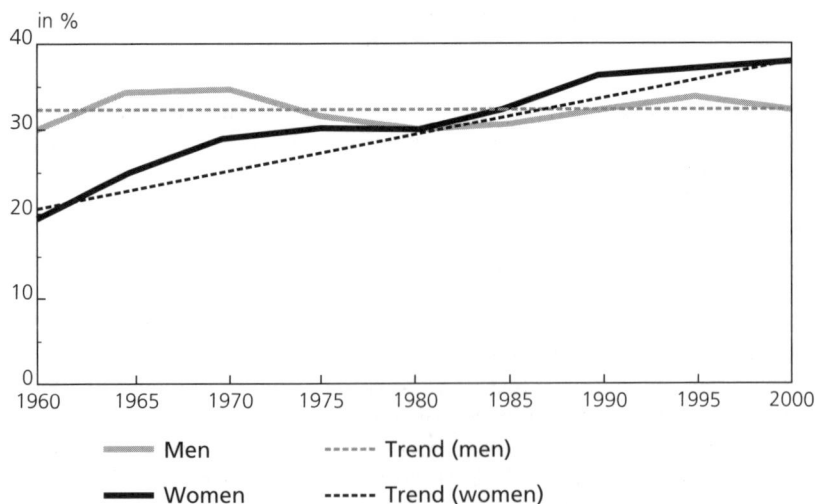

Graph 12.1 Higher education in the United States: the case of generations who reached the age of 25 between 1960 and 2005
Source: Based on the Barro-Lee dataset.

of educational levels by age group, every five years; this assessment is standardized, which allows an international comparison of trends.

In the United States, if we focus our attention on 25-year-olds, we can observe that the figures for men, irrespective of the ups and downs, have been stagnant since the mid-1960s, evidenced by the standard polynomial adjustment of the Excel program. For women, on the other hand, there was a progress that led to their overtaking the men's performance between 1986 and 1990. The proportions of students who started higher education but did not complete a degree rose much higher, of course, but bringing these figures into the discussion would intensify the painful methodological question of the internal stratification of higher education.

On the other hand, the use of proficiency tests carried out at the end of high school to manage and channel the entrance of students into university illuminates the debate. The Scholastic Aptitude Test (SAT) is, alongside other equivalent systems, part of the American tradition, which is not afraid, unlike its French counterpart, to highlight possible intellectual inequalities between individuals. As we have seen many times, the absolute nuclear family does not include in its values an a priori principle of equality. Although we do not really know what these tests actually measure – intelligence, knowledge, the quality of the students' training, their discipline in a test situation, etc. – their evolution has raised many questions in the United States since 1963. Indeed, they registered a fall, until around 1980–4, for tests in mathematics and for verbal tests that were subsequently renamed critical reading. The pre-1963 level was re-established around 2000 for mathematics, but not for the other test, which attempts to measure the student's ability to express facts and ideas.

According to the US statistical yearbook, the average score for the critical reading test dropped from 537 in 1970 to 502 in 1982 and it plateaued out at 501 in 2010. For the maths test, the score dropped from 512 in 1970 to 492 in 1980, rising to 516 in 2010.[7] The numerous modifications undergone by these tests, as well as the enlargement of the populations that take them, suggest that we should err on the side of caution in interpreting them. We can, however, safely say that the blockage of higher education from the mid-1960s or early 1970s did not result from any restriction by the host system but from the fact that an intellectual ceiling had been reached; we are not at all justified in supposing that this halt will last forever. The recent recovery may even mean that, after a pause, progress will resume.

Nor does the attainment of an educational ceiling for the generations that reached the age of 20 or 25 between 1965 and 1975 mean that the average level of American society immediately ceased to rise. At that time, the older generations were characterized by very low rates of higher education, and their gradual replacement by more educated generations continued to raise the average level of society, which therefore started

Table 12.2   Proportion of the population that has completed a course in higher education according to the Barro-Lee dataset, in %

Age group	1950	1980	2010
15–19	0.1	0.1	0.3
20–24	7.9	15.8	17.3
25–29	9.8	27.8	31.6
30–34	9.8	27.8	33.1
35–39	8.8	22.8	35.1
40–44	8.8	22.8	33.9
45–49	7.0	18.8	33.2
50–54	7.0	18.8	33.3
55–59	5.2	13.0	34.8
60–64	5.2	13.0	34.3
65–69	4.0	10.1	30.0
70–74	3.9	10.1	24.3
75 and above	3.9	10.1	19.4
25 and above	7.4	18.1	31.6

Table 12.3   Proportion of college graduates (or above) in the population of over-25s, according to the Statistical Abstract of the United States, in %

1970	10.7
1980	16.2
1990	21.3
1995	23.0
2000	25.6
2005	27.7
2007	28.7
2008	29.4
2009	29.5
2010	29.9

Source: Statistical Abstract of the United States, 2012, p. 151.

to approach, at the pace of demographic replacement, the ceiling rate of 30–35 per cent (the rate of the younger generations). The achievement of this rate by the entire population, all generations included, would mark the end of the upward movement and the beginning of stagnation for society as a whole. In 2015, this point had almost been reached. The comparison of age groups – in 1950, 1980 and 2010 – allows us to observe this inexorable mechanism whereby a level of stagnation is reached by homogenizing educational levels according to generation. I am here using the Barro-Lee dataset again (see Table 12.2). We can see that, in 2010, all adult generations were characterized by rates of between 30 and 35 per cent, with the exception of the 70–74 age group, which reached only

24.3 per cent, and the over-75-year-olds, a little lower still at 19.4 per cent. In these last two age groups, we are dealing with people most of whom are retired and we can thus conclude that, in its active mass, and despite the slight recovery in the youngest generations, American society has, since 2010 or 2015, been in a state of educational stagnation. This is also shown in the US statistical yearbook, which suggests, for its part, a ceiling close to 30 per cent. The revolution in higher education is, for the moment, complete.

The historical significance of stagnation

We need to be aware of the historical importance of this stagnation. Since 1900, the United States had led the way in education. If we conclude this statistical analysis in Hegelian terms, we will say that they were the advance guard of humanity in the development of Spirit. In this sense, the stagnation of the United States is the stagnation of all of us as human beings, as no other country has exceeded this level. The question is that of a limit to the rise in the educational level of humankind.

An examination of the countries following in America's wake will allow us, to a certain extent, to verify the universality of this ceiling, which might, as I have said, be only temporary. In France, for example, the stage of stagnation was reached around 1995 for 25-year-olds, lagging about thirty years behind America, as a result of the later take-off of higher education in France.[8] South Korea, meanwhile, has recently reached a higher rate than the United States, but this performance has been achieved to the detriment of the number of children produced by families, since it has been accompanied by a collapse in birth rate.

Empirically observing an educational stagnation should not lead us to any moralistic interpretation and bring us back to the hackneyed theme of an intellectual decadence brought about by a decline in moral standards. American educational stagnation was not, in fact, a consequence of the libertarian revolution of the 1960s. The generations affected by stagnation, and even by the partial decline in its level, were born and brought up earlier, by the ultra-conformist nuclear families of the 1940s–60s. Historical sequencing shows that 'moral' indicators (in the sense of indicators that reveal morals), such as birth rates and the proportion of births outside marriage, did not begin to shift significantly, downward for the first, upward for the second, until 1960–5. Thus, no decline in moral standards, as the cultural conservatives put it, can explain the fall of SAT scores and the downturn in student numbers.

One very specific factor, however, could have led to the stagnation of intellectual performance in the United States in the 1950s. It was then that television entered the lives of families and individuals, tearing them

211

to some extent away from written culture. By 1958, there were 287 television sets per 1,000 inhabitants in the United States. I mentioned earlier that intensive reading before puberty made *Homo sapiens* more intelligent. It comes as no surprise when we observe that an abandonment of intensive reading reduces the effectiveness of the human brain.

The return of educational inequality

As a result of the expansion of primary and secondary education, the development of higher education was initially seen as pure progress. It had not been realized that the increase in the student population would fragment the homogeneity of the social body. The new cultural stratification was not perceived until it was recognized that the privileged category of the higher educated would not be reached by the whole population. Universal access to primary and then secondary education had nourished an *egalitarian social subconscious* of a democratic kind; the capping of higher education generated, in the United States and elsewhere, an *inegalitarian social subconscious*.

The persistence, in the words of political and social actors, of a conscious egalitarian democratic doctrine does not change this situation. American society is now objectively stratified, as shown in Table 12.4, which now includes, for higher education, courses that were not completed, since the mere fact of having gone beyond high school can be seen as a symbol of belonging to the world of higher education.

The distribution of the over-25s shows us an American society dominated by primary and secondary education in 1980, while at the same time 30 per cent of citizens had already benefited from higher education of one kind or other. The central mass was then secondary, with primary education representing only a residual category. In such a society, simply knowing how to read and write – the egalitarian horizon of the nineteenth century – is no longer the key to joining the body of citizens, but is the characteristic mark of a lower status.

Table 12.4   The new stratification of American society

Level of education reached among over-25-year-olds, in %	1950	1980	2010
No schooling	2.6	1.0	0.4
Primary	45.7	6.3	2.7
Secondary	38.2	62.9	42.9
Higher	13.6	30.0	54.0

Source: Barro-Lee dataset

Thirty years later, in 2010, the group of higher education students exceeded half of the population. But this did not mean the beginning of a re-democratization from above because it was itself stratified: exactly half of the 'highers', 27 per cent of the whole, had benefited from a complete education (BA or higher), the other half from an incomplete education.

We will take full measure of the importance of these cultural categories in Chapter 14, devoted to the ascension of Donald Trump. During the primaries and then in the final clash between Republicans and Democrats, opinion pollsters would carefully distinguish between the voters according to whether they fell into the category 'College, BA' or 'College, no degree'.

The undemocratic consequences of the development of higher education, of which those involved became only belatedly and imperfectly aware, had nevertheless been foreseen, and very early on, by several lucid analysts. In 1958 Michael Young (1915–2002), a British scholar, anticipated the implications of the meritocratic principle, which people in France are always endeavouring to present as by nature egalitarian and republican. *The Rise of the Meritocracy* presents itself as a futuristic novel purportedly written in 2033, in which the author describes the appalling social stratification that resulted from the systematic schooling of the population:

> Under the new dispensation the division between the classes has been sharper than it used to be under the old, the status of the upper classes higher, and that of the lower classes lower. . . . Any historian knows that class conflict was endemic throughout pre-merit times, and, in the light of past experience, might perhaps expect that any rapid diminution in the status of one social class would necessarily aggravate such conflict. The question is: why have the changes of the last century not led to such an issue? Why has society been so stable in spite of the widening gulf between the bottom and the top?
>
> The cardinal reason is that stratification has been in accord with a principle of merit, generally accepted at all levels of society. A century ago the lower classes had an ideology of their own – in essentials the same as that which has now become paramount – and were able to use it as much to advance themselves as to attack their superiors. They denied the right of the upper classes to their position. But in the new conditions the lower classes no longer have a distinctive ideology in conflict with the ethos of society, any more than the lower orders used to in the heyday of feudalism. Since bottom agrees with top that merit should reign, they can only cavil at the means by which the choice has been made, not at the standard which all alike espouse. So much, so good. Yet we would be failing in our duty as sociologists did we not point out that such widespread recognition of merit as the arbiter may condemn to helpless despair the many who have no merit.[9]

Inequality in England and America

Why was it a British sociologist who realized this so early?

With its class structure crystallized by accents and dialects, England has always struggled with equality. Even the democratization of primary education there has not erased the sense of difference between human beings. Its absolute nuclear family, certainly, is content not to define brothers as equals. But we have also noted in this country the place, a minority but structuring place, of an embryonic stem family in the aristocracy, the gentry and the upper layers of the peasantry. And this anthropological type quite openly accepts inequality. So we should not be surprised to find in English culture a strong ability to think or antici-pate inequality, both in sociology and science fiction.

The term eugenics was coined in 1883 by the Englishman Francis Galton (1822–1911), the result of his obsession with inequalities between human beings. In *The Time Machine*, H. G. Wells (1866–1946) imag-ined, as early as 1895, workers and middle classes separating biologically and turning into distinct living species. In 1932, *The Inequality of Man* by John B. S. Haldane (1892–1964) – a biologist and geneticist, a social-ist, Marxist and atheist – emphasized the need for a scientific basis for inequality.[10] *Brave New World*, by Aldous Huxley (1894–1963), also imagined in that same year 1932, albeit ironically, a social stratification programmed by genetics. Michael Young was the heir to this tradition, and his very serious prophetic essay also presented itself as a science-fiction novel.

America, meanwhile, had been liberated by its War of Independence from the explicit claim of inequality between human beings. It then rejected primogeniture. And the United States would have to wait for an objective educational inequality to come into being before it could catch up with England in terms of anti-egalitarian ideological production.

From 1971 however, only a few years after the development of higher education had jammed, Richard J. Herrnstein (1930–94), professor of psychology at Harvard, put the cat among the pigeons by publishing in *The Atlantic Monthly* an article simply called 'IQ'. In it, he states that differences in intelligence quotient and the effects of this quotient on the social performance of individuals ought to ensure that inequality would be long-lived. In 1972, back to square one at Harvard: Christopher Jencks (born in 1936), a professor of sociology, published *Inequality*, which attacked the egalitarian dream of the American 'liberals', i.e. the Left, head on. Relying on masses of numbers and yielding to all the pleasures associated with statistical sleight of hand, he challenged education's ability to engender equality.[11] England, for its part, remained an exporter of inegalitarian ideology. Thus in 1973 Hans J. Eysenck (1917–97) published, under the same title as J. B. S. Haldane in 1932, *The Inequality of Man*, a new version of the argument linking IQ to intrinsic intelligence, academic success and social performance, concluding very classically by passing a final judgement on human nature as a whole.[12] Eysenck, also British, had begun to wax wroth on the subject much earlier, however, since his *Uses and Abuses of Psychology* dated back to 1953.[13] He was already developing the problematic that leads from the measurement of IQ to the notion of a stratified society. The publication of Young's *The Rise of the Meritocracy* came five years later, in 1958.

Looking back, it is now clear that the American texts of the early 1970s, whose intellectual interest was relatively slight compared to the previous British contribution, were indeed the symptoms of an anti-democratic ideological turnaround. They proposed neither more nor less than a naturalistic legitimation of inequality. Young, a Labour supporter and education activist, wanted to warn the British Left before disaster struck. The American ideologues who engaged in this fight contributed to the rise of neoconservatism.

The Bell Curve, co-authored by Richard Herrnstein and Charles Murray, marked the coming of age of inegalitarian ideology.[14] There are the usual clichés about the primacy of IQ. The authors do not have the necessary statistical skills for an analysis of the subject. They are especially blind to the destructive effect on self-esteem that results from being born and raised in a society that tells you that if you are Black, you are inferior. I read this book when it first came out, and it sickened me.

Herrnstein goes no further than Young in his description of the stratified society born of higher education. His argument reveals, however, that in America the question of equality is not based, as it is in England, on the question of class membership but of racial belonging. Basically, for the English an inferior person will always ultimately be a worker, a prole; for an American, the inferior person will always be a Black. The linguistic idioms of the English working-class world are, moreover, often the same as those of the American Black world, which also has its specific accent.

Certainly, Herrnstein poses the question of the inequality of human beings in general and not simply racial terms. But in my opinion, he has far and away less intellectual merit than Young, because the stratified society he claimed to be foretelling already existed when he undertook to write his essay. In 1971, the implosion of the American egalitarian ideal was underway; the Vietnam War (1963–75) had served as a catalyst.

The Vietnam War as a revelation: 'working-class war'

The Second World War had been a great moment of egalitarianism for American society; it was perhaps even the symbol of the maturing of Roosevelt's social democracy. Secondary education was already almost universal; the take-off of higher education was just beginning when all young American men were enlisted in the name of universal conscription. Thus, up until George Bush, Sr, American politicians, whether from the establishment or not, generally had pretty good military careers behind them. After Bush, investigative journalists could start tracking down those who had managed to escape the Vietnam War in cushy desk jobs.

The number of Americans engaged in Vietnam was significant, but did not exhaust the nation's energies. It exceeded 150,000 between 1965 and 1971, plateauing out at 536,000 in 1968. Who was mobilized, who was spared? For an understanding of how this war marked the breakdown of American egalitarianism, we can turn to an extraordinarily sensitive study by Christian Appy, *Working-Class War: American Combat Soldiers and Vietnam*. It shows how much participation in and opposition to war crystallized class sentiments in the United States; in this highly advanced society, classes were already defined by education as well as by position in the relations of production. Describing opposition to the war, Appy writes:

> [M]ost soldiers perceived that the [antiwar] movement was essentially middle class. The image of the antiwar activist dominating the mass media (including the military's) was that of the college radical. For working-class soldiers, college symbolized privilege, and quite apart from the context of Vietnam, college students stirred in many a deep set of class-related emotions: resentment, anger, self-doubt, envy, and ambition. The class gulf was further exacerbated by the knowledge that college students were deferred from the draft.[15]

It was during the Vietnam War that the rift between students and workers, between college and high school graduates, appeared.

When we try to situate the emergence of the same cultural antagonism in France, we find that it was out of synch with America, as the development of higher education and its subsequent stagnation occurred later. In France, solidarity between the two left-wing worlds was still alive in 1968: workers went on strike following the student revolt. There was a residual feeling of condescension towards the real working-class world and its Communist Party only on the side of certain leftists, generally Trotskyists. The opposition between working-class people and the educated classes in France would not appear entrenched until twenty-four

216

years later, during the debate on the 1992 Maastricht Treaty. But by then the confrontation between the working world and the middle classes, between the people and the elites, would be particularly clear, and the language used by those who took part made this obvious.

Those elites were not then in the majority but already had a large-scale presence, since higher education in France then produced 33 per cent college graduates per generation. It would not be long before France entered a period of educational stagnation. It became measurable around 1995. In France as in the United States, a clear (if approximate) temporal coincidence between the beginning of educational stagnation and the emergence of a perception of society as stratified is evident.

Academia: a machine to manufacture inequality

The new educational stratification insidiously spread the feeling that human beings are definitely not equal. In America and England, as we have just seen, professional ideologues formulated the creed of a humankind separated into more or less intelligent and capable groups. In France, the same phenomenon occurred but without calling into question the official egalitarian ideology: here, IQ remains essentially a concept to be treated with suspicion. In these conditions, the development of inegalitarianism in France is still, apart from in phases of political crisis, entirely subconscious.

In France as in the United States, however, we would be wrong to represent the new inegalitarian subconscious as the product of an evolution in the pure world of 'ideas'. Inequality has its machinery. Real individuals are assessed, sorted, assigned to their places, as in the futuristic works of Young or Huxley, by concrete institutions – educational systems whose main function is no longer emancipation but classification and supervision. And it takes a very powerful organization to select and train the one-third of the population who will be defined as part of the college, or so-called 'higher-educated', graduate world.

The university system, together with elite institutions like the *grandes écoles* in France, now plays an important role in the economic and social life of advanced countries, by the number of agents it employs as well as by the fraction of the GDP that it absorbs. We will name this set of people 'Academia', so as to shake off the old images. In the United States, education accounted for 5.4 per cent of total spending in 2012, of which 2.8 per cent was for higher education, or around $450 billion per year.[16] In comparison, note that American military expenditure in the years 2000–15 hovered at between 3.5 and 5.5 per cent of GDP, according to the number of external interventions engaged on, i.e. a central tendency of 4.5 per cent. Academia marks out territories: it has become an essential urban function. Its presence or absence often dictate, for an average city of the post-industrial age, prosperity or decline.

Staying with the United States, the official ideology of the academic world there is now *liberal*, progressive, left-wing – noisily so, of course, if the university concerned is towards the top of the hierarchy of institutions. But the objective function of Academia is to destroy equality. Each institution of higher education assigns each student a place in the social hierarchy. Knowledge, indispensable knowledge, is of course transmitted there, and research, which is just as indispensable, is carried out there. However, since studies are now longer than required for the acquisition of skills or the identification of aptitude for research (master's, doctorate, post-doc, etc.), it is clear that the hierarchization of society has become the primary goal.

It is no longer possible to regard Academia, an unequal structure, as dispensing an ideal of freedom. After all, we no longer embark on graduate studies to emancipate ourselves. Graduate studies are required to reach the top of the social pyramid if one is ambitious, to remain there if one comes from a middle-class background, to avoid slipping down the social order if one is of modest origin. Increasingly severe processes of selection impose on the participants an attitude of submission and conformism to this generalized social competition. Authority, inequality: this is the secret motto of Academia. In the contemporary Anglo-American world, one of the symptoms of the reactionary function of universities is the high salaries paid to those who administrate the machine – much higher than those paid to teachers and researchers. The reforms of the French university system are leading in the same direction. We will see the importance of the role of Academia, a world that thinks it is on the left but is actually organizing inequality and conformism, in the crystallization of ideological alignments in the England of Brexit and the America of Donald Trump.

Economic inequality as a consequence

By 1968, in the United States, the inegalitarian educational subconscious was fully in place. Economic inequality, on the other hand, remained of lesser importance. Again, a simple historical sequence will allow us to distinguish the cause from the effect: it is the cultural sphere that determines the economic.

The curves in the evolution of taxable income, established by Emmanuel Saez and Thomas Piketty for the period 1913–2000, allow us to date the rise of economic inequality: it does indeed follow the rise of educational inequality.[17] Let us follow their lead and distinguish the richest 1 per cent from the next 4 per cent, and finally the next 5 per cent. When

Proportion of national revenue in %, excluding capital gains

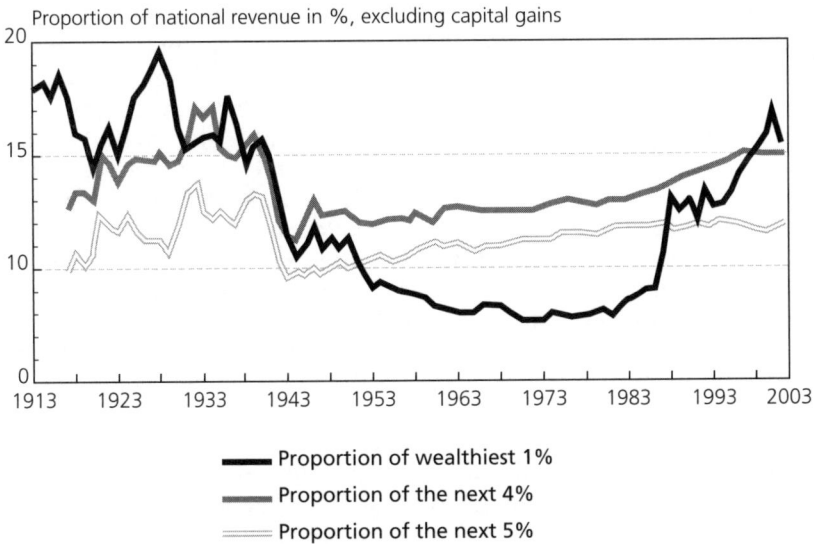

Graph 12.2   The development of the income of the wealthiest people in the United States

Source: Thomas Piketty and Emmanuel Saez, 'Income and Wage Inequality in the United States, 1913–2002', in Anthony Atkinson and Thomas Piketty, *Top Incomes over the 20th Century* (Oxford: Oxford University Press, 2007), p. 147.

aggregated, the 1 per cent, 4 per cent and 5 per cent constitute the 10 per cent, the 'upper decile' generally proposed by the OECD to measure the increase of inequalities. The OECD has made a speciality of hiding the upper class of the 1 per cent away in this upper decile. Let us admit, however, that, overall, the top 10 per cent are rarely disadvantaged and are a good approximation of what is often referred to as the 'upper middle class'.

From 1945 onwards, we observe a slow rise in the incomes of the 5 per cent and the 4 per cent, which together constitute, fraternally mixed together, the least favoured of the favoured, the bulk of the first decile. The incomes of the 1 per cent at the top then evolve downwards, until 1963; then they stagnate until 1980. From this date these 1 per cent show an increase, which gathers pace from 1985 onwards. The progress of the 4 per cent who follow them in the income scale accelerates a little, but in much smaller proportions. For the next 5 per cent, stagnation can be observed as early as 1983.

1980 was a pivotal year: before that date, the increase enjoyed by the 9 per cent could be interpreted as the normal economic effect of an increase in the number of college graduates in the labour force: the development of economic stratification did indeed reflect the new educational

219

stratification. More graduates saw their new skills rewarded with higher incomes. So we are still within a classical economic interpretative framework. After 1980, however, the income of the super-rich achieved escape velocity and freed itself from any technical or economic rationality.

1980 was the year of Reagan's election. Neoliberalism took the lead, in a climate of social war. Inflation peaked at 13.5 per cent in 1981. In June of that year, Paul Volcker raised the Federal Reserve's leading interest rate to 20 per cent. In 1983, the inflation rate fell to 3.2 per cent. It would take too long to list here the measures of deregulation of the labour market and release of capital that created the conditions for the rise of high incomes and the stagnation of low incomes – in short, for a spectacular rise in inequalities. We will simply note that a dramatic change in political direction preceded the emancipation of the rich, a phenomenon utterly distinct from the slight increase in inequality triggered, before 1980, by the new stratification of skills as an effect of the third educational revolution. We are here faced with a complex development but one where the cultural, ideological and political spheres *always* precede the economic.

After 1980, the rise in economic inequality was continuous. The proportion of national income appropriated by the richest 10 per cent increased from 32 per cent in 1972 to 43 per cent in 2002, and that of the richest 1 per cent from 8 per cent to 17 per cent. It then approached what had been its record level at the beginning of the previous century, 18 per cent. The rise of the richest, temporarily halted by the great recession of 2008–10, then resumed, as if nothing decisive had really happened in the economic field. Starting in 2010, a modest resolution of the crisis led to a renewed rise in high incomes but didn't prevent the decline in median household income.

Ideological transformation, political crisis and the rise in material inequalities

To fully understand the conflict between egalitarian America, the heir to universal secondary education and the New Deal, and the new, inegalitarian America, stratified by higher education and embracing the cause of neoliberalism, we must first summarize the succession of political and ideological stages involved.

In the late 1960s and early 1970s, Roosevelt's America was still on the offensive. The presidency of a Republican between 1969 and 1974, Richard Nixon, had not done much to change the post-war equilibrium: ideological hegemony still lay with equality and the state. Between 1969 and 1972, American employers were even forced onto the defensive, threatened by new federal regulations on labour security and the protection of consumers and of the environment. The upper classes, however, eventually reacted. In 1971, Lewis Powell, who was to become a conservative judge in the Supreme Court, had described 'the American economic system' as 'under broad attack. . . . Business must learn the lesson . . . that political power is necessary; that such power must be assiduously cultivated; and that when necessary, it must be used aggressively and with determination – without embarrassment and without the reluctance which has been so characteristic of American business.'[18]

In 1972, three employers' organizations merged to form the Business Roundtable, limited to the CEOs of the largest companies. In the five years that followed, 113 of the 200 most powerful companies were represented in it. SMEs, even more vehement against state regulation, organized themselves equally energetically: between 1970 and 1979, the number of members of the National Federation of Independent Business (NFIB) doubled.[19] These regenerated employers' organizations soon met with a success that was firmly entrenched even before Ronald Reagan came on the scene – indeed, it was evident even in the Carter presidency: in 1978, a Democratic Congress voted for a reduction from 48 per cent to 28 per cent in the top marginal tax rate on capital income.[20]

Let us now survey the whole historical sequence, from an educational, political and economic point of view. The development of higher education fragmented the cultural homogeneity of the social body, which, as early as the mid-1960s, could be described as stratified, ripe for economic inequality. There were now high school Americans on one side and college students on the other. The university system itself was highly differentiated: a chasm separated, in terms of prestige, those students who went to the elite universities and the run-of-the-mill graduates from state colleges. The egalitarian economic dynamic of the previous era, however, rumbled on inertly until the early 1970s, in an America that had yet to grasp the extent to which educational inequality was now its profound reality. Nevertheless, IQ ideologues such as Herrnstein and Jencks, entrenched in the heart of the intellectual establishment at Harvard, embarked on the theoretical shaping of a new inegalitarian creed around 1971–2. By 1972, employers, convinced they were fighting for their lives, engaged in a standoff against the Left and the unions. The dominant economic ideology then quickly changed tack – in rather paradoxical ways, since in order to laud the merits of the free market and justify the withdrawal of the state, it would have to pull things out from a bottom intellectual drawer in which nobody so far had shown the least interest. In 1962, for example, Milton Friedman had published *Capitalism and Freedom*, to general indifference.[21] In the first (and very belated) reprint of the book in 1982, the author emphasized what a flop the book had been in the early 1960s. On the other hand, he described the vast and immediate success

221

of his 1980 book *Free to Choose*[22] – which, in his words, presented the 'same basic philosophy'.

The political and ideological struggle initiated in the early 1970s, against the backdrop of an inegalitarian cultural infrastructure, and in the context of the end of the Vietnam War, which had revealed the new antagonism of the educational classes, culminated around 1980 in the collapse of the egalitarian values of the New Deal and led to the neoconservative revolution. This liberal and inegalitarian revolution, as we have seen, had not needed the election of Reagan to celebrate its first triumphs, which went back to the Carter presidency. Be that as it may, the neoconservative revolution, so fond of deregulation and tax cuts, ensured a happy old age for Milton Friedman. And the big winners in these new class struggles were ultimately not the middle-class graduates, but the 'top incomes' targeted by T. Piketty and E. Saez, the upper 1 per cent. A plutocracy of very high incomes thus flourished in a society that had generally ceased to believe in the ideal of state-regulated equality.

Free trade and the 'providential' march to inequality

We must note the irresistible nature of the march to inequality between 1980 and 2015, just as Tocqueville had to accept the rise of equality, in his time, as 'providential'. The neoconservative revolution seemed, prior to Donald Trump, insensitive to the economic and social contradictions it engendered, even in a country with a 'democratic' tradition where powerful political parties competed for the votes. It is the groundbreaking character of the anti-egalitarian movement that means we can assert the primacy of education and ideology as the decisive factors and note the derivative character of economic evolution. An invisible hand seemed to guide all economic policy decisions towards fiercely inegalitarian programmes. The option of full free trade, which forced American workers to compete with Third World workers who were paid twenty or thirty times less than them, could only be conceived and implemented in a world that no longer wanted to believe in equality.

Free trade drives up corporate profit rates and inequality, as the decades-old textbooks on international economics designed for US students very explicitly point out. Those who promoted free trade knew that it would severely affect the working class and devastate the Black community. But the crushing of wages – its first effect in an advanced country – could have been anticipated by anyone. You don't need a higher education to understand this simple mechanism. While it was the elites who first sang the praises of full free trade, the entire American electorate accepted the augury. Thus, in the 1984 presidential election,

Democrat Walter Mondale, whose programme, supported by the unions, was explicitly protectionist, was crushed by Ronald Reagan.

It is also thanks to an inegalitarian ideological environment, and not for any reason of economic rationality, that the salaries of CEOs and senior executives of companies have been able to soar to such heights, beyond any technical necessity and beyond any moral principle. Let us not waste time dismantling the ravings of the mercenary economists who have claimed to find, on the basis of various completely hermetic models, a justification for this social madness. Inequality was the spirit of the time, and everything became possible. At the helm of the major companies, CEOs began to help themselves to cash, in a strange parodic version of the Marxist-Leninist slogan 'to each according to his needs' adapted for the rich. In 2013, the income of the 'average' CEO of one of the five hundred largest US companies was 204 times that of the average worker. It was only twenty times higher in 1950.

But are we really sure, at this stage of the analysis, that we have explained everything? Is the hypothesis of an educational stratification that engenders an inegalitarian subconscious enough? Yes, certainly, insofar as it is a mechanism generally applicable to the entire advanced world. In Sweden, as in France, Germany and Japan, the new educational stratification did end up leading to greater economic inequality, but later – and to a lesser extent – than in the United States. In the United Kingdom, the rise in inequality, while greater than in Europe, has not yet reached the American level.

The collapse of the value of equality in America was so sudden, so violent, so widespread, that in order to explain it completely, one must dig deep down into the core of the anthropological system.

Far away from the debate that contemporary political economy formalizes under the abstract and universal terms of 'market', 'profit', 'salary', 'taxation' and 'consumer freedom', we will discover an aberrant determination, namely race. Indeed, it can be easily demonstrated that the organization of American society into the categories of Blacks and Whites has played a decisive role in the acceptance and development of ultra-liberal policies. This is because, under the supposed 'rationality' of *Homo oeconomicus*, lies an inability to break free from the dialectic of *us* and *them*.

223

— 13 —

A CRISIS IN BLACK AND WHITE

Readers of Tocqueville, and indeed all those who see America as the first Western democracy, can only marvel at the ease with which, between 1980 and 2015, that country accepted the sudden growth in economic inequality. The neoliberal revolution that took place within the framework of normally functioning representative institutions carried on quite unaffected by any major political shock. As we have seen, the emergence of a new educational stratification largely explains, in the United States as in the rest of the advanced world, the dissolution of the egalitarian subconscious and the crystallization of an inegalitarian subconscious. But why has America's onward march been so easy, much faster than in continental Europe and Japan and even than in the United Kingdom, for all that the latter is so close to the United States in its anthropological basis?

The absolute nuclear family, liberal but non-egalitarian, is common to all the nations of the Anglosphere. It encourages individualism and a break between each generation. It is not, like the French egalitarian nuclear family, or the Russian or Chinese communitarian family, obsessed with an a priori ideal of equality, so it is easy to see why a certain rise in economic inequality has not caused alarm in America. But it is also true that the absolute nuclear family does not define human beings as unequal, in the manner of the German or Japanese stem family. The War of Independence, moreover, allowed America to get rid of the aristocratic primogeniture of the English. In the United States there is no trace of the rules of inequality between children that are typical of the nobility and wealthy peasantry in the United Kingdom. What the American anthropological base might have suggested is an increase in inequalities that occurred more easily than in France – and this hypothesis has been verified – but more slowly than in England, and here the opposite turned out to be the case, as is shown in Table 13.1 and Graph 13.1, taken from Thomas Piketty's research. The proportion of national

Table 13.1   The top 1 per cent in the West: 1900–2000, proportion of national income

	1900	1939	1950	1980	2000
France	19.0	13.3	9.0	7.6	7.6
United Kingdom	19.3	17.0	11.5	5.9	12.7
United States	18.0	15.4	11.4	8.2	16.9
Germany	18.6	16.3	11.6	10.8	11.1
Japan	16.3	18.0	7.7	7.2	8.2
Sweden	27.0	10.3	7.6	4.0	6.0

Source: After Anthony Atkinson and Thomas Piketty, *Top Incomes over the 20th Century* (Oxford: Oxford University Press, 2007).

income absorbed by the top 1 per cent has struggled to take off in France and actually started to do so only in the 2000s; this proportion increased sharply in the United Kingdom but it has soared in the United States, even though the latter's democratic tradition is older and, so everyone thought, stronger than England's.[1]

It is the relative magnitude of the rise in inequality in the United States that needs to be explained. This is impossible unless we start from the very foundation of American democracy, that of a White equality initially defined by the inferiority of Indians and, especially, Blacks: the

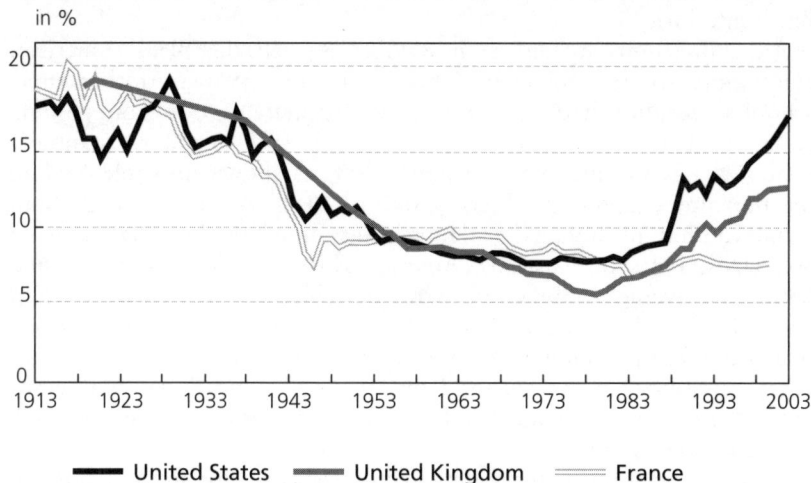

Graph 13.1   The proportion of the wealthiest 1 per cent in the United States, the United Kingdom and France, 1913–2000

Source: Thomas Piketty, 'Top Incomes over the 20th Century: A Summary of Main Findings', in Anthony Atkinson and Thomas Piketty, *Top Incomes over the 20th Century* (Oxford: Oxford University Press, 2007), p. 12.

integration of Blacks into political life has contributed to destabilizing White egalitarian sentiment. Together, a new educational stratification and the struggle for desegregation explain the collapse of equality in America with particular clarity.

Desegregation

By the mid-1950s, 80 per cent of US citizens had benefited from a secondary education. This level of educational development was the mental infrastructure of an optimistic, powerful nation, a major player on the planet. The United States was now facing communism, which was gradually (albeit unwittingly) spreading across the space occupied by the exogamous communitarian family and dominating the heart of Eurasia from Eastern Europe to China. Competition with an egalitarian communist ideology dramatized the question of equality in the United States. In the aftermath of the victory over Nazism, in the context of a global clash, the inferior status imposed on Black Americans became a powerful argument for the Soviet Union.

The United States thus endeavoured to try and include the Black minority in the democratic system. Here we reach a key moment in historical development, since American democratic sentiment had hitherto always defined itself as a White egalitarianism, unthinkable without Indian or Black inferiority.

An endogenous dynamics, however, also led the Black American community to demand civil rights in the mid-1950s. At that time, school segregation had not stopped the dominated group from gaining access to better education, even though it still lagged substantially behind the White majority. Around 1900, as shown in Table 12.1 in the previous chapter, the literacy rate of Black Americans was about equal to that of Italians or Hungarians, much higher than that of Spaniards, Poles or Russians. Among White Americans born around 1900, the average number of years of schooling was close to eight and a half, and among Blacks a mere five. Thirty years later, among Americans born around 1930, Whites received some eleven and a half years' schooling on average, and Blacks nine.[2] Educational democratization had therefore made good progress when the struggle for Black emancipation began.

In 1955, in Montgomery, the second largest city in Alabama, in the Deep South, Rosa Parks launched a boycott of the segregated bus system. This struggle was the result of an initiative from the Black community, which now refused to submit to the segregation that its level of educational development rendered absurd. But, just as importantly, White America, then in an optimistic mood and committed to the anti-communist struggle, had made the Blacks' demand for civil rights its own aim and objective, with the exception of the Deep South.

We can say that, from the point of view of political anthropology, American democracy thereupon tried to escape from its racial matrix. And we need to sense the heroic aspects of such an attempt. We need to understand that, in the context of American history, it was a genuine attempt to soar up to the heavens.

In 1964 and 1965, the Civil Rights Act and the Voting Rights Act showed how the nation was shifting in this direction: the inclusion of Blacks became a priority issue. The United States had decided to put an end to ethnic democracy as a system based on a dominant group and the exclusion of a pariah population. A bold integration policy resorted to busing in order to bring about the desegregation of schools. Affirmative action attempted to compensate for the longstanding backwardness of the Black community, both in education and employment, by reserving places for it in the university system and in the economy, especially in the public sector. The effects of this policy were far from derisory. By the year 2000, the 16.6 per cent of Blacks aged 25 and over with a BA were better educated than the 71.9 per cent of (non-Hispanic) Whites without a BA.[3] Black police officers and firefighters were now part of American life.

The shaking of White democracy

The fact remains that the integration of Blacks into the sociopolitical system weakened the internal egalitarianism of the White group by virtue of a terrible syllogism. If Whites were defined as equal by Black inferiority, the appearance of equality between Blacks and Whites could only destroy the very principle of White equality. Such a syllogism would not have operated in a society with an egalitarian family unconscious, predisposing people to think that if brothers are equal, all human beings are equal. But in a society that considers brothers, and therefore human beings, as different, the disappearance of the Black/White divide can only lead to the rise of a feeling of the non-equality of human beings in general.

Thus, in America, the emancipation of Blacks has, since 1965, contributed to the breakdown of the egalitarian culture and added its effects to the endogenous disintegration of the White group caused by educational stratification, which divides Whites into upper and lower class. This approach, which combines a basic racial sentiment with a new educational stratification, opens up an immense field for investigation that I cannot fully explore in the context of this outline. But one paradox needs to be mentioned here, as it involves the contradiction between the conscious and the subconscious in the American political dynamic.

Conscious ideological life would lead us to view the desire for the emancipation of Blacks by Whites, so manifest and admirable in the mid-1960s, as an extension of the founding principles of American democracy, the effect of an egalitarian dynamic finally breaking free of its initial racial roots. But we are perhaps justified in wondering whether, in a White world where egalitarian sentiment had been shaken by the development of higher education, Black inferiority has not ceased to have a function. The emancipation of the dominated group might well have been desired by a class that had benefited from higher education, that no longer believed in White equality, and that had therefore become indifferent to the Black question.

The logic would then be reversed. The right syllogism would not be: if Blacks become the equals of Whites, equality between Whites themselves loses its meaning, but: if Whites become unequal between themselves, the inferiority of Blacks loses its meaning.

I here raise a cruel question, and in my following discussion I will be pursuing a no less cruel analysis of the persistence of racial sentiment in the United States; but I ask the reader to understand that it is not my intention to activate any kind of anti-American feeling. In my opinion, the subject is crucial because America represents a concrete universal: *Homo americanus* is, in the advanced world, the type closest to the original *Homo sapiens*. The majority of Americans, in any case, are no longer of English origin, and the ease with which the children and grand-children of immigrants, whatever their original values, have adopted the American racial dichotomy and made it their own shows that this dichotomy is not in the least exceptional: it is perfectly compatible with human nature in general.

The persistence of racial sentiment among those with primary and secondary education

By virtue of this cold and dispassionate approach, we can accept, if not understand, how there was an extraordinary mixture of progress and regression in the fate of Black Americans between 1965 and 2015. During this period, racial sentiment persisted amongst a significant proportion of the White population, even if opinion polls tell us the opposite. This is shown by an analysis of marriage, an issue that lies at the heart of the racial question, since, if there is a high rate of intermarriage, races become diluted and eventually disappear. Current polls might make us optimistic: 43 per cent of Americans consider interracial marriages a good thing, 44 per cent say they don't make any difference and only 11 per cent say they are a bad thing. The hostility rate now is only 5 per cent among 18–29-year-olds and 13 per cent in the South.[4] But the reality of social life completely fails to reflect this emancipatory opinion, even if the statistical analysis must lift various veils to reveal the reality of an enduring marital segregation.

Among recent married couples, the rate of intermarriage in 2010 was 17 per cent among Blacks, as against 25 per cent among Asians and Hispanics.[5] Typical of intermarriage among Black Americans, however, was the exclusion of women: 24 per cent of recently married Black men had wed outside their racial category, but only 9 per cent of women had done so. Let us continue to lift the veil of appearances. Wendy Wang, who has provided us with these figures, rightly points out that the relative increase in intermarriage occurred in the context of a collapse of marriage that was particularly striking among Black Americans, since only 31 per cent of them were married in 2010. Let us develop this argument. In 2008, the proportion of births to unmarried mothers was 71.8 per cent for Black American women compared to 40.6 per cent for mothers classified as White and 52.6 per cent for those classified as Hispanic. In other words, the rise in the rate of intermarriage among Black Americans makes little sense for men, and almost none for women. In the racial category targeted by American society as different, the single mother remains the dominant type by far.

There is, however, a slight but real rise in the rate of intermarriage in the higher educated group, where marriages between Black women and White men even display an above-average stability, including homogeneous marriages among Whites.[6] The higher educated may, indeed, be breaking free from the determining factors of a racial conception of social life.

Racial sentiment versus the welfare state: Republicans

In general, however, and in spite of the universalism displayed by society, racial sentiment has endured, particularly in the group of Whites who have attended primary and high schools. It has also been cynically manipulated by some politicians, mainly the higher educated, to accelerate the collapse of the egalitarian socioeconomic system inherited from the New Deal and the Second World War. Having been a motor of White equality until around 1960, racial sentiment became, from 1980, a lever to destroy White economic equality.

In 1991, Thomas and Mary Edsall described this sequence in *Chain Reaction*.[7] Their book is the most important of a cascade of books that, from the early 1990s onwards, have analysed the way the struggle for desegregation perversely led to the shaking up of the American welfare state. Busing, which tried to mix Black and White children in working-class neighbourhoods, and then affirmative action, which imposed Black quotas on the colleges, the police, the fire brigades and all kinds of administrative entities, eventually provoked hostility amongst Whites who were concerned because of the collapse of American industry that resulted from free trade. The struggle for Black emancipation has, in fact, been historically confused with the re-proletarianization of a working class that believed itself to be in the process of definitively moving up into the middle class.

Thus, ordinary Whites fled, whenever they could, to the suburbs, which became independent of the city centres. They removed their children from the public schools. The recruitment of firefighters and Black police as part of affirmative action roused a muted anger among people of Irish or Italian origin, who had hitherto viewed these jobs as their own preserve. The tax system now seemed to be financing a public sector that was bent on favouring Blacks. However, for a population to consent to taxation in a system of democratic representation, group consciousness has to suggest to all the taxpayers involved that state expenditure will benefit not necessarily themselves, but those with whom they feel a sense of solidarity. If we admit that the White population does not feel solidarity with the Black population, that it perceives it as external, we can understand the violence of the American rejection of taxation, a violence that broke out in the form of the anti-tax revolt in California in 1978. Thomas and Mary Edsall also noted the persistent approval by Whites of a local tax that would inevitably benefit them directly.[8] Be that as it may, the revolt against federal taxation reveals the persistence of American racial sentiment just as much as does the only small increase in the rate of intermarriage between Whites and Blacks, the indestructible spatial segregation, and the racial homogeneity of the Black churches. And this remains true despite the opinion polls that tell us that racial sentiment is being eroded, and despite the election of Barack Obama as the first Black president of the United States of America.

The rejection of desegregation has not only affected one-off measures such as busing and affirmative action; it has grown into overall hostility towards the federal state that imposed them. And the struggle for the rights of the fifty states to be respected has provided the Republican Party with the basis for a coded discourse; we can see it as having been tried out under Nixon and having matured with Reagan in 1980. According to this discourse, federal state = pro-Black action, which is undemocratic because it is based on the courts, first and foremost the Supreme Court – institutions dominated at the time by the liberal ideology of Whites with college degrees. Armed with this codified 'dog whistle' rhetoric, the Republican Party, which had been the party of Lincoln and the abolition of slavery, managed to steal Southern White voters from the Democrats, and then make serious inroads into their working-class base in post-Irish and post-Italian milieus in the North. The Republican Party thus became, if we disregard the effects of the way it foregrounded a few Black political leaders, a White party. And the Black vote would reach a level of spectacular communitarization, with 85 per cent or 95 per cent of Blacks voting Democrat, depending on the circumstances.

The hatred of the central desegregating state mainly allowed the Republicans to challenge the legitimacy of welfare, a tax that supposedly benefited minorities to an exaggerated degree. Such was the racial, educational and economic context in which neoconservatism flourished and Reagan was able to attack the state inherited from the New Deal. This was far removed from any economic argument.

The democratic adaptation: jazz and prison

As the Democrats ran out of steam, they read Thomas and Mary Edsall's bestseller, and Bill Clinton used his own coded language, subtly drawing on anti-racist *bien-pensant* wisdom, to ensure that the Black electorate helped vote him into power in 1992, and combining it with a dramatization of the Black problem to gain his share of the White electorate. In *The New Jim Crow*, Michelle Alexander shows how well Clinton understood what was at stake and was keen to avoid giving the Republicans the monopoly of anti-Black sentiment in 1992. On the eve of the decisive New Hampshire primary, he flew to his state of Arkansas to witness the execution of a Black prisoner, a man with a severe mental handicap who, on the very day he was executed, asked for his dessert to be kept for the following morning.[9] The Clinton policy of gaoling Blacks would be as fierce as Reagan's, even if the Democratic president liked to show off by playing the saxophone in the company of Black musicians. Clinton was, according to Alexander, the president whose mandates witnessed the largest increase in the incarceration of young Blacks.[10]

On the other hand, it is the persistence of racial sentiment that has allowed the Republican Party to manipulate White workers and lead them to vote, repeatedly, against their class interests. Throughout this period, the Republican Party has advocated religious values, but used its time in power to reduce, amply and repetitively, the taxes of the rich and to reduce social benefits now perceived as 'Black'; Reagan particularly had 'Welfare queens', single Black mothers supposedly living off the state, in his sights.

At this point I need to emphasize the main weakness of a book known for its excellent demonstration of the ability of American workers to vote against their own interests. In *What's the Matter with Kansas?* (the English edition retitled it *What's the Matter with America?*), Thomas Franks claims that White voters who accepted neoliberalism and fell into the trap of fighting taxation were devoid of racial motivation.[11] This is to

231

miss the main point: the coexistence, within American political culture, of a triumphant universalist language that leads to opinion polls celebrating the victory of desegregation, and powerful and persistent racial stereotypes that are unstated rather than unconscious. Martin Gilens, in *Why Americans Hate Welfare*, showed again in 1999 how the media had imposed the (false) image of a poverty that had become exclusively Black and the (false) idea that public aid was concerned only with Blacks. Alberto Alesina and Edward Glaeser, in their 2004 book *Fighting Poverty in the US and Europe*, added an indispensable comparative dimension to the issue of 'racism against welfare'.[12] According to Alesina and Glaeser, the challenge to the welfare state in the United States, and the fact that it still survives in Europe, are largely the result of American racial division and the greater homogeneity of Europe. But, they ask, how much longer will this situation last?

The pathological dimension of the racial reaction: the large-scale confinement of the Blacks

Before addressing the pathological dimension of the White racial response, we need to remember the climate of cultural crisis during the great period of the struggle for desegregation, between 1965 and 1980. The development of higher education had led to an optimistic state of mind and to the flowering in the 1960s of a dream of emancipation, with a counter-culture that challenged the omnipotence of money and gave birth to the hippie movement and to musical and sexual experimentation (with or without hallucinogenic drugs). It soon became apparent, however, that this evolution entailed a destabilization of attitudes – to anomie in Durkheim's original sense of the term, i.e. a psychosocial state in which aspiration and behaviour cease to be defined and framed by rules. (In American sociology, 'anomie' means a state of social atomization and the isolation of individuals.) The rise in the number of births outside marriage is not the right indicator to observe the development of a crisis of this type, since, as we shall see, a stabilization of moral values is not incompatible with this indicator remaining at a high level. The increase in violence, on the other hand, is a very reliable signal. But the disruption of private behaviour has led to a significant rise in private violence in American society. The least questionable of the indicators is the homicide rate. (The frequency of assault and battery, rape and other delinquent behaviour, not to mention drug offences, is too dependent on the level of reporting to be completely reliable.)

Now, the rate of American homicides plateaued in 1962–3, with 4.6 deaths per 100,000 inhabitants – a much higher rate, of course, than the

European norm. It then rose steadily to 9.8 in 1974, fell to 8.7 in 1976, then rose again to 10.2 in 1980. It hovered above 8 until 1995, then fell rapidly to below 6 by 1999, returning to 4.7 in 2013. This indicator allows us to regard the years 1964–95 as marking a transition crisis, during which American society seemed to lose its bearings.

It is in this context that American society's anxieties once again focused on Black Americans. While free trade was destroying the jobs of Black workers and destabilizing the authority of husbands and fathers, the liberation in moral values was completing the destruction of the Black family, which had been making difficult progress towards greater stability ever since the abolition of slavery. Thus, violence disproportionately affected Black communities, which became America's place of crystallization of all anxieties. In the new and unprecedented context of a relative economic and social stagnation, Blacks once more became the negative pole of America's social and mental organization.

With the struggle against welfare, the fight against crime became one of the elements in the codified language of the Republicans, before being adopted by Clinton's Democratic discourse. In 1982, Reagan launched his 'war on drugs', the beginning of a pathological social saga that led the United States, so used to singing the praises of liberty, to its status as world leader in incarceration. Of the increase in the population of state prisons, 45 per cent was due to the war on drugs.[13] In 1985, the Reagan administration and the Republican Party organized, methodically, a

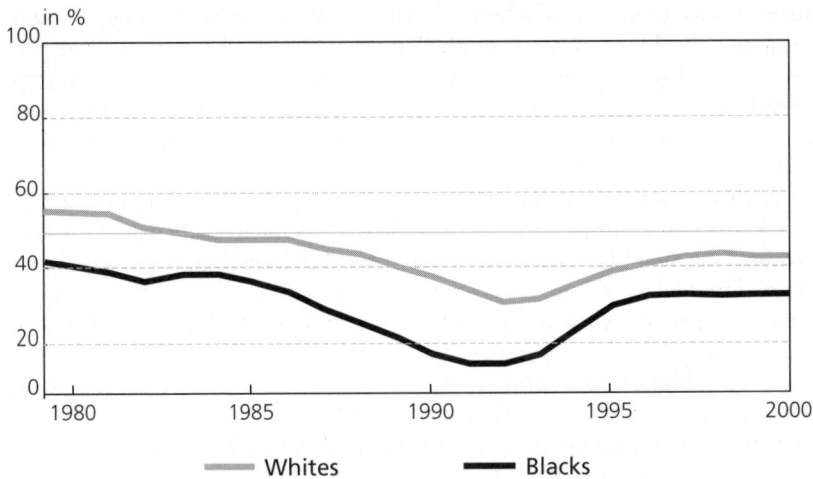

Graph 13.2 Drug use by White and Black pupils in the final year of secondary school

Source: Based on Bruce Western, *Punishment and Inequality in America* (New York: Russell Sage Foundation, 2006), p. 47.

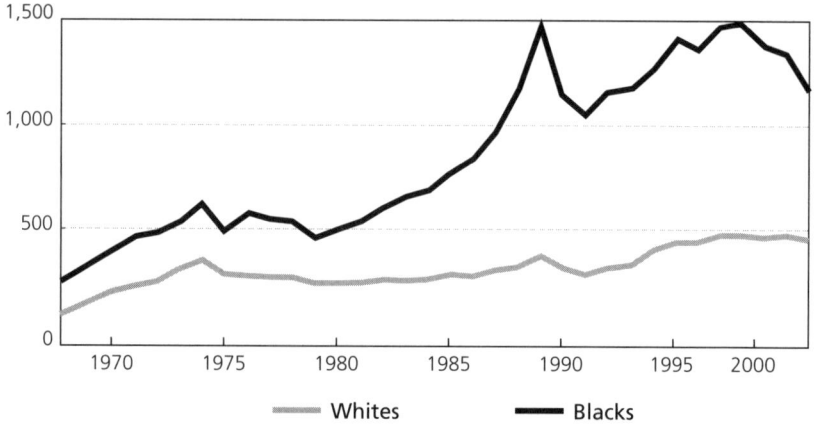

Graph 13.3   Drug-related arrest rates (per 100,000)
Source: Based on Bruce Western, *Punishment and Inequality in America* (New York: Russell Sage Foundation, 2006), p. 46.

serious propaganda operation targeting the crack epidemic; since the American collective consciousness already considered Blacks as a separate category, this led to the young Black male becoming, irrespective of his actual behaviour, the embodiment of an a priori physical threat.[14] Note that the war on drugs was really being waged in a society where its use was falling and where violence had begun to decline; Reagan attacked the Blacks even though Whites were, if all types of drugs are combined, bigger drug users. And if the police and the justice system targeted crack, it is because that drug was cheaper and more heavily used in the ghettos. All the same, the increasing rates of Black incarceration had preceded the crack epidemic.

With the war on drugs, a war declared by Ronald Reagan but that reached a climax under Bill Clinton, America's incarceration rates soared to dizzying heights. White Americans were relatively unaffected. For a man classified as White born between 1965 and 1969, the risk of doing time in a prison cell was only 2.9 per cent; it reached 5.3 per cent if he had not benefited from a higher education; it fell to 0.7 per cent if he had received a higher education (complete or incomplete). For Blacks of the same generation, the overall risk was 20.5 per cent; it rose to 30.2 per cent if the man had not gone to college, and fell to 4.9 per cent if he had received a higher education.[15]

It should be emphasized that in the United States, more than elsewhere, going to gaol means you are marked for life. It leads to an often definitive restriction of your rights to social housing, it limits your job opportunities and, in many cases, means you lose your right to vote. The

234

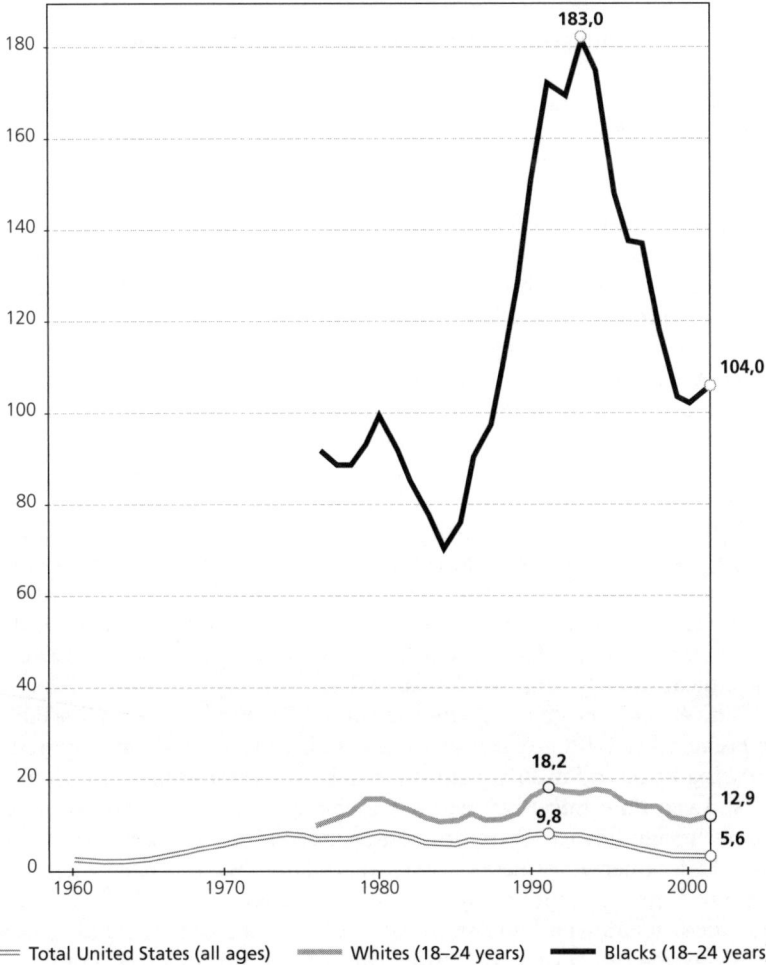

Graph 13.4 Homicide rates between 1960 and 2002 (per 100,000)
Source: Based on Bruce Western, *Punishment and Inequality in America* (New York: Russell Sage Foundation, 2006), p. 170.

duration of imprisonment is in itself a poor indicator of the severity of the punishment, which often consists of a very lengthy exclusion from the social body. That is why Loïc Wacquant's interpretation of mass incarceration as a reincarnation of America's 'peculiar institution' of slavery seems so relevant.[16]

The stratification of the Black community

Anyone who approaches with an unprejudiced mind the facts and figures about Black Americans between, say, 2008 and 2016 must first admit that they make up an inconsistent picture. The president of the country in most of that period was Black, and opinion polls suggest that racial tolerance was at a high level. But the rate of intermarriage, as we have seen, remained low. Moreover, the president's wife was Black too, and the vice-presidential couple, both White, was no less homogeneous. The prisons were full of Blacks. It was the best of times, it was the worst of times. To clarify this confused situation, we need to break free of the illusion produced by the mass communitarian vote of this racial category and accept that, for Black Americans as for Whites, a social stratification based on educational levels was emerging, dramatically in the case of the Blacks: college graduates could swim to safety, those who got no further than secondary school level were left to sink.

According to the data on the Black population in 2015, which point to the resumption of an upward educational movement, clearly so in the case of this minority, 22.5 per cent of the over-25s held a BA, 30.4 per cent had been to college without graduating, 34.1 per cent had a high school diploma and 13 per cent had none of the qualifications issued by the educational system (see Table 13.2).[17]

With *Black Bourgeoisie*, published in 1957 in English after a first edition in French, Franklin Frazier caused a scandal. He not only highlighted the growing differentiation within the Black community; more particularly, he showed how uncertain was the identity of the upper group, its economic insignificance, its cultural dependence on the dominant White world, its inner emptiness.[18] Sixty years later, we too need to think of the Black group, stubbornly classed as a separate bloc by America, as stratified. We must admit the coexistence within it of new middle classes, beneficiaries of affirmative action, and of a sub-proletariat confined to the hyperghetto described by Loïc Wacquant, often destined for prison and social stigmatization. Michelle Alexander, the brilliant author of *The New Jim Crow*, spoke in measured terms of this abandonment

Table 13.2   Education level by race in the United States in 2015

Education of over-25s in %	Blacks	Whites	Hispanics	Asians
College graduates	22.5	36.2	15.5	53.9
College (without graduating)	30.4	27.6	21.3	16.1
High school graduates	34.1	29.5	29.9	19.1
Less	13.0	6.7	33.3	10.9

of the majority of the Black group by its own elites, more anxious to preserve the benefits they derive from affirmative action than to protect young Blacks in the street from the assaults of the police.[19] The Black community vote for the Democratic Party may represent, just as much as the White working-class vote for the Republicans up until Trump, a case of false economic consciousness.

However, nothing forces us to adopt a radically pessimistic view of this issue. America is on the move. The lower social categories are stabilizing, like the whole of American society. Thus the rate of high school dropouts, the main targets for the police, is steadily declining in the Black population.[20]

The liberal gulag in Black and White

At all events, we should not allow ourselves to be blinded by the 'Black question'. The great capacity for self-criticism on the part of American society leads to the regular publication of comparative data concerning Blacks, Whites, Hispanics and Asians; these data could end up producing unwanted side-effects – not only essentializing people by race but also losing sight of the global dynamics of the nation.

Blacks are Americans, and as such they have their place in the general functioning of American society. We have seen the essential role they played right from the start in the definition of White equality and in the American democratic dynamics. We then saw how, in the new context of a stratification brought about by higher education, the 'Black question' served as a launch pad for the neoconservative revolution and the attack on the welfare state inherited from the New Deal, with a subsequent tremendous rise in inequality among Whites. Each time, we find that the fate of Blacks is played out against the fate of Whites, and vice versa. If we follow this argument to its logical conclusion in an attempt to understand the general social function of the mass incarceration of Blacks in the most recent period, we are obliged to observe that, throughout this period, the entire society, with Whites and Blacks fraternally combined, was heading towards social insecurity: so what we need to understand is how the incarceration of Blacks contributed to the overall balance of the United States.

The stability of the American political system, with its two major parties alternating in power and, since about 1978, pursuing policies favourable to the rich, should not lead to an overly functionalist vision that insists too much on the naturalness of the inequalities in a liberal, non-egalitarian anthropological system. The lack of egalitarian values of the French type does not lead to an open acceptance of inequality. This is the fundamental reason, I believe, why the rise in economic inequality has been accompanied by the spread of prisons in the United States, an unmistakable sign of systemic tension.

The per capita incarceration rate in federal and state prisons increased from 100 per 100,000 of the population in 1966–74 to 500 in 2000, and 520 in 2007. It then dropped slightly to 480 in 2013. If we include local prisons, we get the figure of 743 for 2011.[21] Globally, Russia is second in the list, but it lags far behind at 568. In 2009, 1.4 per cent of male adults in the United States were imprisoned: 0.7 per cent of Whites, 1.8 per cent of Hispanics, and 4.7 per cent of Blacks. To fully understand the magnitude of the problem of incarceration in the United States, and to assess the relevance of the concept of the neoliberal gulag, let us begin by following the advice of an analyst of Russian origin, better prepared by history to grasp the sociological significance of the American phenomenon.

Dmitry Orlov, a Russian-American scientist, was born in 1962 in St Petersburg. He arrived in America at the age of 12. In 2006, he wrote a hilarious futurological article on the coming collapse of the United States, in which he maintained, with some excellent arguments, that it would be a harder fall for the Americans, less prepared for survival in extreme conditions than the Russians had been in 1990. *Closing the 'Collapse Gap'* is a feast for the mind.[22]

In the expanded version of this essay, *Reinventing Collapse*, there is a paragraph on prisons which evokes Gogol and Bulgakov. It underlines the relationship between rising inequality and the spread of incarceration.

> The jails race once showed the Soviets with a decisive lead, thanks to their innovative Gulag program. . . . In the end the jails race has been won by the Americans, who are currently holding the world record for the percentage of population held in jail. . . . The American justice system favors the educated, the corporations and the rich, and takes unfair advantage of the uneducated, the private citizen and the poor. It would seem that almost any legal entanglement can be resolved through the judicious application of money, while almost any tussle with the law can result in financial penalties and even imprisonment for those who are forced to rely on public defenders. In essence, any sufficiently complex system of laws is inherently unjust, favoring those few who have the resources to grapple with its extreme complexity. This is clearly the case in the United States where, in civil disputes, those with more money can almost always prevail over those with less, simply by threatening to sue.[23]

The number of lawyers increased from 1.5 to 4 per 1,000 population in the United States between 1965 and 2013, an increase of 2.5 in the rates of legal muddle as well as being an increase of 2.5 in the legal mechanisms whereby the strong dominate the weak.

Table 13.3   Global incarceration rates

Latest figures available in 2011
Prisoners per 100,000 inhabitants

United States	743
Russia	568
Belorussia	381
Ukraine	338
Taiwan	278
Poland	218
New Zealand	199
Hungary	165
Spain	159
United Kingdom	153
Romania	136
Australia	133
Canada	117
Portugal	113
Italy	111
Austria	103
Greece	102
Ireland	100
Belgium	97
France	96
Netherlands	94
Germany	85
Switzerland	79
Sweden	78
Denmark	74
Norway	73
Finland	59
Japan	58
Korea	49

Source: Roy Walmsley, *World Prison Population List* (9th edition), International Centre for Prison Studies.

We are very far here from the neoliberal theory of economist-philosophers who contrast the freedom of the market with state servitude. In view of American incarceration rates, the titles of some bestsellers give one pause: Milton Friedman's *Capitalism and Freedom* appears totally off the wall, Friedrich Hayek's *The Road to Serfdom* downright ironic.[24] The almighty market led to the emergence of a new gulag. The death penalty was reinstated in the United States after 1976, and was soon being liberally enforced, while it was effectively abolished by a moratorium in

Russia. The rise of inequality, in an individualistic context, explains the spread of the American system of repression.

Let us go back to the historical and anthropological sequence. Between 1980 and 2015, the United States experienced a rapid and steady rise in inequality and job insecurity. Individuals experienced a latent fear of not being able to cope with health problems or ageing, a fear that grew more intense the further down the social ladder they were. The spread of the prison system treated this fear with another fear: that of imprisonment. The march of neoliberalism has not been natural or easy, despite the stability of the political system. The American state has, to some degree, changed its function. Elections have remained free; freedom of expression has survived, even though the massive irruption of money into the ideological space – through the creation of think-tanks, newspaper buy-outs and the founding of mercenary TV channels – has changed the conditions of the expression of freedom. But, latent and subtle, a regime of terror has been established by mass incarceration. This is indeed a form of state violence, although many new prisons are built and managed by the private system. But why target Blacks?

Certainly, the threat of confinement hangs over everybody. But Whites, generally, escape it. And we need to bear in mind that racially targeted repression led to one final sinister transformation in White egalitarianism. White equality, having vanished from access to education and the sharing of income, is still there in a negative form: what Whites now have in common is the privilege of not often being incarcerated.

Is this social and economic evolution consistent with the values attached to the absolute, liberal, non-egalitarian nuclear family? My feeling is that the new educational stratification and racial division have taken economic and social inequality beyond the ordinary anthropological factors found in Anglosphere societies. Unless we accept the idea that an anthropological limit has been passed, indeed, we will find it difficult to understand the election of Donald Trump in 2016.

— 14 —

DONALD TRUMP AS WILL AND REPRESENTATION

If the election of Donald Trump, in November 2016, took the American elites, and indeed the entire planet, by surprise, this perfectly illustrates two of the ideas put forward in this book. First, the idea that economic and political clashes are determined by the new educational stratification. And second, the idea that identifies the primitive foundation of democracy, namely its need for an Other – and thus for xenophobia – in order to be born or reborn.

The establishment media have portrayed Trump as vulgar, aberrant, evil or insane; the voters, suffering but rational, have expressed their desire to take America back to its foundations.

The rationality of the vote for Trump

Globalization, initiated and managed by the United States for its own benefit (or so it was thought), did however eventually produce within the American population itself an excess of economic inequality and social insecurity: this was a necessary and sufficient condition for a shift towards a preference for the protectionism of Bernie Sanders or Donald Trump.

To fully understand not only the successful emergence of Donald Trump, but also the blocked emergence of Bernie Sanders, we first need to take a quick look at the long historical sequence that led the United States from its relatively closed position at the beginning of the 1930s to the situation – which still obtains – of maximum openness to trade and immigration.

From the end of the American Civil War to the Crash of 1929, the United States had taken off economically behind the shelter of high tariff barriers. In the early 1930s, tax on imports averaged 50 per cent. Only from 1934, under Franklin D. Roosevelt, did the country start to open

241

up to trade. Customs duties, including both taxed and untaxed products, then rose to an average of 18.4 per cent. They had bottomed out at 1.3 per cent in 2007, when the Great Recession began.

From the beginning of the 1970s, the United States experienced a structural trade deficit from which it has never since emerged, assuming for the whole world the role of universal consumer – i.e., in Keynesian terms, the global regulator of global demand. But by the end of the 1970s, the industrial crisis in America had become apparent; at its heart lay the collapse of the automobile industry. But this was exactly the period in which neoliberal politics accelerated. As we saw in Chapter 12, Reagan was elected in 1980, then triumphantly re-elected in 1984 against Walter Mondale, even though the latter had run on a protectionist platform. The Democrats had adopted their traditional role as direct representatives of the working class, both White and Black. Reagan won by proposing a clever anti-tax cocktail of hostility to welfare, declaring war on a welfare state now perceived as too favourable to Blacks.

The surge in imports began only in the 1960s. The Immigration and Naturalization Act of 1965 then reopened America to immigration, which had been severely restricted since 1924. Economic insecurity was exacerbated by a new feeling of territorial insecurity. The number of inhabitants born abroad rose from 9.7 million out of 181 million inhabitants, 5.4 per cent of the total population, in 1960 to 41.3 million out of 315 million inhabitants, 13.1 per cent of the total, in 2013. By 2009, the number of illegal immigrants, mainly Hispanic, was estimated at 10 million. Obama's America could indeed be described in Popperian terms as an 'open society'.

Between 1980 and 1998 a dramatic increase in inequality in the United States became evident. However, this did not prevent an increase in median household income from $48,500 to $58,000 (in 2015 equivalent terms). Rather than an increase in individual wages, this increase resulted from the additional contribution of women as they entered the labour market and increased the number of dual-earner households.

The years 1999–2015 represented, for the United States, the apogee of the liberal project and the beginning of the crisis of globalization. When China joined the World Trade Organization in December 2001, the threat of a rise in tariffs that might have faced it was removed. The immediate consequence was an acceleration in the crisis in American industry, now subject to a real purge. Between 1965 and 2000, the relative decline in the population employed in the secondary sector did not prevent its stagnation in absolute terms, at around 18 million workers. But between March 2001 and March 2007, this figure dropped by 18 per cent.[1]

The increase in inequality resumed. Between 1999 and 2015, despite a small increase in 2013 and 2014, the median income of US households fell from $58,000 to $56,500. These years included the Great Recession;

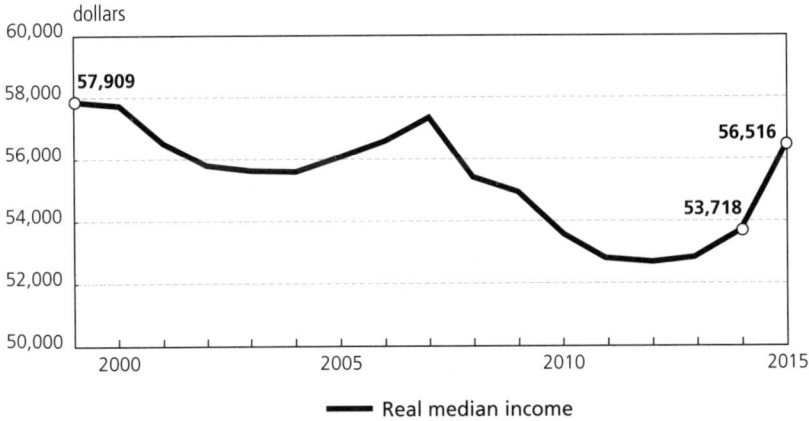

Graph 14.1   Fall in income of American households between 1999 and 2015

Source: United States Census Bureau.

it is unclear whether this is actually over, since, although unemployment, which rose to 10 per cent in 2009, did fall back to 5.5 per cent at the beginning of 2016, the employment rate of the population is still bumping along at just under 60 per cent, compared to 63 per cent before the crisis.

To understand the extent of the stress suffered by the American population at the beginning of the third millennium, we will have to leave the field of economic data and revenues. There will always be a Nobel laureate in economics on hand to assure us, for a small fee, that without free trade the price of the products would have been higher for the consumer. But what if the consumer dies rather than buys?

The judgement of the demographers is final. An article by Anne Case and Angus Deaton published in December 2015 reveals an increase in the death rate among the White population aged 45 to 54 between 1999 and 2013, a phenomenon that has no equivalent in any of the world's other advanced societies.

The main causes of this mortality, as shown in Graph 14.2, are clearly psychosocial: poisoning, alcoholism and suicide. The debate on the benefits of free trade and deregulation is thus closed. It was precisely this increase in adult mortality that seems to me to explain how Donald Trump could first win the nomination as a Republican candidate and then be elected president in 2016; likewise, the increase in Russian infant mortality between 1970 and 1974 allowed me to envisage, as early as 1976, the collapse of the Soviet system.[2]

An article by Justin Pierce and Peter Schott, published in November

Deaths per 100,000

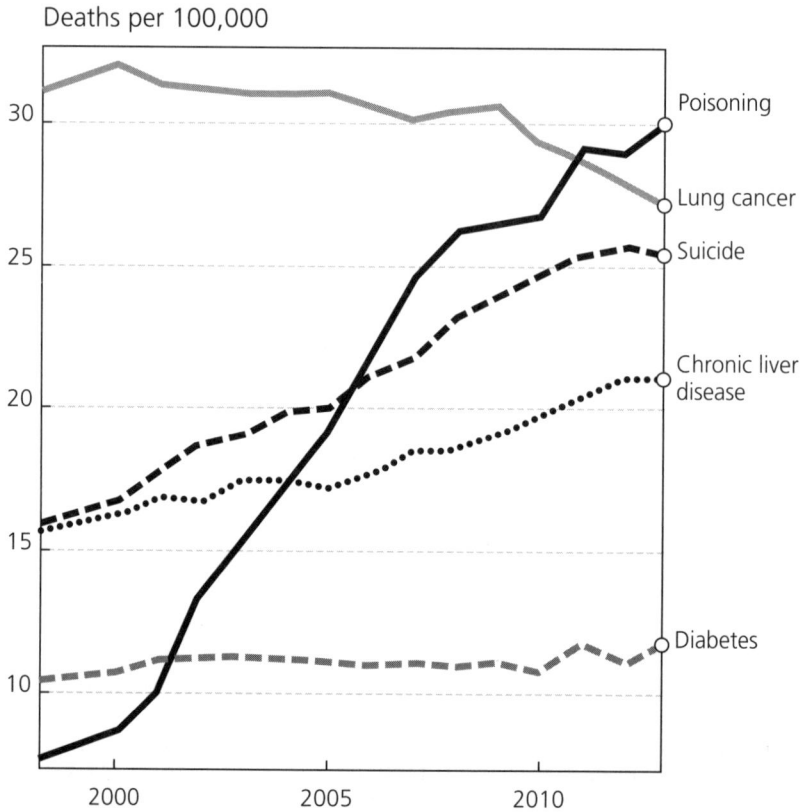

Graph 14.2 The rise in White death rates between 1999 and 2013 (45–54 years)
Source: Anne Case and Angus Deaton, 'Rising Morbidity and Mortality in Midlife among White Non-Hispanic Americans in the 21st Century', *PNAS*, vol. 112, no. 49, 15078–83, December 2015.

2016, established a robust statistical relationship, at US county level, between trade liberalization with China and rising mortality.[3] The specific counties directly affected by Chinese competition at the industrial level saw their mortality rate increase. The analysis concluded that the most significant cause of death appeared to be suicide rather than poisoning. The study by Pierce and Schott is fascinating because of its moral implications: it implicitly turns economists who sign petitions claiming the benefits of free trade into criminals, liable to prosecution by group actions similar to those launched against tobacco companies and pharmaceutical companies.

Table 14.1   Evolution of death rate among 45–54-year-olds by level of education

	Death rate per 100,000 in 2013	Development 1999–2013	External causes	Suicides
Non-Hispanic Whites (total)	415.4	+33.9	+32.9	+9.5
Secondary education or below	735.8	+134.4	+68.7	+17.0
Incomplete higher education	287.8	−3.3	+18.9	+6.0
Complete higher education	178.1	−57.0	+3.6	+3.3
Non-Hispanic Blacks	581.9	−214.8	−6.0	+0.9
Hispanics	269.6	−63.6	−2.9	+0.2

The distribution of additional deaths, analysed in the article by Case and Deaton, reflects educational stratification (see Table 14.1). It is concentrated on those White Americans who have received only a secondary education or less (+134.4 per 100,000). The mortality of those with incomplete college educations stagnated (−3.3), while that of college graduates dropped slightly (−57.0). However, we shouldn't exaggerate the happiness of college graduates. Let us go back, for once, to the economic data: the differential evolution of incomes suggests that the educational advantage is only relative.

It is important to keep in mind, in order to fully understand the shift in the years 2000–16, that if dramatic transformations such as an increase in mortality mainly affect the least educated of White Americans, the economic shift is no longer really favourable to college graduates. Since 2000, in fact, the average income of their households has stagnated, as shown in Graph 14.3.

Higher education now protects you from dropping down the social ladder more than it helps you to climb up it. And this, indeed, lies behind the renewed interest in embarking on long college courses in recent years, a situation that reveals a quest for security rather than a desire for intellectual emancipation. To the extent that higher education is increasingly ensured by student loans, the accumulated debt will be responsible for reducing future income, if it does not lead to some form of economic enslavement of those from modest backgrounds who have had a higher education. One cannot help but be reminded of the indentured servants who, in colonial times, paid for their passage across the Atlantic by years of contractual servitude.

Real median income of households according to educational level
of the head of the household, in 2012 dollars

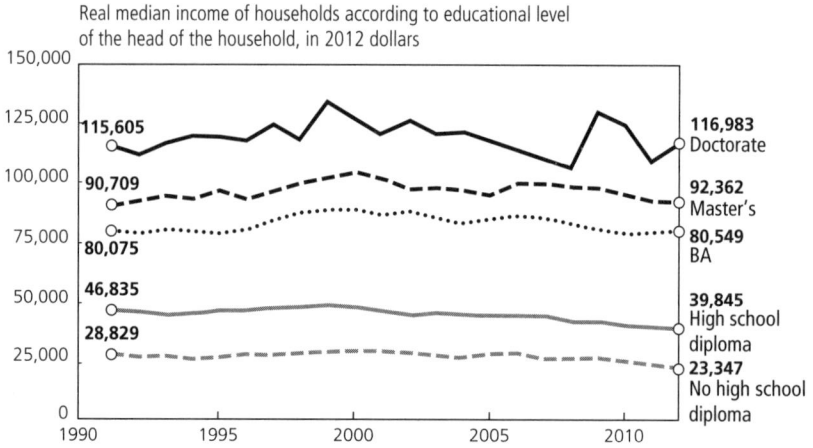

Graph 14.3 Income in relation to education between 1991 and 2012
Source: Russel Sage Foundation, Chartbook of Social Inequality.

Once we come back down to earth from the fairyland of the econo-mists, we can understand the election of Donald Trump. The insults and lies he exchanged with Hillary Clinton cannot hide the fact that, from the point of view of ordinary voters, it was Trump who was telling the truth about American society. It was he who described its sufferings in his book *Crippled America*,[4] while the Democrats celebrated the eternal excellence of America and its 'values' of tolerance and openness.

The socio-demographic structure of the vote for Trump confirms this diagnosis and offers us a true mental X-ray of America as it emerges from the ideology of globalization.

Educational stratification and political choice

One of the striking features of the 2016 US election campaign was the way political clashes were mainly depicted in terms of educational attain-ment. Trump's supporters were regularly portrayed by the establishment press in New York, Washington, Los Angeles and San Francisco as 'under-educated' or 'uncultivated'; Hillary Clinton even described them, in a display of class contempt worthy of nineteenth-century Europe, as 'deplorable'. For commentators, the ideal type of Republican voter was a White who had just managed to graduate from high school. The ideal type of the Democrat, on the other hand, if not a Black or Hispanic, was a college graduate. So-called exit polls only partially verify this depiction; such a vision is a little too simplistic and needs to be qualified.

246

Throughout the following discussion, the totals will never reach 100 per cent because of the presence of an independent candidate, which we have no reason to worry about here.

The distribution of votes by level of income was not particularly significant. We can only note a majority vote of those whose income was less than $50,000 per year in favour of Hillary Clinton (53 per cent against 41 per cent for Trump) – an effect of the overrepresentation of Black and Hispanic minorities in the Democrat electorate. Among Americans who earned more than $100,000, Republicans and Democrats were level pegging. The Republicans are no longer the party of the rich.

The educational criterion, however, appears to be spectacularly discriminating: among male Whites with only a secondary education, complete or not, there was a vote of 71 per cent for Trump and only 23 per cent for Clinton. However, if we look at the overall numbers, combining the races and the sexes, we get less extreme results: Trump only won 51 per cent among those educated only to high school level as against 46 per cent for Clinton. He still won more votes among individuals who had received an incomplete higher education (51 per cent versus 43 per cent), and was only slightly outperformed by Clinton among those who had obtained a college degree (44 per cent versus 49 per cent). The Democrats really took off only at the level of the highest educated, i.e. postgraduates with a higher degree: 58 per cent of these voted for Clinton and only 37 per cent for Trump. This polarization is quite extraordinary because it places the party of the 'Left', the Democrats, on the side of absolute cultural domination, and Clintonism comes across as an illustration of the premonitory nightmare of Michael Young, in a meritocratic system that could lead elected officials to despise educational rejects. Academics are almost all, by definition, postgraduates.

In the aftermath of the election, the commitment of academic elites to free trade appeared more intense and more homogeneous than that of entrepreneurs operating in the market. The world of capital is heterogeneous and pragmatic: it is divided between a sector that derives its surplus profits from underpaid work in China and elsewhere, and another that can only live off work done in the United States. Above all, in the world of capital, there is the floating mass of those who know that money can be made in a protectionist system as much as under free trade: you just need to adapt. Every economic activity must, however, be assessed in its relation to globalization. The young Silicon Valley tycoon who relies on dematerializable work will not have the same relationship to free trade and immigration as an executive for Ford or General Motors whose business requires steel and energy. Faced with Trump, the first will be unleashed, the second will incline to adopt a policy of wait-and-see.

The citadels of the elite: Silicon Valley and Academia

In a premonitory work published in 2014, *The New Class Conflict*, a Californian, Joel Kotkin, had the good sense to see the entrepreneurs of Silicon Valley – the bosses of Google, Amazon and Facebook – despite their young age, and despite the modern and trendy image of themselves which they cultivate, as oligarchs in the making, acting according to their economic interests and already boldly intervening in the political field.[5] For example, Jeff Bezos, the boss of Amazon, has bought the *Washington Post*. Let us preserve human freedom from statistical determinations here: Silicon Valley investor Peter Thiel, who is also gay, supported Trump by speaking in his favour and contributing to the campaign. It is worth noting, in this regard, as a way of taking the measure of local conformism, that a gay community journal went so far as to question the reality of his sexual orientation because he had supported Trump. Be that as it may, exit polls tell us, in fact, that only 14 per cent of the LGBT group supported Trump, compared to 77 per cent for Clinton.

Kotkin refers to Academia, which he calls 'The New Clerisy', as the second heart of established power. The concerns of postgraduates are not fundamentally economic, as their status shelters them from the market. Basically, they are imbued with a sense of intellectual superiority and may as such despise the lower classes as being closed to the values of international or sexual tolerance. So they are running on pure ideology and can express a caste attachment to free trade better than can the business world.

As we have seen above, Academia has become the great machine for sorting the population: it is Academia that enables inequality to flourish, and it is logical to find it remaining faithful to the free trade which nourishes economic inequality (even if the colleges that are not elite are a little less reliable from this point of view). Its love of humankind in general, moreover, renders Academia particularly open to the ideal of immigration, whether legal or not. The material and ideological conditions of maximum hostility to Trump were fulfilled by Academia. The same phenomenon of internationalist conformism had been observed in English Academia, particularly in Cambridge and Oxford: the maniacal hostility to Brexit, before and after the vote, foreshadowed the anti-Trump fury of the great American universities. Academia is on the Left, but it is no longer very fond of the lower classes, those chavs or uncultivated proles, as they are called by an English terminology applied from above, a terminology that is dramatized locally by class attitudes that have never had their equivalent in the United States.[6]

Things can be less taken for granted in France, and they tend to remain unspoken, but Academia, still on the Left, is also undoubtedly one of the most conformist poles of society. Without knowing it or admitting it, it rejects the notions of equality and democracy: by its attachment to authoritarian Europe and its bankrupt currency, by its acceptance of a free trade that destroys workers, and by its tenderness for an untrammelled immigration that basically denies the need for a stable territory in which democracy can work. Less conscious of itself, the conformist magma of French Academia is thicker than anything to be found on the other side of the Channel or the Atlantic.

Let us conclude, at this point, with a broader questioning of the strange relationship which has been established in the advanced world between an Academia on the Left and the defence of economic policies unfavourable to the masses. We cannot confine ourselves to an 'accidentalist' vision of this coincidence: it cannot be by mere chance that so many modern Leftists, well implanted in higher education, are, at the same time, hostile to the lower classes.

The destruction of educational homogeneity, which fostered egalitarian sentiment and democracy, explains, as we have seen, the emergence in advanced societies of an inegalitarian and anti-democratic subconscious. But it was the Left that desired mass education, including higher education. It is thus the Left that has unknowingly guided society towards inequality. The historical and ideological link between the Left and education undoubtedly enables us to understand why and how the inegalitarian drift of the educational system has dragged the Left along with it, transforming it into a new kind of Right, although it will never, ever admit it. And this has occurred in the three major Western democracies.

Economic conflict is replacing racial conflict

The 89 per cent Black vote in favour of Hillary Clinton, when only 8 per cent of Blacks voted for Trump, might lead us to believe that the 2016 election followed the path that has guided US policy ever since Ronald Reagan, and perhaps even since Richard Nixon, in which 'race' membership determines one's trajectory. The fall in Black participation, especially among the young, nonetheless played a significant role in Clinton's failure, and suggests that things are not so simple.

The Republican Party, broken by Trump, had, as we have seen, held its White working-class electorate in a state of false consciousness. It used the technique of racial dogwhistling, onto which an affirmation of religious and moral 'values' was superimposed, to drive an economic policy with disastrous consequences not only for the workers but also for the middle classes. The Republican Party actually brought about the confinement of the Blacks, promised the prohibition of abortion without ever imposing it, and above all brought in ever more tax cuts in favour of the rich. But Donald Trump won, first against the Republican establishment, and then at the heart of the global political system, by ceasing to feed the machine that was fabricating false consciousness, and by bringing the working world back to a certain form of class consciousness. This was the meaning of his attack on free trade and his advocacy of protectionism, the only policy capable of allowing White workers and their Black class brothers and sisters, who were being even more severely mistreated by the collapse of industry, to return to the American middle class.

Whenever confronted with xenophobia or racism, the historian must be able to identify, via a necessary meditation on the universality of the malady, the specific ethnic or racial groups targeted by the dominant group. Current France, for example, demonizes the Arabs rather than the Blacks, and this fact tells us that its supposed 'racism' falls more within the category of 'culturally based xenophobia'. The primary cause of Brexit, namely the massive immigration of Poles to England, deserves even more clearly to be categorized as 'culturally-based xenophobia' of a non-racial kind, since Poles are just as light-skinned as the English.

With his plans to build (or finish) a wall along the southern border of the United States, Trump did not demonize Blacks, but Mexicans. And his attacks did not simply target recent immigrants, legal or illegal. We need to remember those he launched against a judge of Hispanic origin. Such facts, in a modern American context, also mean that Trump distanced himself from the White/Black racial dualism that had become its ideological axis.

The term 'racism' cannot, however, be so quickly abandoned for 'cultural xenophobia' in the case of Trump. The 'Hispanic category' of the American statistical and mental system is a quirk that certainly gives pride of place to the Castilian language, but its main purpose is to target the Indian origin of the majority of Mexicans. 'Hispanic' refers to a simultaneously cultural and racial fixation.

The fact remains that Hispanics are not usually Black, and that anti-Latino 'racism' is not of the same nature as the racism which is directed against the Blacks. As the anti-Mexican wall was its central motive, the concept of xenophobia, which refers to the fear of an exterior other, a phobia with a territorial base, even seems better adapted to describe Trumpism. After all, Blacks and Hispanics, whether the latter are US citizens or legal immigrants, would be among the first beneficiaries of a protectionist economic policy that restores value to manual labour.

If we define Trump's campaign as anti-free trade and xenophobic – the two concepts being associated in a project of economic and ethno-national protection – it is not reasonable to consider it as racist, especially not as anti-Black, even if Trump did not manage, or even really tried, to seduce the Black electorate.

We still need to explain the persistence of the Black Democratic vote. Just as the Republicans, shaken by Trump, ended by basing their programme on the interests of their White working-class electorate,[7] so the Clintonian Democrats rekindled and reintensified the racial concept and managed to maintain their Black electorate in a state of false consciousness. The group's internal stratification played an important role in the persistence of its alienation.

Racial triumphalism and the Clintonian imperial project

From 2010 onwards, the discourse of American political scientists and journalists had a demographic cast: the end of White America was expected, along with the arrival of an electoral majority dominated by minorities – Black, Asian and especially Hispanic. In fact, since 1970, the increase in the 'non-White' fraction of the population had been very significant. But the electoral body still remained 72 per cent White in 2016. Certainly, educational stratification induced the break-up of this group: 'college-educated Whites' seemed destined to support the Democratic Party, those who had not progressed beyond high school the Republican Party. All things considered, the idea was established of a Democratic Party driven by demographic change: the incessant increase of the mass of minorities, added to a civilized White nucleus, would make its future victory inevitable. There were even worries about the survival of the Republican Party, sadly confined to the minority group of under-educated Whites. Such a discourse, of course, contributed greatly to keeping the racial concept alive.

The election of Barack Obama, a Black man educated to a very high level, may have seemed to confirm this perspective. Let us note, moreover, that this perspective was not devoid of a certain grandeur, since it depicted an America capable of 'changing' its racial nature, and of ceasing to be, by its openness to immigration, Latin American and Asian, a White nation of European origin. At the risk of seeming petty, we should nevertheless note the massive support of the financial establishment for Barack Obama then for Hillary Clinton: they were mainly concerned to contribute to the installation of an oligarchy able to control the electoral body by the astute mobilization of the Black and Hispanic mercenary electoral army.

Even when seen as defined by its oligarchic ambitions, the project remained grandiose, since the domination was to be extended to the planetary level, at least in the eyes of Hillary Clinton. It was an 'imperial project', as opposed to Trump's 'national project'.

But it was actually Trump who was able to realize what was obvious – an America outplayed by China and flouted by its allies (Turkish,

251

Saudi and Filipino) – and to tell the American electors what the world was really like. His real claim to fame, however, will have been that he identified Germany as an economic adversary, whose strategic objective now was to finish off an American industry undermined by China.

Clinton's control of the Black electorate: another betrayal by the elites

The imperial project was not reasonable. But, in the very short term, it could ensure the maintenance of a maximum rate of profit in favour of the oligarchy of the top 0.1 per cent on the American income scale, and a more than enviable standard of living for those right behind them within the group of the 1 per cent, which includes, let us remember, a good number of the economists who petitioned against Trump. But in the context of a culture dominated by economism and a political life fuelled by the financial oligarchy, the imperial project seemed perfectly rational.

But how could the Clintonian Democrats, armed with such a project, claim to control the Black electorate, economically destroyed by economic globalization and threatened in its jobs by Mexican immigration?

In the wake of Franklin Frazier, and radicalizing the remarks of Michelle Alexander, we need to take into account the Black group's stratification if we are to understand its 'false consciousness' and its voting discipline. In its lower mass, it is the priority victim of unemployment and gaol, the scapegoat whose sufferings helped stabilize the neoliberal social system between 1980 and 2015. This Black group should have violently opposed the Democratic leadership. But its upper stratum, a beneficiary of affirmative action, could, in spite of persistent territorial and matrimonial segregation, find economic satisfaction in Clinton's globalist and imperial project. The middle and lower classes were quite simply held in thrall by their elites. And the latter were powerfully supported by tradition: after all, ever since President Lyndon Johnson, the Democratic Party had spearheaded the political emancipation of all Blacks.

An episode in the 2016 presidential campaign revealed the domination then exercised by the Clintonian elites over Black voters, willing to vote against their own economic interests.

As I said above, a protectionist turnaround would be economically favourable to the majority of Blacks, less skilled on average than the White population. However, in 2016, within the Democratic Party itself, there was a protectionist candidate. Bernie Sanders should have been supported, in accordance with the logic of class, not only by young Democrats, but also, and with equal enthusiasm, by Blacks. The opposite happened: the 'captive' Black electorate defeated him, revealing a high level of political alienation. Primary after primary, we saw Hillary

Clinton beat Bernie Sanders in states with a high Black population. The correlation coefficient linking a 'vote for Sanders at the primary' and 'proportion of Blacks' was negative at the state total, equal to –0.81.[8] Such an extremely high coefficient, rare in the human sciences, means, according to statistical theory, that nearly two-thirds of the 'variance' of the anti-Sanders vote can be explained by the Black presence. Which simply means that it was the manipulation of the Black electorate that made possible the Clintonian – oligarchic and imperialist – control of the Democratic Party. Without the complaisance of the Black elites, beneficiaries in their own way, and on a very small scale, of the globalist system, such a deviation would not have been possible. Michelle Alexander, meanwhile, supported Bernie Sanders.

The Hispanic problem facing the Democrats

Hispanics now represent 12 per cent of the US electorate. Despite the assaults of Donald Trump, only 66 per cent of Hispanics voted for Hillary Clinton and 28 per cent for Trump. Their basic orientation does not seem strongly Democratic since, in 2004, 40 per cent of Hispanics were already voting for George W. Bush. From the point of view of anthropology and social dynamics, it would be a serious mistake to stick Hispanics and Blacks in the United States into the same conceptual category. Unlike Blacks, Mexicans and most Latinos have a specific and consistent family system.

Franklin Frazier described the Black American family as a fragile entity that, since the end of slavery, had sought to find a stability based on surrounding White values. Undermined in its foundations by the way the man, husband or father, is kept in an inferior status, the Black family is constantly threatened by economic crises and by cultural transformations. With its single mothers taking refuge with their own mothers, the Black family appears at the beginning of the third millennium as a caricature of the unstable nuclear family, with a high rate of divorce – a type that had seemed, in the aftermath of the cultural revolution of the 1960s and 1970s, to be the destiny of the White family in ordinary circles. In 2012, in *The End of Men and the Rise of Women*, Hanna Rosin published a violent book, simultaneously insightful and vulgar, in which she depicted an American society that had overwhelmingly become matriarchal, filled with responsible women and irresponsible men, while leaving intact a slender, patriarchal upper class.[9] In this model, Blacks were an extreme case of the destruction of the male role in the working-class world. Indeed, educational statistics now reveal a female advantage that is even greater in a Black environment than in a White environment.

Mexicans and many other Hispanics, especially when they are of Peruvian or Bolivian origin, promote a very different type of family. As we saw in Chapter 2, the nuclear family with patrilocal temporary residence that characterizes these groups has as its ultimate goal the independence of married children, although it provides them with a phase of cohabitation for a few years with the family of the young husband, possibly followed by an independent establishment that is autonomous but still based nearby. The youngest child has to take care of elderly parents according to a perfectly formalized procedure of ultimogeniture.

Although it has not really favoured the early take-off of Mexico, Peru or Bolivia, this family type does seem to provide a remarkable protection for immigrants subjected to the stress of assimilation. Here again, the infant mortality rate appears to be an excellent indicator. In 2007, the infant mortality rate for White Americans was 5.6 per 1,000 live births, a poor performance when we consider that the rate in Japan and Sweden was 2.5, in France 3.8, in Germany 3.9, in Korea 4.1, in the United Kingdom 4.8, and in Cuba 5.3. This rate was 13.3 for Black (non-Hispanic) Americans, more than twice as high as for Whites, but, surprisingly, only 5.4 per 1,000 for 'Mexicans' and 4.6 for other Latino-Americans, either slightly or significantly below the rate for the dominant White group.[10]

In spite of the very low educational level of Latinos, lower than any other American ethno-racial category, we have already noted elsewhere a high rate of intermarriage among them, much higher than that of the Blacks.

Latinos have long been characterized by significant over-fertility, but this indicator also reveals an accelerating rate of assimilation. The recent decline in the US fertility rate is often attributed to the economic hardships experienced by young couples as a result of the Great Recession. However, while between 2006 and 2013 there was a fall in the fertility rate for Whites, from 1.91 to 1.75 children per woman, and for Blacks, from 2.12 to 1.88, there was a dramatic drop for Hispanics, from 2.85 to 2.15.[11] At the same time that Trump was targeting Hispanics, their demographic alignment, a sure sign of assimilation, was accelerating.

In short, nothing in the trajectory of the Hispanics indicates any proximity or convergence with the Black pariah group. I am not claiming that the process of immigration–assimilation is a path strewn with roses for them; I am simply noting that their difficulties are of a traditional type. It is likely that their destiny will be, with a time lag of 150 years, and in less harsh conditions, the same as the destiny of the Irish Catholics, initially despised and bullied, but finally assimilated.

That's why the Democrats' Hispanic strategy is eventually doomed to fail. Already 28 per cent of them, as I have said, voted for Trump. Why? To be sure, the educative and economic stratification of the group played a part, favouring as it does diversity of choice. The specific nature of the Cuban community, firmly to the political Right due to its anti-Castro mentality, should also be mentioned. But above all we need to admit that the generalizing discourse on non-White minorities flies in the face of American social dynamics. In the field, the way Latinos have adapted well contrasts with the endless flight of Black families. The Watts neighbourhood in Los Angeles, populated mostly by Blacks at the time of the 1965 riots, is now a Hispanic area. Blacks are rapidly moving out of California, even though it had once been hoped that this state, as the west of the West, and with its higher rates of intermarriage, would be the place where American racial obsessions would finally vanish.

Let us finish with the worst, with real sadness, as we reflect on the scary character of the subliminal message delivered by the Democratic Party to assimilating Hispanics: 'We will protect you: for us, you're like Blacks.' For the basic axiom of American society, for those who want to feel at home there, to be human beings among other human beings, is precisely this: you mustn't be Black. In spite of Trump, the Latinos did not save Clinton in 2016, and it seems unlikely that they will provide the Democrats with a guaranteed majority in the decades to come.

A democratic but still xenophobic renewal

The democratic resurgences in the Anglosphere, Brexit and then Trump's election, seem to have been strongly tinged with xenophobia, anti-Polish in England, anti-Mexican in the United States. There is no doubt about this xenophobia, and our habit of identifying liberal democracy and universalism would lead us to deny the authentically democratic nature of the electoral uprisings of the year 2016. If human beings are good, the principle of equality should act externally as well as internally. The equality of the body of citizens should be echoed by the equality of all of humankind. The Democratic Left would have applauded a victory for the protectionist Sanders, but it must consider Trump an abomination. In the same way, the French would have preferred a working class seduced by Mélenchon rather than by Le Pen.

We are here the victims of a false vision of history, of a deductive and philosophical rather than an empirical and anthropological conception of democracy. History shows us by many examples, as I have demonstrated in Chapter 11, that democracy is not, at its source, universalist in essence. Before the emergence of the concept of *isonomia* (the equality of citizens before the law), the birth of Athenian democracy was violently ethnic, with a body of citizens defined as against slaves, against metics, against the citizens of other Greek cities, and against barbarians. Cromwell's revolutionary England, Protestant and nationalist, treated Catholics as pariahs, and was capable of committing atrocities in Ireland in the name of the superiority of the new chosen people. American democracy drew its first energies from hostility to Indians and Blacks, and came to maturity with the racism of President Jackson, Trump's idol and his equal in vulgarity. The general rise of democracy in Europe, between 1789 and 1900, was accompanied by a no less general advance of nationalism, i.e. the definition of the social body as against the Other, most often a neighbouring people perceived as specifically threatening. As far as France is concerned, it was the English in 1793, and the Germans in 1914.

A democracy is a specific people organized, for its own ends, on its own territory. This group defends its border. It is not an abstract collective, deciding for humankind in general. If we accept this historical evidence of a dark, ethnic, national component in the original form of democracy, we can manage to see, and understand, why the resistance to oligarchy and the democratic revival affecting Western 'democracies' one by one, disorganized as these are by the new educational stratification and free trade, are inevitably tinged with xenophobia. Democracy is being reborn, but against the Mexicans in America and against the Poles in England. France's current decision to set itself 'against the Muslims' is dysfunctional, since it targets an internal group that represents, in the younger generation, 10 per cent of the population, and can only lead to the nation imploding. This is just the start of the list, but it still evokes a general movement in which different peoples are returning to democracy, or to 'populism' in the current terminology of the Western oligarchies, in what Tocqueville would have called a 'providential march'. The new inegalitarian educational stratification excludes, however, the possibility of a simple return to the classical democracy of the first half of the twentieth century, one rooted in the cultural homogeneity of universal literacy but lacking a mass university education.

Let us look back at the past history of democracy. Its development, even if not universalist in its foundations, may have appeared to be universal insofar as it existed, if not everywhere, at least in many places. Solidarities were established between parent forms and led to the belated illusion that the many forms in which democracy emerged was the product of an innate universalism. Moreover, only a new dogmatism could compel us to pessimism: pluralist democracy effectively leads to the emancipation of equal individuals within the body of citizens, and it can result, by a dynamic of its own, in the abstract conception of a free citizen equal to others, everywhere, in general. This derivative universalism would end up shedding a positive light on the relations between neighbouring peoples evolving in similar ways. The parallel march of xenophobias, internally emancipatory, could well end up producing a democratic and liberal universality.

Provided that it emancipates the individual within each people, and discerns the same trend in its neighbours, democracy is perfectly capable of reaching a higher stage, a second phase of the demand for the universal. This game has already been played out between the United States, England and France, three nations defined a priori as individualist by their anthropological backgrounds. But where the anthropological foundation did not encourage the emergence of the individual – in Germany, Japan, Russia and China – we have not really seen the burgeoning of a universal conception of liberal democracy.

Global project versus national project

There is a pessimistic interpretation of the American future, in which the conflict between two opposing ideologies of equivalent strength stabilizes. On the one hand, a national, democratic, protectionist and White Republican Party; on the other, a globalist, elitist, imperial and multiracial Democratic Party. The cold civil war that has followed Trump's election suggests such a possibility. The almost equal vote for both candidates, with even a slight advantage for Hillary Clinton, does not suggest that there will be a radical shift to a national vision in the United States. The fact that two leading states such as California and New York are anchored in the Democrat camp, and the predominance of globalism in the main cities and the most prestigious universities, seems to exclude a priori the possibility that the whole of society will swing behind Trump's project.

At a deeper level, the persistent educational divide in American society between the less well educated and the better educated suggests that the establishment of two camps, two ideological fortresses, might just as easily divide America in the long term, and actually condemn it to economic and strategic impotence. The democratic revival would then remain trapped in its xenophobic matrix – an absurd posture for a nation that remains the main global power and the prime orchestrator of our common future.

But there is also an optimistic interpretation that sees Trump's victory and the xenophobic democratic renewal as only a first step, preceding an accelerated advance of democracy towards its universalist second phase. It is not even certain that Trump really represents the first step in this shift. After all, it was under Barack Obama that the democratic, protectionist turn first began.

The 'Buy American provision', adopted in 2009, set aside financing for a recovery plan for infrastructures using materials and products made in the United States. A prolegomenon to the second phase of the democratic renewal, perhaps: but in any case, the rise of protectionism, a central element in the national re-emergence, preceded Trump, and affected the two great American political forces almost simultaneously, even though it is clear that the sociological localization of xenophobia meant that it

257

was Trump who succeeded rather than Sanders. Still, the decline in the belief in free trade affects the whole of American society, a phenomenon that appears rational and reasonable when we realize that college graduates themselves were no longer benefiting from economic globalization and were seeing their revenues stagnate. But then, how can we choose between the two hypotheses: a permanent division of American society, or a majority flocking to support a non-xenophobic national vision?

The economic destiny and the ideological behaviour of the younger generation can enable us to predict the future. With student debt, as we have seen, young generations of graduates will experience an acceleration in the decline in their income. But here again, to really gauge the crisis experienced by young Americans, we will have to dig down to the deepest layers of family and religious behaviour. When the data exist, I will show how widespread this crisis is in Western democracies.

The decline of the absolute nuclear family and the confinement of young people

An age-based analysis of income trends reveals, in all Western democracies except perhaps Australia, that the relative situation of young people is getting worse. As early as 1999, Louis Chauvel highlighted this phenomenon in the case of France, emphasizing that the (long-lasting) crisis did not prevent older generations from bringing their economic careers to a happy conclusion at the very moment when young people were starting to 'slave away' in uncertain and poorly paid jobs.[12] An excellent article in the *Guardian* in 2016 treated the subject in a comparative way.[13]

In the United States, between 1979 and 2010, the growth rate in disposable income for households headed by 25- to 29-year-olds was 9 per cent lower than the average increase, while the growth rate for those aged 65–69 was 28 per cent higher, and that for those aged 70–74 years was 25 per cent higher. Table 14.2 shows that the imbalance was even stronger in the United Kingdom, France, Spain and Italy.

The declining incomes of the youngest sector of the population is a mechanical effect of the neoliberal revolution and, very specifically, of free trade, which crushes with great impartiality all those who do not possess capital. Thus it was the younger generation, together with the workers, who were first to be sacrificed on the altar. Whether or not they are graduates, the supremacy of the market has dramatically increased their economic dependence on their parents. At the very moment when the maturing elites were celebrating more loudly and triumphantly than ever the liberty of the individual, individual young people were suffering a diminution in their own hopes of independence.

Housing has become very difficult for the younger generation. The

Table 14.2   Young and old in the neoliberal revolution

Difference in the average change in household disposable income between 1979 and 2010, as a %, positive or negative, by age

	25–29	65–69	70–74
United Kingdom	–2	62	66
Canada	–4	5	16
Germany	–5	5	9
France	–8	49	31
United States	–9	28	25
Spain	–12	33	31
Italy	–19	12	20
Australia	27	14	2

contrast between ideological affirmation and social reality reached a Brezhnev-type intensity in the Anglosphere on the eve of the Brexit–Trump shift in 2016. In the United States, as in England, Canada and even Australia, the proportion of 18- to 34-year-olds who continued to live with their parents increased: this category included many graduates forced to return home after completion of their university studies.[14] A Pew Research Center study also showed, in May 2016, that the number of 18–34-year-olds living with their parents in the United States had returned to the levels experienced around 1880, a phase of weak nuclearity, as we saw earlier.[15]

At the moment, the American nuclear family is quite simply losing its absolute character: it is clearly undergoing a partial reversion to the temporary co-residence of young people and the undifferentiated family of original times. As we saw, the near perfection of the nuclear family in seventeenth-century England required an agricultural system capable of giving places to young people as servants, and state intervention in favour of the destitute elderly. Similarly, in the United States, a truly absolute nuclear family did not develop until 1950, in the context of full employment and the welfare state inherited from Roosevelt. The neoconservative revolution, by making access to employment difficult and by weakening the state, reversed the trend and brought the American family closer to the undifferentiated nuclear type (i.e., the original model of *Homo sapiens*) for the second time in history.

Given this reversion, it becomes easier to understand the interest of young American graduates for state interventionism, and the enthusiasm of some of them for the 'socialism' of Bernie Sanders. Contrary to what is claimed by the neoliberal catechism, which in practice brings young people back under the authority of the father, the state, for the younger generation in advanced countries, means freedom.[16]

Table 14.3   Young adults living with their parents in Europe in 2008, in %

	Women	Men	Total of 25–34-year-olds
Denmark	0.5	2.8	1.65
Sweden	2.0	3.9	2.95
Norway	2.2	4.7	3.5
Finland	1.9	8.0	4.9
Netherlands	3.1	11.8	7.5
France	8.0	13.0	10.5
Iceland	7.4	15.1	11.2
Belgium	9.0	18.8	13.9
Germany	9.2	18.7	13.9
United Kingdom	10.5	20.0	15.2
Austria	14.7	30.7	22.7
Ireland	17.9	32.2	25.0
Spain	29.8	41.1	35.5
Italy	32.7	47.7	40.2
Portugal	34.9	47.6	41.2

Sources: Eurostat, 'Un homme sur trois et une femme sur cinq âgés de 25 à 34 ans habitent chez leurs parents', no. 149, October 2010.

In Denmark, a country where the absolute nuclear family prevails, the resistance to statism inherited from Lutheran and social democratic times has preserved the absolute nuclear character of the family. Young people benefit from substantial support, which allows them to leave the parental home very quickly. Cécile van de Velde has produced a close study not only of the norm of autonomy among young people in the English tradition, but also the weakening of its practical realization due to the difficulties in getting accommodation. She has also described the sturdy resistance of the Danish nuclear and statist model.[17]

The comparative data provided by Eurostat, shown in Table 14.3, highlight England's current poor 'nuclear' performance after nearly three decades of neoliberalism.[18]

The resistance of American youth to xenophobia

In all educational and racial categories, only 36 per cent of 18–29-year-olds voted for Trump and 55 per cent for Clinton. The gap is important. Among young people classified as White, however, Trump won with 48 per cent of the vote against 43 per cent for his rival. There is, then, a youth factor, which involves a certain distance from Trump's pessimism but, within this age group, is unable to wipe out the strongly

Table 14.4   The American vote by age group in 2016 (%)

Age	Trump	Clinton
18–29	36	55
30–44	41	51
45–64	52	44
65 and over	52	45

pro-Trump orientation of the White group. The younger generation is one of the categories that the system has bullied, and it is not surprising that it participated in the revolt of the electorate. However, its relative resistance to xenophobia impels us to suggest that the optimistic and open dimension of American culture is still alive and well.

We can, moreover, be certain that the ideological evolution of the youngest section of the American electorate is still in its infancy and that an accelerated change is likely in the near future. A crucial element underlines the ideological shift of the American generations who reached adulthood at the turn of the third millennium. It guarantees that phenomena like Trump, Sanders and the challenge of globalization are not short-lived frets and fevers: the most recent studies reveal that religious belief is declining in the United States, and we have noted several times that, historically speaking, this has always paved the way to an ideological revolution.

America has always distinguished itself from Europe by the resistance of its religious beliefs, although, as I said above, the rates of attendance at Sunday services given by opinion polls (40–50 per cent) overestimate actual practice.[19] The number should usually be halved. But if we compare the declared religious practice of the generations who arrived at adulthood around 1950 with those who reached their majority at the beginning of the third millennium, we observe a fall in declared practice: from 40–50 per cent to 20 per cent.[20] The proportion of young adults who declare themselves 'agnostic', 'atheist' or state that their religion is 'nothing in particular' increased from 25 per cent to 35 per cent between 2007 and 2014.[21]

What we are seeing here is probably the terminal secularization of American society, which proves that religiously based neoconservatism is dying on the Republican side and that a general revolution is under way. This fall explains Trump's victory in the Republican camp and the rise of state-friendly attitudes among young people. The resistance of younger generations to Trump, meanwhile, makes it reasonable to imagine, optimistically, a democratic revival which, starting out from a xenophobic matrix, will then pick up speed and reach its universalist second phase.

— 15 —

THE MEMORY OF PLACES

After six chapters on the *longue durée* dynamics of the Anglo-American world, whose family type is nuclear, the time has now come to study the recent evolution of some of the world's great nations whose family structures were, to varying degrees, affected by the patrilineal transformation. Germany and Japan were stem-family countries; in Russia and China, the exogamous communitarian family was the norm. But before we tackle those countries that continue, in interaction with the Anglosphere, to define the game played by the world's powers, we need to take a methodological break. Indeed, the stem family, German or Japanese, no longer exists in the urban areas that now constitute the main residential settlements. In neither Berlin nor Tokyo will you find a population divided into three-generation households; in neither Moscow nor Beijing will there be many households with a father and his married sons. And yet, I will be pursuing my argument in the rest of this outline as if the values of the stem family and those of exogamous communitarian families continued to guide, under the surface, the evolutions and adaptations of these nations. So I need to begin by explaining how, and why, I ended up accepting the hypothesis of such a permanent situation. To do so, I will start by tackling the case of France.

The question is of great interest for the study of France, whose anthropological system rests fundamentally on the contrast between an egalitarian nuclear Paris Basin and a southwestern stem family, though we must not forget the multiplicity of other family forms, a mosaic that in reality makes the 'one and indivisible' nation into the most multicultural of all. For all that, the southwest stem-family households have mostly disappeared, and there are now just as few three-generation households in Toulouse as there are in Berlin or Tokyo. But in France there are still traces, residues of the complex households of the past. A cartography of these residual forms, produced in 2011, reveals, like a radioactive

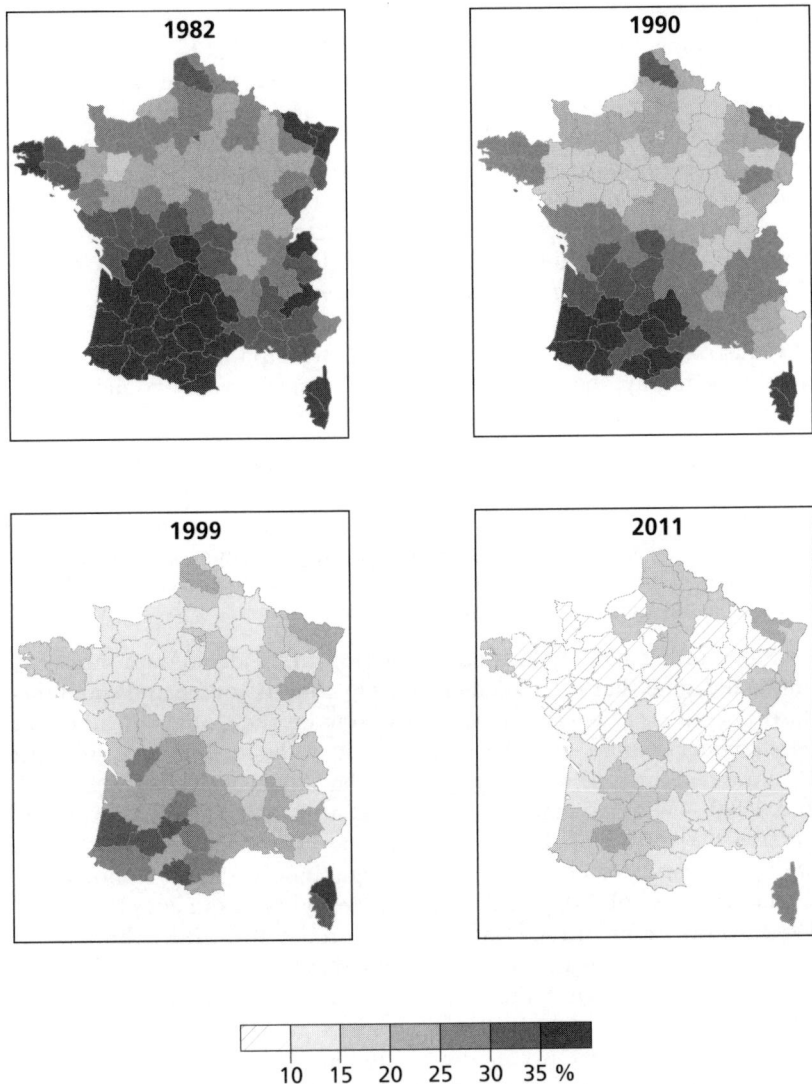

Map 15.1   Cohabitation with relatives between 1982 and 2011 in France
Source: Loïc Trabut and Joëlle Gaymu, 'Habiter seul ou avec des proches après 85 ans en France: de fortes disparités selon les départements', in INED, *Population et Sociétés*, no. 539, December 2016, p. 114.

trace, that domestic complexity was overrepresented in the southwest of France, fading away even more between 1982 and 2011.

The southwest, a pole of development of the stem family between the thirteenth and the nineteenth centuries, has become nuclear. Egalitarian inheritance rules have long since replaced birthright where it was practised, in the Toulouse region as in Germany and Japan.

If we observe the nuclearization of households on a global scale, it may seem easy to prophesy a universal victory of the nuclear family. This was done in 1963 by William Goode, the American sociologist (1917–2003), in *World Revolution and Family Patterns*. He did not see the emancipated couple as a mechanical effect of urban life or a necessity of industrialization. He presented it as the triumph of a certain conception of the family, the victory of an ideology promoted by young people, women and the oppressed:

> The ideology of the conjugal family is a radical one, destructive of the older tradition in almost every society. It grows from a set of more general radical principles which also arouse these groups *politically* in perhaps every underdeveloped country. Its appeal is almost as universal as that of 'redistribution of the land'. It asserts the equality of individuals, as against class, caste, or sex barriers.[1]

Goode rather banally located the origin of this ideology in the West, but he did state that it had detached itself from its source and spontaneously spread everywhere. To read this book on the global spread of the *pure conjugal family* – the American family of the time, in fact, since the absolute nuclear type was at its peak in the United States between 1950 and 1960 – is a fascinating exercise for all those who can nowadays observe the spread of the Western ideology that followed, that of the *pure individual*, detached from the conjugal family, ideally embodied by the homosexual of either sex. Just like the rights of the couple, around 1960, so the rights of the homosexual are today defined by the West as a universal value that needs to be defended everywhere. Homophobia is one of the criticisms of Putin's Russia and many countries in the developing world.

But with Goode we are at the beginning of the 1960s and the universalism of his thesis does not imply, as it does for the ideologues of today, an absolute disregard for the diversity of the world. On the contrary, he was an anthropologist as much as a sociologist and his knowledge of the traditional family systems of the planet – Germany, Russia, China, India, Japan, the Arab world – was remarkable. His book could still serve as an introduction to their study. He knew, moreover, that the Western conjugal model was old and dated back at least a millennium.[2] His description of the rise of conjugal values and nuclear domestic forms is accurate and nuanced. He sensed the self-destructive potential of patrilineal communitarian types, liable to suffocate both men and women. His book highlights the militant feminism of the communist regimes, an element that is forgotten today but that can help us understand the current decline in the status of women in many areas of the post-communist world, such as East Germany and China.[3] Goode also notes that patrilineal and anti-individualist models are anchored in the upper strata of societies, and underlines the relative sexual egalitarianism of dominated social groups.[4]

This last observation appears commonsensical when we realize that patrilineal forms are invented at the top of society and then spread downwards, slowly and always imperfectly. This is a capital lesson in a time of globalization, whose ideology falsely depicts national elites as close to each other, while ordinary people are locked into their respective cultures. In fact, all over the world, ordinary communities remain, to varying degrees, closer to the natural family of *Homo sapiens*, and thus closer to each other, closer to America. And it is the world's elites who, when they are not Anglo-American, French, Dutch or Danish, must make a maximum effort to get closer to the conjugal type, egalitarian with regard to the relations between the sexes, even when they can swan around from one five-star hotel to another, from one airport to another.

Goode is nuanced, but he is keen to demonstrate the convergence of societies and their alignment on a nuclear model. If we identify 'family system' and 'domestic group' (or household), his demonstration is perfect. But if we distinguish between, on the one hand, the family system – i.e., a set of values organizing the relationships between men and women, between parents and children, between brothers and sisters – and, on the other, the domestic group as it can be seen in the census, his demonstration works less well. It is indeed quite conceivable that a system of values may survive the disintegration of the domestic group in which it was embodied in the peasant era. The nuclearization of households does not necessarily imply that of mentalities. Authoritarianism, inegalitarianism and antifeminism can a priori survive in a society made up of nuclear households. The expression 'a priori' here refers only to a logical possibility. Only an empirical demonstration could make us admit that the nuclear household does not always lead to a nuclear mentality, and that the destruction of the complex households of the peasant past does not necessarily lead to an individualistic mentality.

This point is obviously crucial, and I will explain how I myself went from a conception close to Goode's to the conviction that non-individualist, patrilineal or inegalitarian mentalities could survive – and even prosper – in a nuclear household system. My conversion was totally empirical and did not result, I assure you, from any personal preference. Indeed, it took me a long time to understand the mechanism that made this permanence of values possible. To do so, I have had to withdraw from an implicit adherence to a psychoanalytic vision of family relations and the transmission of values. The assumption of a persistence of values is difficult to accept, but fundamental if one wants to understand the current evolution of Germany, Japan, Russia and China; so I will describe briefly the stages of my intellectual conversion.

My initial depiction: a nuclear convergence after the transitional crisis

It was a model akin to Goode's that I had in mind when, in the early 1980s, I connected the geographical distribution of political ideologies with that of the underlying family systems. In this initial model, the disintegration of the Russian, Chinese, Serbian and Vietnamese peasant communitarian family 'released' individuals who, temporarily unfit for liberty, sought in the party, the centralized economy or the police state a substitute for the waning big family. In such a depiction, the totalitarian sociopolitical form was only transitional. The disappearance of the dense households of the past, the lives of the following generations in a 'nuclear' family environment – I confused family and household – had to produce the kind of change that Goode envisioned: a convergence on conjugal and individualistic types. My sequence was a little less angelic than his because, although nuclearization was partly a result of people's desire for freedom, it led them at first to a reflex of panic and a flight away from freedom.

My representation of the transmission of values was implicitly Freudian. I imagined children formatted by their education. Psychoanalysis had attained the status of an official doctrine for my generation and threw up images of an unconscious filled with threatening parenting images: mental prisons, so to speak. The anthropologist translates this as: strong norms were implanted by families into the brains of individuals. A whole literature derived from the Frankfurt School, from Adorno to Fromm, then described the difficulty, for the individual raised in an authoritarian family structure, to live in freedom. My model merely added to this standard interpretation the idea that there are many different family forms, or forms of training, and therefore many different forms of political mentalities, some of them totalitarian but others liberal. And I thought then that, if authoritarian families, egalitarian or not, disappeared with the nuclearization of households in urban areas, the corresponding ideologies would in turn, with time, fade away.

Then would come the time of convergence. The new nuclear families would produce children who, raised according to the liberal norm, could reject the totalitarian transitional ideology, communism in the case of Russia and China, Nazism in the case of Germany.

Nazism was eliminated militarily, so the democratization of Germany cannot be used to verify the model. The endogenous collapse of communism, on the other hand, could be considered as the basis for a demonstration.

Russian history tells us today that communism was only a transitional ideology. Indeed, we find in Russia an announcement of the long sequence leading from communitarian family to family disintegration, then family nuclearization and totalitarianism combined, and finally the disintegration of totalitarianism itself.

As soon as communism fell, I have to admit, I wondered about a possible survival of communitarian traces in the organization of liberalized Russian society. But in the 1990s, it was, oddly enough, the evolution of Western societies themselves that troubled me. Surprisingly permanent features, which only anthropology could explain, led me to abandon the hypothesis that advanced societies were converging on a single liberal type.

The immigration of the 1990s: divergence in the West

Working in the early 1990s on integration into four Western societies – the United States, the United Kingdom, Germany and France – I was surprised to find very different levels of assimilation, measurable by divergent rates of intermarriage for the children of immigrants of Muslim origin. At a time when Western European societies were aligning themselves with the US consumer model, such a finding posed a theoretical problem. How could one explain insignificant rates of intermarriage amongst daughters of Muslim immigrants in England and Germany, when these rates were already substantial in France? Everywhere, cities, suburbs, consumption, the tertiarization of activities and, above all, nuclear households; everywhere the same official political values, democratic and liberal, with elections, an uncensored press, the possibility of unhindered circulation. And yet there was something, hidden in social life, producing a divergence.

The rate of intermarriage is a powerful indicator. It points to the future, since, if they occur in great numbers in a given society, mixed couples who produce children abolish the possibility of that society being racially or ethnically segmented. But the rate of intermarriage also sums up the immediate past: for individuals from distinct groups to marry, they must have been close in their lives as young adults, adolescents and children. At the beginning of intermarriage lies the absence of any taboo on children's games of all origins. So the geographical distribution of populations in the cities plays a role, as does the number and functioning of kindergartens, primary and secondary schools, and finally colleges and

267

universities. The attitude of the parents of the host society, whether they are able or not to let their children out onto the streets, to invite or to forbid, is a key factor. However, we cannot say, a priori, which of these explanatory elements is the most important. We do not know, exactly, what caused the French to open up to intermarriage, while the United Kingdom and Germany remained more closed.

In my book *Le Destin des immigrés* [*The Destiny of Immigrants*], which used data from the early 1990s for those three European countries, I simply measured intermarriage rates, accepted the evidence of a discrepancy and then suggested that a permanence of family values could explain the diversity of integration models.[5] It seemed reasonable to me to hypothesize that, one way or another, the value of equality, among children and adults, identified in the egalitarian nuclear family of the past, was still active in France, and explained the country's ability to produce a high rate of intermarriage. Similarly, if the somewhat blurred value of non-equality in the absolute nuclear family still prevailed in England, and if the value of inequality in the stem family survived in Germany, one could begin to understand the low frequency of intermarriage with the children of immigrants from distant cultures. The rates of intermarriage among Yugoslavs were high in Germany, as were those of West Indians in England. But France was distinguished by higher rates for all groups, European, West Indian and Muslim. Why not admit that, in France, an egalitarian anthropological preconception of human beings was still alive, making it possible to ignore the differences between individuals of very diverse origins and still favouring intermarriage? Conversely, the absence of a universalist presupposition could explain the braking or blocking of marriage with the children of immigrants perceived as being too distant, as happened in England or Germany (albeit in two very different ways in these countries). It would take too long to go into the details of the explanation. It is the theoretical implications of this divergence for an understanding of the transmission mechanism of values that matter here.

In this second phase of my research, the disappearance of visible family differences had led me to describe not so much a determination of attitudes by a *family system*, but rather their determination by an *anthropological system*, a larger concept that encompassed all the relationships between individuals interacting locally. I tried to imagine a more diffuse education of children by adults, including not just parents, but teachers and neighbours as well. But still, I was embarrassed by this permanence of values on national territories, maintained as it was by some obscure mechanism.

The separation of capitalisms

My next work, devoted to economic globalization, confirmed the persistence of these values that I had first grasped, following Peter Laslett and Alan Macfarlane, in the structuring of the peasant families of the seventeenth to the nineteenth centuries. In *L'Illusion économique* [*The Economic Illusion*], I again had to admit the action of invisible forces of an anthropological nature in the divergence of economies, Anglo-American on the one hand, German and Japanese on the other.[6] In this area, however, it was possible to build on previous research. There was a vast literature dealing with the diversity of capitalism. In France, Michel Albert had contrasted, in *Capitalisme contre Capitalisme* [*Capitalism against Capitalism*], the Anglo-Saxon and Rhineland types.[7] In England and the Netherlands, Charles Hampden-Turner and Alfons Trompenaars had defined, in *The Seven Cultures of capitalism*, the value systems structuring American, Japanese, German, British, Swedish and Dutch capitalisms.[8] It only remained for me to find the key to an anthropological reading of these data, to detect in the characteristics of the Anglo-American model – short-termism, the search for the highest rate of profit, the liquidation of industry, financialization and rising inequality – the economic effects of the values of flexibility and indifference to equality of the absolute nuclear family. The values of hierarchical integration and continuity inherited from the stem family reflected, in turn, the powers of resistance of the industrial apparatuses of Germany and Japan, and the preference of their economies for the long term. In both countries, the structural trade surplus perfectly symbolized the asymmetrical vision produced by the inequality of German and Japanese brothers, projected here into the universe of nations and the trade between them.

The inability of all these authors to categorize France – unclassifiable according to Albert,[9] and defying any easy categorization for Hampden-Turner and Trompenaars – confirmed the hypothesis, since France, combining an egalitarian nuclear centre with a stem-family periphery, could, according to the anthropological model, produce a simple capitalism.[10] In central France, liberalism pulls towards Anglo-American flexibility, but equality is opposed to the differentiation of income; on the periphery, in Alsace of course, but especially in the Rhône-Alpes region and in the southwest, where stem families prevail, there is a more German economic sensitivity and a preference for technological continuity.

The infranational persistence of differences in France

In the case of nations, we might be tempted to explain the persistence of values by institutional mechanisms of reproduction. In each of them, a uniform bureaucracy, laws and judicial machinery cover the territory: these institutions can be imagined as ensuring the perpetuation of typical national behaviours. But the case of France destroys this fall-back explanation. The French state, as everyone knows, covers its territory with the same administrative and legal mantle. However, the regional educational and economic developments that Hervé Le Bras and I studied in *Le Mystère français* [*The French Mystery*] are, at the beginning of the third millennium, still conditioned and guided by provincial family systems that are supposed no longer to exist.[11]

That book saw religion as just as important as the family in the determination of mentalities. It thus superimposed on the traditional map of family structures the map of religious practices as they had appeared between 1740 and 1960. The two maps overlapped without fully coinciding. The heart of the Paris Basin, nuclear egalitarian at the family level, had been dechristianized even before the Revolution. The majority of stem-family regions, or of non-egalitarian nuclear-family areas on the periphery, had allowed the survival of active Catholicism until around the 1960s. The correspondence, however, was not absolute. There were combinations of egalitarian nuclear family and strong religious practice, in Lorraine for example, or of stem families and dechristianization, in the Garonne valley, in particular.

Let us now turn to 1975, at the end of France's 'Thirty Glorious Years' of increasing prosperity. Complex households no longer existed, for the most part, outside the rural areas of the southwest, Alsace and Finistère. Catholic religious practice was collapsing where it had survived, in the west, the far north, the east, the southeast of the Massif Central, and the Basque Country. Let us follow the educational revolution of the years 1960–95, in which the number of graduates and students soared. It would be an understatement to say that traces of behaviour remain, induced by old family or religious values. The maps reveal that the very movement of educational progress is guided by 'vanished' family and religious systems. Around 1980, the map of the proportion of high school graduates among young people was a carbon copy of that of the 'vanished' stem family. Towards 1995, the map of the proportion of high school graduates who went on to higher education revealed troubling analogies with the map of an also 'vanished' Catholicism. The economy and political leanings had, as is so often the case, followed education: in areas of poor educational performance, there were high unemployment rates and a strong extreme right-wing vote.

French territory thus remains structured and animated by anthropo-logical and religious forces that are supposed no longer to exist. Again, postulating the stability of values beneath the surface helps us understand the movement of society.

The stem family, with its ideal of continuity and its emphasis on lineage, may explain the extensive periods of education found in the southwest and Finistère. Catholic values of cooperation between indi-viduals may have survived religion and rendered some social fabrics more resilient to the stress of globalization. Taking into account the religious dimension brings us closer to a realistic conception of local cases of the perpetuation of cultures: it forces us to think directly in terms of territory and not only of family.

My co-author and I had decided to introduce the notion of *zombie Catholicism* to refer to a religion that continues to act after its demise – a belief that is simultaneously dead and alive. We could just as well have talked about the *zombie stem family* or, for the northwestern edge of the Massif Central, between Dordogne and Nièvre, the *zombie communitar-ian family*.

The family types that were nuclear in the eighteenth century were still so in the year 2000 and did not apparently need, at first approach, to be called zombie. Yet the permanence of a non-egalitarian mentality in the nuclear inland west suggests that it would not be absurd to refer to a *zombie absolute nuclear family* in this case. The persistent egalitarianism of the Paris Basin, even though the egalitarian inheritance no longer functions properly, due to the lengthening of the average life and the mul-tiplication of stepfamilies, suggests that it might prove useful to resort to the concept of the *zombie egalitarian nuclear family*.

Farewell to Freud

Before working on the data of *Le Mystère français*, I had reached the conclusion, as I said above, that the transmission of values operated not only within the family, but within a territory, between adults and chil-dren, even though the family unit remained a privileged place of repro-duction. But the conception of an 'anthropological system', larger than 'the family', can lead to a truly accurate representation of what a 'family system' is. The researcher who focuses on the mechanism of transmission of values instinctively prioritizes a vertical view of the family, the main axis of which is the succession of generations, even if he is not at all fascinated, as Frédéric Le Play is, by the stem family. But a *family system*, properly viewed, is not only, or even primarily, a typical family placed between its past and its future. A living family system, as I suggested in Chapter 3, where I discussed the original *Homo sapiens* type, is *a set of*

271

families exchanging spouses and producing children within a territory. This is obvious in the case of exogamous systems (i.e., the majority), one of which goes back to *Homo sapiens*. But it remains true of the so-called 'endogamous' systems, in which marriage between cousins, of near or distant degree (which does not prevent a certain proportion of exogamous marriages), also occurs within a territory.

Such a representation is easily compatible with the notion of an anthropological system operating in a given geographical area, and within which all adults contribute, to varying degrees, to the inculcation of norms and values in all children. But we have not yet reached the end of our quest, and truly pierced the mystery of the self-reproduction of values within a territory in the absence of a visible family system, embodied for example in three-generation households.

To imagine territories in which adults inculcate strong norms of behaviour in children is to remain faithful to an implicitly Freudian interpretation of transmission. Starting from the family, I continued to imagine children formatted by their education, whether authoritarian or not.

Working with Hervé Le Bras on *Le Mystère français*, I came to understand that the migrations of individuals, and especially their lack of effects on regional cultures, posed an insoluble problem for the hypothesis of norms strongly inculcated by parents or by adults. The work that Le Bras carried out on migration, now a major phenomenon in France, suggests that we need to ask this crucial question: how can typical regional cultures survive when so many people move away and spend most of their lives elsewhere than where they were born? Despite the intense flow of movement within France, regional temperaments remain. It is exactly as if each place had a memory, immune to the disappearance of the original family and religious structures, to the renewal of the population, to the arrival of individuals from other systems of value and the departure of other individuals to other regions.

Without, however, completely abandoning the assumption of the training of children in the family, or in their neighbourhood and at school, we must seriously question the hypothesis of a regional cultural permanence ensured only by powerful norms at the individual level. For if individuals were indeed the bearers of very strong norms acquired in childhood, migrants would keep them for life and pass them on to their children, and migrations would have the effect of mixing values and destroying the homogeneity of regional systems, eventually creating a national culture as a sort of average.

Finally, the empirical reality shows that migrants are more or less easily detached from their habits and beliefs and reveal a high degree of mimetic adaptability, within local human interactions. This is how they quite often move away from the values that had been theirs in childhood.

We must at this stage think in terms of individuals carrying, not strong values to their host territories, but weak values instead. However, the fundamental paradox is that it is the hypothesis of weak values that makes it possible to explain the persistence of regional temperaments, the phenomenon of a memory of places. If indeed the values supported by the overwhelming majority of the individuals on a given territory are weak, the immigration of individuals who are themselves carriers of weak or relatively weak values, and predisposed to exchange them for those of the host group, does not lead to the dilution of the original system.

Here we find a central element of the *Homo sapiens* matrix, namely flexibility, here associated with the notion of mimetic behaviour. We can therefore conclude our analysis by noting that the hypothesis of weak values at the level of the individuals of the host country can explain the existence of a memory of places.[12]

Weak values and the persistence of nations

This is not to deny the existence of 'strong' values and 'intense' modes of transmission, some of which occur within the family unit itself. Child psychiatry and psychoanalysis have sufficiently emphasized the importance of the first years in the formation of the personality. Between birth and puberty, the development of the body and the mind go hand in hand, and one must even assume that the psyche and intellectual skills are inscribed within the physical architecture of the individual. In Chapter 6 I referred to the transformation of the brain by the intensive practice of reading between the ages of 6 and 10 years, a mechanism associated with the construction of a specific inner personality. But we must admit that these intense modes of transmission do not comprise the totality of the influences that condition human values, beliefs and behaviours. There is also a multiple universe of 'weak' values, beliefs and behaviours, the transmission of which results from quite superficial mimetic processes. The two levels of transmission, far from being contradictory, can combine and strengthen each other. The important thing is to understand how values that are weakly carried by individuals can produce extremely strong, resilient and sustainable systems at group level. In particular, it is not necessary that a belief be lived intensely by individuals for it to live for a long time, sometimes indefinitely, on a territory.

Not all groups that carry values are strictly speaking territorial, even if a certain type of inscription in space – village, city, neighbourhood – is necessary for the daily interactions that give life to value, belief and behaviour. A social milieu or a religious group is largely perpetuated by mimetic phenomena that do not reproduce intense beliefs. The values concerned are not only family values; they may relate to important or insignificant elements of life.

I now realize that my first contact with 'the strength of weak values' was not related to the issue of immigration, although it occurred at the very time when I was working on the rates of intermarriage. Between 1992 and 1995, it was easy to demonstrate to an individual, in a private discussion, the absurdity of the project of a single European currency, but the belief in the inevitability of the euro was invulnerable at the collective level. The weak belief was already carried by a sufficiently broad group, and the individual, convinced for a while, returned to his or her belief at the same time as to his or her milieu after the conversation.

One of the implications of the model linking a 'strong collective value' to 'weak individual values' is less depressing. The concept of the memory of places helps us understand the persistence of national temperaments without demonizing individuals, without making each of them the intense carrier of the values of his or her nation. One can, thanks to the concept of the memory of places, accept as an obvious fact the persistence of German, Japanese, Russian, American, English, Chinese, Arab or Swedish cultures without imagining for a second that every German, Japanese, Russian, American, English, Chinese, Arab or Swedish citizen is a living and immutable archetype. Individuals separated from their group immediately begin to drift away from their original culture, at various speeds, it is true. Let us take our realism to its logical consequences.

The hypothesis of a permanence of national values after the disappearance of complex family forms will now help us to understand, in the last three chapters of this book, the recent evolution of societies that were not characterized, around 1850 or 1900, by the nuclear family. I will begin by studying the 'stem-family societies' of Germany and Japan, homologous but distinct, since their common anthropological basis has not prevented them from really diverging today. I will then show how the continent-wide persistence of stem-family values, as well as the existence of zombie Catholicism, has led to a metamorphosis of the European Union, and especially of the Eurozone. Finally, I will examine the Russian and Chinese 'exogamous communitarian societies', which are very different in terms of the status of women and will inevitably diverge. A comparative examination of the German and Japanese stem-family societies, then of the Russian and Chinese communitarian societies, will enable us to give anthropological factors their fair share without falling into the illusion that they are omnipotent.

— 16 —

STEM-FAMILY SOCIETIES: GERMANY AND JAPAN

To suggest that the advanced nations are diverging contradicts the faith of the Western elites. The dream of an absolute individual must be universal if it is to deal effectively with the obscure, collectivist side of force as embodied, following the whim of the moment, by Islam or Russia. Germany and Japan are part of the Western camp and therefore cannot follow trajectories different from those of societies with an anthropological basis in the nuclear family.

To be honest, the West can cope quite well with the difference of Japan. This difference is there to be seen in the obvious fact that Japan is a largely autonomous culture, which took its first elements, agriculture and writing, from Chinese civilization. Japan itself has always claimed its own specificity, and while it has played a decisive role in globalization, it has refused to take part, since the tragedy of Hiroshima and Nagasaki, in the power play between nations. Its diplomatic role remains insignificant, out of all proportion to its technological power. Its economy is, however, the third largest in the world in terms of gross domestic product and, according to some measures, the largest from a technological point of view. As I said at the beginning of this book, the *World Patent Report* of 2008 tells us that Japan's share in the deposit of exportable patents in 2001–5 was 29.9 per cent as against 28.4 per cent for the United States and 12.3 per cent for Germany, its most immediate competitors. During the 1980s, the rise of the Japanese economy gave the United States some cause for concern, but its long depression in the 1990s finally put paid to hostility towards the Japanese. Of course, there will always be some French academic or other waxing indignant at those who seek a 'culturalist' explanation for the specific economic situation of Japan, even when the Japanese themselves often put forward such an explanation.[1] But overall, this slightly 'different' country, with its literature, manga, robots and cuisine, is praised by all for its positive contribution to world culture.

The case of Germany, a country that is not much in evidence on today's cultural scene, is different. Nazi barbarism posed a real challenge to the proponents of a radical universalist conception. Redefining Germany as 'ordinary' and 'normal' thus appears to your basic occidentalist as a matter of theoretical urgency. Rejecting the idea that the extermination of 6 million Jews was a specifically German phenomenon that could not have been conceived elsewhere in Europe has even become a priority. Some of the best historians of Nazism, such as Ian Kershaw, have felt compelled to participate in what seems to me, personally, a denial of the empirical evidence.[2]

The universalizing attitude may lull us into certain peace of mind, but it stops us understanding the past, present and future historical development of Germany. Deciding that Germany is just a country like any other is to refuse to see its crucial role in the spread of literacy across the planet and in the mental transformation of the years 1550–1650. It is to forget the power of its economic and scientific take-off in the years 1880–1930. It is to ignore its almost superhuman level of military efficiency during two world wars – even though Émile Durkheim had mentioned this efficiency in a controversial essay written in 1915, *L'Allemagne au-dessus de tout* [*Germany Over All, Deutschland über alles*].[3] In this very short text, the founder of quantitative sociology saw wartime Germany as a case of social pathology. But the achievement by the same country, around 1943–4, of a new state of superhuman efficiency in its resistance to the combined forces of the United Kingdom, Russia and the United States would suffice to identify this pathology as the product of a social and mental structure. As Durkheim had foreseen in 1915, the world resisted and Germany's neurotic tension subsided, but only after a Second World War that he could never have imagined. Germany was pacified by force of arms and divided in 1945, and we have endeavoured to forget the terrible power of this nation and its culture. And now we are being punished for it: barely twenty-five years after its reunification, Germany has already rebuilt its eastern area, ruined by communism; it has reorganized Eastern Europe, putting to work the active populations brought up under the old popular democracies; in the West, it has successfully conducted a real industrial blitzkrieg against the weaker nations trapped in the euro; it is proposing a partnership with China and posing as the economic rival of the United States.

Thus, Germany has yet again just revealed an extraordinary capacity for action. In 2015, however, it had only 81 million inhabitants, and was one of the two countries in the world with the most ageing populations, with a median age of 46.3 years. It is nevertheless the third largest exporter, and in 2016, its trade surplus amounted to 8 per cent of its gross domestic product.

How can we not be sensitive to the power to which these results testify, and the intellectual challenge they face us with? Surely they confirm that

Germany is still not a country like any other? However, if we accept the permanence of the values rooted in the stem family, and the effects of these values, we will be able to analyse the specificity of Germany without isolating this people from our common humanity. Japan too, after all, is a country whose historical performances were and remain extraordinary. It was the first of all non-European countries to take off economically in the late nineteenth century and it remains one of the most advanced nations in the world. Its patent production, as we have seen, accounts for almost one-third of the world total. This other country with one of the oldest populations in the world (a median age of 46.5 years) still had only 127 million inhabitants in 2017. The population of Tokyo was 38 million: but the capital was innocent of the ways of the world and litter was unknown there. Yet this incredible nation emerged on a few islands prone to incessant earthquakes.

In reality, so many other peoples where the stem family is the rule develop an 'exceptional' energy and some form of ethnocentrism, such as Koreans, the Basques, the Catalans, the Rwandans and the Bamilekes of Cameroon, that it is not intellectually hard to get away from the idea that Germany or Japan might not be fully part of humankind.[4] Even the folkloric and disturbing case of North Korea verifies the model of a stem family that is able to develop an out-of-the-ordinary efficiency. Its communist regime has mutated, adopting an ethnocentric ideology that affirms the uniqueness of the Korean people. In accordance with the rules of the most traditional stem family, it has adopted a system whereby power is transmitted by lineage to a single heir. Korean totalitarianism was not content with surviving a famine that, between 1995 and 1998, killed between 600,000 and 1 million people. Year after year, it imperturbably manufactures nuclear weapons and ballistic missiles.[5]

Not all these societies can be studied in detail in the present outline. By considering Germany and Japan simultaneously, however, we will be able to distinguish an anthropological determination, common to both countries, from other factors, geographical and historical, that also have their importance. And we will need to explain, beyond the similar structures of their capitalism, their current strategic divergence, with an extraverted Germany that has found its way back onto the international stage and a more introverted Japan that seeks above all to remain itself, under the constraint imposed by the rising power of its close neighbour China.

Low fertility rates in Germany and Japan: the persistence of patrilineality

From a conceptual and practical point of view, nothing is closer to the family structure than the production of children. And demographers

Table 16.1   Status of women, homosexuality and birth rates

	Fertility rate 2015	Status of women	Homosexual marriage on 1 January 2017
France	2.0	1	1
Ireland	2.0	1	1
Sweden	1.9	1	1
United Kingdom	1.9	1	1
United States	1.9	1	1
Australia	1.9	1	0
Russia	1.8	1	0
Norway	1.8	1	1
Belgium	1.8	1	1
Netherlands	1.7	1	1
Finland	1.7	1	1
Denmark	1.7	1	1
Canada	1.6	1	1
Switzerland	1.5	0	0
Austria	1.5	0	0
Japan	1.4	0	0
Italy	1.4	0	0
Germany	1.4	0	0
Spain	1.3	1	1
Greece	1.3	1	0
Taiwan	1.2	0	0
South Korea	1.2	0	0
Portugal	1.2	1	1

form one of the professions that least believe in the notion of the convergence of developed societies. The fact has been theorized, in particular by Zsolt Spéder, director of the Hungarian Institute for Demographic Research, in a well-titled article, 'The Diversity of Family Structure in Europe', which focuses on the way in which couples live together and on the situation of children in Europe at the turn of the millennium.[6] Two successive demographic transitions – the first beginning in France around 1770, the second in the United States around 1960 – have in fact led the advanced countries to very different lower limits of fertility.

Table 16.1 gives the fertility rate for women in the leading developed countries in 2015, in descending order. For the most part, the status of women, as defined by the traditional peasant family system, explains this distribution. At the top of the table are the nuclear-family countries, France and the Anglo-American world, with 1.9 children or more; down below, stem-family countries, the Germanic world, Japan and South Korea, between 1.5 and 1.2. A high status of women is indicated in column 2 by the number 1, a lower status by 0. The third column tells us about the adoption (1) or not (0) of marriage for same-sex couples at the beginning of 2017, a social evolution which, as we shall see, is also related to the anthropological background.[7] The coefficient of correlation linking a high status for women and fertility is relatively strong, equal to +0.60.

The majority of the exceptions to this distribution of fertility by family type can be (easily) explained by deviations in the status of women within a given type: I mentioned above the case of Sweden and Russia, where the stem-family and communitarian-family types do not stop women from having a high status. One could add Finland, where the Swedish stem-family tradition is mixed with a specifically Finnish communitarianism, weakly patrilineal and related to the Russian type.

The very low fertility rate in Taiwan should not surprise us, since the country follows the Chinese communitarian tradition, in its southern variant, which contains traces of the stem family. The island was, in any case, strongly patrilineal in origin. The economic indicator of Italy, at 1.4, is also normal, if we remember the patrilineal impregnation of central and northern Italy.

Canada, at 1.6, is somewhat on the low side compared to a homogeneous Anglo-American world at 1.9. Quebec is not responsible for this deviation. That leaves Denmark, with its absolute nuclear families; its rate of 1.7 is also a bit low, but remains closer to the 1.9 of Sweden than the 1.4 of Germany, its two neighbours.

The low fertility rates in Spain, Portugal and Greece need to be interpreted differently. Spain and Portugal are characterized by a stem-family structure only on their northern edges, between Minho and Catalonia, through Galicia, Asturias and the Basque Country. In addition, Portugal is just as well known to anthropologists for its matriarchal tendencies as is Brittany. The rest of Spain is egalitarian nuclear, as is the centre of Portugal, whose south is characterized by communitarian and matrilocal nuances. Greece is diverse, but Athens and the islands are dominated by a predominantly matrilocal culture.[8]

In their case, we need to mention an extreme drop in the fertility indicator, which has little to do with the low status of women. The drop was the result of a violent effort to catch up with the lifestyles and consumption levels of Northern Europe. Having fewer children has made it possible to reach higher levels of consumption and a standard of apparent modernity more quickly. I propose to describe their case by adopting an amended version of the concept of 'compressed modernity', as proposed by Chyang Kyung-Sup.[9] Catching up, in a short period of time, with the model of advanced countries comes at a cost. The acceleration produces cultural distortions, including an early and sharp drop in the reproduction rate.

The Korean sociologist, however, associates the notion of 'compressed modernity' with the anti-individualism of the Korean stem family, whose values simultaneously include the production of children, educating them until they reach a globally competitive level, and caring for one's elderly parents. Whole swathes of the interpretation, including the notion of individualization without individualism, could be applied to Germany and Japan, advanced countries but countries whose demographic imbalances also result from a mismatch between stem-family values and the ultra-individualism that has come from the West. In Korea, however, it is the temporal compression of modernization – a feature common to the Spanish situation – that helps to explain the extremely low fertility indicator (1.2), a level that Germany and Japan never reached and that the stem family alone cannot adequately explain.

A detailed analysis of national situations would confirm the great diversity of women's statuses in advanced societies. A relatively high fertility rate of 1.9 or 2.0 in 2015 coincides closely with institutional mechanisms that allow women both to work and have children. Tension between the two poles of family and career is particularly high when women have been in higher education and aspire to a profession rather than just a low-skilled job.

Such an interpretation is, I should point out, proposed all too frequently by demographers. It can be found, for example, in 'Why Do English-Speaking Countries Have Relatively High Fertility?', in an almost ethnological form since the notion of Anglosphere appears latent in the very title of the article.[10] In this article, Peter McDonald and Helen Moyle note that a culture in which the couple cooperate – with husbands and wives managing to juggle work and child-rearing – allows for higher fertility in the absence of strong state support. According to these authors, however, recent difficulties should lead to more state intervention.

The contrast between France and Germany in this respect is an obligatory exercise for demographers. In France, crèches and nursery schools quickly free mothers and reduce maternity leave to a very short period; this does not impede their careers, even though it is true that motherhood hinders promotion.[11] In Germany, on the other hand, there is a strong feeling that caring for a child full time is a moral obligation for the mother. Such a conception is not very compatible with the notion of a career. The level of state childcare provision is therefore low in the Federal Republic. But institutions here are simply reflecting mentalities. In France, a 'nuclear' collective mentality assures men and women that it is good to make their children independent as young as possible. In Germany, there is a widespread feeling that mothers who do not take care of their children are practically abandoning them, and there is a terrible expression, '*Rabenmutter*', raven mother, used to designate the woman who aspires to something other than that of homemaker. The

280

Federal Republic has ended up worrying about its fertility and is now undertaking a new type of assistance for families, though this has yet to register much of a demographic effect.

As for East Germany, it had a much higher fertility rate before reunification. State aid, in crèches and employment opportunities for mothers, was massive. In addition, and perhaps most importantly, the explicit ideal of women's emancipation was central to communist ideology.

In Japan, collective pressure cannot be read as clearly in the withdrawal of women from employment; maternal overinvestment in the child is often explained by insufficient 'emotional communication' between husband and wife. Japanese psychiatrists also consider that too strong a link between the child and its mother is potentially pathogenic.[12]

This difference in representations corresponds quite closely to the contrast between the German and Japanese relational styles. German culture values brutal frankness in interpersonal relationships, while Japanese culture is obsessed with the fear of giving offence. It would be absurd, however, to postulate a simple external pressure in the case of the Germans, and merely an internal compulsion in the case of the Japanese, to explain their rejection of the crèche or nursery school. In Chapter 6, I spoke of the simultaneous realization, via Protestantism, of a vertiginous interiority and increased pressure from the local community on the individual. The stem family simultaneously encourages social discipline and the withdrawal of the individual into him- or herself. There is no doubt that in Japan as in Germany, today, internalization and external pressure are combined at a high level in all dimensions of social life.

In both cases, including when the 'modernized' system results in too strong a maternal image, the particular position of the woman reveals the persistence of a level 1 patrilineality, associated with the stem family, even though the stem family has essentially disappeared.

This is not to deny history, or the continuous mutation of social forms; the point is to avoid committing the solecism of a change that inevitably leads to convergence. Demographers, supported by a significant range of statistics, cannot make this mistake; witness Pau Baizán and Teresa Martín-García, who conclude their aforementioned 2006 article:

> To continue our discussion on the differences existing between France and West Germany, these two countries seem to have followed different paths of modernization of their cultural and family models with regard to gender relations. In both countries, the pattern of the man who feeds his family weakened from the 1960s onwards. But while in Germany the approved pattern appears to include a man employed full-time and a woman employed part-time, with the possibility of stopping after the birth of a child, in France, the continuation of employment after pregnancy has become a self-evident model.[13]

The divergence begins in the 'student' phase of life, since these authors note that the French can procreate before having completed higher education – a process that these days can take a very long time. In Germany, the incompatibility is absolute and maximum fertility differences are observed according to educational level.

Childless women

Ron Lesthaeghe has listed the most important elements in the second demographic transition: increase in age at marriage, a greater number of couples living together out of wedlock, increase in the frequency of divorce, delay in procreation, decline in fertility, increase in number of births out of wedlock, increase in the proportion of women who will never have children.[14] As this demographer has shown, the common factor behind these movements is a very simple one – namely, the greater freedom of individuals in their life choices. The variety of levels attained in the various countries by all these parameters, and not only by fertility, would make it possible to draw a complex, contradictory and nuanced picture of current 'modernity'. We would thus see a more moderate increase in the frequency of births outside wedlock in Germany than in France, Scandinavia or the Anglo-American world, as well as a very small increase in Japan. The description of the diversity of fertility levels could also be made more detailed by noting the variety of contraceptive techniques used.

The birth control pill has certainly been a fundamental element in women's emancipation, but it is an innovation to which societies have responded according to their anthropological and religious background, accepting it, rejecting it or complementing it. In the Anglo-American world, dominated by the absolute nuclear family and a now largely zombie Protestantism, there is also a higher prevalence of vasectomy, which can free men from the risk of unwanted procreation and reveals a noteworthy resistance to female power. The use of vasectomy reflects a persistent bilaterality in the way of life rather than a triumph of matriarchy, at least in the well-off classes of American society.[15] In Japan, the rejection and then the low levels of usage of the pill reveal a resistance to women's sexual freedom that is in line with the hypothesis of a persistent level 1 patrilineality.

To officially accept the hypothesis of a social change that does not lead to convergence would allow us to redefine demography as a branch of anthropology. Perhaps we should then talk of demographic anthropology, or anthropological demography.

Not having children has become (yet again, if we bear in mind the numbers of unmarried people in the Europe of the 1900s) a life option for many. The concept of non-procreation is simple, but harder to measure and compare than it seems. As in the case of completed fertility, which records the average number of children born to women in a given generation (or cohort), we have to wait until the latter have reached the end of their fertile lives to measure the rate of non-procreation. The rapid decline in biological fertility from the age of 38 and the low efficiency of assisted reproduction after this age have led many demographers to project what will be the completed fertility, and the proportion of women who have not procreated at age 45 or 50; in other words, they have estimated definitive rates before the cohorts have reached the absolute limit of their reproductive period. The estimates differ in boldness and rigour, and the most recent available years of birth are not the same for all countries; as a result, comparisons are often difficult to make.

In the United States, the proportion of childless women aged 40–44 increased from 10 per cent to 15 per cent between 1976 and 2015, the latter date corresponding to the generation born between 1970 and 1974.[16] In England, this proportion seems to have stabilized at around 18 per cent,[17] and around 16 per cent for Sweden, but in both cases, the birth dates of the cohorts already makes them a bit older.[18] For Germany, I only have figures for the generation born in 1967, but the result was already diverging very clearly from that of societies with a feminist tradition. Non-procreation for this cohort reached 28 per cent.[19] According to the figures for previous cohorts, it can even be estimated that, in the case of completed higher education, the proportion rose to 40 per cent in Germany.[20]

France, like Sweden and Norway, is characterized by a minimal gap between fertility rates according to educational level. In the Anglo-American world, the negative effect of higher education on reproduction is stronger, despite the cultural feminist orientation, and there is a higher rate of reproduction among women from the working and middle classes.

For 43-year-old women born between 1955 and 1959, only 10.4 per cent in France were childless, 10.8 per cent in Norway, 16.2 per cent in the United Kingdom and 16.6 per cent in the United States. For women in these countries with a post-high school education, the lifetime childlessness rate was 13.3 per cent for France, 13 per cent for Norway, 21 per cent for the United Kingdom and 21.2 per cent for the United States.[21] For the two latter countries, however, the most recent period has witnessed a lessening of the contradiction between higher education and procreation, as higher educated women are producing more children. At the master's degree level, the proportion of childless women in the United States aged 40–44 fell from 30 per cent in 1994 to 22 per cent in 2015.[22]

In Japan, the rate of childlessness for women was still only 12.7 per cent for the generation born in 1955, but it seems likely to rise to 22.7 per cent for those born in 1965.[23] The first figure points to a non-Christian cultural base which has never made celibacy or the refusal to procreate an ideal; in the second figure, we need to see the effect of a level 1 patrilineal tradition which accepts that women can be educated but then forces them to choose between child and career.

The existence of a Christian past hostile to sexuality must not be forgotten in the case of European countries, where current rates of non-procreation generally do not exceed those permitted by the anti-sexual radicalism of the Reformation and the Counter-Reformation. In Germany, in the generation born between 1901 and 1905, the proportion of childless women reached 26 per cent. Their marital expectations had without doubt been disrupted by the excessive numbers of men killed during the war, but the rate of non-procreation fell to 7.1 per cent for the generation born in 1935 – probably also handicapped by the excessive mortality levels of men due to the war.[24]

It is fascinating to note that two completely different phenomena could lead to such similar statistical results: the Christian rejection of sexuality in the years 1650–1900 and the glorification of sexuality in the years 1960–2015 led to comparable levels of infertility. Together, the two sexual revolutions, one negative, the other positive, point to a stable anthropological background, one that has been transformed by religion, no doubt, but that always makes sexuality a field of experimentation, sometimes repressing it and sometimes valuing it.

The fact remains that, by 2015, societies that had not been transformed by the patrilineal principle had – in spite of a slight fall due to the great economic recession – reached a level of 1.9 or 2, close to the threshold of 2.1 needed for one generation to replace the previous one. The status of women in these societies can be described as 'functional'. In patrilineal societies, the lowered status of women is dysfunctional because, in the context of a spread of higher education and a broadening of life choices, it leads to a level of fertility insufficient to ensure the reproduction of the population. It should be noted at this point that the societies least distant from the anthropological form that originally characterized *Homo sapiens* currently work better, from a demographic point of view, than those that have been transformed by history.

The recent evolution of attitudes concerning homosexuality, accepted in general by *Homo sapiens*, as we saw in Chapter 3, confirms this interpretation.[25] Not only is there a positive statistical relationship between the high status of women and functional fertility; there is also a correlation between the acceptance of homosexuality and a more or less satisfactory fertility rate. If we assign the value 1 to societies which on 1 January 2017 had already institutionalized same-sex marriage, and the value 0 to those that had not, we obtain a positive correlation coefficient of +0.50 with the total fertility rate – a highly significant figure.

284

More simply, we can calculate an average indicator of 1.74 children per woman for countries accepting same-sex marriage, but only 1.46 for the others. In other words, societies that admit same-sex marriage reproduce better.

In truth, the coefficient of correlation between a high status of women and marriage for all is even higher, at +0.75. The acceptance of homosexual behaviour may well be only an epiphenomenon associated with the emancipation of women. The question is not without its theoretical interest. Should we consider marriage for all as a return to the origin, to a re-emergence of our *Homo sapiens* background? Or is it, in association with the emancipation of women, a real phenomenon of modernity? The attainment by the female sex of an average level of education superior to that of men in certain advanced societies is, in any case, something radically new in human history.

Be that as it may, the hypothesis of a relative naturalness of the nuclear anthropological system, a phenomenon that is still, at the beginning of the third millennium, functional from a demographic point of view, is confirmed. The societies closest to the original background of *Homo sapiens* are better at solving the contradictions of modernity than are societies transformed by patrilineality.

The second demographic transition in the globalization process: a failure to adapt on the part of stem-family societies?

Insisting on the nuances should not make us lose sight of the essential: the parallelism of the demographic trajectories of Germany and Japan, two societies that emerged from a stem-family anthropological form or, in plain and simple terms, two stem-family societies marked by a level 1 patrilineality. This latter does not prohibit the education of women and also assigns a fundamental place to mothers and their qualities as educators. But if they work after graduation, they then have to adopt a male characteristic by not bringing a child into the world. 'Nuclear' societies allow educated women who work to remain women, to bear children. The contrast between these two types of advanced societies stops us confusing change with convergence. But it would be a second solecism to imagine two strictly separate trajectories, the nuclear societies and the stem-family societies living side by side and following different developments purely endogenous to each of them. Demographic change is occurring in an increasingly unified world, and economic globalization is just one of the many dimensions of globalization. The second demographic transition should also be seen as a revolution that first manifested itself in the United States before spreading across the world. Its basic values are indeed derived from a nuclear-family society: they are individualistic, liberal and feminist, and we need to ask whether it is perhaps by attempting to adapt to these values that the German and Japanese stem-family societies have becoming dysfunctional at the demographic level.

We can consider German and Japanese adaptation to globalization, a concept taken here in its purely economic dimension, as exceptionally effective. Both countries, in fact, enjoy structural trade surpluses; a deficit appeared in Japan only after the halting of the production of nuclear energy following the Fukushima catastrophe. There is even, nowadays, an astonishing asymmetry and complementarity in trade: all the countries in the Anglosphere are running at a deficit, while the stem-family societies in general show a trade surplus. However, if we consider demographics as one of the points of application for the concept of globalization (including its cultural and not just its economic values), we need to ask a painful question. What if the low birth rate in Germany or Japan, far from being the simple and direct effect of the stem family, were more subtly a reaction to the American modernity of stem-family societies that are less individualistic and have trouble seeing a child as of any use if women are emancipated and children are treated like royalty?

What would the demographic development of stem-family societies have been like in the absence of Anglosphere pressure? It is impossible to say. How could we imagine an autonomous, purely endogenous development occurring in Germany or Japan? The economic impetus has indeed come from the Anglo-American world and its ability to change through creative destruction. I have noted above the tendency of a too perfect stem-family social structure simply to self-reproduce, or at most engage in a slow improvement of the economic sphere. If this were the model, we could possibly imagine stem-family societies, unstimulated and unbalanced by forces from outside, making very slow progress but finding a way to calibrate the production of children at a rate of 2.1 to make sure that reproduction (one-to-one) replenished each generation. The closed Japan of the Tokugawa era was not far from this near-equilibrium, combining improved technology with stagnating population numbers. The stem family, however, was then far from being perfect in Japan.[26]

Today, Germany and Japan lack 0.7 children per woman, exactly one-third, for the society to be in equilibrium. The imbalance may take time to appear, but it is still huge and it has forced those countries to make certain choices, of absolutely different natures as we shall see. Let us first follow the fate of these children, who are born in too small numbers but are so well brought-up. Already, the educational trajectories of the two great stem-family nations are diverging, for historical rather than anthropological reasons.

The educational divergence of the two stem-family societies

The Barro-Lee database, which I have previously used for the United States, allows us to follow the development of higher education generation by generation. Graphs 16.1–16.4 show, for nine successive generations, the proportion of individuals who graduated from college. The absolute level of the curves should be considered indicative because the educational systems differ enormously from country to country. But the general appearance of the curves describes definite temporal evolutions.

In Graph 16.1, we can see that the United States had a head start, while other nations gradually caught up – leaving it hovering at the same relatively stagnant level. Having started at different levels, Sweden, the United Kingdom and France followed roughly parallel trajectories. Japan is characterized by accelerated growth, which has allowed it to join, with the generation of young people who reached the age of 25 in 2000, the American proportion of 35 per cent of individuals who graduated from college. Sweden and the United Kingdom were at 25 per cent, France only 20 per cent. The contrast between Protestantism and Catholicism seems to have survived the death of religion, and presents a twofold 'zombie' effect, both Protestant and Catholic.

The trajectory of Germany, however, deviates from this model. It started at the same level as Sweden, as one might expect: Sweden was Lutheran, and Germany, although still one-third Catholic, gave birth to Lutheranism. But this nation, which invented universal literacy for the

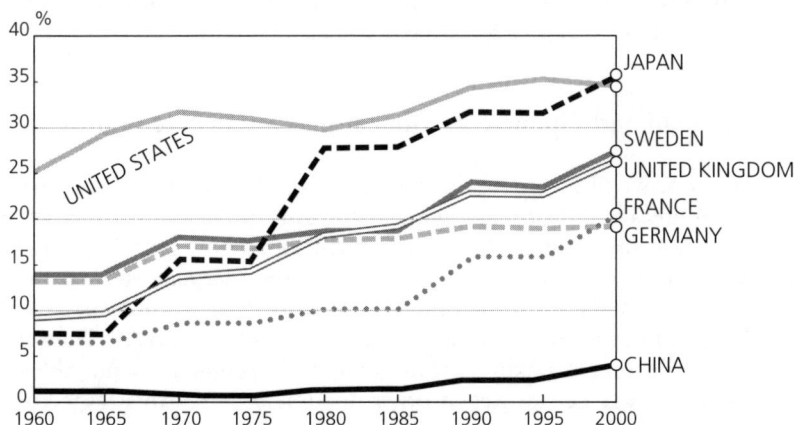

Graph 16.1 Progression of higher education in seven countries

Source: Proportion of the population graduating from college: generations reaching the age of 25 years at the dates indicated. Based on the Barro-Lee database.

entire world, has, since the Second World War, shown only a very slow growth in higher education. France caught up with it between 2001 and 2005. With just 20 per cent of college graduates, Germany ended up diverging strongly from Japan, which reached 35 per cent.

No anthropological determination, whether by family structure or religious background, can explain such a contrast. It is particularly surprising if one bears in mind the prestige of German universities on the eve of the First World War and the intellectual creativity of the country under the Weimar Republic. More than the Japanese take-off, to be expected in a stem-family society catching up, the fact that German growth here came to a halt needs to be explained. And the interpretation can only be historical: Nazism destroyed swathes of high culture and the social strata that promoted it. The Nazis expelled or exterminated a significant proportion of the national elites, both Jewish and non-Jewish. The removal of these people created a lasting vacuum, capable of causing a deviant trajectory taking the shape of a relative underdevelopment of higher education. Japanese militarism had not removed people in the same way. It had dismissed, put under house arrest, imprisoned, but not decimated, the intellectual world; thus, it was an intact cultural class that allowed Japan to catch up after the war. As a result, the educational potential of the stem family was able to produce its usual effects in Japan, which soon caught up with the American level.

German economic elites have survived better. Comparative studies by Anthony Atkinson and Thomas Piketty have shown that the top 1 per cent share of the national income distribution held up fairly well in postwar Germany, a persistence that can be observed above, in Table 13.1.[27]

The progress of higher education according to sex confirms the idea that the German trajectory has been atypical.

German and Japanese patrilinealities, Swedish feminism

In Chapter 5, we observed an extraordinary patrilineal bias in the development of literacy in Germany, with significant differences between men and women in the eighteenth century. I mentioned how learning to read and write strengthened the patrilineality of the German stem family. Sweden's literacy data, on the other hand, show that women very soon caught up, and even overtook men in the eighteenth century.[28] The very wide use of the seal in Japan indicates that many people were not able to sign their marriage certificates or other documents, so in this respect we cannot compare this country for that period.

Graphs 16.2, 16.3 and 16.4, show, for Sweden, Japan and Germany respectively, how the development of higher education is in line with that of primary education, apart from the atypical deviation for Germany.

in %

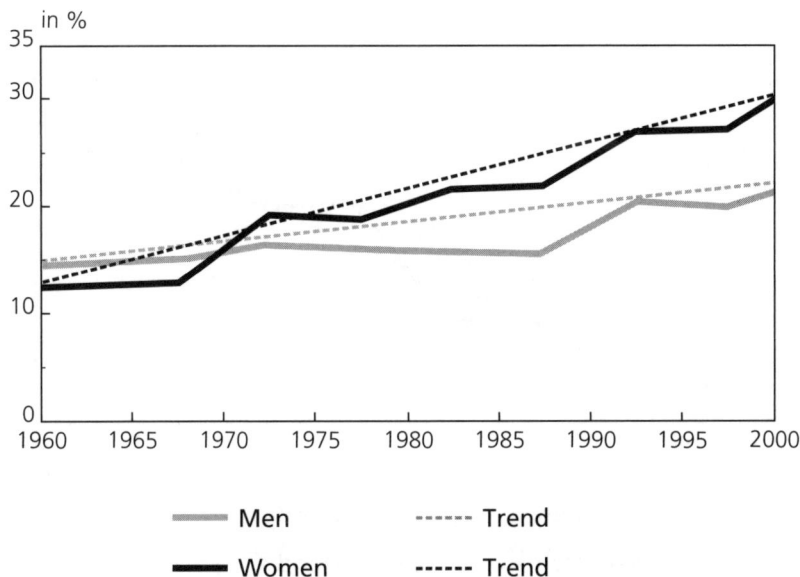

Graph 16.2 Higher education in Sweden
Source: Proportion of the population graduating from college: generations reaching the age of 25 years at the dates indicated. Based on the Barro-Lee database.

In Sweden, there was a small initial gap between men and women, but the latter soon caught up, and – as history repeats itself – overtook the former. In this country, where feminism is today a mark of national identity, in the generation that reached the age of 25 in 2000, the proportion of college graduates was over 30 per cent for women but only 22 per cent for men.

In Japan, men held an initial strong advantage. The gap was bridged only very gradually, but in the context of a rapid rise in rates. From 1991 to 1995, there was an apparent female advantage, which would no doubt disappear if a qualitative study of the higher education diplomas earned was carried out. The types of education followed by women in Japan are often less prestigious.

The curves for Germany reveal, in line with its anthropological matrix, a high initial level for men and a large gap between the two sexes: 23.6 per cent compared to 6.7 per cent. The male advantage was higher than that in Japan (12.0 per cent as against 4.4 per cent) and would lead us to defining, against Western stereotypes, Germany as more patrilineal than Japan. The stem family, however, in Germany as elsewhere, has no difficulty in allowing women and mothers to be educated. There was then a normal linear progression of women to a rate of 19.1 per cent women

289

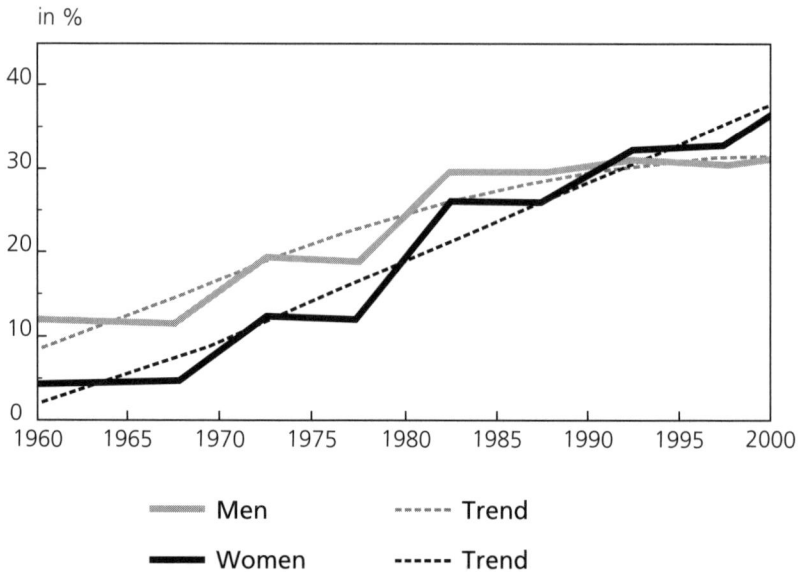

Graph 16.3   Higher education in Japan

college graduates per generation. On the other hand – and here we are moving away from a 'normal' Western trajectory – the proportion of men in higher education slowly started to decline from 23.6 per cent to 20.2 per cent. The two sexes were finally equal, but only after a rather surprising male trajectory.

We need to understand the meaning of this atypical evolution. The foregoing analysis of fertility, or rather infertility, suggests that it cannot be interpreted in terms of the balance between male and female roles: the downward trend for men corresponds to their ever more specialized involvement in industrial training and careers that lie outside higher education. In other words, we are not dealing with a fall in level but with a decline in the universalizing, generalist education provided by . . . the university system.

This German trajectory is so strange that we need to check it against data from another source, the OECD. The statistics proposed by this reliably conformist organization highlight the same phenomenon of a relatively weak development in 'tertiary' education, to use its terminology, with only 28 per cent of 25–34-year-olds in Germany obtaining a diploma of any value, as against 59 per cent in Japan. The Federal Republic is here close to Portugal, the latest country in Western Europe to become literate.

Let us broaden our perspective to other nations. Educational data add

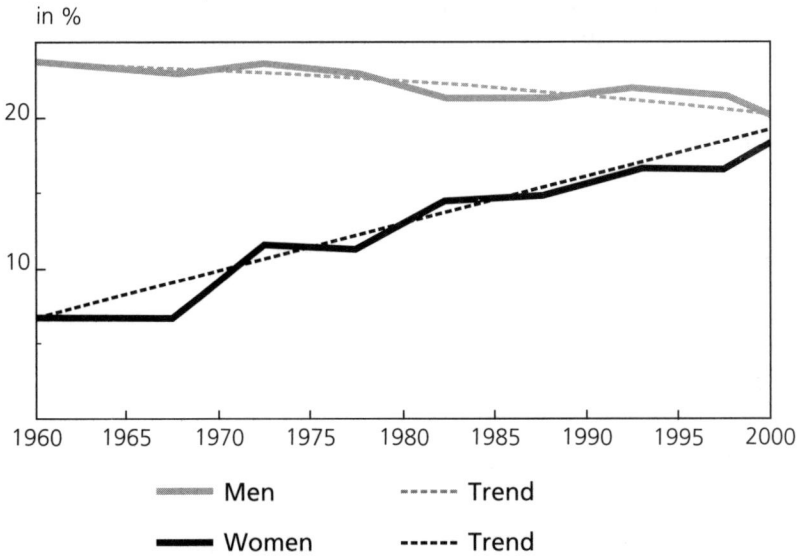

Graph 16.4   Higher education in Germany
Source: Proportion of the population graduating from college: generations reaching the age of 25 years at the dates indicated. Based on the Barro-Lee database.

an essential element to the study of the great divergence of European societies, following lines of force that do not mirror obvious and simple needs such as language or religion. Germanity and Latinity are vanishing. Official Catholicism itself is disappearing. Spain, with its rate of 39 per cent, seems to want to join the leading pack of the advanced nations, all of which, apart from Japan, Canada and Korea, lie somewhere between 40 and 47 per cent. But Italy, at the bottom of the table, with 21 per cent, seems for its part to have given up the attempt to develop a mass superior culture. It is true that these two 'Latin' countries differ greatly in their family structures. In Spain, the egalitarian nuclear family dominates, bordered on the north by a large swathe of stem-family territory. Its anthropological system, predominantly nuclear, is different from what common stereotypes might suggest, being quite feminist, with an element of verticality and authoritarianism in the north. The anthropological system in Italy, dominated by the central communitarian family, is, on the contrary, strongly patrilineal and the major universities are indeed in Emilia-Romagna and Tuscany, i.e. in Bologna and Florence.

The OECD data also allow us to monitor the results given by the Barro-Lee databank for the comparison between men and women. The distribution of college education in the general population aged 25–64

Table 16.2   Higher education according to the OECD. Percentage of 25–34-year-olds in 2011, including all higher education qualifications

Korea	64
Japan	*59*
Canada	57
Ireland	47
Norway	47
United Kingdom	47
Australia	45
Israel	45
France	43
Sweden	43
United States	43
Belgium	42
Netherlands	40
Switzerland	40
Denmark	39
Finland	39
Spain	*39*
Germany	*28*
Portugal	27
Austria	21
Italy	*21*

Source: *Regards sur l'éducation 2013: Les indicateurs de l'OCDE*, p. 38, table A1.3a.

allows a specific sex ratio to be calculated by comparing the proportion of women with a higher education to the proportion of men and multiplying the figure obtained by one hundred. For every one hundred men, we obtain the number of women who have reached this level.

The distribution obtained is typically 'anthropological'.

Unsurprisingly, among the countries with an indicator greater than 125, we find the Scandinavian nations, Russia and Portugal. In these three cases, we are on the periphery of Eurasia, in regions belatedly affected by the patrilineal principle. Even when this principle prevailed, as in Russia, the status of women has remained high, as we have often noted. The Portuguese matriarchy is, like the Breton matriarchy, a commonplace for psychosociologists. However, two anomalies can be noted. Italy shows a rather feminist index of 123, but this must be placed in the context of a stagnation in the development of higher education. The rather low rate of the Netherlands is more disturbing, because it suggests an unsuspected connection with the German world. The inner parts of the country are indeed of the stem-family type, but I dare not reclassify it with Germany, Austria or Switzerland, because of the dominant

292

Table 16.3 The female advantage in higher education. Level of college education in the population aged 25–64 years, in %

	Men	Women	Sex ratio
Sweden	28	40	143
Finland	32	44	138
Portugal	13	18	138
Russia	46	60	130
Denmark	29	37	128
Norway	33	42	127
Italy	13	16	123
Canada	46	56	122
Ireland	34	41	121
Australia	34	41	121
Israel	42	49	117
France	27	31	115
Belgium	32	36	113
United States	39	43	110
Spain	30	32	107
United Kingdom	38	39	103
Japan	47	46	98
Netherlands	33	30	91
Germany	29	24	83
Korea	45	36	80
Austria	22	17	77
Switzerland	38	27	71

Source: 'Niveau de formation tertiaire dans la population de 25–64 ans', table A1.5a, p. 41.

historical role of its coastal parts, the province of Holland in particular. But we will find in the next chapter the problem of this Dutch ambiguity in relation to European authoritarianism.

At the very bottom of the scale, with indices below 100, we find Japan, Korea and all the Germanic countries, Germany being faithfully accompanied by Austria and Switzerland (mainly German-speaking), two countries that are, as it is, dominated by a strongly patrilineal stem family. A comparative analysis of German and Japanese educational developments thus highlights both parallelism and divergence: the patrilineality common to the two nations does not prevent one of them from accelerating and the other one from impeding the development of its university system.

We will now turn to note the survival in these two countries of a strong collective consciousness, in contradiction with the dominant ideology of ultra-individualism, a survival that brings us back to the idea of a strong parallelism between the two nations. Then, however, we will need to try and explain the geopolitical divergence of the two great stem-family nations, major actors in economic globalization.

The resistance of a collective consciousness: zombie nationalism

The resistance of their industrial sectors and the better export performances of Germany and Japan can be explained, as suggested in the previous chapter, by the continuity value of the stem family.

From its invention in Mesopotamia, this anthropological type was designed for its ability to transmit, to perpetuate and improve technology. This basic concern explains the continuity of the German and Japanese productive apparatuses. However, there are some differences between them. The German model remains closer to its rural origins and the medium-sized towns where it flourished. It includes powerful multipurpose groups, but also relies on the dynamism, identified by Hermann Simon, of 'hidden champions', small and medium-sized companies that dominate a narrow niche of global production, and prefer to develop their product, or their range, rather than to diversify.[29] These companies are often located in areas that cannot be described as urban, and they continue, where possible, to prefer family transmission. They preserve the memory of primogeniture. We are here very close to the original stem family. Hermann Simon gives an implicitly ethnic definition of the phenomenon, since he does not distinguish between Germany, Austria and German-speaking Switzerland. In Japan, these hidden champions are on average bigger, and they have less of a global impact. In particular, they are more dependent on big companies and their banks. They are much more 'urban': 74 per cent as against 33 per cent in Germany.[30] We need to note a significant morphological difference between the two nations: Japan is centralized by its urban fabric, since Tokyo has become a megalopolis of nearly 40 million inhabitants, nearly one-third of the country, while Germany remains deconcentrated thanks to a strong network of medium-sized cities. No German city polarizes the whole of the social organization.

The capacity of the Federal Republic to organize collectively appears all the more remarkable. Employers' and professional associations provide the country with a collective action capacity equal to that provided by METI, the central strategic body in Japan. The deficit of engineers that became apparent in Germany in the 1990s provides a good example of the power of its collective reactions. An article published in the *Frankfurter Allgemeine Zeitung*, the leading newspaper of the business world, on 21 September 2016 explained that the mobilization of the *Verein Deutscher Ingenieure* (*Association of German Engineers*) had helped to solve the problem. According to the charts published by the newspaper, the number of those trained as engineers increased from 815,000 to 1,016,000 between 2005 and 2014, and that of individuals employed as engineers rose from 689,000 to 747,000 between 2012 and 2014. In 2014, the number of engineering graduates increased by 7 per cent over the previous year and grew faster than any other group. One out of six graduates in Germany was therefore an engineer in 2014. Given the small size of the student population, one wonders how many were left for more general subjects.[31] Despite decentralization, the German economy reacts like a car with a mysterious driver stepping on the gas. The role of voluntary associations is obviously essential. But none of this would be possible without the existence of a national collective consciousness: Verein *Deutscher* Ingenieure. And indeed, the zombie stem family today guarantees, unlike the nuclear family, the persistence of a collective consciousness of national (not only local or professional) level.

This national collective consciousness gives Germany and Japan, Korea and Catalonia an asymmetrical advantage in the game of globalization. In a nuclear-family country, cultural ultra-individualism and its economic component, ultra-liberalism, have led to a real lowering of customs barriers. The Americans, British and French behave in the manner required by economic theory; they become, when it comes to buying something, *Homo oeconomicus*. Consumers follow their immediate personal interests and choose the cheapest product. They play the game of postnationalism. The abandonment of protectionism (which had allowed their rise to power) therefore places British, American and French capitalisms in a vulnerable situation. They open their markets. But stem-family capitalisms do not offer them an equivalent compensation. Individual German or Japanese consumers do not behave in accordance with economic theory, nor do their elites, since the latter informally control the channels of distribution. Before looking at the price of a product, the Germans and Japanese continue to take an interest in its country of production and, whenever possible, choose their own.

Beyond its capacity for technological transmission, the zombie stem family perpetuates mechanisms of collective integration that oppose the emergence of a postnational *Homo oeconomicus*. The inegalitarian character of this anthropological type, meanwhile, encourages an asymmetrical mentality, a far from universalist vision of the peoples of the Earth, and an a priori difference in nature between, for example, the Germans and others, or between the Japanese and others. The commercial advantage is immense: it entails an initial competitive advantage that will only strengthen over time, since the initial gains are reinvested in the exporting industries. The superiority of German or Japanese technology then becomes a self-fulfilling prophecy, and products may indeed become better.

The case of Japan has always been transparent and one could even say that, in this respect, the country is playing fair. 日本 defines itself as a country apart, and everyone expects it to practise the corresponding economic game. Germany, on the other hand, found its ideological ethnocentrism, with the idea of a German *Sonderweg* ('special path'), proscribed as a result of the Nazi horror. The country is playing its economic game in a Western world that strives to believe, as I said in the introduction to this chapter, in the universalism of the Federal Republic. It can thus be free trade in words and protectionist in action. Its passion for trade surpluses and the constant accumulation of a financial surplus might even be said to define it as mercantilist. Faced with such a mental and ideological mechanism, French elites could not be more naive, as their own zombie egalitarian nuclear family predisposes them to think that human beings, including the Germans, are identical in every place.

In the case of Germany, we ought to think in terms of a strong national feeling that has survived everything. We should even refer to it, in the economic war that resulted from generalized 'free trade', as a zombie nationalism. I hesitate to apply the same term to Japan: this is a country whose national feeling is explicit and which these days probably aspires more to withdrawing from the world than to conquering it.

Economic advantage and demographic crisis

We end up with the paradoxical result that the advanced countries that have been the most successful in globalization, if we focus just on their efficiency in terms of trade, are those that have been protected by their anthropological systems from ultra-individualism, those that have not conformed to the model of *Homo oeconomicus*, those, in short, that have rejected the postulate of globalization. However, we can't say that they are generally efficient. If we go from the economic surface of things to the effects of globalization on the deepest layers of social life – the status of women, sexual behaviour and child-rearing – we find that countries like Germany and Japan have paid a very heavy price, in demographic terms in particular. Their fundamental maladjustment to what, for them, is an exaggerated level of individualism and feminism has led to them no longer ensuring the reproduction of their populations: the long-term preservation of short-term fertility indicators close to 1.4 children per woman implies a final number of children produced by each generation of women that will inexorably approach this very low level. Each year reveals a massive deficit in the number of births. Now, before worrying about the success of its economy, a society must ensure the reproduction of its population.

296

We must therefore consider these fine export performances, in a context of free demographic decline, as the effect of a partial (or limited) rationality. Much has been made of the short-termism of the Anglo-Saxon economies, but we must admit that their demographic reproduction, at least, is safe. If one adopts a broader conception of efficiency, which includes demographic performance in addition to industrial performance, it is the German and Japanese companies that are short-termist, since their economic success seems to entail demographic exhaustion. But that brings us to our point: it is at this stage that the parallelism between the two great stem-family societies breaks down. Germany and Japan have reacted in completely different ways to the demographic threat, one largely opening up to immigration, the other, at the present stage, accepting the decline of its population and its power.

German extraversion and Japanese introversion

The false image of a Germany less ready than France or the United States to accept immigrants was shattered when, in 2015, the country opened up to the flow of refugees from Syria and Afghanistan. The truth is that this nation has a long and daring history of using foreign labour and assimilating immigrants. Prussia, which brought about German unity, was not just a military, but an experimental society, whose rise to power was partly the result of an innovative use of immigration; it was able to take advantage, in particular, of the massive arrival of Huguenots driven out by Louis XIV. Around 1700, in Berlin, one inhabitant in three was French. The Revocation of the Edict of Nantes in 1685 not only deprived France of educated Protestants, but enriched Prussia and England.[32] Jumping over the centuries, we can also mention the import of millions of foreign workers by German industry during the Second World War, planned and managed by bosses who were admittedly inclined to Nazism, but were first and foremost pragmatic.

In the Federal Republic, the drop in the number of births began between 1965 and 1975, and resulted in empty adult classes from 1995 onwards.

Future historians of Germany will no doubt choose the demographic question as the main issue in the years 1995–2050. Maintaining the labour force will have been, from 1995 to 2017 at least, a necessary condition of commercial power. At the beginning of this struggle for survival, the fall of the Berlin Wall at first offered a miraculous solution: the immigration of Germans from the East, then of Soviets of 'German nationality'. An educated and trained workforce, easily assimilated, were able to fill the first holes in the age pyramid. On the eve of the wave of Syrian and Afghan migrants, Germany already had an impressive proportion of foreign-born people on its soil: 13.3 per cent in 2012. It had

Table 16.4   Foreigners among the nations in 2012, in %

	Foreigners	Born abroad
United States	6.8	13.0
United Kingdom	7.5	11.9
Germany	8.8	13.3
Sweden	7.0	15.5
France	6.4	11.9
Japan	1.6	–
Korea	1.9	–
Russia	0.4	7.9

Source: OECD data.

overtaken the 13 per cent of the United States and, above all, the 11.9 per cent of France. Only Sweden was higher, with 15.5 per cent.

For Japan, we must make do with the proportion of foreigners, but the proportion of persons born abroad would not be very different, given the difficulty of obtaining naturalization in this country; in 2012 there were just 1.6 per cent foreigners in Japan as against 8.8 per cent in Germany. One can, of course, already see the beginnings of a flow of migrants into the country, technically necessary to fill the deficits of numbers apparent in its economy. Still, we must note Japan's refusal to use mass immigration to solve its demographic problem. In these conditions, its population has been decreasing since 2010. Japan has indeed renounced power.

The main explanation for the divergence between the demographic policies of Germany and Japan lies in the attachment of Japanese culture to its ideal of a homogeneous social body, a concept highly compatible with the values of integration and asymmetry in the stem family. However, the same values do not prevent Germany from being open. But here, a difference between the Japanese stem family and the German stem family could shed light on the ultimate cause of the divergence of attitudes and policies. The German anthropological system is fiercely exogamous, like that of all European family types modified by Christianity. The radical exogamy of Christianity did not affect Japan. Exogamy was tempered by a genuine tolerance towards marriage between first cousins; the rate of such marriages reached 11 per cent in the aftermath of the Second World War. It has since fallen, and is now tending to zero. This rather high proportion probably did not go back very far. It must have appeared in the Tokugawa period, from the beginning of the seventeenth century, when Japan was closed off from the world; this was precisely the period when it rejected Christian attempts at infiltration. Often, a village's withdrawal into endogamy was motivated by the desire to preserve the monopoly of a modern technique, paper-making, for example.[33]

298

What we observe in Japan is fundamentally a dialectic of openness and closure that connects all levels: politics, economics, family. It hardly seems possible to distinguish the level from which the slight movement towards endogamy started.

Family endogamy is not returning in present-day Japan, but the country did what it could to preserve its economic autonomy, just as Germany was entering a phase of extreme extraversion. The Federal Republic has reached a rate of openness to trade that is astonishing for a country of more than 80 million inhabitants, a respectable size that would permit the preservation of a significant domestic trade. As a proportion of GDP, German exports increased from 31 per cent in 2000 to 47 per cent in 2015. Japan, too, had to open up over the same period, but, starting at 11 per cent, its exports did not amount to more than 18 per cent of GDP in 2015. And in 2015, imports and exports balanced. In Germany, imports were curbed at a ceiling of 39 per cent.[34] The larger size of the Japanese population cannot in itself explain such a difference in openness.

While Germany was defining production channels that assimilated East European labour, taking the risk of lowering the quality of its products, the priority for Japan seems to have been preserving the autonomy of its production lines. Japan even maintained its civilian nuclear industry after Fukushima, despite the permanent threat of an earthquake. Japanese introversion is the opposite of German extraversion.

If one sought a perfect equivalent to Germany in Asia, it would be found in Korea. The Korean stem family is exogamous, and the country contains 31.6 per cent Christians (24.0 per cent Protestants, 7.6 per cent Catholics), compared with 24.2 per cent Buddhists. This country, whose demographic crisis is more recent, has still taken in a higher proportion of foreigners than Japan, though immigration is admittedly facilitated by the existence of 'ethnic' Koreans in North China. An anthropologist of the American culturalist tradition would consider Korean culture as extraverted, favourable to the expression of feelings, in contrast to Japanese culture that favours reserve.

Nothing is more instructive than reading, in the appendices of an ambitious study comparing the evolution of family values in Japan, South Korea, Taiwan and China, the report of a discussion between Japanese and other opinion pollsters. Japanese pollsters require an even distribution of possible answers, which forces respondents to choose between the positive and the negative. (The existence of a central answer allows the individual to take refuge, so as not to express an opinion.) But Japanese researchers ultimately did not win their case, and throughout the study, whatever the theme under discussion, the Japanese sample is distinguished by its rate of non-response.[35] Here again, common-sense categories – Europe against Asia for example – do not work, since Korea and Taiwan tend towards European extraversion.

Here, perhaps, we can finally agree with the idea that Japan really is a distinct country. But its difference, its introversion, its endogamy are, like its stem family, the products of a fairly recent history, extending at most from the fifteenth to the twentieth centuries.

— 17 —

THE METAMORPHOSIS OF EUROPE

Ever since its enlargement to the East and the establishment of the single currency in the West, Europe seems to have become dysfunctional. We cannot, however, understand the continent's malaise if we continue to be in thrall to the two great intellectual principles that guided the construction of Europe: a belief in the primacy of economic determinations and the hypothesis that, in a consumer society, nations will converge. The project might have been successful in a world where the economy was the engine of history and levels of economic efficiency could draw closer, from North to South and from West to East. Our world, however, is different. As I am systematically trying to show in this book, deeper forces – educational, religious and family forces – underlie economic development. In the last chapter, I referred to the diversity of the paths followed by the advance of higher education in Europe. I will now descend to the anthropological base and study how its family and religious diversity has brought about a metamorphosis of the European Union. I will come to the rather surprising conclusion that, far from being monstrous, today's Europe is exactly what it was bound to be, by virtue of the vision of history developed in this book.

Before studying the economic and demographic divergence of nations, I will set out a schematic portrait of their anthropological diversity, proposing a map of family structures which, combined with Map 8.1 of the levels of religious impregnation, will lead to a general map revealing the geographical distribution of the values of authority and inequality across the continent.

Diversity of family forms on the edges of Eurasia

Agriculture, the city, writing and the state all reached Western Europe only belatedly, so this part of the continent presents itself to the

301

anthropologist as a conservatory of archaic family forms. Family types in Poland, Romania, Belgium, Brittany, the Vendée region, the Italy of Piedmont, Lombardy and Liguria, and the France of the Mediterranean coast were nuclear but still practised temporary co-residence in the peasant environment, with a significant patrilineal element in Romania, northern Italy, Provence and Languedoc. In the East, we find, as in the heart of Asia, communitarian types: this is true of Russia, inland Finland, the three Baltic countries, Slovakia, part of Hungary, Bulgaria, Serbia and Albania. In the north of this communitarian area, the status of women is as high as on the western fringe of the continent. In the south, it is lower; but everywhere, even in the Muslim part of Bosnia, in Albania and Kosovo, the system is exogamous. It excludes the possibility of marriage between cousins.

Map 17.1, however, reveals that the predominant family type in the European Union is the stem family, which represents the first stage of patrilineal transformation. It was the dominant peasant type in countries and regions today occupied by just over 180 million inhabitants. Such a mass would represent 36 per cent of a Union including Switzerland and Norway but before the departure of the United Kingdom. The relative mass of the stem family rises to 40 per cent after the departure of the British, and reaches 46 per cent in the Eurozone alone. To the extent that no other type covers more than 20 per cent of the Union, it must be admitted that Western Europe, on its mainland, is predominantly a stem-family area. Germany comprises only 18 per cent of the Union (plus Switzerland) without the United Kingdom, 25 per cent of the Eurozone. If we add Austria and German-speaking Switzerland, where the stem family reigns together with the German language, we reach 21 per cent of the Union (plus Switzerland) without the United Kingdom. Together, Germany and Austria account for 27 per cent of the Eurozone.

In the construction of Europe, the non-German stem family thus plays a very significant part: it is found in Sweden, in the interior of the Netherlands, in the Czech Republic, in Slovenia, in the Veneto, in Alsace, in Occitania, and in the north of the Iberian Peninsula. It accounts for 47 per cent of the total stem family – almost half. So it would be wrong to see Germany, or even the whole of the Germanic world, as being mainly responsible for values of authority and inequality or, in other words, a preference for the integration of the individual into a hierarchical system, in Europe. The stem family accounts for 31 per cent of families in Spain, 29 per cent in France and Portugal, and 11 per cent in Italy.

In the Eurozone, if we now turn to the heart of the European political construction, the egalitarian nuclear family accounts for only 27 per cent, which is small compared to the 46 per cent of the stem family. However, the significance of nuclear and egalitarian values can be increased to

302

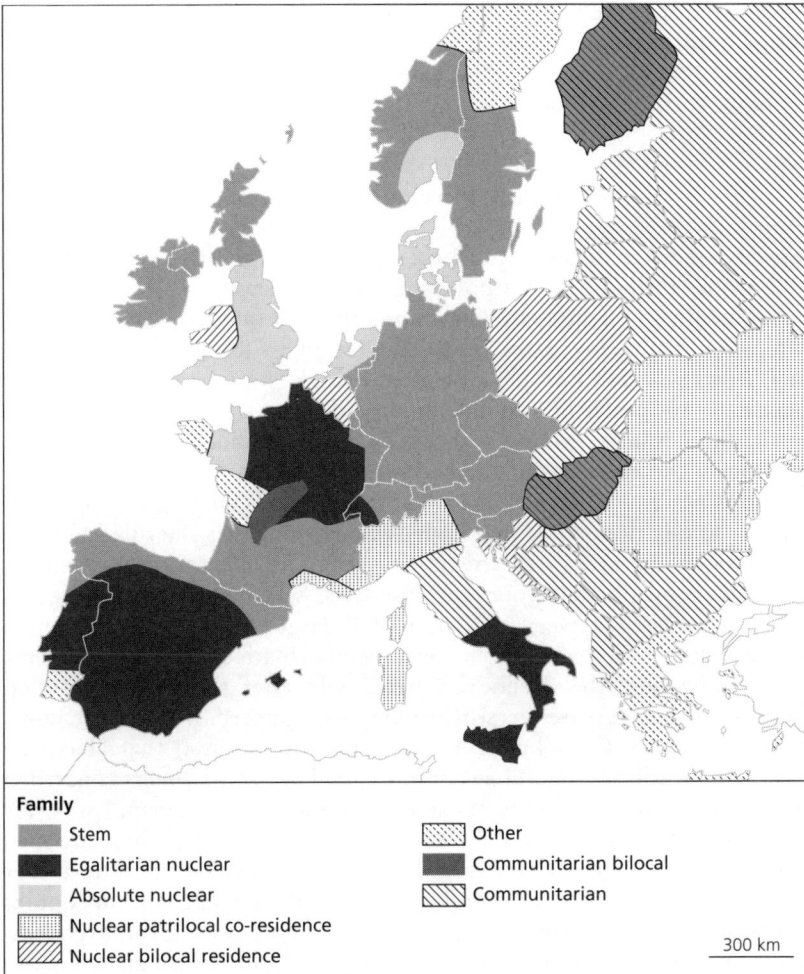

Map 17.1   Family types in Europe

34 per cent if the patrilocal nuclear family of northern Italy and the Mediterranean coast of France is taken into account.

What the stem-family map shows, in fact, is a central Germanic block that overflows into the Netherlands, the Czech Republic, the extreme east of France, Slovenia and northeast Italy. To these areas we need to add autonomous centres in Sweden, Occitania, Catalonia, the Basque Country, Galicia and northwest Portugal. Sweden is the other stem-family country, but it has only 9.6 million inhabitants, and its family

303

type, feminist to the highest degree, remains atypical and imperfect. By its actual anthropological mass, the second stem-family country in Europe is in fact France, with 19 million stem-family inhabitants, and the third is Spain, with 14 million.

The diversity of religious impregnation

It is customary to distinguish between three main varieties of Christianity in Europe: Orthodoxy, Catholicism and Protestantism. I do not have enough data on Orthodox religious practice and therefore cannot define, for this variant, any dates of secularization in terms of locality. But in *L'Invention de l'Europe*, I defined a single era in which Protestants ceased to be practising, and two eras, distinct according to locality, for Catholicism. As Map 8.1 shows (p. 142), in much of the Church's territory – the Paris Basin, and the south of Spain, Italy and Portugal – religious practice collapsed in 1740–50, in regions where the egalitarian nuclear family dominated and large-scale farming was the rule.[1] In these long-secularized areas, the strength of religious integration is minimal, residual or nil. In the Protestant countries, where the ebb of religious practice occurred between 1870 and 1930, larger traces can be imagined. In areas that remained Catholic until the aftermath of the Second World War, and where the decline occurred only after the Second Vatican Council, an even greater persistence may be supposed. It is in the regions of France where Catholicism has only just disappeared that Hervé Le Bras and I identified a *zombie Catholicism*. The *départements* concerned showed an educational dynamic and an economic performance superior to those of the others. As I showed in *Who is Charlie?*,[2] these are also parts of the country where social attitudes predispose one to accept authority, inequality and hierarchical social forms. In the current context of spiritual and economic crisis, we observe a particular form, hypocritical in its way, of Islamophobia. But zombie Catholicism is a phenomenon of European scale; indeed, it is intercontinental if we include Quebec in its constellation. In this last, archetypal region, the negative fixation on the religion of Muhammad is very easy to detect, given the absence of a large Muslim population. In the case of European countries other than France and Belgium, I do not have satisfactory data to deal with Islamophobia in terms of zombie Catholicism. I also pointed out in *Who is Charlie?* that Protestantism in the Netherlands, Denmark and northern Germany was even better able than Catholicism to stimulate a xenophobia of a religious character. This is because the expression of the value of inequality is more frank in Protestantism, where it is bolstered by the doctrine of predestination which distinguishes the elect from the damned. Protestantism from the outset demanded that the Bible be translated into the vernacular, and it has always been linked, if not with nationalism, at least with the first expression of national identity.

On the economic level, on the other hand, zombie Catholicism is easy to identify. The way that Flanders, the Veneto, Bavaria and Baden-Württemberg have caught up in their respective national areas is proof of this. In the case of Germany, we can even see how the Weberian hypothesis of an association between progress and Protestantism no longer works, since the two most dynamic *Länder* are predominantly Catholic.

The principle of submission to the priest lay at the heart of the Counter-Reformation. On the ideological level, therefore, zombie Catholicism encourages hierarchical, authoritarian and inegalitarian behaviour, even where a leftist shift has changed the apparent political alignment of the voters. In France, as I pointed out in *Who is Charlie?*, the 'conquest' of Catholic regions by the Socialist Party in fact led to the party becoming attuned to the authoritarian and inegalitarian cultural values of zombie Catholicism. The so-called 'deuxième Gauche' ('second Left'), emerging from the conservative and Catholic Right, won over the Left, and then France, not to the values of freedom and equality, but on the contrary to those of authority and inequality. The movement has been reinforced by the educational and economic success of Catholic regions whose power has spread.

The new educational stratification has everywhere added its own inegalitarian effect to that of the intrinsic values of the stem family or the principle of the priest's superiority. France converted, under Jacques Delors and a now rigorist Socialist Party, to the strong franc, then to the euro, a currency designed to be honoured and served rather than to be useful to economic life. In the mental trajectory of the populations and social groups that remained Catholic until around 1960, God was replaced by a monetary golden calf. The spirit of the Republic has been betrayed, but the wisdom of the Bible tells us that gold is a substitute of a religious or, rather, an anti-religious nature. At journey's end, the French elites, converted to the ideology of the stem-family, became the clumsy managers of a society that had remained liberal and egalitarian at its heart, and they could only divinize Germany, the European ideal type of the stem-family society.

France, by virtue of its anthropological diversity, is a wonderful field of experimentation. In particular, it is in France that we can identify the mechanism of the transubstantiation of Catholic values. A similar survey needs to be carried for the entire zombie Catholic sphere. One could then observe a great diversity of trajectories. Even in France, the inner western region, with its absolute nuclear family, was not conquered by the Socialist Party, but remained formally 'right-wing'. The northeast of Italy has gone over to the Northern League, the bulk of Catholic Germany has remained faithful to the CDU, Bavaria to the CSU. In Flanders, Christian democracy has stayed on top, but needs to reckon with the rise of anti-Francophone and anti-Arab nationalists. It is quite possible that the Netherlands, whose historic heart was maritime and Protestant, will have experienced a rise in power of the Catholic zombie southeast, similar to that which affected France, where the secular and republican heart has ended up being dominated by its periphery. However, the virulent Islamophobia, palpable even in this country of 'tolerance', suggests the presence of a strong resistance from its Protestant centre.

But still we can postulate the persistence, after the collapse of religious practice – measurable directly by polls or indirectly by the fall of fertility – of the authoritarian and inegalitarian dimension of Counter-Reformation Catholicism. The eclipse of the universal Church, which ensured the unification of these particular worlds, has, where family structures were inegalitarian, liberated ethnocentric tendencies: in Flanders, in the Basque Country, in Ireland and in Quebec. But we must also assume the persistence, in zombie Catholic areas, of traces of Christian universalism and a moderation of xenophobia that has no equivalent in Protestant territory.

Together, the zombie Catholic regions comprise, after the stem family, a second constellation within the European Union. It often, but not always, overlaps with the first. Like the stem family, zombie Catholicism weighs relatively more in the Eurozone than in the Union as a whole. The Germanic world appears to be a little less central in this zone. Zombie Catholicism brings together the values of authority and inequality found in non-stem-family regions: the interior of western France, with its absolute nuclear families, Old Castile and León in Spain, with their egalitarian nuclear families, communitarian central Italy, and half of northern Italy, with their nuclear families with patrilocal temporary residence.

I will not attempt here to systematically and carefully combine family and religious values. A long debate on Protestantism's relationship to authority and inequality would be necessary, and probably inconclusive. After all, as well as preaching the metaphysical inequality of human beings, Lutheranism and Calvinism have massively insisted on their equality and their freedom from priests. I will content myself with a pragmatic combination of the imprints of Catholic and Protestant stem families (see Map 17.2, which combines Maps 8.1 and 17.1).

The stem family and zombie Catholicism can collaborate in the making and maintaining of an authoritarian and inegalitarian local culture. Areas where both forces coincide are characterized by a maximum integration of individuals into the hierarchical model. The stem family can also exist without any trace of the Church: in most of Occitania and Catalonia, the stem family did not prevent an early dechristianization. The Protestant world, which (as we saw in Chapter 5) had an initial affinity with the

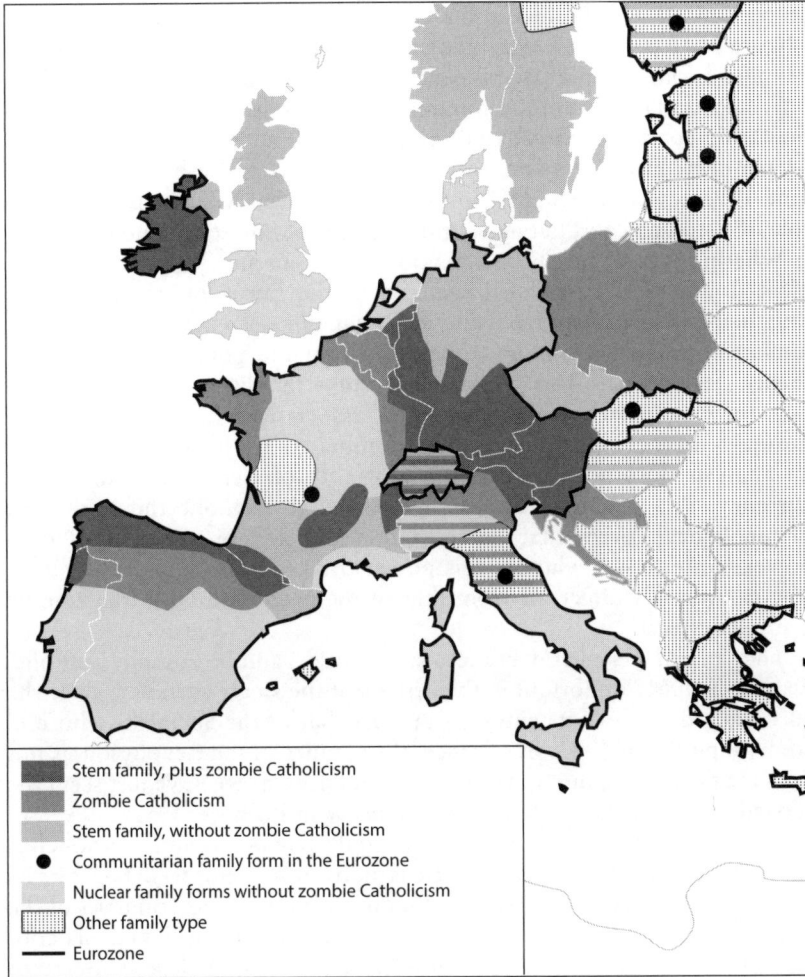

Legend:
- Stem family, plus zombie Catholicism
- Zombie Catholicism
- Stem family, without zombie Catholicism
- ● Communitarian family form in the Eurozone
- Nuclear family forms without zombie Catholicism
- Other family type
- —— Eurozone

Map 17.2 Authority and inequality in Europe

stem family of Germany and Sweden, cannot by definition be zombie Catholic.

In our continent-wide assessment of the potential of authority and inequality, we need to pay special attention to the zombie Catholic but non-stem-family regions, which constitute as it were a second circle dominated, albeit more weakly than in zones of Protestant stem families or zones where stem family and zombie Catholicism coincide, by a hierarchical temperament and a tradition of integration of the individual. I estimated the proportion of the Eurozone dominated by the stem family at

46 per cent. If we add the zombie Catholic non-stem-family areas, we get a figure of 56 per cent. Let us take our assessment of anti-individualism to its logical conclusion: if we take into account the authoritarianism of the provinces and nations of the communitarian tradition of central Italy and the Baltic coast, which are egalitarian but still authoritarian, we obtain 61 per cent. In Estonia and Latvia, the influence of Lutheranism adds a hint of Protestant inequality. In my next chapter I will be discussing the role of Estonians and Latvians in the genesis of Soviet communism.

Whether it is of family or religious origin, an authoritarian temperament dominates in the local societies of the Eurozone. Anthropology thus helps us get away from the idea that this currency, with its harsh human consequences, is an anomaly. From the point of view of the theory developed in this book, which links family, religion and ideology, the euro (and the austerity policy associated with it) is simply the normal currency in a Europe not dominated by liberal values. Such an analysis does not question the centrality of Germany in the single currency. But it emphasizes the existence, throughout the Eurozone, of ideological forces that prefer rigour and adhere to the ideal of a power from above, whether this power derives from that of the father (the stem-family effect) or from that of the priest and God (the zombie Catholic effect).

The role of peripheral France, stem family and/or zombie Catholic, was particularly important in the genesis of the single currency, since the euro was the idea of its elites, or at least that of the Socialists who had come to power in 1981. But France, the country of the Revolution, is not only the eldest daughter of the Church, but also, as we have just seen, the second most important stem-family country in Europe.

Whether associated with the stem family or not, zombie Catholicism is at the heart of the Eurozone. Cartography even seems to define it as its real basis, since its bastions can be found in almost all the countries of the Eurozone, with Finland, Estonia and Latvia alone lying outside its constellation. However, historical anthropology simply makes us aware of a commonplace: the importance of Christian Democracy, and therefore of the Catholic Church, in the genesis of the European community. The principle of the memory of places, established in Chapter 15, helps us accept the hypothesis of a persistence of religious values, and their transfiguration into the design and defence of a currency made to dominate human beings rather than to serve them.

Note that with the exception of Finland, Estonia and Latvia, which chose the euro for fear of Russia, the fully Protestant countries remained outside the zone. Norway did not belong to the Union. But Denmark and Sweden, both Lutheran countries, kept their currency, as did the United Kingdom with its Calvinist tradition. The strong national dimension of what we can call *zombie Protestantism* is still active and has most often been able to preserve monetary independence and, in the end, independence *tout court*.

Germany, at the time of its entry into the single currency was dominated by its Right, solidly established in Catholic areas. Reunification with East Germany has since reshaped the country, giving it a Protestant majority; this has certainly resulted in a general orientation that is becoming more national than European. It is always touching to hear French Socialists waiting for German Social Democrats, those 'men and women of the Left', to come to power and thus – they surmise – usher in a Germany more open to the demands of France, Italy and Spain. But they should of course be preparing for the complete opposite, since the Social Democratic Party, solidly implanted in Protestant areas, just as Nazism was, fosters nationalism more than does Christian Democracy, the heir of the Catholic *Zentrum* and connected by religion to the Latin world.

I mentioned above some of my doubts as to the still 'Protestant' character of the Netherlands. Whatever the answer to this question, it is clear that this small nation, Germany's outlet on the Rhine, had little choice but to enter the euro.

We now need to investigate how the management of an enlarged Europe, inside and outside the Eurozone, has implemented the value of the inequality of human beings, common to the stem family and the majority of areas of zombie Catholic culture.

The triumph of inequality in Europe

A country-by-country survey of wealth produced per capita in 2014 (i.e., gross domestic product per capita) is a very good illustration of the principle of persistence and the memory of places in action. Decades of bureaucratic experimentation, monetary invention and acceptance or rejection of the Eurozone have not changed the traditional geographical and cultural distribution of economic efficiency. In 2006, Jacques Sapir asked the question of how difficult it is for European countries to converge.[3] This is shown in Table 17.1, which shows, in descending order, GDP per capita for the countries of Europe, regardless of their membership of the European Union or the euro. Norway and Russia are included. Stem-family countries correspond to a grey box, which is lighter if the anthropological type only concerns half the population. Protestant countries are in italics. The Netherlands is classified among the Protestant countries, emphasizing its role in the economic and scientific take-off of the seventeenth century. Values are calculated in parity of purchasing power, so as to take into account the price of the goods and services to be purchased in the various countries. The top of the table, unsurprisingly, shows a mixture of Protestantism and stem family. It is

309

Table 17.1   GDP per capita in 2014 in the countries of Europe (in $$, in purchasing power)

Norway	65,970
Switzerland	59,600
Luxembourg	57,830
Netherlands	47,660
Germany	46,840
Sweden	46,710
Denmark	46,160
Austria	45,040
Belgium	43,030
Ireland	40,820
Finland	40,000
France	39,720
United Kingdom	38,370
Italy	34,710
Spain	32,860
Slovenia	28,650
Portugal	28,010
Malta	27,020
Czech Republic	26,970
Greece	26,130
Slovakia	25,970
Estonia	25,690
Lithuania	25,390
Russia	24,710
Poland	24,090
Hungary	23,830
Latvia	23,150
Croatia	20,560
Romania	19,030
Belorussia	17,610
Bulgaria	15,850
Montenegro	14,510
Macedonia	12,600
Serbia	12,150
Albania	10,210
Bosnia-Herzegovina	10,020
Ukraine	8,560
Moldavia	5,480

no longer the advanced Protestant Europe of the seventeenth century. It is no longer even that of the beginning of the twentieth century, since Austria, with its stem families, and now released from active Catholicism, has joined the leading group. The influence of Protestantism in England

310

has failed to prevent the United Kingdom from falling to the same level as France, in the middle. The ranking is still evolving, since France, for example, paralysed by a single currency unfavourable to its egalitarian nuclear centre, continues to decline and will, if the trend persists, end up being closer to Italy and Spain than to the club of rich nations. One can even imagine it being overtaken by the Czech Republic, with its stem families; actually, this would bring things back to the pre-war situation.

Nominal wage costs by country, the indicator that counts for firms that relocate or subcontract and for workers who emigrate temporarily, display much larger gaps. Eurostat data on the median hourly wage expressed in euros are shown in Table 17.2, again in decreasing order. In 2014, this indicator fell from 25.4 in Denmark to 1.7 in Bulgaria – i.e., a factor of 15 to 1. Within the Eurozone, the gaps range from 18.3 for Luxembourg to 3.1 for Lithuania, a factor of 6 to 1.

Thus, the integration of the former communist countries has not led to a convergence of standards of living, but to the establishment of a

Table 17.2   Median hourly wage in 2014 in European countries

Denmark	25.4
Ireland	20.2
Sweden	18.5
Luxembourg	18.3
Belgium	17.3
Finland	17.2
Netherlands	16.0
Malta	15.6
Germany	15.3
France	14.8
United Kingdom	14.7
Austria	13.8
Italy	12.3
Spain	9.8
Cyprus	8.4
Slovenia	7.3
Portugal	5.1
Estonia	4.9
Czech Republic	4.6
Slovakia	4.4
Poland	4.3
Hungary	3.6
Latvia	3.4
Lithuania	3.1
Romania	2.0
Bulgaria	1.7

differentiated and unequal system in which the active populations who were well educated by the communist regime serve as an underpaid workforce, at levels that support the comparison with China. Poland has become the queen of household appliances, Slovakia and Romania dominate car production. The Union now has a kind of inner China. If we consider the European Union as a single entity, the continental reorganization of its production has made the distribution of incomes within each of the component nations an obsolete indicator of the level of inequality, especially if we are comparing 'American democracy' with 'European democracy'. It is now a commonplace to consider the United States as more inegalitarian than Europe. However, if we make our calculations across the Union as a whole, rather than nation-by-nation, we discover that, between 1990 and 2015, the triumph of 'ultra-liberal' inequality found Europe to be the most congenial of territories.

The industrial Blitzkrieg in the West

There is not even a slight convergence in the west of the continent. The drop in relative GDP per capita in France had already suggested this pessimistic conclusion. The old divide between Southern Europe and Northern Europe has, on the contrary, been reaffirmed. The particularly dogmatic internal free trade in the Union has led to the emergence of comparative advantages that economic theory ignores because it forgets that *Homo oeconomicus* does not evolve in a vacuum, but within ways of life defined by family structures and religious traditions. Stem family and Protestantism, zombie forces maintained by the memory of places despite migration and cultural exchanges, continue to ensure the radical heterogeneity of the European economic area, in the West as well as in the East.

The euro has aggravated the competition between strong and weak economies, preventing the latter from protecting themselves by devaluing a too-effective competition. Italian and French industries could not resist Germanic and Scandinavian competition. A misunderstanding of the mechanisms of commercial competition at work in the world explains the Europeans' miscalculation. One of the commonplaces of globalization is, as we know, that there is a primary and unique effect of competition between the expensive labour force of the advanced countries and the cheap labour of the developing countries. Now this phenomenon certainly exists, and it is indeed central. We have just seen its existence within the European Union, with companies to the West taking advantage of the underpaid labour force from the East. But we must take our analysis further.

312

For advanced nations struggling to keep the developed part of their industry and garner trade surpluses, the most effective defence is to turn against their economic and social neighbours, who are close to them in their standards of living and wage rates. A study by Patrick Artus highlighted this phenomenon in 2009 in a book entitled *L'Allemagne, un modèle pour la France?* [*Germany, A Model for France?*][4] He raised the question of the effects that Germany was seeking by implementing a labour cost reduction policy and came to the conclusion that it was directed against its partners in the Union. Let us put the problem in its most general terms. A reduction in Northern Europe of 20 per cent of the labour cost cannot be a hostile move against a country such as China or Indonesia, where wage rates are ten or twenty times lower. It is necessarily directed against close rivals, whose incomes are, if not equal, at least comparable.

An authoritarian and collective German culture has made it acceptable for a wage freeze to be applied, along with this essentially nationalist policy of competitive disinflation. (Here again, we find that there is an anthropological foundation for all economic behaviour.) Now of all the large and medium-sized nations in Europe, France was traditionally the closest to Germany in terms of standards of living and industrial specializations, and in terms of volume of trade, too. Beyond the embraces exchanged by their leaders, who tirelessly celebrate the end of wars that no longer have any concrete meaning for the under-70s, the present historical truth is that Germany has declared economic war on France and is, indeed, winning it. The euro, a French idea, whose official goal was to tie down the Deutschmark, has proved just as effective as the Maginot Line.

The demographic destruction of Eastern and then Southern Europe

The brutal integration of Eastern Europe into Western Europe led not only to the triumph of economic inequality, but also to a demographic disaster. The exceptional gap between the wage levels in the East and the West triggered major migratory movements, the first of which was the exodus to the Federal Republic of the young assets of the late German Democratic Republic. The most famous migration now is the mass entry of Poles into the United Kingdom, which ended up ensuring the electoral victory of Brexit, as too many English cities had been hosting too many migrants. In France in 2005, the fear of Polish plumbers contributed to the victory of the 'noes' to a referendum on Europe. In the former people's democracies, this exodus added its effects to the drop in fertility caused by the collapse of the security structures with which the socialist state looked after its individuals.

313

The European media system is worried by the rise of conservative and xenophobic forces in Poland and Hungary and the persistence of corruption in Romania and Bulgaria, but day after day it refuses to analyse the process of social and human destruction that began for these nations with integration into the Union. This indifference has a functional value for Western capital. The very low wages of Eastern Europe allow companies that have established subsidiaries to achieve superprofits which, while failing to ensure the flourishing of the personal and family life of Poles, Hungarians, Romanians or Bulgarians, ensure the happiness of Western investors. Thus the positive image of the old liberalized popular democracies, maintained by the French, German and other media, better reflects the happiness of Western capitalists, the owners of these media, than the worries of the active populations concerned in the East, who are very badly paid, and whose medical and pension systems have been largely destroyed by integration into the globalized economic area. The cruel reality is that far from being new Eldorados, Poland, Hungary and other countries are places of fundamental anxiety about the future. The anxiety that dominates these countries, whose levels of wealth are low but which, for the time being, are not showing any rise in mortality rates, is similar to the discomfort of the American White population who voted for Trump.

Other demographic indicators than mortality will guide us here. The overall population change between 1995 and 2015, the natural growth rate and the balance of migration in 2015 all indicate that East European countries are currently wagering on their survival as nations. Table 17.3 shows that, between 1995 and 2015, the Baltic countries, Romania and Bulgaria experienced population falls of between 10 and 22 per cent. The shrinking of the populations in Croatia, Poland and Hungary is just beginning, while only the Czech and Slovak Republics remain in equilibrium.

This geographical distribution suggests that proximity to Germany tends to be a source of protection. Economic and educational effects are intermingled here, however, since countries that are not too threatened have more often been characterized, since at least the pre-war period, by educational levels higher than those of Romania or Bulgaria.

Table 17.4, which shows the natural increase and the migration balance for 2015, shows the most recent developments but does not project the deficit of births brought about by the falling fertility rate into the future. Only Germany is managing to overcompensate for its negative natural growth by mass immigration. In Eastern Europe as a whole, declining fertility and emigration are combining to reduce the population. It should be noted that Estonia now has a positive migration balance, which enables it to offset its birth rate deficit. Slovenia and the Czech and Slovak Republics also show a positive migration balance,

314

Table 17.3   Decrease or maintenance in population levels between 1995 and 2015

	Population in millions 1995	Population 2015	Evolution 1995–2015
Lithuania	3.7	2.9	−21.6
Latvia	2.5	2	−20.0
Bulgaria	8.5	7.2	−15.3
Estonia	1.5	1.3	−13.3
Romania	22.7	19.9	−12.3
Croatia	4.5	4.2	−6.6
Hungary	10.2	9.9	−2.9
Poland	38.6	38	−1.55
Germany	81.7	81.2	−0.6
Slovenia	2.0	2.0	0
Slovakia	5.4	5.4	0
Czech Republic	10.4	10.5	+1.0
Greece	10.5	10.9	+3.8
Portugal	9.9	10.4	+5.1
Italy	57.7	60.8	+5.3
Finland	5.1	5.4	+5.9
Austria	8.1	8.6	+6.2
Sweden	8.9	9.7	+9.0
Netherlands	15.5	16.9	+9.0
Denmark	5.2	5.7	+9.6
Belgium	10.2	11.2	+9.8
United Kingdom	58.6	64.8	+10.6
France	58.1	66.4	+14.3
Switzerland	7	8.2	+17.1
Spain	39.1	46.4	+18.6
Norway	4.3	5.2	+20.9
Ireland	3.6	4.6	+27.8
Luxembourg	0.4	0.6	+50.0
TOTAL	493.9	520.3	+5.3

perhaps a sign of their final integration into the German area – a historically logical result, since these nations were part of the Austro-Hungarian Empire.

Spain and Portugal, on the other hand, have joined the bulk of Eastern Europe in population decline by natural deficit of births and emigration. In Italy, immigration is positive but insufficient to prevent population decline.

Table 17.4   Natural population growth and balance of migration in 2015, in thousands

	Natural growth	Balance of migration
Germany	−187	+1151.5
Italy	−161.8	+31.7
Romania	−75.7	−35.0
Bulgaria	−44.2	−4.2
Hungary	−39.4	+14.4
Greece	−29.0	−64.5
Poland	−25.6	−12.8
Portugal	−23.0	−10.5
Croatia	−16.7	−17.9
Lithuania	−10.3	−22.4
Latvia	−6.5	−10.6
Spain	−2.8	−8.4
Estonia	−1.3	+2.7
Czech Republic	−0.4	+16.0
Slovenia	+0.8	+0.5
Austria	+1.3	+122.9
Slovakia	+1.8	+3.1
Luxembourg	+2.1	+11.2
Finland	+3.0	+12.6
Denmark	+5.7	+41.9
Belgium	+11.7	+69.1
Switzerland	+17.6	+70.0
Norway	+18.3	+29.2
Netherlands	+23.0	+55.4
Sweden	+24.0	+79.7
Ireland	+36.0	−6.4
United Kingdom	+174.4	+399.7
France	+200.6	+45.8

The 'demographic' foreign policy of Germany

We must consider the European demographic system as a whole, interacting with the EU's economic system. Eastern workers have, through local work or migration, been integrated into the continental mechanism for optimizing the rate of profit. But in the case of Germany, the search, not only for labour but also for immigration to make up population figures, has become an obsession for employers and the government.

Year after year, Germany has to plug the yawning void at the base of its age pyramid created by its low birth rate. Its industrial strength and prestige allow it to cast its net ever more widely and more boldly, and even recklessly in 2015. We cannot understand German foreign policy if we forget this demographic goal: the search for immigrants is now one of Berlin's top priorities. This axiom makes it possible to understand behaviours that are otherwise difficult to explain.

It opens up the possibility, in particular, of a new interpretation of the austerity policy imposed on the south of the Eurozone by Germany, with the collaboration of leaders of France, and highlights a certain form of rationality – that limited and terrible rationality which leads to treating a problem as purely technical, losing sight of all the human and moral implications of the 'solutions' put forward.

Austerity policies are squeezing European domestic demand – with the result that American economists, the French people, and indeed all those who think that the economy should serve human beings and their lives, view them as perfectly irrational. But for a Germany whose dream is now spreading across the globe and includes Chinese and American consumers, the Eurozone is no longer the priority market. And although Southern Europe still contributes significantly to the absorption of German production, it is gradually becoming a reserve of labour first and foremost. The destruction of the economies of the South no longer seems irrational, but functional. The contraction of the Spanish, Greek, Italian and Portuguese productive apparatus is freeing workers who are both young and qualified. I admit that this rather daring hypothesis came to me when I read an article by Arnaud Leparmentier published in *Le Monde* on 27 February 2013. I quote the beginning of the text of this loyal Europeanist:

They are beautiful, young and bright. They are the new immigrants to Germany. 'Die neuen Gastarbeiter', as *Der Spiegel* put it on its front page. These 'new guest workers' are no longer the Turkish peasants of Anatolia from the 1960s who came to get the car factories up and running in Germany. They are Italian, Spanish, Greek or Eastern European. Graduates of the best universities of their country, they form 'the young elite of Europe for the German economy'. This week, the German weekly displays an insolence worthy of the British *The Economist*. It makes fun of the world, just as Germany cocks a snook at Europe.

'Deutschland AG' refuses to relocate its factories, even when it loses the industrial battle. Its neo-protectionism has led it to block the merger between Airbus and British Aerospace, so that it could protect its Bavarian factories. And now it is plundering the talent of the Latin world, which flocks to escape endemic unemployment. The 'German dream' shamelessly celebrated by *Der Spiegel* is the nightmare of Europe.

The frankness of *Der Spiegel* largely compensates for the lack of data on the discussions and decisions made in German government and business circles. We need to accept the explanatory power of the migratory axiom if we are to shed light on German foreign policy. In accordance with the principle of Occam's razor, this axiom allows us, from a minimum of facts, to provide a maximum of explanations.

Table 17.5   Origins of migrants to Germany (positive migratory balances)

Country or continent	2015	2010–2015	Proportion of the total (%)
Europe	457,405	1,756,035	60
European Union	382,449	1,559,941	54
Romania	86,274	319,426	11
Poland	63,279	354,150	12
Italy	35,870	140,131	5
Bulgaria	37,850	155,831	5
Croatia	36,727	77,774	3
Spain	11,255	90,332	3
Hungary	18,197	110,640	4
Serbia	8,242	39,499	1
Greece	15,519	88,612	3
Asia	577,481	913,092	31
Syria	316,732	409,666	14
Afghanistan	89,931	127,921	4
China	10,315	39,164	1
India	10,214	39,156	1
Pakistan	21,581	41,617	1
Africa	82,520	194,031	7
America	8,229	36,563	1
Oceania	192	659	0

The rush to the East

Let us pursue the implications of this migratory axiom, this time eastwards. The axiom undoubtedly explains the activism of the Federal Republic in Ukrainian affairs, whose logic is quite independent of the geopolitical dreams of the United States, Brzezinski-style,[5] i.e. anti-Russian and global. Ukraine is a large political entity, but has not managed to construct a state for itself since its separation from Russia. Its fertility rate is 1.5 children per woman, its migratory balance is heavily in deficit. Its population fell from 51.3 million in 1990 to 45.5 in 2013, a fall of 11.3 per cent. Its middle classes are taking flight, which makes any political stabilization unlikely: the construction of a state is only ever the institutional crystallization of the management of society by its middle classes. Western pressure on Ukraine is fuelling the instability of a country that is being transformed year by year from a newly born country into a labour pool.

It is in this context that we have to interpret the German intervention in Ukrainian affairs, and first of all the visits of Martin Schulz and Angela Merkel to Kiev. Let us forget the ditty they sang in favour of the necessary defence of 'Western values', since a decaying society cannot give life to any political value. But then, there is a better possibility than formal integration with Europe (hardly conceivable now, in any case): the disintegration of Ukraine could provide Germany with an abundant supply of labour and immigrants. In these conditions, maintaining chaos in Ukraine could well appear, yet again, to be a 'rational' goal. Let us say, however, that at the present stage this policy has not been a great success and has especially benefited . . . Russia, where immigration from Ukraine is very significant.

A bridge too far: migrant, patrilineal and endogamous communities

The German demographic deficit, renewed year by year due to an inadequate completed fertility rate, is a problem that never stops growing. The limited rationality of the German mercantilist system, which tirelessly seeks commercial and monetary power, exacerbates the problem until it becomes insoluble. More and more immigrants: such is the logic of the system, which includes at its heart the vague awareness of an ultimate impossibility. The resulting feeling of vertigo finally suggested to Germany, in 2015, a leap into the void: it summoned and opened its doors to a massive flow of refugees from Syria and Afghanistan, but also from other countries belonging to the Arab or Muslim sphere.

In the belief that she was affirming universal values, Angela Merkel in fact yielded to the illusion of an abstract *Homo oeconomicus*, devoid of any specific culture. Worse, she claimed to be importing en masse this *Homo oeconomicus* that does not exist outside his or her own culture. So it was not individuals who might integrate into German culture who entered the Federal Republic in 2015 and early 2016, but communities able to turn in on themselves if necessary.

Until then, the appeal to foreign labour in Germany had more or less respected an unspoken but effective anthropological code. The few difficulties created by the assimilation of Turkish migrants in the 1960s, whose rate of intermarriage was still tiny around 1990, masked the overall success of the integration of populations from Eastern Europe. I already noted, in *Le Destin des immigrés* [*The Destiny of Immigrants*], the high intermarriage rates of immigrants of Yugoslav origin and their children.[6] It is quite possible, indeed, that the Turkish difficulties, by diverting people's attention, favoured this silent and rapid assimilation of the populations of Slavic origin. Under these conditions, such a process could be regarded as a surreptitious version of the American assimilation system, which, by excluding Blacks, permitted the integration of Whites of all origins, Asians and even some Indians who survived the conquest.

Immigration from Eastern Europe after 1990 only made this model more general. The populations concerned had family values that were not so very different from the German system. Like the latter, their fundamental characteristic was an absolute exogamy. Neither in Poland, nor in Russia, nor in Romania do you ever marry your cousin. Orthodoxy, Protestantism and Catholicism do not differ much on this point, because all these beliefs come from the same Christian trunk, which, before they separated, showed a strenuous desire to militate against marriage between cousins and inbreeding in the kinship network. The flow of migrants from Eastern Europe was also an ordered process, divided up by languages and nations. It posed no risk for the continuity of the German social and anthropological system.

On the other hand, with the 2015 influx, the migratory model has taken off. The majority of new immigrants, including those from Syria and Afghanistan, bring with them a specific family system, the endogamous communitarian family. Its patrilineal principle is even stronger than that of the exogamous communitarian family. Remember the possible levels: a level 1 patrilineality corresponds to the German stem family, a level 2 patrilineality to the Serbian exogamous communitarian family, and a level 3 patrilineality to the Arab endogamous communitarian family. (The Russian family, on the other hand, has a perfect patrilineal communitarian architecture and should theoretically be classed as level 2, but its educational performance suggests that the status of women in it is rather higher than in the German stem family.)

In the Arab Middle East, the rate of first cousin marriages hovers at around 35 per cent. This is much more than in Turkey, a country where nuclear and communitarian forms of family mix, and where the endogamy rate is around 15 per cent (8 per cent in the west and south, 20 per cent in the north and east).[7]

The sudden eruption of an endogamous communitarian mass into Germany, if prolonged, should logically result in bracketing the principle of the memory of places. The mimetic adaptation of immigrants, carriers of values that are often 'weak', generally ensures, as I said in chapter 15, the permanence of the host society's anthropological system. The memory of places, however, requires limited and continuous flows of migrants for it to function. The arrival in just a few months of a block of immigrants or a group is a quite different phenomenon. In order to give our thoughts a resolutely technical turn, free from all anti-Muslim or anti-Arab prejudices, we can cite a French example of the dysfunctioning of the memory of places, with a completely different ideological sense. The arrival of returnees from Algeria, 800,000 of whom settled in a very short time on the Mediterranean coast of France, created a lasting deviation in the local political culture, which shifted towards an anti-Arab stance and, from the mid-1980s, led to a high vote for the National Front. Nothing in the Provençal or Languedoc culture predisposed people to this specific hostility. The local background has been modified. A new xenophobia has been introduced, which itself is now being perpetuated, in accordance with the principle of a damaged memory of places.

We do not know if the migratory flows of 2015 and early 2016 to Germany, which slowed down or stopped as an awareness of the social risk grew, will have been sufficient to produce a distortion of the national culture. But with an initial flow of the order of half a million in 2015, with the family reunions that will follow, we can predict, without absolute certainty, of course, the stabilization and growth of a small separate population living in parallel with the Turkish group. Like Édouard Husson, we must therefore imagine a Germany increasingly concerned about its internal stability and cohesion.[8] Here we come to the final paradox: the extraversion of the German economy ought finally to lead, like the Japanese choice of introversion, to the country turning in on itself. The real risk is that of the internal hardening of a German society in which anxiety leads to a policing of the differences in ways of life. The authoritarianism and the spirit of system inherent in German culture would facilitate such a development.

Post-democratic Europe: a normal world

The word that designates Europe is still the same, though nobody is aware that it has changed its nature since German reunification and its enlargement to the former people's democracies and the Baltic countries. From its foundation in 1990, the European Union has been described as a system of free and equal nations. Some of them, namely France and Germany, and then the United Kingdom, were a little more equal than others, certainly, but their disagreements subsumed those of all concerned, including the small countries. Liberal democracy was the common political form, even though the internal functioning of each unit was specific: the French, German, British, Italian, Spanish, Swedish and Dutch party systems were all different from each other. As has just been suggested by the use of the expression 'free and equal nations', the ideological centre of gravity of the system was France, in the name of the values of the egalitarian nuclear family.

This perception is out of date. Authority and inequality are the concepts that now describe the European system. A hierarchy of nations, more or less rich, more or less powerful, more or less dominated, has appeared, and thus a political entity whose practical values are the opposite of its founding values. Authority and inequality are not typical of Germany alone. The stem family and zombie Catholicism produce, as we have seen, the map of a preference for hierarchy that goes far beyond that most powerful of the nations of the Union.

Considering the situation of Europe to be abnormal, 'monstrous' even, makes sense only if we remain at the level of the conscious values of liberal democracy, Anglo-American and French in origin; if we continue to think that the objective of the Union is abundance in a situation of freedom and equality for its citizens and nations, we cannot fail to conclude that it is witnessing a tragic failure. This, indeed, is how all its peoples, and no doubt its elites, see it. But if we take the time to go down to the deep, subconscious and unconscious layers of the lives of nations, in those educational, religious and family strata that are the basis of life, we can only conclude that everything is normal in Europe.

The emergence of a new educational stratification separating the more highly educated from the rest of the population has led everywhere, as in the United States, to an erosion of the democratic feeling that was once rooted in the homogeneity of mass literacy. In America, this movement has been fostered by traces of Protestant metaphysical inequality and, above all, by a liberal and non-egalitarian family structure whose values tolerate large income disparities. But in America, the individual remains free, and strict inequality is inconceivable. Thus, the sufferings of the White population eventually led to a revolt and the election of Donald Trump. In accordance with the anthropological perspective developed in this book, this revolt was, at first, xenophobic. America will have to travel once again, if it can, the path that leads from a primitive democracy hostile to foreigners to a more mature democracy that accepts its share of universality.

On the majority of the European territory, on the other hand, and particularly in the Eurozone, the dominant family and religious base is authoritarian and inegalitarian. It can lead much further than in America to the weakening of democracy that results from the new educational stratification – in other words, to its complete withering away. We have already reached this point. The vote of the peoples in the Eurozone no longer counts. The Greeks, Dutch and French can reject whatever they want by referendum, but their vote will itself be rejected by their ruling classes. The German political system, at the heart of the system, could be considered truly democratic if its political elites did not practise, in the Bundestag as in the European Parliament, the union of the Left and the Right. Why not, after all? Is this practice not in conformity with the Swiss model, of whose democratic character everyone sings the praises? And then, the German people remains, despite its acceptance of a power from above, free in its democracy. But if Germany sets the tone, Europe, for sure, will turn into a vast 'ethnic democracy', a system in which one dominant people alone exercises the fullness of its rights.

323

Let us say it again: nothing about this situation is an accident, a regrettable deviation from history. The political, economic and social system that has developed in Europe, with its hierarchy of peoples, its austerity, its economic inequalities and its absence of representative democracy, is the normal form to which the stem family must give birth, with the help of zombie Catholicism (with, in central Italy, the Baltic states and Finland, a supplementary battalion provided by the communitarian family, which strengthens authoritarianism without encouraging inequality). The rise in inequality, which is higher in Europe as a whole than it is in the United States, is normal because the inegalitarian potential of the stem family in a situation of ethnic diversity is higher than that of the absolute nuclear family.

The revolution in higher education certainly gives the hierarchical principle a new depth, and the history that reveals itself to us is also, for the most part, new. But we must also admit that continental Europe, liberated by the emergence of Germany from its American tutelage, is now reverting to the normal course of its history, which has never been, apart from the Netherlands, Belgium, France and Denmark, liberal and democratic. Consider the Europe of 1935: authoritarian regimes ruled everywhere, after the collapse of the democracies implanted since 1918 under Anglo-American and French influence. Continental Europe invented communism, fascism and Nazism. Depicting it as the birthplace of liberal democracy is a pure intellectual swindle.

The last element in normality: revolts against the system occur in countries where the nuclear family, which carries genuine liberal values, is dominant, or has been. England alone is attempting to bid farewell to the European Union, but it is also the only country, with little Denmark, where an absolute nuclear family structure underpins a uniform and powerful liberal democratic tradition. Scotland and Northern Ireland, with more authoritarian traditions rooted in stem-family forms, did not vote for Brexit. The most notable electoral revolts, in the west of the Eurozone, were those of the Netherlands and France, whose historical hearts are based on the nuclear family, absolute in the first case, egalitarian in the second. To the east, Poland has undifferentiated nuclear families.

With Viktor Orbán's Hungary, we are faced with an exception, since in this country communitarian family forms coexist with stem families and probably undifferentiated nuclear families. We must also emphasize the tense coexistence, in the Magyar religious traditions, of Catholic, Calvinist and Jewish components, even if the latter was greatly weakened by the Shoah. The national sentiment that results from this subtle blend is powerful, but specific. We need to accept that this country, which rose against the USSR in 1956 and subsequently tore down the Iron Curtain in 1989 by allowing Germans from the GDR to pass to the West, is the

324

exception that proves the rule. But in Hungary as in Poland, France, the Netherlands and England, the revolt against the European Union undeniably includes a xenophobic component. Again, all this is normal. As in the United States, the democratic revival must start off again in Europe, where possible, from the ethnic foundation of primordial democracy, perhaps while awaiting the better days of a universalization of the concept.

Nuclear family types are in a small minority in continental Europe, and so the success of these revolts is by no means guaranteed outside the United Kingdom, especially as, in the Netherlands and in France, the stem family and zombie Catholicism have perhaps taken control of these two national systems, independently of any German intervention. So what we may need to prepare ourselves for, particularly in the Eurozone, is the prospect of the abolition of democracy.

Be that as it may, Germany's grip over the continent is currently firm. The single currency has locked eighteen weaker nations into a network of obligations that are technically difficult to break. The trade surpluses of the Federal Republic give its business and diplomatic worlds considerable means to buy employees and companies. Let us not forget, above all, the authoritarian and inegalitarian substratum of many regions in the Eurozone, which feel an affinity with the dominant power, and whose servitude is essentially voluntary.

——18——

COMMUNITARIAN SOCIETIES: RUSSIA AND CHINA

For the West of the years 2000–16, Russia again became something of a *bête noire*. It is quite difficult to understand how this poor country, with only 144 million inhabitants in 2015 (hardly more than Japan) could so polarize the attention of the Anglosphere and the European Union when, at the same time, these had populations of 450 and 438 million respectively. With Japan and South Korea, the geopolitical West then had more than 1 billion inhabitants, nearly seven and a half times the figure in Russia. However, during the 2016 US presidential campaign, Vladimir Putin's country occupied a central place: Donald Trump's plan to turn him into a partner rather than a force for evil sparked real outrage among the Democrats, and convinced them that they now held a winning card against their rival. In France, in the years 2010–15, it became well-nigh impossible to express a moderate opinion on Russia in any press organ, including on the anti-establishment Left. However, it was this Russia which, through its sacrifices in the Second World War, helped decisively to destroy the Wehrmacht and made it possible for France to be liberated by the American, British and Canadian armies. Moscow's recovery of the Crimea and the seizure of independence by the Russian part of Ukraine, events that the old view of a people's right to self-determination would have defined as legitimate adjustments, were and are still considered, in France and elsewhere, as abominations. Quite apart from the historical amnesia this involves and the failure to take geopolitical realities into account, what is staggering is the way the Russian threat has been exaggerated. By 1996, Russia had nearly imploded; as Jacques Sapir wrote, the demonetization of its economy had brought it to the verge of chaos.[1] Such a disintegration would have led to the Siberian provinces breaking away. Straddling Europe and Asia, Russia is admittedly still the largest country in the world, but it is firmly surrounded by a network of US bases. And while its army is again operational, as we have seen in Syria, it is still very reduced in size. Obviously, the part played by this new

Satan in the eyes of the West has nothing to do with practical reason, but mainly stems from the symbolic order.

After 1945, the emergence and success of communism gave rise to the counter-definition of a magical 'Western world' that simultaneously included the founding countries of liberal democracy (the United States, England and France) and those that had invented right-wing totalitarianism (Italy and Germany). So it is easy to understand why the fall of the Berlin Wall produced such disarray in the often ageing geopolitical establishment, which was suddenly deprived of its main structuring element – especially since, in spite of everything, even at the height of the crisis Russia had preserved the nuclear capacity to annihilate the United States.

In fact, Russia remained the only element of balance capable of stopping an America drunk on victory from thinking that it was now the master of the world. In view of what happened in Iraq in 2003, we should still be grateful to Russia for, yet again, even if inadvertently, helping to safeguard our space of freedom. But mistrust of Russia has still continued to rise in tandem with its recovery. The cultural dimension of this rejection has become explicit: Vladimir Putin's authoritarian democracy has become in itself, as a stabilized model, an object of hatred.

Between 2015 and 2017, the West's attitude began to change – or rather, to become more differentiated. The political Right in America, Britain and France seemed to be showing more tolerance towards the Russian difference, and the hard Right even went so far as to develop a certain fascination for the Putin model. The liberal Left, on the other hand, in the United States as elsewhere, persisted in its fierce hostility. Across the West, Media and Academia were the main forums in which detestation of Putin and his country were expressed. In the opinion of Russian researchers who, with a certain amount of humour, try to gauge hostility towards Russia, German newspapers are the most justified. How can we manage without the concept of *Russophobia* if we are to explain this situation? Symmetrically, we sense that the opposite attitude is also emerging, though it registers a lower-intensity commitment: Russophilia. I cannot, in this outline, track the inventory of these two attitudes or analyse their evolution in every country. Such an analysis would need to combine geopolitical reason with a study of values. Swedish Russophobia, for example, has something to do with geographical proximity. But even in the case of this small country of fewer than 10 million inhabitants, insignificant from the point of view of Russia – after all, wasn't Sweden toppled as a Baltic power during the Great Northern War between 1700 and 1721? – an irrational, anthropological and cultural element is becoming apparent. Finland, which belonged to the Russian Empire and fought against Moscow in 1939–40 and 1941–4, is well aware that present-day Russia, whose territory is already too vast for its population, needs dynamic economic partners and not new possessions. Russophobia is a fascinating phenomenon that deserves a complete book. Here, I shall merely examine how historical anthropology can shed light on the case of Russia and evaluate its persistent features.

The permanence of communitarian values obviously explains the emergence, after the disorder of the 1990s and 2000s, of a stable authoritarian democracy, combining elections and a unanimist vote. Indeed, there is nothing in the electoral process to prevent Vladimir Putin being indefinitely re-elected to head the system, either as president or as prime minister. Control of the media is not the fundamental cause of permanence in power; authoritarianism is rooted in the people, and draws on communitarian values that are constantly being reproduced by the memory of places. We should in any case see a parallel between the continuity of Russian power and the way a single party or bloc tends to remain in government in Germany and Japan: stem-family democracies also reveal a certain electoral verticality. In Germany, the union of the Left and the Right makes it possible, if necessary, to maintain the continuity of political positions decided at the top of the social pyramid. In Japan, with few exceptions, the Liberal Democratic Party remains in power, and the factional struggles within its ruling group, constitute the reality of political debate.

Historical anthropology will also help us to understand the strength of Russia and the reason why this nation has so quickly become a major geopolitical actor, as important, but in a different way, as Germany and Japan in the globalized world.

It is the power of collective integration that, in this case too, has given Russia, in the age of ultra-individualism, a competitive advantage in the balance of power in its confrontation with a world that is, after all, three times larger and ten times richer than itself: the Anglosphere.

From the exogamous communitarian family to communism

It is the coincidence between the map of the 'fully achieved' communism of the mid-1970s, as it appeared in the aftermath of the Vietnam War, and the map of the exogamous communitarian family – including Russia, Serbia, Albania, China, Vietnam, central Italy and the interior of Finland – that led me to formulate, in 1983, the hypothesis of a general relationship between peasant family systems and the ideologies that emerged when mass literacy came to the societies involved. Admittedly, this hypothesis owes much to the partial formulation proposed by Alan Macfarlane to explain English individualism.[2] But to tell the truth, as Pascal Tripier-Constantin has shown me, the pupils of Frédéric Le Play had foreseen the 'communist' potential of the Russian anthropological substratum even before the 1917 Revolution and Stalinist collectivization.[3] Anatole

Leroy-Beaulieu's survey, entitled *L'Empire des Tsars et les Russes* [*The Empire of the Tsars and the Russians*] was prophetic. I quote the text of the fourth edition published in 1897–8:

> The great patriarchal family under the authority of the father or the elder, and the village communities under the authority of the *mir*, have already shaped [the Russian] for common life, and thus for association. As soon as he starts a job, and in particular as soon as he leaves his village, the *muzhik* joins an *artel* ... The *artel*, with its Communist tendencies and its practical solidarity, is the spontaneous form, the national form of association ... The *artel* is like a large family or a small community, egalitarian and united, which carries over the close relations and the patriarchal manners of the village into the family ...
>
> The state strives to maintain a patriarchal character in industrial life ... Then, whether muzhiks or employers, the Russians of any class are disrespectful of the law as they are deferential towards the authorities ... It should come as no surprise that this country, accustomed to seeing any initiative coming down from on high, eventually joined or surpassed the most democratic states of Europe, on the adventurous paths of state socialism.[4]

Written no later than twenty years before the October Revolution, these lines do not detract from the tactical genius of Lenin, who was first party builder, then organizer of the great coup and finally the unyielding leader in the Civil War of 1918–21. But Lenin was also the pragmatic leader who authorized the return of the market through the New Economic Policy (NEP) in 1921–8. It was after him that the essential new development, from the anthropological point of view, took place: the irresistible rise to power of the collectivist dream realized by Stalin after 1929 – something that cannot be explained without the hypothesis of a Russian anthropological substratum that predisposed the country to embark on this experience.

The continuity of regional nuances: Putin and Lukashenko

Anatole Leroy-Beaulieu presents a nuanced regional picture of family structures in the Empire. The rapid expansion of the population from a founding nucleus in the West did not create much diversity in Russia. But it is precisely in the West that some significant differences must be noted; the early and persistent impact of these differences, aided by a memory of places internal to the Russian space, are tangible. Leroy-Beaulieu knew that the Ukrainian (Little Russian) family was more nuclear, more individualistic, and more anarchic too, and maintained a freer status for women.[5] It is worth adding that the epicentre of Russian

329

communitarianism was located in northwest Russia and Belorussia, as Kovalewsky noted in 1914.[6] Recent studies by Mikolaj Szoltysek on the Polish-Lithuanian state have revealed that by the end of the eighteenth century there was a sharp split between Poland, whose family system was nuclear and bilateral, and Belorussia, where it was communitarian and patrilineal. The Polish nuclear family tolerated the co-residence of generations – sons could accommodate their elderly fathers, for example. But in the case of a young couple settling for a time with their parents, there was explicit bilocality. The wife's family was chosen in 42 per cent of cases in Poland. In Belarus, this rate fell to 18 per cent, i.e. an 82 per cent rate for patrilocality; the co-residence of brothers, extremely rare in Poland, was commonplace in Belorussia.[7] With 82 per cent patrilocality, we are certainly far from the Chinese figure of 99 per cent, and even lower than in nineteenth-century central Russia, since the rate there would reach 95 per cent.[8] As in the Baltic countries, the communitarian Belarussan family was powerful, but still had traces of bilaterality.[9] I imagine, however, that communitarianism grew stronger in all the Russias in the nineteenth century, at least until the abolition of serfdom in 1861.

In Belarus and the northwest of present Russia, we are very close to the origin of communitarianism, perhaps born of a confrontation between the Germanic stem family and Mongolian patrilineal organization. The trading republic of Novgorod, a little to the southwest of St Petersburg, belongs to this region and was part of the Hanseatic League. I mentioned it in Chapter 11 in connection with the democratic and oligarchic forms that preceded authoritarian systems. We may raise the question of whether it is not part of the epicentre of the communitarian transformation. But the question remains open, since it seems that in the fourteenth century, the Hanseatic League did not practise primogeniture; rather, in its trade associations we can see the multiple family solidarities of undifferentiated periods, solidarities that were often horizontal and bilateral.[10] But let us now turn to the transition crisis that resulted from literacy.

The elections to the Constituent Assembly of 1917, dissolved by the Bolsheviks, fixed a unique and crucial image of the political temperaments to be found in the Empire on the eve of the October coup. Lenin's party had not obtained a majority and was outdistanced – by a considerable margin – by the socialist revolutionaries amid the bulk of the peasantry. In Ukraine, the national parties won easily. The Bolsheviks, however, controlled Moscow, St Petersburg, the central industrial region and – as Oliver Radkey noted in 1950 – Belarus.[11] He focuses on the example of the province of Vitebsk, where the Bolsheviks received an absolute majority of votes, 287,101 out of 560,538, the social revolutionaries only getting 150,279.[12] The Bolshevik party was deeply rooted to a remarkable degree in much of Belarus. And the hypothesis of an association between communism as an ideology and peasant family communitarianism is confirmed by an observation of the nuances of Russian regional diversity.

Let us stay in the region of strong communitarianism, but leave Russia for the Baltic countries, where the same hypothesis holds good. And, at a time when the Latvian European Commissioners are delivering a harsh verdict on the economic management of France, let us not forget the way their nation played a prominent part in the communist revolution. Radkey mentions Estonia in his book, but in his appendices he notes the case of Livonia and that of the powerful Latvian vote in favour of Leninism. Baltic participation was not only electoral: the role of the Latvian guard was decisive in the October *coup d'état*, and Lenin later told the Latvians how much he trusted them. Latvian activists were particularly active in founding the communist political police. The Bolsheviks had obtained 40 per cent of the votes in Estonia, 51 per cent in St Petersburg, 56 per cent in Moscow and 71 per cent in Livonia, when their average score in the Empire was only 24 per cent.[13]

From the beginning, then, the relative power of Bolshevism mirrored that of the underlying family communitarianism. It can be seen today that while the collapse of communism is indeed the effect of a cultural evolution towards greater individual autonomy, it has not abolished those anthropological foundations. The authoritarian democracy that dominates Russia at the beginning of the third millennium seems more the expression of a political temperament of the Russian people than the effect of the machinations of one man and his clan. The memory of places, however, is even more useful, since it provides us with the fascinating example of a Belarus that was more communitarian on the level of the family before 1900, more Bolshevik in 1917, and today is more attached than Russia to authoritarianism. President Lukashenko is now the only 'old-fashioned' dictator on the European continent, but the citizens of Belarus seem perfectly happy with the situation – and we will see that their society is functioning quite satisfactorily.

The recovery of Russia: proof by demography

In my first book, published in 1976, I predicted (as the reader will recall) the collapse of the Soviet system after noting the rise in the Russian infant mortality rate, that is to say an increase in the number of deaths among children under the age of 1 between 1970 and 1974. To assess the recovery of Russia since the year 2000, it seems fair to trust the same indicator. Graph 18.1 shows how it has changed since 1990 in Russia, Belorussia Ukraine, and, by way of comparison with the outside world, in Poland and the United States.

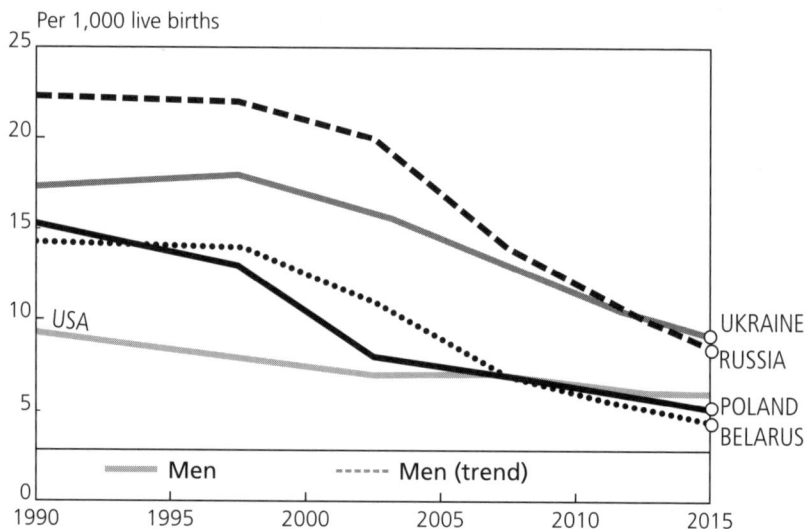

Graph 18.1 Infant mortality in the East

Infant mortality rates make it possible to follow the improvement in the living conditions of newborn infants west of the former Soviet sphere. We also see how slow the progress of the United States has been. The high child mortality rates among Black Americans, as I said above, are not solely responsible for this poor performance, since the infant mortality rate among Whites, at 5.0 per thousand (2013) already exceeds that of Poland, and would hardly put America in a very good position in the Western sphere.

Even more striking than the rapid progress of Russia is that of Belarus, which is now doing even better than Poland, reaching a level of 3.6 per thousand – comparable to France's 3.3 per thousand and Germany's 3.4 per thousand. Russia only achieves 7.0 per thousand, but the vastness of the Russian Federation and the presence on its territory of a multitude of ethnic groups with less medical provision than the properly Russian population must be taken into account in assessing this rate. Such minorities do not exist in these numbers on Ukrainian territory. But that accurate seismograph, the infant mortality rate, now places Ukraine behind, at 8.1, while in 1990 it was ahead of Russia with 17 per thousand as against Russia's 22.

Some sharp economic indicators point to the rapid improvement in living conditions in Russia at the beginning of the third millennium, such as the proportion of the population whose cash income is below the subsistence level, which fell from 29 per cent in 2000 to 13.2 per cent in 2009.[14] But pure economism, obsessed with GDP, exports and the money supply, prevents us from appreciating the extent of Russia's recovery. What the nineteenth century called 'moral statistics' allows us to get right close up to reality. The suicide rate plummeted from 39.5 per 100,000 population in 2001 to 18.4 in 2014 (–53 per cent), the homicide rate from 30.0 per 100,000 in 2003 to 8.7 in 2014 (–71 per cent), and the rate of deaths from alcohol poisoning from 30.0 in 2003 to 6.5 in 2014 (–78 per cent).

Overall mortality rates, abnormally high before the fall of communism, especially for men, began to decline, and life expectancy increased; between 2005 and 2014 it rose from 59 to 65 years for men.[15]

Russian fertility

The best explanation for the stability of the regime lies far from Western conspiracy theories. It is that under Vladimir Putin, Russian society has regained its balance, right down to its lower strata. Russia has survived the challenges of the 1990s – yet again, we might be tempted to say, given the great number of challenges this country has overcome in its history. This nation has regained civil peace, security and, quite definitely, human relationships that are becoming gentler and more reliable. That is why it is resisting the fall in the price of oil or gas whose in-house strategists are waiting, in vain, for the collapse of the 'Putin regime'.

The most impressive fact for a demographer, however, is the rise in the Russian fertility rate to 1.8 children per woman, well above the European average and that of countries like Germany, Japan, Italy or Spain, because in this respect Russia seems to be succeeding in something that none of the very low-fertility countries of the West has even attempted: an active policy of support for second and third births.[16] Is this a cyclical upswing? What will be the final fertility rate of Russian women born after a particular date? It is too early to say, and professional opinions on the issue are divided. However, the drop in mortality and the rise in fertility allowed the natural growth rate to become positive again in 2009. Russia, thus stabilized, has also once again become the centre of a migratory system that includes most of the former Soviet Union. Workers from Ukraine, the Caucasus and Central Asia ensure a continuous flow of labour. The net migration to Russia is invariably positive, unlike that of the former peoples' democracies or the Baltic countries, and it is clear that Russia, defying the forecasts of many experts, is not about to collapse. On the contrary: located to the east of a European Union threatened by demographic contraction, it is now a centre of resistance to decline. The CIA, whose reports on the world situation had predicted a spontaneous liquefaction of the historical adversary, is extremely disappointed.[17]

The final outcome of the Russian population policy is still open to debate, but probably because the experiment is unique and leaves Westerners incredulous. The fixation on short-term economic objectives prevents them from tackling the main problem of their societies: the renewal of the population. If the situation is satisfactory in the United States and in northwest Europe, all the better. If it is disastrous, as in the rest of Europe, too bad. Only economic performance is worthy of interest and demographic passivity is needed. But one elementary decisive factor is never taken into account: the professional insecurity of the free market combined with the shrinking of income due to austerity contribute to depressing fertility rates. The contraction of domestic demand ends in a contraction of life.

Admittedly, the demographic action of the Russian state benefits, as we have said, from a favourable anthropological terrain. The lands of Orthodox tradition did not undergo the wave of control of sexuality that followed the Protestant Reformation and the Catholic Counter-Reformation. Russia, even more than the rest of Eastern Europe, escaped the European marriage model which, between 1700 and 1900, imposed a late age of union and the sterilization of a proportion of the population resulting from celibacy. In Russia, only 5 per cent of women born between 1960 and 1965 do not have children between the ages of 40 and 44.[18] Early marriage and low levels of infertility remain features of Russian demography. But yet again we need to hypothesize, as in the case of France, Scandinavia and the Anglo-Saxon world, that the high status of women facilitates the reconciliation between maternal life and general social activity.

A transformation in the kinship system?

I have repeatedly stressed the recent character of patrilineality and the still high status of women in the Russian tradition. Some authors are currently debating a possible reversion of the system of kinship in Russia to bilaterality, such as Elisabeth Gessat-Anstett on the basis of an ethnological study conducted in the province of Yaroslavl.[19] The coexistence of a patrilineal onomastic (which adds 'son or daughter of so-and-so' to the first and last names) and the central role of mothers and grandmothers in household organization suggests that, in the Russian urban world, there is a bilinear system that superimposes patrilineal and matrilineal features. Even more than in the United States, progress in higher education opens up the possibility of a matriarchal transformation in Russia.

In order to assess the higher education revolution in Russia, I did not use the Barro-Lee database, the figures of which contradict those of the

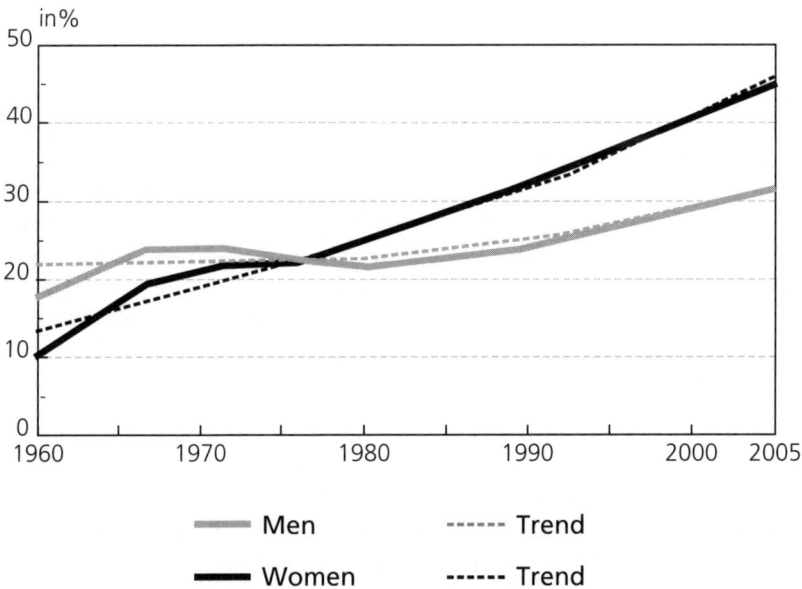

Graph 18.2 Progress of higher education in Russia
Source: Proportion of the population with a college degree: generations reaching the age of 25 on the dates indicated. Russian 2010 census.

OECD; I preferred to carry out a direct analysis of the results of the 2010 Russian census.[20]

Starting with the generation that was 25 years old in the years 1976–80, the proportion of women with full higher education has caught up with that of men. These advances in higher education played a powerful role in shaking up communist ideology, a product of the first educational transition, typical of a 'primary' period in which the overwhelming majority could read, write and count, but no more, with the exception of a small minority.

Among the Russians who reached the age of 25 in 2005, the number of women with a college education, for a male base of 100, was 144. Sweden, which wants to restore military service to counter an improbable Russian attack, will have to fight especially hard on the doctrinal level if it wants to hold onto its position of being the most feminist nation in the world.

The antithesis of the Anglo-American world

The principle of the memory of places now helps to show why Russia is always perceived, despite the disintegration of the Soviet system, as the antagonist par excellence of the Anglo-American world. It is because the values underlying the two worlds are, term by term, polar opposites. On the territory of the United States, England, Canada and Australia, the absolute nuclear family continues to reproduce an ideal of freedom, indifferent to the notion of equality. In Russia, the communitarian family has disappeared, but its values of authority and equality continue to be perpetuated by the mimicry of family and social behaviour. Exogamy and a high status for women are, however, common to both systems.

The collapse of communism, both a religion and an economic system, led to a decade of helplessness and suffering, in a Russia fundamentally unfit for the unbridled economic liberalism proposed to it by the triumphant West. The people have survived, largely because individuals left to themselves by the state have been able to rely on family, local and regional solidarities that cannot be analysed, or even perceived, in terms of a classical economic or political sciences approach. With Putin, a new ruling group eventually emerged, which managed to realign the social system with its anthropological substratum. The oligarchs who appeared during the era of the troubles have been quelled. A market economy tempered by a strong state has been put in place. It now draws revenues from the exploitation of natural resources, including gas and oil. A protectionist regime has been established to allow the survival, or rather the reconstruction, of the industrial apparatus. The deep ideological sense of Moscow's adoption of a protectionist system is the refusal of the Russian ruling class to see the people sold off as a cheap labour force to globalized capitalism. And it is precisely this unexpected determination that explains Western Russophobia: should not the elites of the globalized world share this concern? The Chinese Communist Party is irreproachable, as are the regimes born in Eastern Europe after the fall of communism.

But Russia, 'de-communized', can hold all the elections it wants: it remains, as in its totalitarian age, a counter-model in a world that has moved towards a fierce ultra-individualism. The United States' slide into inegalitarianism has, in one sense, meant that the ideological gap between Putin's Russia and Obama's United States was just as significant as that between the two nations at the time of Nikita Khrushchev and John F. Kennedy. As a result, it is possible that the establishment of a protectionist system in the United States might promote, beyond the inevitable military rivalry, a real Russian–American ideological rapprochement.

Russia, like other advanced nations, has experienced the emergence of a new educational stratification, and the inexorable rise of an inegalitarian social subconscious. As elsewhere, the desirable cultural homogeneity of mass literacy has been destroyed. The revolution in higher education was undoubtedly the final development that led to the disintegration of communist ideology, just as it had led to the shaking of American democracy or the collapse of the Catholic Church where the latter had survived. At the end of the 1980s, the dying Soviet regime even tried to block the development of universities, on this occasion abandoning one of the fundamental principles of communism which, like Judaism and Protestantism, saw the progress of education as one of its cardinal values.

The Russian anthropological base, however, imposes a limit on inequality.

We are here at the heart of Russian reconstruction: the values that have emerged from the communitarian family ensure the persistence of an integrated concept of the nation. As in Germany or Japan, this integrated conception has given Russia a competitive advantage over an Anglosphere that is admittedly much larger, much richer, and better armed. This is why Vladimir Putin's country – like those of Angela Merkel and Shinzo Abe – occupies a place in the world that is out of proportion to its demographic reality. The disproportion between the geopolitical importance of Russia and the volume of its GDP is also particularly dramatic. In 2016, in current prices, GDP amounted to only $1,200 billion, compared with $18,700 billion in the United States, $12,300 in China, $4,200 in Japan, $3,500 in Germany, $3,000 in the United Kingdom and $2,500 in France. A calculation in purchasing power parities, which approximate the actual consumption level of the population, halves the differences, but the raw values show how far Russia lies outside the heart of the world order.

Military specialization and the equality of nations

The specialization of Russia, in the globalized world, is different from that of Germany or Japan. It is military rather than commercial. Mathematical skill, patriotism and systemic inertia have made weaponry, already the heart of the Soviet economic system, a Russian speciality. The persistent hostility of the United States has even led to a surprising rebirth of the sector, and in particular to the development of a sophisticated and cheap defensive technology. Russian mobile missiles, capable of neutralizing any airspace, have in theory allowed the world to escape the omnipotence of the US Air Force. Without this breakthrough, we could not understand the Russian intervention in Syria. With a modernized nuclear force, exportable missiles and renewed IT expertise, Russia has once again become the natural counterweight to the United States.

337

Such a role fits perfectly well with the egalitarian values intrinsic to communitarianism.

Let us go over the sequence, in some respects a subliminal one, which links family relations to an a priori vision of the relations between peoples.

The German and Japanese stem family – a zombie version, since we are discussing the present – leads to an ethnocentric sequence: children are unequal, human beings are unequal, peoples are unequal.

The absolute nuclear family found in Britain and America generates a soft differentialist sequence: children are different, human beings are different, peoples are different.

But like the French egalitarian nuclear family, the Russian communitarian family triggers a universalist sequence: children in the French sequence, sons in the Russian sequence, are equal; human beings are equal, peoples are equal. Like the French Revolution, the communist revolution was therefore aggressively universalist and planned to extend the system invented in Russia to the rest of the world. The Soviet Union and the Communist International expressed this visceral egalitarianism on the institutional level, during a phase when the Russian population and power were expanding. In a phase when the population is dwindling and power diminishing, the imperial dream has transformed into a more peaceful vision of the necessary equality of nations. Vladimir Putin and Sergei Lavrov, Minister of Foreign Affairs, have both written their plans for a multipolar world, in which Russia must protect the equality and autonomy of nations. The integrated, almost familial, concept of the people (*narod*) that characterizes Russia prevents Moscow from fantasizing French-style about the dissolution of nations in these times of atomized, liberal humanity. In a world where most nations are small in size and militarily insignificant, the allure of the Russian approach is obvious, and very exasperating for the American geopoliticians who still think in terms of being all-powerful.

China as an ideological object

The benevolence from which China has benefited in the North American and European media contrasts with the severity applied to Russia. If Russian authoritarian democracy is never forgiven for the least failing, Chinese liberal totalitarianism can commit only venial sins. Beijing, with its one-party regime, basically a police state, albeit one tempered by corruption, has only had a few vague and formal reproaches directed against it. Why? Because between 1980 and 2015, China, a country of 1.36 billion inhabitants (in 2013), became not only the workshop of the world, but especially, for the well-off Westerner, the paradise of super-profit. Selling goods produced by a Chinese underpaid labour force in the markets of advanced countries meant that, for a few decades, undreamt-of margins could be attained. This financial dream has turned into a false conscience, a refusal to understand that it is impossible to perpetuate the model – an illusion shared by Westerners and the Chinese themselves.

Of course, there are a few sensible writers who analyse, in moderate and cautious terms, the internal structures and imbalances of the Chinese economy.[21] But they are very few and far between.

In 2007–8, the advanced countries entered a crisis period and, in 2017, it was China's turn to face the wall of reality. Donald Trump and his advisers, such as Peter Navarro, prefer to talk of China as a problem rather than a miracle.[22] And indeed, given the incredible weight of investments in the country's GDP, the official growth rate, slightly lower than 7 per cent in 2016, is likely soon be approaching zero.

Those who sing the praises of globalization have also for decades extolled the rise of the Chinese middle class and the flourishing of a market of nouveaux riches that has become the horizon of the free world. It is obviously not a question here of denying China's progress, the improvement in its living standards, the rise in GDP per capita and even the rise in wages. But such progress is simply to be expected for a fully literate population which practises birth control and is no longer constrained in its economic activity by a mad Maoist state.

And how can we fail to perceive, in the Chinese model, the trace of a Stalinist-type economy, with its investment rate of 43 per cent of GDP in 2016, the persistent restriction on domestic consumption, the militarization of the economy, and the incessant anti-corruption campaigns, which simply mean that there is no free market in China guaranteed by stable and secure institutions? The depiction of the leaders of the Chinese Communist Party as brilliant economic strategists (as opposed to incompetent Russians) has been particularly ridiculous. China has not chosen its destiny. It has agreed to integrate its workforce into the system under the guidance of the United States and, in addition, the European Union and Japan.

Today's China was invented by the West, and very early on – witness the conclusion of the classic *Imperialism: A Study* by John A. Hobson, an analyst of imperialism before Rudolf Hilferding and Lenin. This anti-conformist intellectual had in fact considered the configuration of the present world as early as 1902, and we find in him a prophetic power superior to that of H. G. Wells.

> We have foreshadowed the possibility of an even larger alliance of Western States, a European federation of great Powers which, so far from forwarding the cause of world-civilisation, might engender the gigantic peril of a Western parasitism, a group of advanced industrial nations, whose upper classes drew a vast tribute from Asia and Africa,

with which they supported great tame masses of retainers, no longer engaged in the staple industries of agriculture and manufacture, but kept in the performance of personal or minor industrial services under the control of a new financial aristocracy. Let those who would scout such a theory as undeserving of consideration examine the economic and social condition of districts in Southern England today ... and reflect upon the vast extension of such a system which might be rendered feasible by the subjection of China to the economic control of similar groups of financiers, investors, and political and business officials.[23]

Hobson, who lived at a time of intense rivalry between the pre-1914 European powers, had simply forgotten ... America. Yet it's up to America to fulfil his prophecy, before it tries to escape its consequences once the dream of financiers has become a nightmare of the Western masses.

Yes, Chinese leaders have been manipulated rather than manipulative, and they should wake up to the realities: a reversal of attitude in the West could not fail to reveal the strategic powerlessness of Beijing. Already, Chinese leaders are struggling to curb the outflow of capital from their country. This financial leakage should not be considered as the quantitative, mechanical effect of trade surpluses. In a country in real development, these surpluses would not exist. The country should be a net importer of capital and its trade balance should show a deficit.

But the reality is that economic extraversion – a growth driven too exclusively by exports – has pulled the Chinese economy out of the normal trajectory where the speed and shape of growth would be defined by those of the underlying educational development. The advance of higher education in China is fast, as shown in Graph 18.3, but the rates achieved are very low compared to those of the United States, Europe or Japan. We have already seen this in Graph 16.1, which compares the major powers of globalization: 4 per cent of college graduates aged 30–34 years in China, in the generation that turned 25 in 2000, compared to 36 per cent in Japan, 35 per cent in the United States, 27 per cent in Sweden, 26 per cent in the United Kingdom, and 20 per cent in Germany and France. The ranking of the advanced countries is, of course, questionable, given the diversity of educational systems and qualifications issued, but the Chinese are definitely lagging behind.

This comparison allows us to ridicule another, or rather to unveil its ideological character: Shanghai's ranking of universities. How can the most advanced countries grant a country that is so little advanced in educational terms the right to award them grades, prizes and certificates of merit? This unheard-of privilege, somewhat evocative of the Feast of Fools, a carnivalesque inversion of statuses, is only one of the components

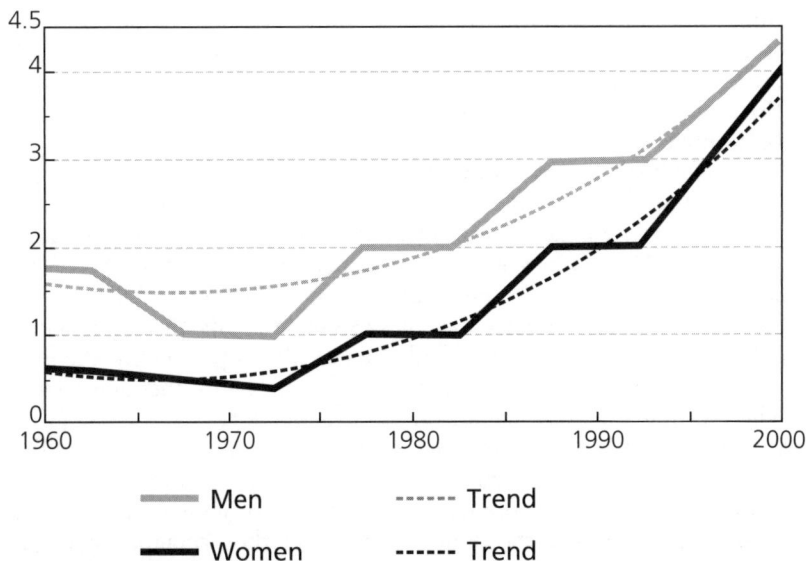

Graph 18.3   Progress of higher education in China
Source: Percentage of the population with a college degree: generations reaching the age of 25 at the dates indicated.

of the ideological system that has made China the horizon of the world, or rather the horizon of profit.

The scepticism of demographers

Once again, demography helps us to lift the veil of ideology. The demographic profession is not optimistic about China. Demographers know all too well that the dynamism of the 1980s largely relied on what they call, colloquially, the 'demographic bonus': the decline in fertility, combined with the small number of elderly people, produced a situation in which the burden of the inactive population was minimal. Workers are abundant and, as we have seen, competitive in the global market. But the bonus can only be transient. Soon the population will be ageing, the 'demographic burden' will increase, and things will start to slow down. The median age of the Chinese population increased from 27.3 years in 1950 to 34.1 in 2010. According to UN projections, it will reach 42.1 in 2030 and 46.3 in 2050. However, China has not had time to set up a social security and old-age insurance system; it has, for the most part, merely reinstated in law the duty of children to care for their parents. An individual precautionary principle imposes its obligations: the Chinese

341

savings rate is as abnormally high as the investment rate. As it has become customary to say, the Chinese will be old before they are rich, and the transition to maturity will have far more dramatic consequences in their country than in the United States or in Europe.

Not only is the population ageing; there has been a brain drain, a loss of substance that completes the flight of capital. In 2012, according to the World Bank, the net migration balance showed a deficit of 1.5 million individuals, even if in 2013 the OECD counted only 500,000 immigrants from China. Many of them were students, since China sends 22 per cent of mobile students to the West. In 2015, the Chinese Ministry of Education recorded the departure of 523,000 students abroad, welcoming the fact that the return rate had risen to 70–80 per cent in the most recent years. The great Western recession favoured this phenomenon.

The fact remains that China, far from belonging, like Russia, to the club of nations that prey on manual workers and brainpower – a position which is enough to define a country as a member of the dominant geopolitical group – is one of those countries that are losing human substance due to emigration, and the middle classes are thus being depleted. Its negative migratory balance is not dramatic, given the mass of its population, but the qualitative effect of these losses cannot be underestimated. It is the best scientists who do not go back to China. Worse still, the Chinese who aspire to freedom of expression are obviously overrepresented among the emigrants who settle abroad. Geographic flows thus reinforce China's authoritarian system by constantly purging it of its potentially more liberal elements.

A persistent patrilineal dynamics, in China and elsewhere

On the scale of patrilineality levels, China occupies level 2, which corresponds to a communitarian family system formed a little over two millennia ago. The lowering of the status of women has led, in the north and centre of the country, to rates of patrilocality that, as we have seen, exceed 99 per cent. On the southeast coast, between Canton and Shanghai, traces of the stem family (or even nuclear family) and a higher status for women had survived until the revolution, with residual rates of matrilocal marriage sometimes as high as 10 per cent.

Chinese communism had drawn from its Russian model a desire to elevate the status of women in society and had tried to repress patrilineality. Ever since its fall, and even as Western ideologues praised China's accession to modernity, the patrilineal principle has re-emerged in force, and probably even resumed its advance. The collapse of the state's security structures has sent people back to their families and traditional customs, in China as in East Germany, but it would probably be wrong to attribute the fall in women's status to this single doctrinal and institutional change. We can also see it happening in India, where it cannot be explained by the collapse of communism.

In China, women's higher education is certainly catching up with men's, at a minimal level for the time being. But the persistence of the patrilineal principle is demonstrated by a preference of parents for boys, which is strikingly evident from the statistics of Chinese births. There is no need here to conduct an opinion poll. Modern prenatal sex screening techniques can 'pick' a boy, by performing selective abortions of female foetuses. At 1.7 children per woman, Chinese fertility rates are low, though not as low as in Japan or South Korea. But the probability of a couple not having a boy, at a birth rate of fewer than 3 children per woman, rises to a noticeable degree. In several articles, Christophe Guimolto, doubtless the world's leading specialist on the subject, has made a global inventory of the rise in sex ratio at birth – i.e., the number of boys per 100 girls coming into the world.[24] For Eurasian populations, the natural rate is around 105–6, with more boys being conceived than girls.

Table 18.1 ranks the sex ratios of exogamous communitarian family countries in descending order and presents for comparison several countries of nuclear, stem and endogamous communitarian family. Exogamous communitarian family countries are lightly shaded, those where this type is well represented but shares the national space with others are a shade darker. With an index equal to 107, we may suspect that selective abortion is being practised; above, this is almost certain. With a sex ratio of 118, China is in the lead and for a while its cultural influence extended to South Korea, a stem-family country where the current rate of 107 is simply the residue of a crisis, more or less overcome, in which the index had risen to 115 in 1994. The supremacy of China in this respect is nevertheless partly an illusion, since some states in the north of India reach 120. The Indian national rate of 111 incorporates the relative feminism of South India, which acts as a moderating influence.

Muslim countries, except Pakistan, appear immune to selective abortion, perhaps because of religious prohibition, probably more due to endogamy. In an endogamous communitarian system, a girl will be destined to wed her cousin. Her destiny is not to leave her family through marriage: from her conception to her death, she will belong to the same group and her life will be protected.

In this context, the rate of 110 in Pakistan – where the frequency of marriages between first cousins, however, is 50 per cent, one of the highest in the Muslim world – reveals the subterranean persistence of a cultural closeness between Muslims, Hindus, and the Sikhs of ancient Punjab. The region has long practised old-style infanticide of female infants, before adopting the more modern technique of selective abortion. The very high index in Muslim Azerbaijan, 117, shows that the

Table 18.1   The sex ratio in communitarian societies and several others, in 2010

China	118
Azerbaijan	117
Armenia	115
Georgia	112
Albania	112
Vietnam	111
India	111
Pakistan	110
Kosovo	110
Montenegro	110
Singapore	108
Macedonia	108
South Korea	107
Bosnia	107
Serbia	107
Italy	106
Russia	106
Sweden	106
Germany	106
Japan	106
Bulgaria	106
Estonia	106
Hungary	106
Lithuania	106
France	105
United States	105
United Kingdom	105
Algeria	105
Slovakia	105
Iran	105
Saudi Arabia	105
Israel	105
Latvia	105
Finland	104

latter continues to 'belong' to the southern periphery of the Soviet world, where abortion was a standard technique of birth control. Soviet habits prevail over Islam and endogamy, facilitating selective foeticide. Georgia and Armenia, despite all the internal conflicts in the Caucasus region, persist in behaving in this regard as cultural cousins.

The sex ratio is a cruel indicator for those geopoliticians who tried to 'sell' us Georgia or Kosovo as Western countries, and Russia as different

344

from our way of life. The Russian sex ratio is obviously normal, like those of the Baltic countries, Finland, Slovakia and Bulgaria. But the ratios in Georgia (112) or of Kosovo (110) show how these two countries are not part of the Western sphere, if a high status for women is indeed a component of Western identity. We would like to see Sweden worrying a little more vigorously about these infringements of women's rights.

These figures bear witness to a re-emergence. Even more significant is the rise in the sex ratio in southern China and southern India, where a relative feminism had survived.[25] These recent developments suggest that despite the global discourse on the emancipation of women, the patrilineal principle, which manifested itself around 3000 BCE in Mesopotamia, and about 1400 BCE in China, is now completing the conquest of the two nation-continents of Asia, namely China and India.

The memory of places: authority and equality in China

The quantitative imbalance between the sexes, together with the ageing population, seems to spell out a rather dark demographic future for China. But we need above all to understand what the rise in sex ratio at birth means in terms of mentalities, and return to our concept of the memory of places.

Despite the effects of globalization and the country's export success, China's traditional values, established by nearly three and a half millennia of evolution towards patrilineality, remain alive and sometimes even continue to spread. We can therefore postulate a persistence of communitarian values associated with a strong patrilineal principle, with authoritarianism and egalitarianism. The leading role of the Communist Party and the omnipotence of the police testify to authoritarianism. But the egalitarianism of the anthropological system is also a factor – the very same egalitarianism that allowed China to undertake a radical communist revolution. The hierarchical systems of the German and Japanese type, based on the stem family, come with a principle of inequality that stabilizes the social order. The latent egalitarianism of Chinese values, in a phase where economic inequalities are rising sharply, is a threat to the balance of the social and political system. The leaders know this, or feel it, and live not only with the corruption entailed by the reshaping of patrilineal family ties, but also in fear of their people. An internal hardening of the regime weighs heavily on the Chinese people, for whom the regime manufactures alluring but dangerous toys.

The xenophobic nationalism maintained by the Communist Party, which has in this respect become much closer to fascism than to Marxism-Leninism, is poisoning the life of neighbouring Japan, which (as we saw in Chapter 16) has renounced power and expansionism in

Asia. I have no intention, of course, of forgetting the violence displayed by Japanese colonialism, but I would note that it was no worse than the violence inflicted by French colonialism in Algeria or during the wars on the Native American Indians in the United States, and was far removed from what the Shoah represented for humankind as a whole. The Chinese communicators' insistence on reminding us of the Nanking massacres has something pathetic about it, coming from a country where the crazed economic policy of the Communist Party had, in the Great Leap Forward, and in the absence of any foreign intervention, entailed the deaths of 30 million Chinese.

We would be wrong, however, to exaggerate Chinese expansionism. Anti-Japanese xenophobia and expansion into the South Seas are a tactical adjustment to a difficult internal situation rather than a real imperial gambit. China is so populous that its internal gravitational system prevents it from practising any real expansionism: its mass makes it a sort of black star that retains and concentrates matter rather than dilating it.

At the international level, Chinese egalitarianism leads to a vision similar to that promoted by Russia: a multipolar world made up of equivalent nations. In the stable state, China presents itself as a reasonable and reliable actor on the world stage, even if we have seen emerging, at the end of the phase of economic expansion, a few megalomaniac theories on the Chinese civilizational state, such as the one presented in *The China Wave* by Zhang Weiwei, who depicts the internal authoritarianism of the system as a positive value and an ontological challenge to Western democracy.[26] The emigration of millions of Chinese students to North America, Europe and Japan suggests something quite different.

Struck by the slowdown in global demand, suffering the brunt of the decline in the resulting growth rate, faced with a major demographic imbalance, and experiencing growing inequality in the context of an egalitarian culture: with its 1.3 billion inhabitants, China is one of the major poles of global instability at the beginning of the third millennium.

Russia as both an accident and a necessity

I would like to end this chapter with a brief reflection on Russia's place in the anthropological and ideological history of the world. The Russian family system is exogamous communitarian and, as such, finds its place in the same typological 'box' as China, Vietnam, Serbia, Albania and central Italy. In the twentieth century, all these countries and regions produced communism, either through revolution or through a stable electoral establishment. Can we draw from this coincidence the conclusion that they represent exactly the same thing as Russia, and that, basically, communist ideology could have been born in any of them?

Russia's advance on China in terms of mass literacy alone would exclude such a possibility. But we need to take the analysis further. In contemporary Russian history there is a creativity, a capacity for invention, sometimes murderous in its intensity, that has gone beyond what a mere difference in educational development could explain. The special role of women in the family system is a fundamental structural feature that distinguishes Russia from its typological companions, and seems to have spared the country what might be called 'the patrilineal trap'. One of the central theses of this book is that, after the invention of agriculture, the civilizations born in the Middle East, in China and in West Africa all conceived, applied and reinforced a patrilineality that, as time went by, lowered the status of women and paralysed society.

Marginalizing or locking women away in their homes means slowing down their education, then that of their sons, destined to be locked away in a patrilineal network. Men too cease to be individuals in their own right. They dominate patrilineal societies as a group, but as individuals they often remain children. This is the reason for a paradox common in the world of patrilineality: the man dominates in the public square, but at home his wife treats him like a little boy. A society thus constituted cannot remain creative indefinitely. The anti-feminist involution of the original centres of civilization explains the cessation of their historical development, and the centrifugal geographical movement of progress, from Mesopotamia to England, from China to Japan.

The individual did indeed become locked away inside kinship networks in Russia, but very belatedly, and women's status was not seriously diminished. That is why Russia happens to be, in the universe of patrilineality, an exception. It benefits, so to speak, from the collective integration that the communitarian family allows and thus finds in itself resources of high-level social cohesion. But the status of women acts as a corrective, which explains the incessant Russian creativity in intellectual, scientific and military spheres, right up until the most recent period, for better and for worse.

Russia thus invented communism, but who can say with certainty that China would have been able to do so? Engaged in this stifling and bloody adventure, Russia still found the energy to defeat Nazi Germany between 1941 and 1945, with one of the best pieces of equipment used in the war, the T34 tank: everyone agrees that it was the best of the time. Even today, surviving a decade of disintegration, Russia has just upgraded its military technology by manufacturing the S-400 missile systems, able to neutralize any air superiority.

To pastiche Hegel, I would like finally to emphasize Russia's paradoxical place in history. This nation was capable of imposing an intolerable communist system, with universalist aspirations, on itself, but it saved the world. To have sacrificed so much to defeat Nazism must be counted

347

as a major contribution to world history. But does Russia really represent something universal? The analysis of its anthropological infrastructure, which is communitarian and feminist, shows that Russia was originally just an anthropological oddity, an accident of history.

ENVOI

One can hardly conclude an outline of human history because history, of course, does not stop. Moreover, as I said at the beginning of this book, my aim was to provide a better description rather than an explanation in any absolute sense. And if you don't know the meaning of history, how can you imagine how it will end? I hope, however, to have convinced the reader that it is possible to understand it a little less badly if one is prepared to delve down into the deepest layers of the lives of societies, to subconscious and unconscious levels.

The sense of helplessness that grips today's elites and the most advanced peoples of the world is the result of an ignorance of the forces that tirelessly express and produce events that are supposedly incomprehensible: inequality and decline in the standard of living against a backdrop of technological progress, nihilism in religious expression, xenophobia, and conflicts between nations at a time when the concept of nation is deemed to be outdated.

The educational dynamic is subconscious. In this respect, the stagnation of the United States, which since 1945 has set the direction of history for the entire developed world, largely explains the feeling of regression that has invaded us in spite of technological progress. The spread of this sentiment is encouraged by the fact that America remains, par excellence, the place of innovation. And neither Japan, nor Germany, nor Russia, nor China has laid out another path.

At a deeper level, the persistent divergence between anthropological systems hinders the pragmatic management of the interaction between nations. The crystallization of religious systems in a zombie form contributes to the persistence of the forces of separation. But no one can claim to manage the most advanced world if they refuse to perceive its profound diversity, a diversity that is renewed again and again by a memory of places that itself results itself from the differentiation of family types defined by 5,000 years of evolution. Technology does not

349

wipe out the way of life, which remains that of nuclear or stem families, not forgetting the accidental feminist communitarianism of Russia. The universal human being exists, of course, in the original form of *Homo sapiens*, to which America remains close, or in the useful ideological dream of France. But as for nations, they are specific.

The ideology of globalization is based on an assumption of homogeneity. But this is impossible to achieve. This ideology, suddenly, threatens to lead us to conflicts of power aggravated by clashes of values. In Europe, when certain anthropological substrata impose their values without the knowledge of the actors, liberal democracy, as I think I have shown, can metamorphose into an inegalitarian autocracy.

I also hope that, by highlighting the archaic nature of its anthropological foundations, I have helped convince the West that a little modesty is in order. In particular, it is the very primitiveness of America that has made it successful. And this country continues, unbeknown to us, to impose on the world the weight of its founding racial division: I have described at length the complex interaction of democracy, the drive towards oligarchy, and the persistent White/Black polarity in the United States. This analysis allows us to grasp the astonishing contribution of racism to the ultra-liberal revolution.

We urgently need to accept the hypothesis of the divergence of nations, resulting from the differentiation of family systems, if we have the peace of the world at heart.

Admittedly, on the educational level, a certain global convergence can be noted. The developed world seems to have reached an educational and demographic limit. When a nation exceeds this level, as defined by the United States, it seems to pay for it by a subfertility which, by reducing the absolute number of men and women, compensates for the higher proportion of those who go on to higher education. Sweden and Russia may be exceptions.

Anyway, if the ceiling stays in place, the floor rises.

The old third world is advancing in primary, secondary and higher education, and it is getting closer, from one generation to another, to the advanced world. However, it lives under the constant threat of having its grey matter pillaged by a developed world that is beginning to fail.

An educational recovery in the United States, of course, would contradict this movement towards homogenization, again opening up the gap between advanced countries and those that are catching up. Without being inconceivable, this is nevertheless unlikely. America lacks a minimum of mental verticality, stem-family structures that would facilitate discipline in education, and a greater efficiency in cultural transmission in general. The United States will continue to tread its traditional path of looting human resources here and there across the planet. Given the demographic size reached by this nation-continent, its needs will very soon be

350

considerable. China, another nation-continent, busy exporting not only its goods but also its people, should fear this prospect.

Be this as it may, the tendency to more educational homogeneity, for the time being, prevails.

We must be prepared to approach history by its two major dimensions.

The subconscious, educational level, with or without homogenization, represents its universal dimension. Everywhere, the trajectory of education, despite its lags and differences in rhythm, is the same for the whole species *Homo sapiens*. It comprises the reality of globalization. But throughout the advanced world, a new educational stratification has broken the unity of the body of citizens. A new, inegalitarian subconscious has pulverized the ideologies and remnants of religion left over from the age of primary education. The crisis of democracy and the rise in populism are universal phenomena.

A second, anthropological dimension implies, on the contrary, at least a persistent separation between peoples or, worse, a divergence that might increase.

Whatever happens to progress, some nations will remain liberal and others authoritarian. In some countries, a certain egalitarianism stemming from the anthropological background will resist the tendency to oligarchy, while in others an inegalitarian tradition will reinforce it.

The emancipation of women is a false universal. True, it can be found everywhere, and it is sometimes where we would least expect it that it manifests itself most forcefully, as in Russia, for example. But in most societies with a patrilineal background, and to varying degrees depending on the intensity of the principle, it causes major dysfunctions in the demographic field, as in Germany, Japan and China.

A concrete analysis of the major nations also reveals the coexistence of stable systems (the United States, Russia and probably also Japan, which has accepted its demographic decline) and unstable systems (Germany and China, because they have set goals that their demographic and educational base has rendered inaccessible). To what will this coexistence give birth?

I will abstain from proposing any solutions that would help us surmount the contradictory movement of a history that is torn between the educational universal and anthropological divergence. I will limit myself here to a strict Weberian neutrality: the role of the researcher is to enlighten human beings as to the forces that move them, not to propose a solution, that is to say a new ideology. It is for all actors, if they agree to see themselves as they are in history, to discuss and decide on these matters. The relationship of politicians to history makes it unlikely, however, that an awareness of long-term forces will emerge among them. But who knows?

POSTSCRIPT: THE FUTURE OF
LIBERAL DEMOCRACY

I would like, finally, to focus the analysis on the fate of the West in the narrowest sense, that part of the world that really invented liberal democracy, with three nations of now unequal size at its heart: the United Kingdom, the United States and France. My world. The months between June 2016 and June 2017 were a kind of *annus mirabilis* of 'populism', which saw the success of Brexit, the election of Donald Trump and the collapse of the French party system with a second round setting a far Right party against Emmanuel Macron, a young inspector of finances (the higher rank for students graduating from the École nationale d'administration, ENA) from the heart of the French state and banking establishment. This year can be described, on the Anglo-American side, as that of democratic renewal, protectionism, xenophobia and a return to nationalism. For the moment, France has taken the opposite path of reaffirming the postnational, European, free trade, globalist path, indifferent to the issue of borders and immigration. The vote for the National Front, in the first as in the second round, was after all modest, even after a five-year term that had produced a 25 per cent increase in unemployment (already high to begin with) and that was punctuated by the violence of terrorism.

Nevertheless, an analysis of the electoral results reveals that, in all three cases, educational level played a decisive role in the vote. Everywhere, in line with the view of history proposed in this book, higher education broke up the cultural homogeneity of the liberal democracies and created 'worlds above' attached to the values of openness, and 'worlds below' demanding that a nation should have the right to control its borders and to consider the interests of its citizens as a priority. In each of the three cases, Academia represents the heart of the universalist and liberal world, enraged by Brexit in England, by Trump in the United States, and by the National Front in France, signing and publishing petitions and injunctions intended for their teachers, their students and their 'misinformed' fellow citizens. The corporate world, generally globalist, was generally, except perhaps in France, more inclined to wait and see. A researcher is here so close to his or her own universe of reference – Academia – that a renewed caution is imperative. The researcher in particular, and his or her readers too, must again remember the Weberian precept of neutrality. It is not a question of judging, but of understanding and trying to catch a glimpse of the direction the world is taking, an intellectual attitude that does not exclude the use of the right to irony.

One clarification of a sociological order is needed. The identification of educational stratification as the cause of ideological cleavage means that the problem is structural and, in a sense, insoluble. Universal literacy, the basis of modern democracy, is, despite what some declinists say, still in place, but a division of society into primary, secondary and higher 'meritocratic orders' has been superimposed on it. The higher order is itself finely graduated by the prestige levels of the various degrees and university qualifications. Meritocratic selection cannot function without the basis of literacy on which the order created by the college-educated rests. Advanced societies must therefore live in a state of tension: universal primary education indefatigably nourishes the possibility of democracy, higher education no less tirelessly nourishes a higher class, which, because it is selected by merit, thinks itself intellectually and morally superior in rights. This superiority is a collective illusion: the homogeneity and conformism engendered by the mechanism of selection produce the ultimate paradox of a 'world above' subject to intellectual introversion, unsuited to individual thought. So in a sociological sense, it can be said that the 'world above' is idiotic and somewhat immoral. But, like the primary people, this 'mass elite' is built to last. True, it strives to preserve its own children from school competition, through various mechanisms, and itself attempts to undermine the meritocratic principle. Since academic success ultimately leads, from a systemic point of view, only to money, meritocracy lives under the permanent threat of being captured and closed off by plutocracy. But Academia, that sorting machine for human beings, is itself rich and solid, and it seems capable of reproducing for many years to come our society of orders, foremost among which is this mass elite entangled in its intellectual difficulties.

Common sense tells us that no brutal choice can solve the contradiction between egalitarianism, which results from primary education, and inegalitarianism, which stems from higher education, and that advanced societies, if they want to remain coherent and viable, must provide an average path. In short, we must reconcile the values of the people below and those of the people above, the security of peoples and openness to the world. Because a democracy cannot function without the people, the denunciation of populism is absurd. Because a democracy cannot work without elites, who represent and guide, the denunciation of the elites as such is just as absurd. A stubborn prolongation of the confrontation between populism and elitism, if it were to continue, could lead only to social disintegration. Remember that in each of the three countries concerned, the people and the elites speak the same language: English or French. Exogamy renders social strata porous. A hypothesis that would make the higher educated a racial variety gradually separating out from the species *Homo sapiens* is far less likely than the imaginings of H. G. Wells's *The Time Machine*.

We can now better grasp the dilemma facing liberal democracy if we make the effort to compare the currently divergent destinies of the three founding countries. Three levels of negotiation between each 'people' and its 'elite' are already detectable.

France defines a zero level of negotiation. The 'populist' aspiration to redefining a protective nation has been not just contained but repressed. Voting for the National Front still constitutes a taboo for two-thirds of voters. In the second round of the presidential election in May 2017, only a minority voted for the far Right in all groups, whether based on education, income, age or occupation, with the exception of workers. But including blank ballots and abstainers would have revealed that the National Front polled a minority even among workers. French society, violently polarized in an asymmetrical fashion, is still moving towards openness – towards self-dissolution in Europe and in free trade. A third of its population is rotting economically and morally, and raging at its inescapable impotence.

The United States is engaged in a negotiation between its people and its medium-level elites which, at the time of writing, has led American society into what might be called 'dynamic schizophrenia'. Donald Trump was elected with a numerical vote slightly lower than Hillary Clinton's. The American electoral system, which gave him a majority in the Electoral College, meant that he won. But not everyone recognizes the legitimacy of this bête noire of the establishment. The America of the upper strata – the America of the highly qualified, of Silicon Valley, of well-established journalists – did not disarm. It has mobilized against the new president in what many consider a cold civil war. The existence of numerous countervailing powers, including an independent judiciary, has led to the establishment of trench warfare.

Let us imagine that, at this stage, the outcome of the conflict is uncertain. But we must keep in mind that an analysis in educational terms means that the real choice for America is not between Trump and the establishment, but between negotiation and disintegration. The hypothesis of a total victory for Trump is unthinkable, while a return of globalist triumphalism is equally inconceivable.

In the United Kingdom, negotiation between the people and the elites seems to have resulted, rather quickly, in a result that would be

354

unthinkable in France or the United States: agreement. Brexit, too, won the votes of the less well-educated. The rage of academics and journalists of the centre-left establishment in Britain was and remains every bit as intense as the rage of the anti-Trump camp in the United States. But to our surprise we witnessed an unlikely spectacle: the Conservative Party, led by Theresa May, accepted the popular verdict and is preparing to manage the United Kingdom's exit from the European Union.

The important thing here is not to award good or bad marks for democracy, or certificates of xenophobia. We must remember that a significant degree of rejection of foreigners is common to the French National Front vote (anti-Arab), to Trump's electorate (anti-Mexican) and to the Brexiteers (anti-Polish). The main thing is to understand the differences now being revealed between the French, American and British trajectories.

This ultimate divergence between advanced societies, even within the narrow club of nations that founded modern democracy, is itself a paradox, since there is no doubt that, of the three societies, the British is the least egalitarian in temperament. I have insisted at length on the importance in England of a real sense of aristocratic inequality, associated with an embryonic stem family in the noble and peasant strata of the seventeenth century. I have shown how, in the United States, racial sentiment, despite the indifference of the absolute nuclear family to equality, allowed the emergence of a White egalitarianism. In France, egalitarianism is even more deeply rooted, since the egalitarian nuclear family structures of the Paris Basin predispose to an a priori egalitarian vision of men and women, even if the stem-family periphery in France moderates this predisposition. Paris remains, from the point of view of the anthropology of advanced societies, the capital of egalitarian liberalism.

Yet, in an absolutely counterintuitive way, what we must observe is that it is easier to take into account the aspirations of the people – in the United Kingdom – where the society in question is less egalitarian in temperament. Admittedly, in England, there is an open academic contempt for 'chavs', a term that condenses all the graciousness of the similar terms 'prolo' in France and 'redneck' in America. But it is also in England that we already find the best intellectual formulations of the legitimacy of the people's aspirations to territorial and social security, formulations that do not reject the equivalent legitimacy of the aspirations of the 'world above' to openness and mobility. In Exodus, published in 2013 but already a classic, Paul Collier, a development economist, gave a nuanced analysis of the phenomenon of migration; while he completely understood the migrants' point of view, he did not consider the right of advanced peoples to preserve a certain level of self-esteem and cultural stability to be a priori illegitimate.[1] More recently, in 2017, David Goodhart, founder of the liberal left-wing magazine *Prospect*, wrote *The Road to Somewhere*, in which he noted the need to take into account the aspirations of the people from below.[2] His description of society, very similar to ours, contrasts the *Anywheres* with the *Somewheres* and the need in each society, not only the United Kingdom, for a negotiation between the two visions of the world. He resorts to the magnificent expression 'decent populism', which, far from being an oxymoron, expresses an escape from primitive binary thought and, for liberal democracies, shows the only way out if they want to avoid fragmentation and disintegration. Goodhart's description is nuanced, but his interpretation is basically somewhat mono-factorial, and accurate: he places the emergence of the massive group of the higher educated at the heart of the mechanism of ideological polarization. We are all students of Michael Young. But why has England managed so easily to define a new social pact ahead of her sisters in liberal democracy? The differences in social structure between France, the United States and the United Kingdom are too numerous for us easily to identify, when the process is not complete, the reasons why it is in the most aristocratic of the great liberal democracies that populism is the best integrated.

Let us evoke pell-mell the differences that characterize our three democracies. America is continental, racial from the beginning, military and imperial. France and the United Kingdom are medium-sized countries, deprived of empires, and where aggressive nationalism has become unthinkable. Educational stratification is older and almost stabilized in the United States, recent in France and the United Kingdom. The two nations of the Anglosphere emerged from Protestant culture, France from the Catholic tradition.

France, moreover, has renounced its monetary autonomy, and the process of national decomposition is more advanced. Its executive no longer has the capacity to decide on an independent economic policy. One could even say that France, if it still has privileged classes, no longer has a ruling class, simply because there is nothing essential to rule. In France, it is now impossible to make the essential decisions, which are economic in kind.

Confronted with so many different factors, it is very difficult to propose a rigorous interpretation of the way the British are ahead in defining a new pact between elite and nation, on the basis of the acceptance of a 'decent populism'. I will, however, take the risk, advancing a hypothesis in the spirit of the general logic of the outline of human history I have put forward here.

Let us start from Young's hypothesis: that of a meritocracy that undermines egalitarian sentiment because anyone selected by the school system ends up thinking himself or herself as intrinsically superior. Let's not lose sight, first of all, of the fact that the meritocratic ideal is the child of

356

democracy. It is the perverse effect of an egalitarian aspiration to equality of opportunity – an equality of opportunity that ends up creating an inequality of merit. The more a society is originally egalitarian and democratic in temperament, the stronger the meritocratic ideal will be and – this is where the paradox becomes apparent – the more powerful will be the inegalitarian perversion that is inadvertently engendered. In other words, the more the school system reigns supreme, in accordance with the meritocratic ideal, the more efficient the sorting system for human beings will be. Where the ideal of an aristocracy of birth coexists with the school system and the mechanisms for the out-of-school transmission of status, there are counterbalances to the ferocity of the inegalitarian sorting system run by Academia.

This interpretation will be given an individualistic and moral formulation. Meritocrats, who sometimes come from the people, but more often from the lower or middle ranks of the middle class, think that they owe everything to their intelligence and work, to their merit. Far from aspiring to give life to equality in deeds and not just words, meritocrats too often consider anyone who has not followed them in their upwards trajectory as, depending on their temperament, less talented, stupid or dumb – highly likely to vote for Trump or for the National Front. On the other hand, those who have inherited their privileged status, whether aristocrat or not, know well, deep down, how much they owe to their ancestors. They will not be so inclined to spontaneously express contempt for those who have failed in their studies. In the case of a full aristocratic tradition, the spirit of which may have been transmitted to the members of the lower middle and working classes, there will be not just modesty but the notion of *noblesse oblige*, that there are duties that come with privilege.

We must seriously consider the possibility that, if the United States, and especially France, have been less successful in recognizing the anxiety of ordinary people, this is a perverse effect of the egalitarianism that prevails there, and of a meritocratic ideal that is too dominant. Symmetrically, the way the British Conservative Party has elegantly taken over its nation might be the result of an aristocratic tradition that transcends individuals and classes. The value of a human being is not, in the United Kingdom, determined by the selective machinery of the university system, not even Oxford and Cambridge.

That history too will continue its course. America, after a time of hesitation, should follow England's example and come to a great compromise between the people and the elites. France's destiny is much more obscure. It is already partially welded to the destiny of Germany, where the people are following in the footsteps of their elites, even though the economic and demographic rationality of the latter is limited. But for France, the time will soon come for vital decisions to be made, decisions that will redefine the relationship between the people and their elites, decisions that are basically of a sociological and moral nature, but that will take the form of a geopolitical choice between Germany and the Anglo-American world.

NOTES

Preface

1   See John Cleese and Jamie Lee Curtis in *A Fish Called Wanda*; Hugh Grant and Andie MacDowell in *Four Weddings and a Funeral*, etc.
2   Youssef Courbage and Emmanuel Todd, *A Convergence of Civilizations. The Transformation of Muslim Societies Around the World*, trans. George Holoch (New York: Columbia University Press, 2011).

Introduction

1   'Real Median Household Income in the United States', Federal Reserve Bank of St Louis.
2   'Rising Morbidity and Mortality in Midlife among White Non-Hispanic Americans in the 21st Century', *PNAS*; www.pnas.org/cgi/doi/10.1073/pnas.1518393112.
3   Joseph Stiglitz, *Freefall. America, Free Markets and the Sinking of the World Economy* (New York: Norton, 2010); Paul Krugman, *End this Depression Now!* (New York: Norton, 2012); Thomas Piketty, *Capital in the Twenty-First Century*, trans. Arthur Goldhammer (Cambridge, MA: Belknap Press of Harvard University Press, 2014).
4   James K. Galbraith, *The Predator State* (New York: Free Press, 2008); Pierre-Noël Giraud, *L'Homme inutile* (Paris: Odile Jacob, 2015).
5   Joseph Stiglitz and Paul Krugman began their 'critical' careers after winning the Nobel Prize for Economics, awarded by the Royal Bank of Sweden; but, even after they were released from the need to win the highest recognition, they were unable to break this fundamental taboo.
6   Friedrich List, *The National System of Political Economy*, trans. Sampson S. Lloyd (London: Longmans, Green and Co., 1909); John Maynard Keynes, *La Pauvreté dans l'abondance* (Paris: Gallimard, 2000) [this is a collection of essays by Keynes translated into French, including his radio talk 'Poverty in Plenty: Is the Economic System Self-Adjusting?', available in D. Moggridge (ed.), *The Collected Writings of John Maynard Keynes*, vol. 13 (London:

Macmillan, 1973). Trans. note]; Ha-Joon Chang, *Kicking Away the Ladder, Developmental Strategy in Historical Perspective* (London: Anthem Press, 2003).

7 Emmanuel Todd, *L'Illusion économique* (Paris: Gallimard, 1999), especially chap. 6.

8 Robert Skidelsky, *Keynes. The Return of the Master* (New York: Public Affairs, 2009).

9 Estimated from the age structure of the population as given in Tony Wrigley and Roger Schofield, *The Population History of England, 1541–1871* (Cambridge: Cambridge University Press, 1989), pp. 203, 204–5, 218.

10 Emmanuel Todd, *La Troisième Planète. Structures familiales et systèmes idéologiques* (Paris: Seuil, 1983), trans. David Garrioch as *The Explanation of Ideology. Family Structures and Social Systems* (Oxford: Blackwell, 1985); and *L'Enfance du monde. Structures familiales et développement* (Paris: Seuil, 1984), trans. Richard Boulind as *The Causes of Progress. Culture, Authority and Change* (Oxford: Blackwell, 1987). These books have been published together in one volume as *La Diversité du monde. Structures familiales et modernité* (Paris: Seuil, Points Essais, 2017).

11 Hervé Le Bras and Emmanuel Todd, *Le Mystère français* (Paris: Seuil and République des Idées, 2013); Emmanuel Todd, *Who Is Charlie? Xenophobia and the New Middle Class*, trans. Andrew Brown (Cambridge: Polity, 2015).

12 Andrew M. Greeley and Michael Hout, 'Americans' Increasing Belief in Life after Death: Religious Competition and Acculturation', *American Sociological Review*, vol. 64, no. 6, December 1999, pp. 813–35; see especially the chart on p. 817.

13 Emmanuel Todd, *L'Origine des systèmes familiaux* (Paris: Gallimard, 2011).

14 Bilateral: treating paternal and maternal relations as equivalent. 'Undifferentiated' or 'cognatic' are other terms used to describe these kinship groups.

15 In Britain and the United States, the term 'Anglosphere' often refers to a political project aiming at, if not the unification, at least the coordination of American, British, Australian, Canadian and New Zealand powers. This is never the case in the present book.

16 William W. Rostow, *The Stages of Economic Growth. A Non-Communist Manifesto* (Cambridge: Cambridge University Press, 1960). I am using the dates indicated in the diagram on p. xviii of the preface to the third edition (1990).

17 Daron Acemoglu and James A. Robinson, *Why Nations Fail. The Origins of Power, Prosperity and Poverty* (New York: Random House, 2012).

18 The concept of the Anglosphere was introduced by James C. Bennett in *The Anglosphere Challenge. How the English-Speaking Nations Will Lead the Way in the 21st Century* (Lanham, MD: Rowman and Littlefield, 2004). The theme of the nuclear family as a substratum appears in this work, but only marginally. It appears fully developed in James C. Bennett and Michael Lotus, *America 3.0. Rebooting American Prosperity in the 21st Century. Why America's Greatest Days Are Yet to Come* (New York: Encounter Books, 2013).

19 *World Patent Report 2008*, p. 16.

20 Peter Laslett, 'Mean Household Size in England Since the 16th Century', in Peter Laslett, Richard Wall, et al., *Household and Family in Past Time*

(Cambridge: Cambridge University Press, 1972), pp. 125–58. I was working on my thesis at the time, and taking a mischievous pleasure in finding and analysing, in Tuscany, Brittany and Sweden, households more complex than those that could be found in England.

21 Lutz Berkner, 'The Stem Family and the Developmental Cycle of the Peasant Household: an 18th-Century Austrian Example', *American Historical Review*, vol. 77, no. 2, April 1972, pp. 398–418.

22 Locke attacks Filmer in the first of his *Two Treatises of Government*, published anonymously in 1689.

23 Robert H. Lowie, *The History of Ethnological Theory* (New York: Farrar and Rinehart, 1937).

24 Saïd and Chérif Kouachi were responsible for the *Charlie Hebdo* killings in January 2015; Salah and Brahim Abdeslam were involved in the attacks in Paris on 13 November 2015. (Trans. note.)

Chapter 1 The Differentiation of Family Systems: Eurasia

1 For America, estimates of the date of settlement (which may have involved several waves of migration) vary between 30,000 and 10,000 years BCE.

2 Brenna M. Henna, Luigi Luca Cavalli-Sforza and Marcus W. Feldman, 'The Great Human Expansion', in *Proceedings of the National Academy of Sciences*, vol. 109, no. 44, October 2012. See also Luigi Luca Cavalli-Sforza, Paolo Menozzi and Alberto Piazza, *The History and Geography of Human Genes* (Princeton, NJ: Princeton University Press, 1994).

3 Marta D. Costa, Martin B. Richards, et al., 'A Substantial Prehistoric European Ancestry amongst Ashkenazi Maternal Lineages'; http://www.nature.com/ncomms/2013/131008/ncomms3543/full/ncomms3543.html.

4 Adolphus P. Elkin, *Les Aborigènes australiens* (Paris: Gallimard, 1967), p. 29.

5 See the excellent *Principles of Evolutionary Medicine* by Peter Gluckman et al. (Oxford: Oxford University Press, 2009).

6 Emmanuel Todd, *L'Origine des systèmes familiaux* (Paris: Gallimard, 2011).

7 There are still traces of this in the footnotes of Claude Lévi-Strauss's *The Elementary Structures of Kinship*, revised edition trans. James Harle Bell, John Richard von Sturmer and Rodney Needham) (Boston, MA: Beacon Press, 1977), pp. 176–7, 404; but George Murdock is even more radical since, in *Social Structure* (New York: Macmillan Company, 1949), he rejects from the start any analysis of spatial contiguities on principle. He uses the simple correlation coefficient to establish relations between characteristics, which a priori excludes spatial proximity as a factor.

8 I forgot to mention, in the chapters of *OSF* devoted to Europe, the biblical obsession with birthright (on which St Augustine insists at length in *The City of God*) as an important cultural element in understanding the emergence of the European stem family. It is in some ways the equivalent, if you will, of the Chinese Tang code in Japan.

9 German kinship terminology is more or less the same as ours. For Japan, see Chie Nakane, *Kinship and Economic Organization in Rural Japan* (London: Athlone Press, 1967), pp. 32–3.

10 Marshall D. Sahlins, 'The Segmentary Lineage: An Organization of Predatory

Expansion', *American Anthropologist*, New Series, vol. 63, no. 2, part 1, April 1961, pp. 322–45; Frank Lorimer, *Culture and Human Fertility. A Study of the Relations of Cultural Conditions to Fertility in Non-industrial and Transitional Societies* (Paris: Unesco, 1954), especially pp. 90–4. Lorimer discusses Lowie's conclusions about the primordial nature of the nuclear family and the association between complex structures and development. At this stage, the association between the use of iron and patrilineality is apparent (p. 63).

11 This is shown in Antoinette Fauve-Chamoux and Emiko Ochiai (eds.),*The Stem Family in Eurasian Perspective* (Bern: Peter Lang, 2009).

12 David Le Bris, William N. Goetzmann and Sébastien Pouget, 'Alternative Paths to the Development of the Corporate Form', a presentation given in Florence on 1 May 2016.

13 Akira Hayami, 'The Myth of Primogeniture and Impartible Inheritance in Tokugawa Japan', *Journal of Family History*, vol. 8, no. 1, spring 1983, pp. 3–29.

14 Dionigi Albera, *Au Fil des générations. Terre, pouvoir et parenté dans l'Europe alpine (XIVe–XXe siècles)* (Grenoble: Presses universitaires de Grenoble, 2011), esp. pp. 484–91.

Chapter 2 The Differentiation of Family Systems: Indian America and Africa

1 Hans Buechler and Judith-Maria Buechler, *The Bolivian Aymara* (New York: Holt, Rinehart and Winston, 1971); H. Tschopik, 'The Aymara of Chucuito, Peru', *Anthropological Papers of the American Museum of Natural History*, vol. 44, no. 2, 1951; Jean-Louis Christinat, *Des Parrains pour la vie. Parenté rituelle dans une communauté des Andes péruviennes* (Neuchâtel: Éditions de l'Institut d'ethnologie, and Paris: Éditions de la Maison des sciences de l'homme, 1989); William J. McEwen, *Changing Rural Society. A Study of Communities in Bolivia* (Oxford: Oxford University Press, 1975); George Korb, *Ticaco: An Aymara Indian Community* (Ithaca, NY: Cornell University Press, 1966); Hugo Nutini, *San Bernardino Contla. Marriage and Family Structure in a Tlaxcalan Municipio* (Pittsburgh, PA: University of Pittsburgh Press, 1968); David L. Robichaux, 'Residence Rules and Ultimogeniture in Tlaxcala and Mesoamerica', *Ethnology*, vol. XXXVI, no. 2, spring 1997, pp. 149–71; M. Salovesa, 'Post-Marital Residence in San Bartolome de los Llanos, Chiapas', in Hugo Nutini et al., *Essays on Mexican Kinship* (Pittsburgh, PA: University of Pittsburgh Press, 1976), pp. 207–17; Evon Vogt, *Ethnology. Handbook of Middle American Indians*, vol. 8 (Austin, TX: University of Texas Press, 1969); Marie-Noëlle Chamoux, *Indiens de la Sierra. La communauté paysanne au Mexique* (Paris: L'Harmattan, 1981).

2 Robichaux, 'Residence Rules and Ultimogeniture in Tlaxcala and Mesoamerica', p. 150.

3 Christinat, *Des Parrains pour la vie*, p. 20.

4 Robert McCaa, 'The Nahua *calli* of Ancient Mexico. Household, Family and Gender', *Continuity and Change*, vol. 18, no. 1, 2003, pp. 23–48.

5 Robert Lowie, *Primitive Society* (New York: Boni and Liveright, 1919),

chap. 4; and George Peter Murdock, *Social Structure* (New York: Macmillan Company, 1949), chap. 1.

6 I am using here the data from George Peter Murdock, *Ethnographic Atlas* (Pittsburgh, PA: University of Pittsburgh Press, 1967). There are traces of primogeniture among the Siane, the Motu, the Manam, and the Abelam.

7 The most accessible surveys of African family and kinship systems are George Peter Murdock, *Africa, its Peoples and their Culture History* (New York: McGraw Hill, 1959), and Jean Poirier et al., *Ethnologie régionale*, vol. I, *Afrique et Océanie* (Paris: Gallimard, 1972).

8 Henri Léridon, 'Afrique subsaharienne: une transition démographique explosive', *Futuribles,* no. 407, July–August 2015.

9 The pygmy family is influenced by the surrounding patrilineal and patrilocal groups, but remains nuclear. See Murdock, *Africa*, p. 51. The !Kung Bushmen are also influenced by their patrilineal environment, but they are even closer to the original type (Murdock, *Africa*, pp. 55–6, and Lorna Marshall, 'Marriage among !Kung Bushmen', *Africa*, vol. 4, 1959, pp. 335–65).

10 Gluckman et al., *Principles of Evolutionary Medicine* (Oxford: Oxford University Press, 2009), p. 141.

11 George Peter Murdock, 'Ethnographic Atlas: A Summary', *Ethnology*, vol. VI, no. 2, 1967, pp. 109–235.

12 Murdock, *Africa*, p. 67.

13 Peter Bellwood, *First Farmers: The Origins of Agricultural Societies* (Oxford: Blackwell, 2005), chap. 5.

14 Meyer Fortes, *The Web of Kinship among the Tallensi* (Oxford: Oxford University Press, 1949); see chap. 3.

15 Richard Henderson, *The King in Every Man. Evolutionary Trends in Onitsha Ibo Society and Culture* (New Haven, CT, and London: Yale University Press, 1972), p. 150 on birthright; Jeremy Eades, *The Yoruba Today* (Cambridge: Cambridge University Press, 1980), p. 55 (the Yoruba place a great deal of emphasis on primogeniture, but with an archaic element, the passage from elder brother to younger brother); Jean Hurault, *La Structure sociale des Bamilékés* (Paris and The Hague: Mouton, 1962), p. 50.

16 I am here using the date given by Murdock in *Africa*, p. 21, but without any certainty.

17 Abdoulaye Bara Diop, *La Famille Wolof* (Paris: Karthala, 1985), p. 15; Pace Lloyd, 'Agnatic and Cognatic Descent among the Yoruba', *Man, New series*, vol. 1, no. 4, December 1966, pp. 484–99.

18 Meyer Fortes, 'Kinship and Marriage among the Ashanti', in Alfred Radcliffe-Brown, Daryll Forde, et al., *African Systems of Kinship and Marriage* (Oxford: Oxford University Press, 1950), pp. 252–84.

19 Audrey Richards, 'Some Types of Family Structure amongst the Central Bantu', in Radcliffe-Brown, Forde, et al., *African Systems of Kinship and Marriage*, pp. 207–51.

20 See also James Clyde Mitchell, *The Yao Village* (Manchester: Manchester University Press, 1956).

21 Mitchell, *The Yao Village*, p. 157. Succession by the elder son of the elder sister, with a shift towards succession by direct primogeniture, shows the frequent link between matrilineality and primogeniture.

22 Murdock, *Social Structure*, p. 28.
23 Ron Lesthaeghe et al., *Reproduction and Social Organization in Sub-Saharan Africa* (Berkeley, CA: University of California Press, 1989); see the maps on pp. 270–7.
24 Ian Knight, *The Anatomy of the Zulu Army from Shaka to Cetshwayo, 1818–1879* (London: Greenhill Books, 1999).
25 According to Mark Twain, writing in 1872, the Goshute branch of the Shoshone were 'the wretchedest type of mankind I have ever seen, up to this writing' (*Roughing It*, chap. 19, available online at https://www.gutenberg.org/files/3177/3177-h/3177-h.htm).
26 *Basin-Plateau Aboriginal Sociopolitical Groups* (Salt Lake City, UT: University of Utah Press, 1997); first issued by the United States Government Printing Office, 1938.
27 Thomas Headland, 'Kinship and Social Behavior among Agta Negrito Hunter-Gatherers', *Ethnology*, vol. XXVI, no. 4, October 1987, pp. 261–80, 270.
28 Stella Go, 'The Filipino Family in the Eighties: A Review of Research', in *The Changing Family in Asia: Bangladesh, India, Japan, Philippines, Thailand*, Social and Human Sciences in Asia and the Pacific, RUSHSAP Series on Monographs and Occasional Papers, Bangkok: UNESCO Principal Regional Office for Asia and the Pacific, pp. 239–306, especially pp. 258–9.
29 Peter Czap, '"A Large Family: The Peasant's Greatest Wealth": Serf Households in Mishino, Russia, 1814–1858', in Richard Wall et al., *Family Forms in Historic Europe* (Cambridge: Cambridge University Press, 1983), pp. 105–50; Emmanuel Todd, *La Diversité du monde. Structures familiales et modernité* (Paris: Seuil, Points Essais, 2017), see table on p. 398.

Chapter 3 *Homo Sapiens*

1 Vernon Reynolds, 'Kinship and Family among Monkeys, Apes and Man', *Man*, vol. 3, no. 2, June 1968, pp. 209–23.
2 Michael Gurven and Hillard Kaplan, 'Longevity among Hunter-Gatherers: A Cross-Cultural Examination', *Population and Development Review*, vol. 33, no. 2, June 2007, pp. 321–65. According to the authors: 'Our conclusion is that there is a characteristic life span for our species, in which mortality decreases sharply from infancy through childhood, followed by a period in which mortality rates remain essentially constant to about age 40 years, after which mortality rises steadily in Gompertz fashion. The modal age of adult death is about seven decades, before which time humans remain vigorous producers, and after which senescence rapidly occurs and people die. We hypothesize that human bodies are designed to function well for about seven decades in the environment in which our species evolved. Mortality rates differ among populations and among periods, especially in risks of violent death' (p. 322).
3 Gurven and Kaplan, 'Longevity among Hunter-Gatherers', p. 335.
4 Priscille Touraille, *Hommes grands, femmes petites: une évolution coûteuse* (Paris: Éditions de la Maison des sciences de l'homme, 2008), pp. 126–7.
5 Alain Testart, 'Essai sur les fondements de la division sexuelle du travail chez les chasseurs-cueilleurs', *Cahiers de l'Homme*, Paris, EHESS, 1986.

6   Lorna Marshall, 'Marriage among !Kung Bushmen', *Africa*, vol. 4, 1959, pp. 335–65, esp. p. 364).

7   Richard Lee and Irven Devore (eds.), *Man the Hunter* (New Brunswick, NJ: Aldine Transaction, 1968).

8   In his coding system, George Murdock sets the limit at 66 per cent.

9   Marshall, 'Marriage among !Kung Bushmen'.

10 James George Frazer, *Folk-Lore in the Old Testament. Studies in Comparative Religion, Legend and Law* (London: Macmillan, 1919).

11 Kaj Arhem, *Makuna Social Organization. Study in Descent, Alliance and the Formation of Corporate Groups in the North-western Amazon* (Uppsala: Academiae Upsaliensis, 1981), pp. 186–7.

12 Laurent Barry, *La Parenté* (Paris: Gallimard, 2008), pp. 82–107.

13 See Chapter 2 above, p. 58.

14 Edward Westermarck, *The History of Human Marriage* (London, Macmillan, 1891), p. 51.

15 Westermarck, *The History of Human Marriage*, p. 353.

16 My model of the divergence of family systems unfortunately renders a great swathe of historical thinking obsolete, but it is with unmixed joy that I note that one of its collateral victims is Edward O. Wilson, the pope of sociobiology. His interpretation of Darwinism is typically differentialist. The universalist reading of Darwin never loses sight of the unity of the human species, which is expressed by the inter-fertility of all human phenotypes and is explained by the length necessary for the process of separation of animal species. Darwin himself draws on the incommensurability of geological and biological times to explain the extreme rarity of intermediate types. Darwinism of a differentialist tendency, or social Darwinism, or sociobiology, reveals quite the opposite: a latent preference for the internal differentiation of the human species. Highly dependent in practice on the standard model of the evolution of the family – from the complex to the simple – *differentialist Darwinism* assumes that the least economically developed peoples are the closest to animality in their family organization. This leads to Wilson, in his *On Human Nature*, spouting nonsense about the selective infanticide of female infants, a consequence of hypergamy, a practice found in northern India which consists of a woman attempting to marry a man of a condition superior to her own. But this a bad example. The family system of northern India is far removed from the original system of humanity. It is the product of a long history and its cruellest characteristic must be interpreted in terms of sophistication, not of primitiveness, even if it is true that the lowering of women's status has resulted in the cultural paralysis of civilization in northern India, expressed as ever by very low literacy rates in the regions concerned. It is *Homo anglo-americanus* (whether he or she be a sociobiologist or not . . .) who remains closest to the original *Homo sapiens* in terms of lifestyle. But Wilson can be reassured that his family 'primitiveness' does not bring him any closer to the monkey. There is, as we have seen, no stable marital bond among chimpanzees. The division between the species is radical.

17 Westermarck, *The History of Human Marriage*, p. 20.

18 Westermarck, *The History of Human Marriage*, p. 239.

19 Westermarck, *The History of Human Marriage*, p. 505.

20 Clellan Ford and Franck Beach, *Patterns of Sexual Behaviour* (New York: Harper, 1951), chaps. 6 and 7.

21 Alexander Carr-Saunders, *The Population Problem. A Study in Human Evolution* (Oxford: Clarendon Press, 1922), chap. 7.

22 Charles Darwin, *The Descent of Man, and Selection in Relation to Sex*, 2 vols (London: John Murray, 1871; second edn enlarged by the author, 1879), see esp. chap. 5.

23 Pierre Guichard, *Structures sociales 'orientales' et 'occidentales' dans l'Espagne musulmane* (Paris: Mouton, 1977).

24 Konrad Lorenz, *On Aggression*, trans. Marjorie Latzke (London: Routledge, 1996).

25 Adam Ferguson, *On the History of Civil Society*, Part I, section IV; http://oll.libertyfund.org/titles/ferguson-an-essay-on-the-history-of-civil-society. Ferguson was born in Atholl, Perthshire, and served as chaplain in a regiment of Highlanders: he was acquainted with the morality of this 'backward' people. He espoused the Whig modernity of his day, but never adopted a simplistic evolutionism of the 'backward'/'modern' type.

26 '[W]e are obliged to observe, that men have always appeared among animals a distinct and a superior race; that neither the possession of similar organs, nor the approximation of shape, nor the use of the hand, nor the continued intercourse with this sovereign artist, has enabled any other species to blend their nature or their inventions with his; that, in his rudest state, he is found to be above them; and in his greatest degeneracy, never descends to their level. He is, in short, a man in every condition' (Ferguson, *On the History of Civil Society*, Part I, section I).

27 Ferguson, *On the History of Civil Society*, Part I, section IV.

Chapter 4 Judaism and Early Christianity: Family and Literacy

1 Emmanuel Todd, *Le Destin des immigrés. Assimilation et ségrégation dans les démocraties occidentales* (Paris: Seuil, Points Essais, 1997). See especially the discussion of 'unity versus difference: the stem family and monotheism', pp. 168–72.

2 André Chouraqui, *La Vie quotidienne des hommes de la Bible* (Paris: Hachette, 1978), pp. 159–62.

3 Baruch Halpern, 'Jerusalem and the Lineages in the 17th Century BCE: Kinship and the Rise of Individual Moral Liability', in Baruch Halpern and Deborah W. Hobson, 'Law and Ideology in Monarchic Israel', *Journal for the Study of the Old Testament*, Supplement Series 124, 1991, pp. 11–107.

4 Israel Finkelstein and Neil Asher Silberman, *The Bible Unearthed. Archaeology's New Vision of Ancient Israel and the Origin of its Sacred Texts* (New York: Touchstone, 2002); Mario Liverani, *Israel's History and the History of Israel*, trans. Chiara Peri and Philip R. Davies (London: Equinox, 2005).

5 Christophe Lemardelé, 'Structures familiales et idéologie religieuse dans l'ancien Israël. Contribution pour une compréhension du "monothéisme" biblique', *Semitica et Classica*, no. 9, 2016, pp. 43–60.

6 Finkelstein and Silberman, *The Bible Unearthed*, p. 109.

7 James George Frazer, *Folk-Lore in the Old Testament. Studies in Comparative Religion, Legend and Law* (London: Macmillan, 1919), pp. 429–33.

8 Thomas Römer, Jean-Daniel Macchi and Christophe Nihan (eds.),

Introduction à l'Ancien Testament (Geneva: Labor et Fides, 2004; new edn revised and enlarged, 2009).

9 Sarah B. Pomeroy, *Families in Classical and Hellenistic Greece* (Oxford: Clarendon Press, 1997), p. 127.

10 William V. Harris, *Ancient Literacy* (Cambridge, MA: Harvard University Press, 1989), pp. 136, 239, 252.

11 Erich S. Gruen, *Diaspora. Jews amidst Greeks and Romans* (Cambridge, MA: Harvard University Press, 2002).

12 Shaye J. D. Cohen, *The Beginnings of Jewishness. Boundaries, Varieties, Uncertainties* (Berkeley, CA: University of California Press, 2000).

13 Cohen, *The Beginnings of Jewishness*, p. 307.

14 Maristella Botticini and Zvi Eckstein, *The Chosen Few. How Education Shaped Jewish History, 70–1492* (Princeton, NJ: Princeton University Press, 2012).

15 Cohen, *The Beginnings of Jewishness*, p. 185.

16 Cohen, *The Beginnings of Jewishness*, p. 203.

17 Catherine Hezser, *Jewish Literacy in Roman Palestine* (Tübingen: Mohr Siebeck, 2001), p. 496.

18 Harris, *Ancient Literacy*.

19 Harris, *Ancient Literacy*, p. 259.

20 This book, remarkable for its attempt at historical modelling, cannot be too highly recommended. Its one failing is that it overestimates these populations, whether Jewish or not, in all periods. But it is probably right in its analysis of the varying roles and changing proportion of the Jews in ancient and mediaeval times.

21 Joel Perlmann, 'Literacy among the Jews of Russia in 1897: A Reanalysis of Census Data', *Working Paper*, no. 182, December 1996.

22 Christopher R. Friedrichs, 'Jewish Household Structure in an Early Modern Town: The Worms Ghetto Census of 1610', *History of the Family*, no. 8, 2003, pp. 481–93 (for houses), and Gerald L. Soliday, 'The Jews of Early Modern Marburg, 1640s–1800. A Case Study in Family and Household Organization', *History of the Family*, no. 8, 2003, pp. 495–516 (for households).

23 Zenon Guldon and Waldemar Kowalski, 'The Jewish Population and Family in the Polish-Lithuanian Commonwealth in the Second Half of the 18th Century', *History of the Family*, no. 8, 2003, pp. 517–530; Andrejs Plakans, 'Age and Family Structures among the Jews of Mitau, Kurland, 1833–1834', *History of the Family*, no. 8, 2003, pp. 545–61; Soliday, 'The Jews of Early Modern Marburg'.

24 Elisabeth Goldschmidt, Amiram Ronen and Ilana Ronen, 'Changing Marriage Systems in the Jewish Communities of Israel', *Annals of Human Genetics*, no. 24, 1960, pp. 191–204.

25 Myriam Khlat, 'Les mariages consanguins à Beyrouth', *Cahiers de l'INED*, no. 125, 1989, p. 93.

26 St Augustine, *The City of God*, trans. Marcus Dods (Peabody, MA: Hendrickson Publishers, 2009), p. 452.

27 Flavius Josephus, *Against Apion*, trans. William Whiston, sections 25 and 26; http://www.gutenberg.org/files/2849/2849-h/2849-h.htm; (my emphasis).

28 Tacitus, *Histories*, book 5, trans. W. Hamilton Fyfe; http://www.gutenberg.org/files/16927/16927-h/ii.html#conquest_Judea (my emphasis).

29 Flavius Josephus, *The Wars of the Jews*, trans. William Whiston, II, 8; https://www.gutenberg.org/files/2850/2850-h/2850-h.htm#link2noteref-6.

30 Matthew 10:21–22.

31 Rodney Stark, *The Rise of Christianity. How the Obscure, Marginal, Jesus Movement Became the Dominant Religious Force in the Western World in a Few Centuries* (New York: HarperCollins, 1997). The whole of chap. 3 is dedicated to the problem.

32 Botticini and Eckstein, *The Chosen Few*; this is the book's general thesis (see chart, p. 18).

33 Dominique Lhuillier-Martinetti, *L'Individu dans la famille à Rome au IVe siècle d'après l'œuvre d'Ambroise de Milan* (Rennes: Presses universitaires de Rennes, 2008), p. 88.

34 Peter Brown, *The Body and Society, Men, Women and Sexual Renunciation in Early Christianity* (New York: Columbia University Press, 2008), p. 145.

35 Stephen Neill, *A History of Christian Missions* (London: Penguin, 1964), pp. 88–90.

36 Stark, *The Rise of Christianity*, p. 107.

37 St Augustine, *The City of God*, XV, 16.

38 Peter Brown, *Through the Eye of a Needle. Wealth, the Fall of Rome and the Making of Christianity, 350–550 AD* (Princeton, NJ: Princeton University Press, 2012), p. 76.

39 There is an extraordinary description of this chaos in Stark, *The Rise of Christianity*, chap. 7.

40 Peter Kropotkin, *Mutual Aid. A Factor of Evolution* (New York: New York University Press, 1972; first published in 1902); Anton Pannekoek and Patrick Tort, *Darwinisme et Marxisme* (Paris: Les Éditions Arkhê, 2011; first published in 1909).

Chapter 5 Germany, Protestantism and Universal Literacy

1 William V. Harris, *Ancient Literacy* (Cambridge, MA: Harvard University Press, 1989), p. 141.

2 Egil Johansson, 'The History of Literacy in Sweden in Comparison with Some Other Countries', *Educational Reports*, no. 12, 1977, pp. 9–10.

3 Richard L. Gawthrop, 'Literacy Drives in Pre-industrial Germany', in Robert F. Arnove and Harvey J. Graff, *National Literacy Campaigns and Movements. Historical and Comparative Perspectives* (New Brunswick, NJ, and London: Transaction, 1987 and 2008), pp. 29–48; esp. p. 34.

4 UNESCO, *Le Défi de l'alphabétisation*, p. 177.

5 See Emmanuel Todd, *L'Enfance du monde. Structures familiales et développement* (1984); this is the central thesis in the book; reprinted in Emmanuel Todd, *La Diversité du monde. Structures familiales et diversité* (Paris: Seuil, Points Essais, 2017).

6 UNESCO, *Le Défi de l'alphabétisation: un état des lieux*; http://www.unesco.org/education/GMR2006/full/chap7_fr.pdf, p. 176.

7 Luther, *De Servo Arbitrio* and Erasmus, *De Libero Arbitrio Diatribe sive Collatio*.

8 Martin Luther, 'On the Bondage of the Will', in *Luther and Erasmus. Free Will and Salvation*, ed. E. Gordon Rupp and Philip S. Watson (Louisville,

KY, and London: Westminster John Knox Press, The Library of Christian Classics, 1969), pp. 243, 250.

9 Emmanuel Todd, *L'Invention de l'Europe* (Paris: Seuil, Points Essais, 1996), pp. 135–40, 507.

10 Mikolaj Szoltysek et al., 'Variation spatiale des structures des ménages en Allemagne au xixe siècle', *Population*, vol. 69, no. 1, 2014, pp. 57–84.

11 Hans Bödeker et al., *Alphabetisierung und Literalisierung in Deutschland in der Frühen Neuzeit* (Tübingen: Max Niemeyer Verlag, 1999), p. 44.

12 Bödeker et al., *Alphabetisierung und Literalisierung in Deutschland in der Frühen Neuzeit*, p. 113.

13 Roger Schofield, 'Dimensions of Illiteracy in England, 1750–1850', *Explorations in Economic History*, vol. 10, no. 4, 1973, pp. 437–54.

14 François Furet and Jacques Ozouf, *Lire et Écrire. L'alphabétisation des Français de Calvin à Jules Ferry*, vol. 2 (Paris: Éditions de Minuit, 1977), pp. 206, 238.

15 Kenneth Lockridge, *Literacy in Colonial New England* (New York: Norton, 1974), p. 39.

16 1897 census, Table IIIa.

17 1926 census, Book 5, Table 1.

Chapter 6 The Great European Mental Transformation

1 Felipe Pegado et al., 'Timing the Impact of Literacy on Visual Processing', *PNAS*, vol. 111, no. 49, November 2014.

2 David Riesman, *The Lonely Crowd* (Yale, CT, and London: Yale University Press, 2001), p. 89–90.

3 Riesman, *The Lonely Crowd*, p. 90.

4 See above, p. 61.

5 John Hajnal, 'European Marriage Patterns in Perspective', in David V. Glass and David E. C. Eversley (eds.), *Population in History. Essays in Historical Demography* (London: Edward Arnold, 1965), pp. 101–43.

6 Tony Wrigley and Roger Schofield, *The Population History of England, 1541–1871* (Cambridge: Cambridge University Press, 1989), p. 255.

7 Wrigley and Schofield, *The Population History of England, 1541–1871*, p. 260.

8 Robert Muchembled, *A History of Violence: From the End of the Middle Ages to the Present*, trans. Jean Birrell (Cambridge: Polity, 2012), pp. 33–4.

9 Muchembled, *A History of Violence*, p. 31

10 Muchembled, *A History of Violence*, p. 1.

11 Muchembled, *A History of Violence*, p. 28.

12 Norbert Elias, *The Civilizing Process: The History of Manners, and State Formation and Civilization* (Oxford: Basil Blackwell, 1994); first German edn, *Über den Prozess der Zivilisation* (Basel: Verlag Haus zum Falken, 1939).

13 Pierre Chaunu, *La Civilisation de l'Europe classique*, second edn (Paris: Arthaud, 1984), p. 378.

14 Hugh Trevor-Roper, *The European Witch-Craze of the 16th and 17th Centuries* (London: Pelican Books, 1969); Robert Mandrou, *Magistrats et Sorciers en France au xviie siècle* (Paris: Plon, 1968); Alan Macfarlane,

Witchcraft in Tudor and Stuart England. A Regional and Comparative Study (Abingdon: Routledge and Kegan Paul, 1970); Robert Muchembled, *Les Derniers Bûchers, Un village de Flandre et ses sorcières sous Louis XIV* (Paris: Ramsay, 1981).

15 See above, p. 108.

16 Keith Wrightson and David Levine, *Poverty and Piety in an English Village. Terling 1525–1700* (New York: Academic Press, 1979); esp. chap. 5, 'Conflict and Control: The Villagers and the Courts'.

17 For all these figures, see André Corvisier, *Armées et sociétés en Europe de 1494 à 1789* (Paris: PUF, 1976), p. 126.

18 Peter K. Taylor, *Indentured to Liberty. Peasant Life and the Hessian Military State* (Ithaca, NY: Cornell University Press, 1994), p. 87.

19 Taylor, *Indentured to Liberty*, chap. 3, 'Military Taxation, Recruitment Policy and the Ideology of "Das Ganze Haus"' ['the undivided house'].

20 Liah Greenfeld, *The Spirit of Capitalism. Nationalism and Economic Growth* (Cambridge, MA: Harvard University Press, 2001).

21 Akira Hayami, 'The Myth of Primogeniture and Impartible Inheritance in Tokugawa Japan', *Journal of Family History*, vol. 8, no. 1, spring 1983, pp. 3–29.

Chapter 7 Educational Take-off and Economic Development

1 William W. Rostow, *The Stages of Economic Growth: A Non-Communist Manifesto*, 3rd edn (Cambridge: Cambridge University Press, 1990).

2 It does not, however, mark its beginning, since demographic transition is most often preceded by a decline in mortality.

3 Daron Acemoglu and James A. Robinson, *Why Nations Fail. The Origins of Power, Prosperity and Poverty* (New York: Random House, 2012).

4 This is what I did in my *L'Enfance du monde. Structures familiales et développement* (Paris: Seuil, 1984).

5 Emmanuel Matteudi, *Structures familiales et développement local* (Paris: L'Harmattan, 1997).

Chapter 8 Secularization and the Crisis of Transition

1 Lucien Febvre, *The Problem of Unbelief in the Sixteenth Century: The Religion of Rabelais*, trans. Beatrice Gottlieb (Cambridge, MA and London: Harvard University Press, 1982).

2 Hervé Le Bras and Emmanuel Todd, *L'Invention de la France*, 2nd edn (Paris: Gallimard, 2012), pp. 259–61.

3 See above, Chapter 4, p. 90.

4 Note that Russia too had some 26 million inhabitants in 1789.

5 Le Bras and Todd, *L'Invention de la France*.

6 See Emmanuel Todd, *L'Invention de l'Europe* (Paris: Seuil, Points Essais, 1996), map 44, p. 317.

7 On Amida or Pure Land Buddhism, see Emmanuel Todd, *Le Destin des immigrés. Assimilation et ségrégation dans les démocraties occidentales* (Paris: Seuil, Points Essais, 1997), pp. 169–72.

8 For a presentation of Shinto, see Satoshi Yamaguchi, *Shinto from an International Perspective* (Tokyo: Ebisu-Kosyo Publication Company, 2012).
9 William W. Rostow, *The Stages of Economic Growth. A Non-Communist Manifesto*, 3rd edn (Cambridge: Cambridge University Press, 1990).
10 Emmanuel Todd, *La Troisième Planète. Structures familiales et systèmes idéologiques* (Paris: Seuil, 1983), trans. David Garrioch as *The Explanation of Ideology. Family Structures and Social Systems* (Oxford: Blackwell, 1985).
11 Peter Laslett, *The World We Have Lost*, 2nd edn (London: Methuen, 1971).
12 Alan Macfarlane, *The Origins of English Individualism* (Oxford: Basil Blackwell, 1978).

Chapter 9 The English Matrix of Globalization

1 The Roman conquest of Britain began in 43 CE.
2 Emmanuel Todd, *Le Destin des immigrés. Assimilation et ségrégation dans les démocraties occidentales* (Paris: Seuil, Points Essais, 1997), chap. 3.
3 To follow the growth of the Anglosphere, see Colin McEvedy and Richard Jones, *Atlas of World Population History* (London: Penguin, 1978); Tony Wrigley and Roger Schofield, *The Population History of England, 1541–1871* (Cambridge: Cambridge University Press, 1989); and James Belich, *Replenishing the Earth. The Settler Revolution and the Rise of the Anglo-World, 1783–1939* (Oxford: Oxford University Press, 2009).
4 Published as *The Invention of the Modern World* (*The Fortnightly Review*, Odd Volume 3, 2014), p. 313.
5 Marc Bloch, *Les Rois thaumaturges* (Paris: Gallimard, 1983; first published in 1924).
6 Charles Petit-Dutaillis, *La Monarchie féodale en France et en Angleterre. Xe–XIIIe siècle* (Paris: Albin Michel, 1971; first published in 1933); esp. pp. 122, 127, 133.
7 Petit-Dutaillis, *La Monarchie féodale en France et en Angleterre.*
8 Alan Macfarlane, *The Origins of English Individualism* (Oxford: Basil Blackwell, 1978).
9 Emmanuel Todd, *L'Origine des systèmes familiaux* (Paris: Gallimard, 2011), pp. 140–2.
10 See for example Douglas J. V. Fisher, *The Anglo-Saxon Age c. 400–1042* (London: Longman, 1973), esp. pp. 118, 120–1, 122, 216.
11 Peter Laslett, *Family Life and Illicit Love in Earlier Generations* (Cambridge: Cambridge University Press, 1977), 'Clayworth and Cogenhoe', pp. 50–101, 96–7.
12 Peter Laslett, 'Family, Kinship and Collectivity as Systems of Support in Pre-Industrial Europe: A Consideration of the Nuclear-Hardship Hypothesis', *Continuity and Change*, vol. 3, no. 2, 1988, pp. 153–75.
13 Richard Smith, 'Charity, Self-Interest and Welfare: Reflections from Demographic and Family History', in Martin Daunton et al., *Charity, Self-interest and Welfare in the English Past* (London: University College London Press, 1996), pp. 23–49; see also pp. 36–8.
14 See Richard Smith, who draws on Mary Barker-Read, 'The Treatment of the Aged Poor in Five Selected West Kent Parishes From Settlement to Speenhamland (1662–1797)', PhD thesis, London, Open University, 1988.

See also William Newman Brown, 'The Receipt of Poor-Relief and Family Situation: Aldenham, Hertfordshire, 1630–90', in Richard Smith et al., *Land, Kinship and the Life Cycle* (Cambridge: Cambridge University Press, 1984), pp. 405–22.

15 David Thomson, 'The Welfare of the Elderly in the Past. A Family or Community Responsibility', in Margaret Pelling and Richard Smith (eds.), *Life, Death and the Elderly* (Abingdon: Routledge, 1991), pp. 194–221, 204, 214.

16 Pelling and Smith, *Life, Death and the Elderly*, p. 31.

17 Laslett, *Family Life and Illicit Love in Earlier Generations*, pp. 65–86.

18 Keith Wrightson and David Levine, *Poverty and Piety in an English Village. Terling 1525–1700* (New York: Academic Press, 1979), pp. 82–7. The comparisons drawn by Wrightson and Levine with the measurements I myself carried out for kinship networks in the communities of Longuenesse, Wisques and Hallines, in the Pas-de-Calais on the eve of the French Revolution, in a major agricultural region, suggest there was a particular weakening in the English kinship network.

19 Wrightson and Levine, *Poverty and Piety in an English Village*, p. 79.

20 Emmanuel Todd, 'Seven Peasant Communities in Pre-Industrial Europe', PhD thesis, typescript, Cambridge, 1975.

21 Peter Laslett, *The World We Have Lost*, 2nd edn (London: Methuen, 1971), p. 56.

22 Steve Hindle, *The State and Social Change in Early Modern England, 1550–1640* (Basingstoke: Palgrave, 2002), pp. 206, 236.

23 Todd, *L'Origine des systèmes familiaux*, p. 457.

24 Todd, *L'Origine des systèmes familiaux*, pp. 402–3.

25 David Cressy, *Literacy and the Social Order. Reading and Writing in Tudor and Stuart England* (Cambridge: Cambridge University Press, 1980), esp. pp. 118–41. See also Wrightson and Levine, *Poverty and Piety in an English Village*, pp. 145–51.

26 Keith Wrightson, *English Society, 1580–1680* (Abingdon: Routledge, 2003), pp. 179–81.

27 Karl Polanyi, *The Great Transformation* (Boston, MA: Beacon Press, 2001; first published in 1944), p. 82.

28 Steven Ruggles, *Prolonged Connections. The Rise of the Extended Family in 19th-Century England and America* (Madison, WI: University of Wisconsin Press, 1987); see especially the chart on p. 5. The first studies produced by Peter Laslett and the Cambridge Group exaggerated the degree to which the structure of English households remained constant, probably because Laslett simply observed mean household size over the long period. See, for example, Peter Laslett, 'Mean Household Size in England since the 16th Century', in Laslett, Wall, et al., *Household and Family in Past Time*, pp. 125–58.

29 Michael Anderson, *Family Structure in 19th-Century Lancashire* (Cambridge: Cambridge University Press, 1971), pp. 44, 85.

30 In French, the word '*domaine*' is also used for the '*réserve*', but the former sometimes refers to the terroir as a whole.

31 See Max Weber, *The Agrarian Sociology of Ancient Societies*, trans. R. I. Frank (London: Verso, 2013).

32 Marc Bloch, *Seigneurie française et manoir anglais* (Paris: Armand Colin, 1967), p. 17. This was a lecture series given in 1936.

33 Michael Postan, *The Mediaeval Economy and Society* (Harmondsworth: Pelican Books, 1975), p. 87.

34 Its destiny seems to have been linked to the fluctuations in Germany's prestige. Frederic W. Maitland – in *Domesday Book and Beyond, Three Essays in the Early History of England* (London: Fontana, 1969; first published in 1897) – had followed those German historians who sought to connect the social structures of their time to original ethnic groups, with Germanic freedom at the heart of the fantasy. In 1896, Ernest E. Williams published *Made in Germany*, a bestseller that expressed anxiety about the triumph of German industry. Already! And it was after the Second World War that the importance of Rome to the history of England was again acknowledged. The state of Europe in 2017, dominated by Germany, suggests a new surge of Germanism.

35 Frederic Seebohm, *The English Village Community, Examined in its Relation to the Manorial and Tribal Systems and to the Common or Open Field System of Husbandry* (Cambridge: Cambridge University Press, 2012; first published in 1883).

36 George Homans, *English Villagers of the 13th Century* (New York: Harper and Row, 1970; first published in 1941).

37 Richard Smith, 'Families and Their Land in an Area of Partible Inheritance: Redgrave, Suffolk 1260–1320', Richard Smith et al., *Land, Kinship and the Life Cycle* (Cambridge: Cambridge University Press, 1984), pp. 135–95.

38 See Seebohm, *The English Village Community*, maps between pp. 86 and 87.

39 Postan, *The Mediaeval Economy and Society*, pp. 160–73.

40 Tony Wrigley and Roger Schofield, *The Population History of England, 1541–1871* (Cambridge: Cambridge University Press, 1989), p. 260.

41 David Cressy, *Literacy and the Social Order. Reading and Writing in Tudor and Stuart England* (Cambridge: Cambridge University Press, 1980); see charts on pp. 159–63.

42 On the connection between literacy and revolution, see Lawrence Stone, 'The Education Revolution in England 1560–1640', *Past and Present*, no. 28, July 1964, pp. 41–80, and 'Literacy and Education in England, 1640–1900', *Past and Present*, no. 42, February 1969, pp. 63–139.

43 Lawrence Stone, 'Interpersonal Violence in English Society, 1300–1980', *Past and Present*, no. 101, November 1983, pp. 22–33 (pp. 31–2).

Chapter 10 *Homo Americanus*

1 David Hackett Fischer, *Albion's Seeds. Four British Folkways in America* (Oxford: Oxford University Press, 1989).

2 Kenneth Lockridge, *A New England Town. The First Hundred Years* (New York: Norton, 1985).

3 Lockridge, *A New England Town*, pp. 64, 139–40.

4 Philip Greven, 'The Average Size of Families and Households in the Province of Massachusetts and in the United States in 1790: An Overview', in Peter Laslett, Richard Wall, et al., *Household and Family in Past Time* (Cambridge: Cambridge University Press, 1972), pp. 545–60. But see also the critique in John Demos, 'Demography and Psychology in the Historical Study of Family

Life: A Personal Report', in Laslett, Wall, et al., *Household and Family in Past Time*, pp. 561–9.

5 Philip Greven, *Four Generations. Population, Land, and Family in Colonial Andover* (Ithaca, NY: Cornell University Press, 1970).

6 Toby Ditz, *Property and Kinship. Inheritance in Early Connecticut, 1750–1820* (Princeton, NJ: Princeton University Press, 1986).

7 Mary Ryan, *Cradle of the Middle Class. The Family in Oneida County, New York, 1790–1865* (Cambridge: Cambridge University Press, 1981).

8 Daniel Snydacker, 'Kinship and Community in Rural Pennsylvania, 1749–1820', *Journal of Interdisciplinary History*, vol. 13, no. 1, summer 1982, pp. 41–61. On the Quaker family, see also Barry Levy, '"Tender Plants": Quaker Farmers and Children in the Delaware Valley, 1681–1735', *Journal of Family History*, vol. 3, no. 116, 1978.

9 Ditz, *Property and Kinship*, p. 165.

10 Greven, *Four Generations*, p. 206.

11 Greven, *Four Generations*, p. 212.

12 Greven, *Four Generations*, p. 214.

13 Ryan, *Cradle of the Middle Class*, p. 252.

14 Ryan, *Cradle of the Middle Class*, p. 255.

15 See Table 7.1, p. 132.

16 C. Wright Mills, quoted in Ryan, *Cradle of the Middle Class*, p. 14.

17 Steven Ruggles, *Prolonged Connections. The Rise of the Extended Family in 19th-Century England and America* (Madison, WI: University of Wisconsin Press, 1987), chart, p. 5.

18 Natasha Pilkauskas and Melissa Martison, 'Three-Generation Family Households in Early Childhood: Comparisons between the United States, the United Kingdom, and Australia', *Demographic Research*, vol. XXX, article 60; http://www.demographic-research.org.

19 Kirk Hadaway, Penny Marler and Mark Chaves, 'What the Polls Don't Show: A Closer Look at US Church Attendance', *American Sociological Review*, vol. 58, December 1993, pp. 741–52.

20 Robert Putnam and David Campbell, *American Grace. How Religion Divides and Unites Us* (New York: Simon and Schuster, 2010), pp. 83–4.

21 Peter Laslett, *Family Life and Illicit Love in Earlier Generations* (Cambridge: Cambridge University Press, 1977), 'Clayworth and Cogenhoe', pp. 65–86.

22 Raven Molloy, Christopher Smith and Abigail Wozniak, 'Internal Migration in the United States', *Journal of Economic Perspectives*, vol. 25, no. 3, pp. 173–96.

23 On the Irish, I am here correcting what I wrote in my *Le Destin des immigrés. Assimilation et ségrégation dans les démocraties occidentales* (Paris: Seuil, Points Essais, 1997). The Irish were described there, on the basis of monographic studies conducted in the twentieth century, as bearers of the stem family. The historical analysis presented in my *L'Origine des systèmes familiaux* (Paris: Gallimard, 2011), however, shows the extremely belated nature of the Irish stem family, after the Great Famine (1845–52). Stem family and emigration to the United States can be considered two parallel consequences of the Great Famine. The emigrants were, for the most part, carriers of the old family system.

24 See, for example, Todd, *Le Destin des Immigrés*, pp. 75–80, on the destruction of Norwegian and Jewish family models.

25 Geoffrey Gorer, *The American People. A Study in National Character*, revised edn (New York: Norton, 1964).

26 Gorer, *The American People*, chap. 3.

27 Gorer, *The American People*, chap. 2.

28 Ruth Lidz and Theodore Lidz, 'The Family Environment of Schizophrenic Patients', *American Journal of Psychiatry*, vol. 106, 1949, pp. 332–45; Suzanne Reichard and Carl Tillman, 'Patterns of Parent–Child Relationships in Schizophrenia', *Psychiatry*, vol. 13, 1950, pp. 247–57; J. C. Mark, 'Attitudes of Mothers of Male Schizophrenics toward Child Behavior', *Journal of Abnormal and Social Psychology*, vol. 48, 1953, pp. 185–9; C. W. Wahl, 'Some Antecedent Factors in the Family Histories of 568 Schizophrenics of the United States Navy', *American Journal of Psychiatry*, vol. 113, 1956, pp. 201–10; Melvin Kohn and John Clausen, 'Parental Authority Behavior and Schizophrenia', *American Journal of Orthopsychiatry*, vol. 26, 1956, pp. 297–313.

29 William Novak and Moshe Waldoks, *The Big Book of Jewish Humor* (New York: Perennial Library, 1981), p. 268.

30 Martin Ottenheimer, *Forbidden Relatives. The American Myth of Cousin Marriage* (Champaign, IL: University of Illinois Press, 1996), p. 27.

31 Ottenheimer, *Forbidden Relatives*, p. 59.

32 Robert Muchembled, *A History of Violence: From the End of the Middle Ages to the Present*, trans. Jean Birrell (Cambridge: Polity, 2012), and *Le Temps des supplices* (Paris: Armand Colin, 1992).

33 Lawrence Stone, 'Interpersonal Violence in English Society, 1300–1980', pp. 22–33; esp. the chart on p. 26.

34 Jean-Claude Chesnais, *Histoire de la violence* (Paris: Laffont, 1981), p. 35.

35 Eric Monkonnen, *Murder in New York City* (Berkeley, CA: University of California Press, 2001), p. 11.

36 See above, pp. 75–7.

37 Franklin Frazier, *The Black Family in America* (Notre-Dame, IN: University of Notre Dame Press, 2001; first published in 1939).

38 Katarzyna Bryc et al., 'The Genetic Ancestry of African Americans, Latinos, and European Americans across the United States', *American Journal of Human Genetics,* vol. 96, no. 1, pp. 37–53, January 2015, p. 43.

39 Michael Young and Peter Willmott, *Family and Kinship in East London*, revised edn (London: Pelican Books, 1962; first published in 1957).

40 Lee Rainwater and William Yancey, *The Moynihan Report and the Politics of Controversy* (Cambridge, MA: MIT Press, 1967). This contains the text of the Moynihan report, from which these figures are taken.

Chapter 11 Democracy Is Always Primitive

1 Raul S. Manglapus, *Will of the People. Original Democracy in Non-Western Societies* (New York: Greenwood Press, 1987).

2 Thorkild Jacobsen, 'Primitive Democracy in Ancient Mesopotamia', *Journal of Near Eastern Studies*, vol. 2, no. 3, July 1943, pp. 159–72.

3 See above, Chapter 9, pp. 156–7.

4 On the Iroquois, see the classic work by Lewis H. Morgan, *League of the Iroquois* (New York: Citadel Press, 1993; first published in 1851).

5 Emmanuel Todd, *L'Origine des systèmes familiaux* (Paris: Gallimard, 2011), pp. 430–9.

6 Jérôme-Luther Viret, *Valeurs et pouvoir. La reproduction familiale et sociale en Île-de-France. Écouen et Villiers-le-Bel (1560–1685)* (Paris: Presses de l'université de Paris-Sorbonne, 2004).

7 Brian Downing, *The Military Revolution and Political Change. Origins of Democracy and Autocracy in Early Modern Europe* (Princeton, NJ: Princeton University Press, 1992).

8 Downing, *The Military Revolution and Political Change*, p. 3.

9 John Plumb, 'The Growth of the Electorate in England from 1600 to 1715', *Past & Present*, no. 45, November 1969, pp. 90–116.

10 John Calvin, *The Institutes of the Christian Religion*, trans. Henry Beveridge (Grand Rapids, MI: Christian Classics Ethereal Library), p. 568; http://www.ntslibrary.com/PDF%20Books/Calvin%20Institutes%20of%20Christian%20Religion.pdf.

11 Alexis de Tocqueville, *Democracy in America*, trans. Henry Reeve (A Penn State Electronic Classics Series Publication, 2002), pp. 75–6; http://seas3.elte.hu/coursematerial/LojkoMiklos/Alexis-de-Tocqueville-Democracy-in-America.pdf.

12 I summarize here the argument and conclusion of chapter 2 of my *Le Destin des Immigrés. Assimilation et ségrégation dans les démocraties occidentales* (Paris: Seuil, Points Essais, 1997), 'Differentialism and Democracy in America (1630–1840)'.

13 Pierre L. van den Berghe, *Race and Racism. A Comparative Perspective* (New York and Sydney: John Wiley, 1967), p. 77.

14 See above, p. 182.

15 Loïc Wacquant, 'America's New Peculiar Institution. On the Prison as a Surrogate Ghetto', *Theoretical Criminology*, vol. 4, no. 3, 2000; Michelle Alexander, *The New Jim Crow. Mass Incarceration in the Age of Colour Blindness* (New York: The New Press, 2010 and 2012).

Chapter 12 Democracy Undermined by Higher Education

1 Angus Maddison, *The World Economy. A Millennial Perspective*, Development Center Studies OECD, 2001, p. 261.

2 Claudia Goldin and Lawrence Katz, *The Race between Education and Technology* (Cambridge, MA: Harvard University Press, 2008), p. 198.

3 Goldin and Katz, *The Race between Education and Technology*, p. 26.

4 Thomas Piketty and Emmanuel Saez, 'Income and Wage Inequality in the United States, 1913–2002', in Anthony Atkinson and Thomas Piketty (eds.), *Top Incomes over the 20th Century* (Oxford: Oxford University Press, 2007), pp. 141–225, p. 147.

5 Goldin and Katz, *The Race between Education and Technology*, p. 249.

6 See for example Josipa Roksa et al., 'United States: Changes in Higher Education and Social Stratification', in Yossi Shavit, Richard Arum and Adam Gamoran (eds.), *Stratification in Higher Education. A Comparative Study* (Stanford, CA: Stanford University Press, 2007), pp. 165–91.

7 *Statistical Abstract of the United States*, 2012, p. 173.

8 Emmanuel Todd, *Après la démocratie* (Paris: Gallimard, Folio, 2008), p. 63.

9 Michael Young, *The Rise of the Meritocracy* (London: Penguin, 1958), pp. 123–4.
10 John B. S. Haldane, *The Inequality of Man* (London: Chatto & Windus, 1932).
11 Christopher Jencks, *Inequality. A Reassessment of the Effect of Family and Schooling in America* (New York: Basic Books, 1972).
12 Hans J. Eysenck, *The Inequality of Man* (London: Maurice Temple Smith, 1973).
13 Hans Eysenck, *The Uses and Abuses of Psychology* (London: Penguin, 1953).
14 Richard Herrnstein and Charles Murray, *Intelligence and Class Structure in American Life* (New York: The Free Press, 1994).
15 Christian G. Appy, *Working-Class War. American Combat Soldiers and Vietnam* (Chapel Hill, NC: University of North Carolina Press, 1993), p. 220.
16 National Center for Education Statistics.
17 Piketty and Saez, 'Income and Wage Inequality in the United States, 1913–2002'.
18 http://scalar.usc.edu/works/growing-apart-a-political-history-of-american-inequality/the-powell-memorandum.
19 My discussion of this 'business moment' draws on Jacob S. Hacker and Paul Pierson, *Winner Take-All Politics* (New York: Simon and Schuster, 2010), chap. 5, 'The Politics of Organized Combat'. The book offers a remarkable study of the political and organizational dimension of the neoliberal revolution.
20 Hacker and Pierson, *Winner Take-All Politics*, p. 134.
21 Milton Friedman, *Capitalism and Freedom* (Chicago, IL: University of Chicago Press, 1962).
22 Milton Friedman, *Free to Choose* (San Diego, CA: Harcourt, 1980).

Chapter 13 A Crisis in Black and White

1 See also Camille Landais, 'Les Hauts revenus en France (1998–2006): une explosion des inégalités?', (Paris, School of Economics, June 2007.
2 Claudia Goldin and Lawrence Katz, *The Race between Education and Technology* (Cambridge, MA: Harvard University Press, 2008), p. 23.
3 National Center for Education Statistics, *Status and Trends in the Education of Blacks*, September 2003, p. 107.
4 Pew Research Center, 'The Rise of Intermarriage', February 2012.
5 *Statistical Abstract of the United States*, 2012.
6 Wendy Wang, 'The Rise of Intermarriage, Rates, Characteristics Vary by Race and Gender', Pew Research Center, February 2012, chap. 3.
7 Thomas and Mary Edsall, *Chain Reaction. The Impact of Race, Rights and Taxes on American Politics* (New York: Norton, 1991).
8 Edsall and Edsall, *Chain Reaction*, p. 228.
9 Michelle Alexander, *The New Jim Crow. Mass Incarceration in the Age of Colour Blindness* (New York: The New Press, 2010 and 2012), p. 56.
10 Alexander, *The New Jim Crow*.
11 Thomas Franks, *What's the Matter with America? The Resistible Rise of the American Right* (London: Vintage Books, 2005), p. 179.

12 Martin Gilens, *Why Americans Hate Welfare. Race, Media and the Politics of Antipoverty Policy* (Chicago, IL: University of Chicago Press, 1999); Alberto Alesina and Edward Glaeser, *Fighting Poverty in the US and Europe* (Oxford: Oxford University Press, 2004). See also Ian Haney López, *Dog Whistle Politics. How Coded Racial Appeals have Reinvented Racism and Wrecked the Middle Class* (Oxford: Oxford University Press, 2014).
13 Bruce Western, *Punishment and Inequality in America* (New York: Russell Sage Foundation, 2006), p. 50.
14 Alexander, *The New Jim Crow*, p. 5.
15 Alexander, *The New Jim Crow*, p. 33.
16 Loïc Wacquant, 'America's New Peculiar Institution. On the Prison as a Surrogate Ghetto', *Theoretical Criminology*, vol. 4, no. 3, 2000.
17 Camille L. Ryan and Kurt Bauman, 'Educational Attainment in the United States: 2015', United States Census, *Current Population Reports*, March 2016; see the table on p. 2.
18 E. Franklin Frazier, *Black Bourgeoisie* (New York: The Free Press, 1957).
19 Alexander, *The New Jim Crow*. See her conclusion, pp. 244 et seq.: 'The Racial Bribe. Let Us Give It Back'.
20 It dropped from 21 per cent to 13 per cent between 1972 and 2000. See *Status and Trends in the Education of Blacks*, National Center for Education Statistics, US Department of Education, 2003, p. 40.
21 Roy Walmsley, *World Prison Population List* (9th edition), International Centre for Prison Studies.
22 First published in December 2006 in *Energy Bulletin*.
23 Dmitry Orlov, *Reinventing Collapse. The Soviet Experience and American Prospects* (Gabriola Island, Canada: New Society Publishers, 2011), pp. 46–7.
24 Milton Friedman, *Capitalism and Freedom* (Chicago, IL: University of Chicago Press, 1962); Friedrich Hayek, *The Road to Serfdom* (Abingdon: Routledge, 1944).

Chapter 14 Donald Trump as Will and Representation

1 Justin R. Pierce and Peter K. Schott, 'The Surprisingly Swift Decline of US Manufacturing Employment', *Finance and Economics Discussion Series*, Washington, DC, Board of Governors of the Federal Reserve System, April 2014.
2 Emmanuel Todd, *La Chute finale. Essai sur la décomposition de la sphère soviétique* (Paris: Robert Laffont, 1976).
3 Justin R. Pierce and Peter K. Schott, 'Trade Liberalization and Mortality: Evidence from US Counties', *Finance and Economics Discussion Series*, no. 94, Washington, DC, Board of Governors of the Federal Reserve System, 2016.
4 Donald Trump, *Crippled America. How to Make America Great Again* (New York: Threshold Editions, 2015).
5 Joel Kotkin, *The New Class Conflict* (Candor, NY: Telos Press Publishing, 2014).
6 See the magnificent essay on the subject by Owen Jones, *Chavs. The Demonization of the Working Class* (London: Verso, 2011).

7 For an analysis of the way the Republican Party has fallen into line with its electorate, see Michael Lind, 'This Is What the Future of American Politics Looks Like', *Politico Magazine*, 22 May 2016.

8 A correlation coefficient varies between -1 and $+1$. Negative or positive, it is stronger as it approaches an absolute value equal to 1.

9 Hanna Rosin, *The End of Men and the Rise of Women* (London: Viking Penguin, 2012).

10 Center for Disease Control, M. F. MacDorman and T. J. Mathews, 'Understanding Racial and Ethnic Disparities in US Infant Mortality Rates', NCHS Data Brief, no. 74, September 2011.

11 CDC, *National Vital Statistical Report*, vol. 64, no. 1, table 8. The categories of 'Blacks' and 'Whites' are non-Hispanic.

12 Louis Chauvel, *Le Destin des générations. Structure sociale et cohortes en France au XXe siècle* (Paris: PUF, 1999).

13 'Revealed: The 30-Year Economic Betrayal Dragging down Generation Y's Income', 7 March 2016.

14 In the United States, the proportion of men aged 25–34 living with their parents increased by 30 per cent between 2000 and 2011. In the United Kingdom, the proportion of 20–34-year-olds living with their parents increased by 20 per cent between 1997 and 2011. In Australia, the proportion of 15–34-year-olds living with their parents increased by 8 per cent between 1996 and 2006. In Canada, the proportion of 20–29-year-olds living with their parents increased by 16 per cent between 1981 and 2006.

15 Richard Fry, 'For First Time in Modern Era, Living with Parents Edges Out Other Living Arrangements for 18–34-Year-Olds', Washington, Pew Research Center, 24 May 2016.

16 The contradiction might not have existed in the eyes of a Friedrich Hayek, born in a stem-family country: he would probably not have seen the freedom of the market and submission to the father as antagonistic notions.

17 Cécile Van de Velde, *Devenir adulte. Sociologie comparée de la jeunesse en Europe* (Paris: PUF, 2008), esp. pp. 100–8. The diagram on p. 67 gives an idea of the importance of Danish nuclearity in 1994–7.

18 The current 'decohabitation' of young people is not just the effect of a nuclear family norm inherited from the past. The possibility of living together as an unmarried couple is a new factor that explains why Sweden and France show good results, while young Spaniards and young Italians are still trapped. But the performance gap between Denmark and the United Kingdom, which have the same absolute nuclear tradition, is highly significant.

19 C. Kirk Hadaway, Penny L. Marler and Mark Chavez, 'What the Polls Don't Show: A Closer Look at US Church Attendance', *American Sociological Review*, vol. 58, December 1993, pp. 741–52.

20 Robert Putnam and David Campbell, *American Grace. How Religion Divides and Unites Us* (New York: Simon and Schuster, 2010), p. 74.

21 Michael Dimock, 'How America Changed during Obama's Presidency', Washington, DC, Pew Research Center, 2017.

Chapter 15 The Memory of Places

1 William J. Goode, *World Revolution and Family Patterns* (New York: The Free Press, 1970), p. 19.
2 Goode, *World Revolution and Family Patterns*, p. 22.
3 Goode, *World Revolution and Family Patterns*, p. 20.
4 Goode, *World Revolution and Family Patterns*, p. 17.
5 Emmanuel Todd, *Le Destin des immigrés. Assimilation et ségrégation dans les démocraties occidentales* (Paris: Seuil, Points Essais, 1997).
6 Emmanuel Todd, *L'Illusion économique* (Paris: Gallimard, 1999).
7 Michel Albert, *Capitalisme contre capitalisme* (Paris: Seuil, 1991).
8 Charles Hampden-Turner and Alfons Trompenaars, *The Seven Cultures of Capitalism* (New York: Doubleday, 1993). See also that classic of business schools: Michael E. Porter, *The Competitive Advantage of Nations* (New York: The Free Press, 1990).
9 Albert, *Capitalisme contre capitalisme*, p. 266.
10 Hampden-Turner and Trompenaars, *The Seven Cultures of Capitalism*.
11 Hervé Le Bras and Emmanuel Todd, *Le Mystère français* (Paris: Seuil and République des idées, 2013).
12 The expression 'memory of places' ('*mémoire des lieux*') comes from Hervé Le Bras.

Chapter 16 Stem-Family Societies: Germany and Japan

1 Sébastien Lechevalier, *La Grande Transformation du capitalisme japonais (1980–2010)* (Paris: Presses de Sciences Po, 2011), p. 75.
2 Ian Kershaw, *The Nazi Dictatorship. Problems and Perspectives of Interpretation* (London: Hodder Arnold, 2000).
3 Émile Durkheim, *L'Allemagne au-dessus de tout* (Paris: Colin, 1915).
4 On the stem-family area of Africa where the Bamileke are found, see Chapter 2. The Bamileke are known for their educational and economic dynamism. See Jean-Pierre Warnier, *L'Esprit d'entreprise au Cameroun* (Paris: Karthala, 1993), and Jean Hurault, *La Structure sociale des Bamilékés* (Paris and The Hague: Mouton, 1962).
5 On the transformation of the Korean system, see the wonderful book by Philippe Pons, *Corée du Nord. Un état-guérilla en mutation* (Paris: Gallimard, 2016), p. 168 for the emergence of an ethnic conception of the nation and pp. 336–8 for a discussion of the numbers affected by famine.
6 Zsolt Spéder, 'The Diversity of Family Structure in Europe. A Survey on Partnership, Parenting and Childhood across Europe around the Millennium', *Demográfia*, vol. 50, no. 5, 2007, pp. 105–34.
7 The Bundestag brought Germany into line with the West by adopting same-sex marriages in a stealth vote on 30 June 2017.
8 See Emmanuel Todd, *L'Origine des systèmes familiaux* (Paris: Gallimard, 2011), pp. 310–11, 327–30.
9 Chyang Kyung-Sup, 'Individualization without Individualism: Compressed Modernity and Obfuscated Family Crisis in East Asia', *Journal of Intimate and Public Spheres*, Pilot Issue, March 2010, pp. 23–39.

10 Peter McDonald and Helen Moyle, 'Why Do English-Speaking Countries Have Relatively High Fertility?', *Journal of Population Research*, no. 27, 2010, pp. 247–73, esp. pp. 263–4.
11 Pau Baizán and Teresa Martín-García, 'Endogeneity and Joint Determinants of Educational Enrolment and First-Birth Timing in France and West Germany', *Genus*, vol. 62, no. 2, 2006, pp. 89–117.
12 Sechiyama Kaku, *Patriarchy in East Asia. A Comparative Sociology of Gender* (Leiden: Brill, 2013), p. 133.
13 Baizán and Martín-García, 'Endogeneity and Joint Determinants of Educational Enrolment and First-Birth Timing in France and West Germany', p. 97.
14 Ron Lesthaeghe, 'The Unfolding Story of the Second Demographic Transition', *Population and Development Review*, vol. 36, no. 2, 2010.
15 EngenderHealth (Firm), *Contraceptive Sterilization: Global Issues and Trends*, 2002; Michael L. Eisenberg et al., 'Racial Differences in Vasectomy Utilization in the United States: Data from the National Survey of Family Growth', *Urology*, vol. 74, no. 5, November 2009, pp. 1020–4. The use of vasectomy in men aged between 30 and 45 years is 14.1 per cent for Whites and 3.7 per cent for Blacks. The income level is an important explanatory factor: from 5.6 per cent below $25,000, the rate increases to 16.5 per cent above $50,000.
16 Gretchen Livingston, 'Childlessness Falls, Family Size Grows Among Highly Educated Women', Pew Research Center, May 2015. See also Gladys Martinez, Kimberly Daniels and Anjani Chandra, 'Fertility of Men and Women Aged 15–44 years in the United States: National Survey of Family Growth', *National Health Statistics Reports*, no. 51, April 2012.
17 Martina Portandi and Simon Witworth, 'Lifelong Childlessness in England and Wales', *Longitudinal and Life Course Studies*, 2010, vol. 1, no. 2, pp. 155–69.
18 Jan M. Hoem, Gerda Neyer and Gunnar Andersson, 'The Relationship between Educational Field, Educational Level, and Childlessness among Swedish Women Born in 1955–1959', *Demographic Research*, vol. 14, article 15, May 2006. See also Jan M. Hoem, 'Why Does Sweden Have Such High Fertility?', *Demographic Research*, vol. 13, article 22, November 2005, pp. 559–72.
19 Toshihiko Hara, 'Increasing Childlessness in Germany and Japan. Towards a Childless Society?', *International Journal of Japanese Sociology*, vol. 17, no. 1, November 2008, pp. 42–62. See also María-José Gonzalez and Teresa Jurado-Guerrero, 'Remaining Childless in Affluent Economies. A Comparison of France, West Germany, Italy and Spain, 1994–2001', *European Journal of Population*, no. 22, 2006, pp. 317–52.
20 Heike Wirth and Kerstin Dümmler, 'The Influence of Qualification on Women's Childlessness between 1970 and 2001 in Western Germany', *Zeitschrift für Bevölkerungswissenschaft*, vol. 30, no. 2/3, 2005, pp. 313–36, esp. pp. 323, 325.
21 Michael Rendall et al., 'Increasingly Heterogeneous Ages at First Birth by Education in Southern European and Anglo-American Family-Policy Regimes. A Seven-Country Comparison by Birth Cohort', *Population Studies*, vol. 64, no. 3, 2010, pp. 209–27. See also Olivia Ekert-Jaffé et al., 'Fécondité,

calendrier des naissances et milieu social en France et en Grande-Bretagne', *Population*, vol. 57, no. 3, 2002, pp. 485–518.

22 Michael Dimock, 'How America Changed during Obama's Presidency', Washington, DC, Pew Research Center, 2017.

23 Hara, 'Increasing Childlessness in Germany and Japan'.

24 Jürgen Dorbritz, 'Germany: Family Diversity with Low Actual and Desired Fertility', *Demographic Research*, vol. 19, article 17, July 2008, pp. 557–98.

25 See above, p. 73.

26 The population varied between 25 and 27 million between 1720 and 1820. See Akira Hayami, *The Historical Demography of Pre-modern Japan* (Tokyo: University of Tokyo Press, 1997), p. 46.

27 See above, Table 13.1, p. 225.

28 See above, Chapter 5, p. 113.

29 Hermann Simon, *Hidden Champions of the 21st Century* (Berlin: Springer, 2009).

30 Stefan Lippert, *World Class beyond Toyota. Japanese Hidden Champions and their International Peers* (Tokyo: Kenichi Ohmae Graduate School of Business, 2010).

31 *Frankfurter Allgemeine Zeitung*, 'Kind, werd Ingenieur!', 21 September 2016.

32 Sebastian Haffner, *The Rise and Fall of Prussia* (London: Phoenix, 1998), p. 37.

33 On all these points, see Emmanuel Todd, *L'Origine des systèmes familiaux* (Paris: Gallimard, 2011), pp. 187–90.

34 World Bank, *World Development Indicators*, 4.8 Structure of Demand.

35 Noriko Iwai, Tokio Yasuda et al., *Family Values in East Asia. A Comparison among Japan, South Korea, China, and Taiwan Based on East Asian Social Survey 2006* (Kyoto: Nakanishiya, 2011), pp. 96–7, 'The Japanese Preference for Neither Agree nor Disagree'.

Chapter 17 The Metamorphosis of Europe

1 Emmanuel Todd, *L'Invention de l'Europe* (Paris: Seuil, Points Essais, 1996), chap. VI.

2 Emmanuel Todd, *Who is Charlie? Xenophobia and the New Middle Class*, trans. Andrew Brown (Cambridge: Polity, 2015).

3 Jacques Sapir, *La Fin de l'euro-libéralisme* (Paris: Seuil, 2006), chap. 2, section II.

4 Patrick Artus et al., *L'Allemagne, un modèle pour la France?* (Paris: PUF, 2009).

5 Zbigniew Brzezinski was President Carter's National Security Advisor.

6 Emmanuel Todd, *Le Destin des immigrés. Assimilation et ségrégation dans les démocraties occidentales* (Paris: Seuil, Points Essais, 1997), chap. 8, on 'Assimilation and segregation in Germany'.

7 Emmanuel Todd, *L'Origine des systèmes familiaux* (Paris: Gallimard, 2011), table XI-3, pp. 507–8.

8 *Atlantico*, 26 August 2016. His conclusion: 'Let us be prepared to live with a Germany that is more and more self-centred, more and more politically divided, and less and less ready for European compromise.'

Chapter 18 Communitarian Societies: Russia and China

1 Jacques Sapir, 'À l'épreuve des faits. Bilan des politiques macroéconomiques mises en œuvre en Russie', in *Revue d'études comparatives est-ouest*, vol. 30, no. 23, 1999, pp. 153–213; 'Troc, inflation et monnaie en Russie: tentative d'élucidation d'un paradoxe', in Sophie Brama, Mathilde Mesnard and Yves Zlotowski (eds.), *La Transition monétaire en Russie. Avatars de la monnaie, crise de la finance (1990–2000)* (Paris: L'Harmattan, 2002), pp. 49–82.

2 See above, Chapter 9, p. 155.

3 Pascal Tripier-Constantin has pointed me to some of the followers of Le Play who anticipated the 'communist' direction Russia was starting to pursue before the First World War, including:

- Léon Poinsard, the economist of the Le Play group in the years 1890– 1910, who wrote a very interesting study on free trade and protectionism.
- Edmond Desmolins, one of the founders of the 'Social Science' group in 1886. See, for example, the 'Conférence contradictoire sur le social-isme entre M. Paul Lafargue, député, et M. E. Desmolins, directeur de Science Sociale' ('Contradictory conference on socialism between M. Paul Lafargue, *député*, and M. E. Desmolins, director of Social Science') to the Geographical Society on 21 May 1892, with M. Funck-Brentano in the chair. Here, Desmolins clearly associates a communitarian system with communism, but he often talks in terms of 'inferior races'.
- Paul Descamps proposes a more neutral sociology based on Le Play's work. In a text entitled 'L'humanité évolue-t-elle vers le socialisme?' ['Does humanity evolve towards socialism?'] published in 1906, he writes: 'Let us first observe, with M. Alfassa, that the Russian peasant family is a communist association'. And he goes on: 'According to the information we currently have, communist corporations have been reported only in Russia. One might conclude that they can exist only by recruiting their members from an environment where family education has previously trained individuals to communism. This seems pretty logical; the cor-poration is responsible solely for giving technical education and not for educating the character.'

4 Anatole Leroy-Beaulieu, *L'Empire des Tsars et les Russes* (Paris: Robert Laffont, 'Bouquins', 1991), pp. 445–7.

5 Leroy-Beaulieu, *L'Empire des Tsars et les Russes*, pp. 90, 370. See also D. B. Shimkin and Pedro Sanjuan, 'Culture and World View. A Method of Analysis Applied to Rural Russia', *American Anthropologist*, vol. 55, no. 3, August 1953, pp. 329–48.

6 Maxime Kovalewsky, *La Russie sociale* (Paris: Giard et Brière, 1914), p. 106.

7 *Rethinking East-Central Europe: Family Systems and Co-residence in the Polish-Lithuanian Commonweath* (Bern: Peter Lang, 2015), pp. 539–40. I am not doing justice here to the power and finesse of Szoltysek's work; he studies economic and demographic determinants to assess the proper role of systems of family values in determining behaviour. I think, nevertheless, that his thinking struggles somewhat with the theoretical weight of the stem family and with John Hajnal's discussions of age at marriage, a heritage of

the historical research of the last forty years. A simple typological break, accepting the hypothesis of an imperfect nuclear family and integrating the potential co-residence of relatives as a systemic element, would greatly simplify the analysis. Szoltysek's text about Poland is permeated by the reality of an optional bilateral relationship and the vagueness of the rules that characterize the undifferentiated nuclear family.

8 Emmanuel Todd, *L'Origine des systèmes familiaux* (Paris: Gallimard, 2011), p. 95 for Russia; p. 115 for China.

9 Todd, *L'Origine des systèmes familiaux*, pp. 316–17 on traces of matrilocality and stem-family influences in forms of communitarianism in the Baltic.

10 Philippe Dollinger, *La Hanse, XIIe–XVIIe siècles* (Paris: Aubier-Montaigne, 1988), pp. 207–9. The reference is however too succinct for us to be entirely certain.

11 Oliver H. Radkey, *Russia Goes to the Polls. The Election to the All-Russian Constituent Assembly, 1917* (Ithaca, NY: Cornell University Press, 1990).

12 Radkey, *Russia Goes to the Polls*, p. 33.

13 Radkey, *Russia Goes to the Polls*, general table, pp. 148–51.

14 Lidia Prokofieva, 'Pauvreté et inégalités en Russie', Ceriscope Pauvreté, 2012; http://ceriscope.sciences-po.fr/pauvrete/content/part5/la-pauvrete-et-l-inegalite-en-russie?page=1.

15 See also Piotr Grigoriev et al., 'The Recent Mortality Decline in Russia: Beginning of the Cardiovascular Revolution?', *Population and Development Review*, vol. 40, no. 1, March 2011, pp. 107–29.

16 Sergei Zakharov, 'Russian Federation. From the First to the Second Demographic Transition', *Demographic Research*, vol. 19, article 24, July 2008, pp. 907, 972; Serafima Chirkova, 'Do Pro-Natalist Policies Reverse Depopulation in Russia?', *Working Paper*, University of Santiago de Chile, October 2013.

17 *Global Trends 2030s. Alternative Worlds*. A publication of the National Intelligence Council, 2012.

18 Anneli Miettinen, et al., *Increasing Childlessness in Europe. Time Trends and Country Differences*, Väestöliitto, Väestöliiton Väestöntutkimuslaitoksen työpaperi 2014, *Working Paper* no. 5; https://www.vaestoliitto.fi/.../Working+paper+5_Increasing+Childlessness+in+ Europe_1.pdf.

19 Elisabeth Gessat-Anstett, *Liens de parenté en Russie post-soviétique* (Paris: L'Harmattan, 2004).

20 These, and the translation of the tables, were provided by Alain Blum, whom I thank here. I am solely responsible for the interpretation of the data.

21 For example, Barry Naughton, *The Chinese Economy. Transitions and Growth* (Cambridge, MA: MIT Press, 2007).

22 Peter Navarro, *Death by China. Confronting the Dragon. A Global Call to Action* (London: Pearson, 2011).

23 John A. Hobson, *Imperialism. A Study* (London: Unwin Hyman, 1988; first published 1902), p. 364.

24 Christophe Z. Guilmoto, 'La masculinisation des naissances. État des lieux et des connaissances', *Population*, vol. 70, no. 2, 2015, pp. 204–65, and 'Missing Girls. A Globalizing Issue', in James D. Wright et al., *International Encyclopedia of the Social & Behavioral Sciences*, 2nd edn, vol. 15 (Oxford: Elsevier, 2015), pp. 608–13. See also Isabelle Attané, Chistophe Z. Guilmoto, et al., *Watering the Neighbour's Garden. The Growing Demographic Female*

Deficit in Asia (Paris: CICRED, 2007); Tulsi Patel et al., *Selective Abortion in India. Gender, Society and New Reproductive Technologies* (New Delhi: Sage Publications, 2007).

25 Christophe Z. Guilmoto, 'A Spatial and Statistical Examination of Child Sex-Ratio in China and India', in Isabelle Attané and Jacques Véron, *Gender Discriminations Among Young Children in Asia* (Pondichéry: IFP-Ceped, 2005), pp. 133–65; Todd, *L'Origine des systèmes familiaux*, pp. 155–6.

26 Zhang Weiwei, *The China Wave. Rise of a Civilizational State* (New Jersey, World Century Publishing Corporation, 2012).

Postscript: The Future of Liberal Democracy

1 Paul Collier, *Exodus. Immigration and Multiculturalism in the 21st Century* (London: Penguin Books, 2013).

2 David Goodhart, *The Road to Somewhere. The Populist Revolt and the Future of Politics* (London: Hurst and Company, 2017).

INDEX

Illustrations are indicated by page numbers in bold.

life expectancy, 6, 333
literacy, 85, 102, 112, 113–14, 147,
205, 335, 347
matrimonial exchange statistics, 67
military specialization, 337–8, 347
Mongol conquest, 92
mortality rate, 331–3
Muscovite Russia, 92
natural resources, 336
New Economic Policy, 329
Novgorod, 191, 330
Orthodox Christianity, 92, 334
patrilineality, 21, 41, 92, 114, 292,
321, 334
persistence of values, 336–7
population ageing, 6
population size, 326
private violence, 333
protectionism, 336
quadrilateral exogamy, 69
Revolution, 147, 328, 338
Russophobia, 21, 326–8, 336
and the Second World War, 326,
347–8
secularization, 147
sex ratio at birth, 345
shift towards matriarchy, 13
social stratification, 336–7
suicide rate, 333
universalism, 200, 338, 347–8, 350
Russian Civil War, 329
Russian Revolution, 147, 328, 338
Russophobia, 21, 326–8, 336
Rwanda, 53, 150, 277
Ryan, Mary, 176, 177

Saez, Emmanuel, 200, 207, 218–19,
222
Sahlins, Marshall, 41
Salazar, António de Oliveira, 9
same-sex marriage, 278
Sanders, Bernie, 3, 241, 252–3, 255,
258, 259
Sapir, Jacques, 309, 326
Scandinavia, 10, 11, 33, 292
see also Denmark; Finland; Iceland;
Norway; Sweden
Schofield, Roger, 118, 170
Scholastic Aptitude Tests (SATs), 209,
211

Schott, Peter, 243–4
Schröder, Gerhard, 114
Schulz, Martin, 319--20
Schumpeter, Joseph, 137
science fiction, 136–7, 214
scientific revolution, 23, 135, 139, 144
Scotland
absolute nuclear family, 38
literacy, 11, 103
Protestantism, 11, 103
Scottish Enlightenment, 76
stem family, 38, 324
witch-hunting, 120
Seal, Anil, 28
Second Vatican Council, 304
Second World War, 11, 144, 206, 216,
275, 276, 297, 326, 347–8
secondary education, 5, 205–7, 212,
226, 350
secularization
and current transformation of
advanced countries, 5
Czech Republic, 142–3
decline of Catholicism, 140–3, **142**,
145, 291, 304
decline of Hinduism, 146
decline of Islam, 17, 146
decline of Protestantism, 143–5,
304
and declining birth rates, 143,
144–5, 147
and egalitarianism, 141
Europe, 140–4, **142**, 304
France, 140–1, 143, 144, 147, 270
Germany, 147
Hungary, 143
and ideological crises, 144–7, 261
Iran, 17
Italy, 141
Japan, 146
and literacy, 139, 144–7
Russia, 147
and the scientific revolution, 139,
144
Spain, 141
United States, 261
and zombie traces of religion, 9–10
sedentarization, 5, 35, 100, 183
Seebohm, Frederic, 166
Senegal, 51, 56